Jay Gre

# Men Who Kill Men

## The Shadowy World of Serial Killers who Target their Fellow Men

Green Witch Publications

Published by Green Witch Publications

Cover images are used with thanks.

Also by Jay Greenwich

*Skinless Meat*
*The Unfortunate Victims*
*The Dark, Dirty Underbelly*
*Fables for the 21st Century Vol. 1*
*Fables for the 21st Century Vol. 2*
*America's Unidentified Serial Killers*

Dedicated to the victims

# Author's note

This is a book about serial killers – secretive psychopaths whose priority is to kill and kill again. They don't want to be caught, and they take steps to avoid being caught, and so evidence about their crimes and their motives must be viewed through the lens of subjectivity. A degree of license – as well as caution – is necessary when describing the acts of serial killers, and I attempt to take this into account when writing about them.

The theories I posit are merely that – theories. At best, they are guesses – but *informed* guesses, I hope, based upon the best evidence available. Again, inevitably, unreliable evidence can leak in and muddy the waters – but when this happens I try to take a balanced view based upon the weight of probabilities. If I have made any errors in my writing, these are mine and mine alone, and I will be happy to make amendments or additions should I become aware of them. I am always pleased to hear the thoughtful criticisms of my readers, and I can be found under Jay Greenwich on Facebook.

In writing this book, I attempted to standardise the use of names. For those under 18 years of age I generally (but not exclusively) use first names. Those in adulthood are generally referred to by their surnames. When I omit more up-to-date information, this is generally because it is irrelevant, unreliable, potentially libellous or, frankly, spurious.

I write using British English, and, whilst acknowledging that this may not be to everyone's taste, I trust in the wisdom of the reader to recognise this. Direct quotations, unless translated into English from another language, remain as they were originally written.

I resolved to keep this book relevant and interesting and I hope you enjoy reading it as much as I enjoyed researching and writing it.

Fantasy, abandoned by reason, produces impossible monsters …

- Francesco Goya, c. 1799

# Contents

# Foreword

THE VAST MAJORITY of serial killers are men, who project their lethal loathing of women onto female sex workers, hitchhikers, college girls and other prospective female objects.

However, a proportion of serial killers vent their rage on their own gender, and some of the world's most infamous murderers have names which are instantly recognisable - John Wayne Gacy, Jeffrey Dahmer, Andrew Cunanan.

These killers, like their women-hating counterparts, are capable of the most heinous crimes - rape, torture, mutilation, necrophilia, cannibalism. They can often be prolific, taking dozens of victims in their nefarious careers.

Just why this should be so is a subject of debate. Perhaps self-hatred, or the perceived hatred of society, impels these killers to inflict appalling acts of cruelty on their fellow man. These accounts of some of the most notorious homosexual serial killers imaginable must, of necessity, describe and discuss their crimes. To gloss over the crimes would be to depreciate the value of the victims' lives. That is not to say that one should take a perverse interest in the inevitable suffering and gore that accompanies such murder. Throughout this book I have striven to maintain a balance between the need to inform the reader and the requirement to maintain due respect for the victims and their families; certainly, it was my intention to do so. This book is dedicated to the victims.

*- J.G., September 2020*

# Men Who Kill Men

## The Shadowy World of Serial Killers who Target their Fellow Men

# Charles "Carl" Panzram
(active 1915-1929)

BY THE AGE OF 39, one of the world's most unrepentant men, Carl Panzram, a serial robber, burglar, arsonist, rapist and murderer, had spent more than half his life behind bars. In a one-man demonstration of obsessive loathing for himself and the human race he had engaged in a jaw-dropping campaign of brutality and mayhem that was both relentless and remorseless. What was most notable about Panzram's nihilist philosophy towards his fellow man was his almost complete and utter lack of regret for anything that he had done. In the pencilled autobiography[1] he smuggled out of prison via a sympathetic warden, he confessed that:

> *I am sorry for only two things. These two things are I am sorry that I have mistreated some few animals in my lifetime and I am sorry that I am unable to murder the whole damed [sic] human race.*

Prison was not going to help him, for he knew he was well beyond help, and in any case, he freely admitted to having no desire to be rehabilitated. Instead, he wished to return the good-will of others in a kind of twisted payback:

> *The only thanks you or your kind will ever get from me for your efforts on my behalf is that I wish you all had one neck and I had my hands on it. My only desire is to reform people who try to reform me. I believe the only way to reform*

---

[1] Published as Thomas E. Gaddis and James O. Long *Killer: A Journal of Murder* (Macmillan, 1970).

*people is to kill them.*[2]

Panzram ended his life as bitterly and angrily as he had lived it. There were few public expressions of emotional strain from the witnesses present, although a person in the crowd gleefully shouted, "Here they come!" as Panzram walked briskly to the platform and faced the crowd in the closure defiantly, his teeth clenched, with menace in his eyes. Before the sentence was carried out, the prisoner cursed his mother for bringing him into the world as well as "the whole damned human race".

In his last moments he spat in the hangman's face as the black hood was being put in place over his head. When asked if he had any final words he berated the executioner for taking too long: "Hurry it up, you Hoosier bastard! I could kill a dozen men while you're screwing around!" It was a fitting end to a dreadful existence and, given Panzram's early start in life, it was little wonder that this was the point to which it had led.

Charles Panzram was born on 28 June September 1891 in East Grand Forks, Minnesota, the son of two East Prussian immigrant farmers, Johann and Matilda Panzram. The young Carl's childhood appeared to have been quite typical for the offspring of hardworking, immigrant farmers of the time – just like many other children's, including those of his five siblings. His four brothers and a sister, although all experiencing much the same life experiences, appeared to have grown up honest and decent people, and the very traits that afflicted their aberrant brother seemed to have completely passed them by.

From an early age Panzram recognised himself as different from others.

*All of my family are as the average human beings are.*

---

[2] From a letter sent on 23 May 1930 to the Social for the Abolishment of Capital Punishment. They were campaigning to spare him the death penalty.

_They are honest and hard working [sic] people. All except
myself. I have been a human animal ever since I was born.
When I was very young at five or six years of age, I was a
thief and a liar, and a mean, despicable one at that. The
older I got the meaner I got._

When Panzram was aged around seven or eight, his father
simply got up and departed, leaving Matilda to raise the six offspring on her own on the small clapped-out farm. The older
brothers were not far behind and moved out as soon as their ages
allowed them. One of the brothers died. This left Panzram, his
sister and an older brother. Panzram and his sister went to school
during the day, and after school they were put to work on the
farm alongside their mother – from daylight to sundown, and
sometimes long after darkness had fallen. It was around this
time that Panzram began his career of crime (initially indulging
in petty thievery), a vocation that would carry on right throughout his lifetime, escalating in seriousness along the way until it
became that nothing was off limits.

There is no doubt that the young boy suffered immensely during his formative years. He was beaten regularly by his older
brothers, often for no reason. Shortly after his father left,
Panzram began to drink alcohol and by 1899, at the age of eight,
he was before the juvenile court for being drunk and disorderly.
In 1903, a string of burglaries landed him in reform school.
Here, he was being beaten severely, often for a trifle, and he felt
the injustice of it keenly, for he was struck and kicked for right
or wrong, totally at the whim of his punishers. He wrote:

_Everyone thought it was all right to deceive me, lie to me,
kick me around whenever they felt like it, and they felt like
it pretty regular. At this time, that is the way my life was
lived until I was about eleven years old._

This brand of punishment was meted out, it seemed, by the
strongest, and by the age of 11 Panzram began to suspect that

this treatment was wrong. He realised that other people didn't live like this and that there were other corners of the world besides his own. He wanted to leave his "miserable home" and in the end he did so. He ran away.

But before he did, he cast his eyes towards a wealthier neighbour's home and decided that "he had too much and I had too little". So he broke in and stole those items which, to his eyes, had the most value: some apples, some cake and a pistol.

Thereafter, Panzram's intention was to seek a better life in the west.[3] Munching on the cake and apples, he caught a freight train, imagining that in the west he would become a cowboy and shoot Indians. However, he either lost his bearings or mistook a connection, for somewhere along the line he was caught and returned home. There, he received another ferocious punishment ("beaten half to death") and sent to jail and then to the Minnesota State Training School at Red Wing, Minnesota.

This was no boarding school. It was more like a prison facility for grown-up violent and criminal men. He was abused appallingly – verbally, physically and sexually – and the ill-treatment was to have a profoundly negative effect upon the boy. He quickly learned, through regular demonstration and example, just how inhumane humans could be.

At first they tried to beat Christianity into him. The consequences could easily have been foreseen; the more they punished Panzram the more he hated them and their religion. He was beaten and whipped for wrongdoings of both omission and commission so it seemed that everything he did was wrong. In his mind he knew that he was being unjustly punished but he could do little to fight back; after all, his attackers were so much bigger and stronger that he was. And it seemed that the punishments dealt out to the boy were divers and creative. He

---

[3] "Go West, young man, and grow up with the country." Attributed to Horace Greeley, urging the young to seek a better life in the new frontiers of America.

remembered them all in his memoires. He underwent torture by use of "the whip, the Paddle, the Snorting-pole, the Humming Bird, the Hose, the Jacket". He was "chained up frontwards, backwards, bucked and gagged, spread-eagled, water-cured, starved, beaten, thrown into sweat boxes and half-cooked, thrown into ice-cold dungeons and half frozen".

The abuse began upon his first day at the facility. First, an oral examination. The Manager, Mr George Mann, asked Panzram questions about his parents: *Was his father insane, was he a drunkard, was he lazy or industrious? Was his mother a prostitute, a drunkard? Was she ignorant or educated?* Then Panzram was stripped naked and the physical examination began. Mr Mann made checks for lice and any kind of disease. He examined the boy's penis and rectum and asked if he had ever masturbated or committed fornication or sodomy, or had anyone ever committed sodomy upon him, explaining in great detail what those terms meant.

Mr Mann was a very religious man and great emphasis was placed upon religious education. Prayers were mandatory. After getting out of bed in the morning, before each meal, and then just before bedtime. On Sundays there was Sunday school in the morning and church in the afternoon. Failure to memorise Sunday school lessons meant a thrashing. Panzram recounted getting beaten every Saturday night and about three or four times during the week also, again for random acts of omission or commission. It was just like being at home on the farm. He remembered the creative methods of punishment for doing wrong that were used to teach him to do right. The most popular, he recounted, was a trip to the "paint shop", a room that was so called because "there they used to paint our bodies black and blue". In this room the boys were stripped naked, bent over a wooden block and covered in a large towel doused in salted water. They were then whipped with a large belt that had small holes punched through it. After many lashes of the belt blisters would form where the skin had come up through the holes. The blisters would burst and the salt water would do the rest. By any other name the treatment was nothing less than torture.

Panzram, perhaps not without some justification, laid the entire blame for his demise at the foot of the Minnesota State Training School. He was able to get some revenge on his abusers. Waiting upon the officers' table in the dining room he used to urinate in their soup or drinks and masturbate into their desserts, and then he'd stand and watch as they tucked in, delighting when they told him how much they'd enjoyed their meal.

Panzram attempted to escape from the facility on one occasion but was caught. He was beaten nearly to death, he recalled, but then was put back to work in the officers' dining room. In revenge he put rat poison in Mr Mann's rice pudding, but he was caught again and for his crime he was brutally beaten and relieved of his dining room duties and placed in the school band. Meanwhile, Panzram was plotting his revenge. He eventually figured out a way to punish his tormentors, burning down the building that housed the Paint Shop on 7 July 1905, causing $100,000 of damage.

Panzram was to learn a valuable lesson from some of the cleverer boys. They told him to act like a very good boy, to tell everyone that he loved Jesus, and to say that he wanted to go home in order to be a good boy, and to go to school and learn to be a preacher. Panzram did as was suggested and after being at the school a total of two years he earned his freedom by telling the parole board "all the lies and hot air" he could.

However, according to Panzram, the Minnesota State Training School had been his undoing:

*When I first went to the Minnesota State Training School I was about eleven years old, lively, healthy, and very mischievous, innocent and ignorant. The Law immediately proceeded to educate me to be a good, clean, upright Christian citizen and a credit to the human race. They trained me all right in that Training School. There during my two years I was trained by two different sets of people to have two differnet [sic] sets of morals. The good people tried to train me*

> _to be good and the, bad people did train me to be bad. The method that the good people used in training me was to beat goodness into me and beat all the badness out of me. They done their best but their best wasn't good enough to accomplish the task they set out to do._

His lessons had been for naught other than to teach him how to avoid detection. "In that was I first found out how to use religion as a cloak of hypocrisy to cover up my rascalities," he confessed, apparently with some pride, going on to add:

> _I had been taught by Christians how to be a hypocrite and I had learned more about stealing, lying, hating, burning and killing. I had learned that a boy's penus [sic] could be used for something besides to urinate with and that a rectum would be used for other purposes than crepitating._

Instead of "correcting" or "reforming" Panzram, the School, with its systematic regime of physical and sexual abuse, had had the opposite effect.

> _I made up my mind that I would rob, burn, destroy, and kill everywhere I went and everybody I could as long as I lived. That's the way I was reformed in the Minnesota State Training School._

Nevertheless, he was released from the School and he would leave forever changed.

Panzram caught the train home and was set to work on the farm immediately. However, he told his mother that he wished to study to be a preacher and so skilled at lying was he that he was sent to the German Lutheran Church and School nearby in North Dakota. It wasn't long before the pupils there worked out that he'd been to reform school and they began to tease him. So he beat them up. They told their parents, who in turn told the preacher, who in turn started to whip Panzram regularly.

One day, Panzram fought back, but, despite being a big, strong boy, he was no match for the preacher. Defeated, Panzram considered another means by which to overcome his new tormentor. He found it in the shape of his brother's Colt pistol.

The next day, when the preacher began to lay into the boy again, Panzram warned him off. The preacher assumed the boy was bluffing and, instead of ceasing, now ordered him to the front of the class to receive a whipping. Panzram refused to leave his seat so the preacher attempted to pull him from it. Then a scuffle ensued, during which the pistol fell from Panzram's pocket. All the preacher could say was, "*Mine Gott, mine Gott,*" paralysed with fear. Panzram retrieved the gun, pointed it straight at the preacher's head and then pulled the trigger – three times. The gun did not go off.

Casually leaving behind the uproar, Panzram walked home, thinking he would be patted on the back for his heroic act. Instead he was knocked to the floor with a punch to the head, beaten so hard he was nearly killed and strangled by his brother who wanted to know what had become of the gun.

That night Panzram ran away from home a second time. He'd given up his desire to be a preacher and reverted to original plan – to be a cowboy and shoot Indians. He was 14 years-of-age.

For the next four months or so Panzram hoboed across America, jumping freight trains, sleeping in sheds and haystacks whilst begging for food with hard-luck stories about being an orphan and saying how much he loved Jesus. Sometimes he earned money by working; other times he stole what he needed.

Then two events happened which were to change Panzram's outlook irrevocably. One night, travelling alone in a box car in the west, he decided to approach "four big, burly bums" in order to have a chat. He told them of the train carriage he'd just left, which was warm and had straw on the floor. The four men, apparently friendly, became interested and went with him to the carriage. Then the train pulled out and the men began to tell the boy they would buy him silk underwear and diamonds. In fact, they promised him the world – if only he would do something for them.

Panzram, upon hearing what the men wanted, told them he didn't want to do it. However, his declination mattered little to the men, for what they couldn't achieve by persuasion they took instead by force, despite the boy pleading for them to stop. He learned an awful lesson from the incident:

> *I left that box-car a sadder, sicker but wiser boy than I was when I entered it. After that I always went alone whenever and wherever possible.*

Sometime later, Panzram was travelling in a small town on a Sunday afternoon. He was broke and hungry and so he approached some "loafers" who were drinking in a livery stable. He told them his hard-luck story and how he loved Jesus, hoping to gain some food for his trouble. Instead he got sympathy and whiskey, as the men offered him a small drink, and then a bigger one, until he was so drunk he didn't know what was happening. When he awoke later he realised he had been raped a second time.

These two experiences taught Panzram lessons he hadn't wanted to learn, but which he nevertheless never forgot. He learned to look with suspicion and hatred upon everyone. He learned that sodomy could give more pleasure to the giver than to the receiver. And he learned that the use of force and might could get him what he wanted.

Panzram spent further time inside after being caught in the act of petty larceny burglary. Now an older and much bigger boy, he got into a few scrapes and the officers had orders to watch him closely. One of the wardens, Officer Bushart, took such pleasure in making Panzram's life a misery by nagging at him incessantly that Panzram decided to kill him. One evening, whilst the warden was having his shoes shined, Panzram took the opportunity to sneak up behind him and whack him on the top of his head with a hard, heavy oak board. The blow didn't kill the warden as intended, but it *did* make him ill for a while and it put a stop to the nagging.

Inevitably, punishments followed for Panzram in the form of being locked up, hard work and even harder beatings. The wardens even took him to a hospital where he was subjected to a circumcision, an attempt, ostensibly, to turn him into a good boy by preventing him from masturbating.

Eventually, Panzram and another inmate, Jimmie Benson, made a successful escape. Feeling mean, Panzram thought that as he couldn't go back to punish the screws at the reform school (who'd be on the lookout for them), he'd raise hell elsewhere. As the two boys made their way east they stole what they could, burned everything they could and sabotaged rail cars so that wheat harvests would pour from the carriages onto the tracks as the trains travelled.

The two boys separated at Fargo, North Dakota and Panzram returned home for a few days before heading back west. After a spell on the coast he went to Montana where he enlisted in the US Army sometime around 1905 or 1906. He was only a couple of months into duty when he was sentenced to three years in the US Military Prison at Fort Leavenworth, Kansas. He tried, unsuccessfully, to escape. Then he burned down the prison shops, causing another $100,000 of damage, without suspicion falling upon him.

Panzram's court proceedings were reviewed by the Secretary of War, William Howard Taft, who recommended three years. After 37 months' imprisonment he was released in 1910, claiming that he was a reformed character and that he loved Jesus. (Years later, in 1920, it would be Panzram's delight to rob Taft of about $40,000 worth of jewellery and liberty bonds.)

By now Panzram was 20-years-old, 6-feet tall and weighing around 190lbs. All the hard prison work had turned him into a strong brute of a man and by his own admission he "was the spirit of meanness personified". It would prove to be an accurate assessment. After earning his freedom from the chain gang, Panzram travelled to Houston, Texas. When he got there the town was ablaze and he enjoyed the spectacle very much. Some people asked for his help to save some valuables, which he did, although he kept the salvaged items for himself.

Panzram then met up with a "quarter-breed Indian" in Kalamath Falls, Oregon. They spent a week travelling together when they happened upon a man who had $35 on him. Panzram and the Indian led the man into the desert, robbed and bound him. As the man was now incapacitated, Panzram decided to rape him. Then he and the Indian left the hogtied man in the desert. "He is still there unless the buzzards and coyotes have finished the last of him long ago," Panzram wrote.

Panzram and the Indian parted ways. Panzram went south to Mexico, joined the Foreign Legion, then promptly deserted. He stole a horse and rode it to death in his efforts to make it back to the US border and onwards to Fresno, California. On the way he indulged in an orgy of mayhem and destruction, stealing whatever he could, setting fire to anything from chicken coops to entire prairies and shooting at livestock and farmers' houses. He also raped other hobos with abandon, and he wasn't fussy: "I rode 'em old and young, tall and short, white and black." On one occasion he and two travelling hobos were aboard a train when they were discovered by the brakeman. Panzram stole his money and raped him at gunpoint. He then forced his two companions to sodomise the man too. Then, under threat, he forced the three men off the moving train.

He was in and out of jail during the next months, using his time incarcerated to rape as often as he could. ("I got to be an experienced wolf. I knew more about sodomy than old boy Oscar Wilde ever thought of knowing.") In one spell inside, Panzram managed to escape from his cell. He then sabotaged the locks of the other cells so that no one could get in or out and then proceeded to attempt to burn down the prison. He was overcome and failed in that attempt, but he later burned down the prison shops, causing yet another $100,000 worth of damage.

In 1914, Panzram was eventually released only to be detained again following a burglary. He was told if he pleaded guilty he would be offered a lighter sentence. He did plead guilty, but he was given the maximum sentence of seven years in the State Prison at Salem, Oregon in 1914, from which he tried to escape several times.

What followed then could have been a turning point in Panzram's life. An idealistic new warden arrived at the prison. Spud Murphy introduced a new regime with no enforced religion, no physical punishment, plenty of books to read, regular meals and regular exercise. In a radical test of trust, Murphy told Panzram that he could leave the prison if he would not try to make his escape. Panzram readily agreed to this, thinking that escape was assuredly his intention.

The gates were opened and Panzram was free to go wherever he pleased. However, dumbfounded, he simply sat around for a while before returning to the prison that evening and demanding to be let back in.

Panzram ended up accepting a job in the prison, something that he had never done for any of the other wardens in other prisons. He joined the baseball team and ended up carrying the flag when the team played at outside games in other towns around Oregon. He was put to work outside the prison walls as a "trusty". He was able to spend time alone beyond the confines of the prison, just walking around, passing time. For around eight months he never made any attempt to escape.

It was too good to last. One night, Panzram stayed out too late and got drunk in the company of a "very pretty and affectionate" girl. He heard the sound of a freight train whistle and reckoned that it was calling to him. He answered the call and a week later he was robbing a house near Eugene, Oregon, finding and donning some nice new clothes and taking a pistol and some bullets. "When I left there I felt that I would rather die than be brought back to the prison to face Spud Murphy." It seemed that Panzram still felt the embers of a nearly dead sense of remorse.

Nevertheless, he was caught and sentenced yet again to prison. He did not serve the full sentence. After a few months in May 1918, he sawed through the bars of his cell and broke out for the final time, never to return to the northwest again.

It was at this time, in August 1920, that Panzram burglarised the New Haven, Connecticut mansion of William Howard Taft, who Panzram had held responsible for the sentence after the court martial. He fenced the goods, and with the funds he later received, and the .45 calibre handgun he had stolen from Taft's house, the violence now escalated into a murder spree that would span eight years and many countries.

Panzram bought a yacht, the *Akista*. He lured sailors away from New York bars with the promise of good money and easy work. Instead, he got them drunk, raped them, shot them dead with Taft's pistol and dumped their bodies in Long Island Sound. Others became suspicious of the disappearing sailors – but not before 10 sailors had been killed, so Panzram claimed – and the murder spree only ended when the yacht ran aground near Atlantic City, New Jersey, an accident which spared the lives of two potential victims.

Following a six-month spell in jail in Bridgeport, Connecticut, Panzram retrieved his gun, got into a gun battle with cops (the cops won) and was indicted for aggravated assault and incitement to riot. He got out on bail and immediately left the country, setting forth for Congo in Africa, landing at Matidi in the Congo and then moving onwards to Luanda in Angola. There, he worked as the foreman of an oil rig, which he later burned down. Whilst in Luanda, Panzram "decided to get me a nigger girl", paying excessively for what he believed to be a virgin. The girl was aged around 11 or 12 but, according to Panzram, she was not a virgin and so he quibbled the deal with the girl's father. He did not get his money back; instead he got a girl of around 8-years-of-age. Again, Panzram contested that he'd been given a virgin. At this point he decided to look for a boy instead and ended up taking a local by force. The boy told Panzram's boss and Panzram was fired and chased out of town. He ended up back in Luanda again. Whilst sitting outside the US Consulate,

*... a little nigger boy about 11 or 12 years old came bumming around. He was looking for something. He found it*

*too. I took him out to a gravel pit around 1/4 mile from the main camp ... I left him there, but first I committed sodomy on him, and then killed him. His brains were coming out of his ears when I left him and he will never be any deader. He is still there.*

Then Panzram moved down the coast to Lobito Bay, bringing havoc with him. The murder of six native Africans was premeditated and cold-bloodedly executed:

*There I hired a canoe and 6 niggers and went out hunting in the bay and back waters. I was looking for crocodiles. I found them, plenty. They were all hungry. I fed them. I shot all six of those niggers and dumped em in. The crocks done the rest. I stole their canoe and went back to town, tied the canoe to the dock and that night someone stole the canoe from me.*

After robbing a Spanish prostitute, Panzram realised that the police were after him. He stowed away on board a ship, the *West Nono*, but was kicked off on the Gold Coast. He caught further ships, landing in Las Palmas, Gran Canaria; Lisbon, Portugal; and Avenmouth, England, before finally signing aboard a ship heading for New York in the summer of 1992.

In Salem, Massachusetts, Panzram murdered a boy of around 11 or 12 years-of-age by beating his brains out with a rock. "I tried a little sodomy on his first. I left him laying there with his brains coming out of his ears."

Then he went to New York ("robbing and hell-raising as I came"), to Jacksonville, Florida, New Orleans (where he robbed a hospital drug-room and sold cocaine, morphine and opium), eventually ending up in Yonkers, New York where he "taught the fine art of sodomy" to a 15-year-old boy called George Walosin, a relationship which seems to have been consensual.

In June 1923, he stole a yacht which he was happy to know had belonged to the Police Commissioner, picked up Walosin, and sailed to Kingston, New York. A man there attempted to steal the boat so Panzram shot him, killing him with a gun stolen from the Police Commissioner, and disposing of the body by dumping it overboard.

Panzram and Walosin sailed downriver, Panzram stealing what he could on the way. However Walosin, who had witnessed the murder of the would-be thief, became skittish and jumped overboard and swam to shore. He reported the crime to the police and an alert was raised for the captain of the yacht. Panzram was arrested yet again and eventually sentenced to five years.

He tried to escape prison on 9 July 1923 but failed in the attempt. He sold the ownership of the stolen yacht to his lawyer[4] in exchange for bail money, then skipped bail. Whilst in New Haven, Panzram later asserted that he sodomised another boy and then strangled him to death.

He planned to travel to China and got a job as a bathroom steward on the US Grant. His plan went awry when he got fired for being drunk and fighting, and the next day, 26 August, he was arrested for robbery in Larchmont, New York and charged with sodomy, burglary, robbery and breaking out of jail. He was found guilty and served his five-year sentence in Sing Sing Prison and Dannemora Prison (where he tried to burn down the shops). Again he tried to make his escape but failed, succeeding only in breaking his ankles, twisting his back and rupturing his testicles, one of which was later surgically removed. He also tried to murder another prisoner by beating him with a 10lb club but he failed in this enterprise.

After his time was up in prison, Panzram was discharged in July 1928. He was told that he was "pure as a lily, free from all sin, [and] to go and sin no more". Small chance. Within two days of leaving he'd murdered 14-year-old Alexander Uszacke,

---

[4] The lawyer lost the boat when the rightful owner turned up.

a newsboy in Philadelphia, Pennsylvania, and committed further burglaries in Baltimore, Maryland and Washington D.C. He was caught again in Baltimore for stealing a radio and some jewellery and this time he would not escape.

During his interrogation, Panzram confessed to having killed another boy earlier that month, 12-year-old George Henry McMahon in New Salem, Connecticut. He wrote of his ambitions to commit mass killings or anarchy by poisoning a city's water supply with arsenic or scuttling a British warship in New York Harbour in order to provoke a war between the US and Britain. He received a sentence of 25 years to life. Sometime after this, he was caught chipping away at the bars to his cell. For this he was beaten, handcuffed to a pole and hoisted up so that his toes barely touched the floor.

Upon his arrival at Leavenworth Prison, Panzram had warned that he would "kill the first man that bothers me". This man was Robert Warnke, a prison laundry foreman known for writing up small infractions of the prison rules. Panzram beat Warnke to death with an iron bar on 20 June 1929, and the small, balding supervisor became his 22nd and last victim. Panzram was condemned to death for this crime and he refused to allow any appeal of the sentence, even writing to President Hoover that he would reject any pardon or commutation should either be offered to him.

Henry Lesser was the sympathetic prison warden who gave the condemned man some money to buy cigarettes, and to whom Panzram later gave the handwritten autobiography that detailed his nihilistic viewpoint and the particulars of his crimes. He must have realised that he would never leave prison again. The document began with a full list of the 17 institutions in which he had been in, followed by the following statement:

*In my lifetime I have murdered 21 human beings, I have committed thousands of burglaries, robberies, larcenies, arsons and last but not least I have committed sodomy on more than 1,000 male human beings. For all these things I*

_am not the least bit sorry. I have no conscience so that does
not worry me. I don't believe in man, God nor devil. I hate
the whole damed [sic] human race including myself._

The night before his sentence was carried out, Panzram paced
his prison cell restlessly, singing to himself a pornographic little
song he'd composed.

Prisoner no. 31614 was hanged on 5 September 1930. He was
buried in a grave marked only by his given number within the
shadow of the Leavenworth's walls. Henry Lesser preserved the
documents given to him, but so dreadful were the confessions
therein that it took 40 years to find a publisher brave enough to
release them.

In his writings, Panzram had revealed himself to be a man of
intelligence, wit and some introspection. He was clear, in his
own mind at least, why he had turned out the way he had, blaming
his early childhood physical and sexual abuses and the tortures
he had received inside prison for creating the unrepentant,
destructive criminal rapist and murderer he would become. He
wasn't motivated by sexual lust or power; he was motivated by
rage, giving back in return exactly what he had received. In a
letter to the renowned Dr Karl Menninger, written from prison,
he asked an unflinching self-analytical question: "Is it unnatural
that I should have absorbed these things and have become what
I am today, a treacherous, degenerate, brutal, human savage, devoid
of all decent feeling, without conscience, morals, pity,
sympathy, principle or any single good trait? Why am I what I
am? I'll tell you why. I did not make myself what I am. Others
had the making of me."

He may have been correct in that analysis.

# Henry Lee Lucas & Ottis Elwood Toole
[active 1961-1983]

THE TRUTH ABOUT THE LIVES of Henry Lee Lucas and Ottis Elwood Toole is just about as murky as it can get. The former was an admitted serial killer and necrophiliac, the latter a self-confessed serial killer, rapist, arsonist and cannibal as well as the suspect in several unsolved murders. Lucas was convicted for 11 murders in total and sentenced to death for the killing of a woman known at the time only as "Orange Socks". Toole was convicted on three counts of murder and had confessed to a further four. He was sentenced to death for the murder of a 65-year-old man and a six-year-old boy. Between the two of them the pair confessed to literally hundreds of murders.

However, as the accounts started to sound simply implausible and each man individually recanted his confession, it began to seem as though the two men were simply fabulists engaging in a spectacular hoax, and eventually their death sentences were commuted to life imprisonment. So did Henry Lee Lucas and his diabolic sidekick Ottis Toole indiscriminately kill men, women and children to become two of the world's most monstrous and prolific serial killers? Or, as compliant police witnesses, did they fabricate stories of murder so that we should view them as little more than a serial fantasists? The jury is still out.

Henry Lee Lucas' early life was about as miserable as one could imagine. He was born on 23 August 1936 in Blacksburg, Virginia to a prostitute mother, Viola Lucas, and an alcoholic former railroad employee, Anderson Lucas. Anderson had lost his legs in a train accident of his own making: he had been lying on the track inebriated when the train ran over and amputated his legs, an event which earned him an unkind nickname, "No Legs".

The Lucas family were poverty-stricken. Viola was unable to look after her eight other children and they were variously sent to other relatives, institutions and foster care, but for some reason she decided to keep Henry, her last-born, and his half-brother, Andrew. They lived in a small four-room log cabin in the Appalachians. It had dirt floors and no running water or electricity. Henry's parents, both chronic alcoholics, brewed "moonshine" whiskey. Henry was an alcoholic himself by the age of 10 after his father gave him the taste for the homebrewed concoction. Otherwise, the boy, it appears, was left to fend much for himself. As his mother would only cook for herself, the malnourished youngster soon learned to steal food from neighbouring farms or stores in town. Not surprisingly, he became a juvenile delinquent and spent a great deal of his teenage years in young offenders' institutions. He'd begun to steal, he said, as soon as he'd learned to run.

Henry received little education and had some learning difficulties. Anderson earned extra money by selling pencils and moonshine on street corners; Viola sold her own body. Henry was forced to work on chores, often from dawn till dusk, and any deviations from his mother's instructions brought him swift and severe punishment. It was "a nightmare that would not end", he would later report.

Viola was a quick-tempered and violent woman. She would beat Henry and his half-brother mercilessly, often for no reason. On one occasion she attacked Henry so hard with a plank of wood it caused his scalp to be split to the bone and put him in a coma for three days. His misdemeanour had been to refuse to pick wood for the fireplace. He was brought to hospital at the insistence of Viola's sleazy live-in lover and pimp, "Uncle Bernie", and to avoid prosecution the two concocted story about Henry having fallen down the stairs. Henry, fearing further reprisal should he do otherwise, backed them up.

In another episode, whilst playing with a knife with his half-brother, Henry accidentally slashed his left eye. The wound received no medical attention at the time and became infected. A later incident occurred at school, whilst Henry was still recovering: a teacher, wanting to hit someone, accidentally hit Henry with a ruler instead. The wound in his eye reopened. This time the orb had to be removed and replaced with a glass eye, which cause Henry's face to slacken and become odd-looking.

Viola was unquestionably a sadist. She would beat both Henry and her husband regularly. She forbade Henry from expressing love towards anything. Noticing that he took pleasure in a pet mule she asked him if he liked it. When he replied that he did, she went into the house, returned with a shotgun and killed the animal. She then beat Henry because of the expense she incurred in having to have the carcass carted away.

Viola, a prostitute who earned most of the family's meagre income by servicing strangers, would force both Henry and her husband to watch her ply her trade. The family all shared a bedroom in the small house. Viola was so insistent that her two sons would watch her having sex that she would punish them harshly if they attempted to avoid doing so. On one occasion in December 1949, Anderson, disgusted, left the house, dragging himself into the cold night air during a blizzard. There, he caught a fatal dose of hypothermia. The only person to have shown young Henry any kindness now died, leaving the 10-year-old boy alone to the ministrations of his vicious mother. After this, Henry became increasingly angry and embittered.

Due to their mother's proclivities it was perhaps inevitable that the Lucas boys' own relationship with sex would became tainted. Henry himself reported having sexual relations with his half-brother as a teenager. He was also introduced to the torture and killing of animals by "Uncle Bernie", would taught him to trap and rape animals, and then to slit their throats. For his own additional pleasure Henry would sometime skin animals alive.

As an act of humiliation that must have been difficult for Henry to endure, Viola forced him to dress in female clothes.[1]

---

[1] Purportedly, she cross-dressed him so that she could pimp him out to males and females alike.

She sent him to school wearing girls' clothes (but always shoeless). She further taunted him by curling his long hair into ringlets. A teacher who took pity on Henry gave him trousers and a shirt to wear and cut his hair. In payment for this kindness, Viola came into school and berated the teacher for interfering.

Although Henry received some care and attention at school, the persistent beatings at home began to take their toll. Henry was gripped by seizures. He would often complain of "noises" in his head and that he could heard "voices" that taunted him day and night, including his mother's. He would dream of a life without torment and desired escape.

Lucas claimed to have committed his first murder in 1951 at the age of 15. He was anxious to try sex with a human, he later told authorities. For this he chose a girl, 17-year-old Laura Burnley. He attempted to pick her up at a bus stop near Lynchburg, Virginia. When she resisted his charms he strangled her and buried the corpse in woods.[2]

After a series of burglaries in 1954 Lucas got a four-year prison term. He walked away from a road gang on 14 September 1957 and made his way to the house of his half-sister, Opal, in Tecumseh, Michigan, only for the authorities topick him up from there three months later. He was formally discharged from prison on 2 September 1959 and returned to his sister's house again.

By 20 January 1960, Lucas was engaged to marry a girl called Stella, a pen-pal with whom he had corresponded whilst incarcerated. Whilst he was celebrating the engagement, his septuagenarian mother turned up on the doorstep and interrupted the party. Viola, disapproving of her son's fiancée, ordered him to cancel the engagement and return with her to the family home in Blacksburg. They began to argue back-and-forth about the

---

[2] The murder remained unsolved and the killer unidentified for three decades until Lucas confessed to the crime in 1983. He later recanted the confession.

engagement and upcoming nuptials. In the end, Lucas stabbed his mother in the neck and left her to bleed to death.[3]

He was tracked down and arrested for matricide in Toledo, Ohio and in due course he was sentenced to 20-40 years in jail. During his time inside he repeatedly told anyone who would listen that he wasn't ready to be released and that he would kill again if set free. He also spent some time in a hospital for the criminally insane, where he was diagnosed as a sadist, a psychopath and a sexual deviant. Nevertheless, due to prison overcrowding Lucas was released after 10 years. "I'll leave you a present on the way out," he reportedly told prison guards on the day of his release, later claiming that he had killed two women within sight of the prison walls that same day.[4]

Lucas was back inside within the year. His crime – the attempted kidnapping of a 15-year-old girl and violating his parole by carrying a firearm. However, it was back on the outside, in 1976, when he met his partner-in-crime, Ottis Toole, at a soup kitchen.

Ottis Elwood Toole was born in Jacksonville, Florida in 1947. Like Lucas' background, Toole's was far from idyllic and he too appeared to suffer abuse just as extreme and disturbing at the hands of his parents, Bill and Sarah. His upbringing was undoubtedly harsh beyond measure. His malignant, dominating mother would abuse him and force him to wear girls' clothes, mockingly calling him "Susan". She was a deeply religious woman whose hyper-fundamentalist "hell-fire and brimstone" brand of Christianity relied more upon punishment than kindness. Ottis' father, a chronic alcoholic, regularly beat and belittled him, and subjected him to involuntary incest at the hands of

---

[3] Some accounts report that it took Viola around 50 hours to die. Others state that Lucas raped her dying or dead body. He later recanted his confession that he had committed incestuous necrophilia.

[4] This has not been confirmed by prison authorities. No evidence to support Lucas' claim has been unearthed.

several close relatives. His grandmother, a Satanist who indulged in grave-robbing and self-mutilation, introduced him to these practices, taking him along to dig bodies from graves to use in her cult worship services and allegedly partaking in the eating of human flesh. She used to call Ottis a "Devil's Child".

Ottis held an early fascination with fire and was an admitted pyromaniac and arsonist, sexually aroused by fire and enjoyed setting fire to houses just to watch them burn. "The bigger the fires, the more I get excited," he said. Like Lucas, Ottis had a learning disability; his IQ was considered to be around the 50-75 percentile. Psychiatrists likewise labelled him drug-dependent, illiterate, retarded, schizophrenic and psychopathic, one of them writing about his ability to act on impulse without the slightest sense of right or wrong:

> *"Life itself, to him, is so unmeaning, and the distinction between living and dead people so blurred, that killing is no more than swatting an annoying fly ... He trivializes the distinction between living and dead, believing himself to be dead. Retarded and illiterate, he has been out of control since early childhood. A severely drug-dependent individual, he is unsafe under any conditions outside of a secure prison, and perhaps unsafe there."[5]*

The early beatings and rape imprinted themselves upon Ottis' psyche and were the impetus for all that followed. By the age of 14, he was a dropout from school, addicted to drugs and alcohol.

As though that were not enough, Ottis was a homosexual, which made him an aberration in the Bible Belt of the Deep South. Referring to his inclinations, he once said about women, "Tried 'em. Don't like 'em." He was often to be found in a dull

---

[5] Conducted by the University Hospital of Jacksonville at the time of his arrest in 1983.

haze under the stupor of alcohol and barbiturates (stolen from his mother), frequenting the gay taverns of downtown Jacksonville and occasionally crossdressing. He was not an attractive boy. Already in his mid-teens, standing at six-feet in height he was dead-eyed and snaggle-toothed, and standing on street corners dressed in women's clothes to prostitute himself he would have looked positively Neanderthal in appearance. It's a wonder he got *any* takers. Nevertheless, he was *someone's* type and a travelling salesman picked him up in 1963. Whatever happened on that occasion (it may have been that Ottis was a willing partner who changed his mind, or he may have been forced by the salesman to have sex), Ottis nevertheless proceeded to drive the man over with his own vehicle. It is said that this was his first murder. He fled the scene, not returning to the city until some years later. In the meantime he had been picked up by police a number of times for auto theft, larceny and lewd behaviour including crossdressing, indecent exposure, voyeuristic peeping and propositioning a police officer in a pornographic movie theatre.

These were wandering years for Lucas, travelling throughout the American East. He married during this time (1975-1977) but, accused of sexually interfering with his stepdaughter, left rather than face the repercussions. He moved back in with Opal in Michigan and was at this time accused of molesting a granddaughter. The next day he asked to borrow a truck for a pick-up job, but instead he drove himself to Jacksonville.

In 1976, when he was doing on-and-off menial work, Lucas met his dreadful partner. It was a chance encounter. They met in line at a Jacksonville soup kitchen, struck up a conversation, and were astonished at just how much they appeared to have in common. Toole, who was living with his mother and other family members in a squalid suburb, invited the homeless Lucas back home with him.

Lucas' presence would not have been surprising at the Toole household: Ottis was always bringing men back for sex – sometimes for payment, sometimes just for pleasure. Toole and Ottis stayed together for a while, and everyone, it seemed, got along just fine, enjoying a period of relative stability. During this time, Lucas became close to Ottis' adolescent niece, Frieda "Becky" Powell, who, like Lucas and Toole, had a mild intellectual disability. Then one day, the pair decided they had had enough of domestic life and so, looking for adventure, they packed their bags and hit the road.

Henry and Ottis then waged a crime spree of enormous but mostly unverifiable proportions – robbing stores and banks, stealing anything and everything and wantonly killing people. They would kill for a car ... for sex ... for fun ... and anyone who drifted across their path was at peril. They murdered constantly and relentlessly, each of them vying to prove to the other who was the more lethal. Sometimes, if they were in too much of a hurry to stop and kill a hitchhiker, they would simply run them over and keep driving.

One murder occurred in western Georgia during the robbery of a convenience store. As Lucas was binding the clerk she began to scream. He informed her that if she didn't keep quiet he would shoot her. The woman obeyed. Whilst Lucas and Toole were dividing their spoils, Lucas noticed that the clerk was trying to loosen the knot. He coolly walked towards her and shot her in the head with a .22 calibre pistol and then proceeded to load cases of beer into their car. As he was doing that, Toole had sex with the corpse.

Another crime occurred on the I-35 when they chanced upon a young male and female walking along the road whose car had run out of fuel. Toole simply pulled over, got out of the car and shot the boy, disposing of the body in a culvert. Lucas fought with the girl, overpowering her and forcing into the car. Toole drove off whilst Lucas raped the girl repeatedly. At a distant spot, Toole jammed the brakes, dragged the girl from the car and shot her several times, leaving the body at the side of the road. The reason Toole had stopped the car was jealousy. He disapproved of Lucas having sex with a living person other than himself. This didn't matter much to Lucas; he himself admitted preferring sex with the dead.

The indignities didn't stop at killing and necrophilia, however. It was Toole's particular pleasure to partake of the flesh itself by eating it, and he never made a secret of his cannibalistic feasts. In conversation with a journalist, Billy Bob Barton, in 1996, Toole expounded upon his dietary preferences for young boys:

*"I've eaten my share. First I go out and catch me a little boy ... grab him, tie him up, use a gag, put him in the trunk of my car and drive him out to my place out in the swamps ... After the fucking then you strip them naked and hang them upside down by ankles; then slit their throat with a knife, slit the belly and take out the guts, the liver, the heart. Cut off the head. Let the blood drain."*

He described the cooking method:

*"A pit. A bar-q-que pit. Charcoal so there ain't much smoke. Take down the body, put the metal spit through them. Put it into the asshole, through the body and out the neck, wire the meat to the spit, put it on the spit-holder over the coals. Damn tasty."*

He described the taste:

*"Same as a roasted piglet. Boys and girls taste about the same when you roast them 8-10-years-old. The flavour is a shade different when they're teenagers. The boys are gamier than the girls. Give me the roasted meat of a boy age 14 and a girl age 14 and I can tell the difference when you use a spicy sauce."*

He boasted about his discriminatory palate:

*"Teenagers make a nice roast, I do favour a rump roast*

*from a teen. Younger ones. I think I prefer ribs. Juicy. Tasty. You ought to try some."*

He regaled with apparent pleasure how others had taken the blame for his crimes:

*"I got me a Chinese girl out by Colorado Springs in 1974, cut her throat and she had a friend and I stabbed her up too. The cop got a guy named Estep for that case but I did it. Cops don't always get the right person."* [6]

Investigators later released a transcript of a 1983 telephone conversation between the two as they reminisced about their abominable killing and cannibalistic practices. It was apparent that they were both willing parties, aware of what they were doing, but unable to accept full responsibility for it.

*Lucas: I got just about every law enforcement agency in the country talking to me. I'll continue to talk as long as they treat me like a man.*

*Toole: If they get rowdy with me, I just freeze up on 'em.*

*Lucas: Ottis, I don't want you to think I'm doing this as a revenge.*

*Toole: No, I don't want you to hold anything back on me.*

*Lucas: See, we got so many of them, Ottis. We got to turn up the bodies ... Now this boy and the girl, I don't know anything about.*

*Toole: Well, maybe that's the two I killed my own self. Just like that Mexican that wasn't going to let me out of the house. I took an axe and chopped him all up ... What made*

[6] Park Estep was convicted for the 1974 murder of attempted murder of a masseuse, Yon Cha Lee, and the murder of Sun Ok Cousin. He was later released on first parole hearing but not formally cleared of the crimes.

*me – I been meaning to ask you. That time when I cooked some of those people. Why'd I do that?*

*Lucas: I think it was just the hands doing it. I know a lot of the things we done, in human sight are impossible to believe.*

*Toole: When we took 'em out and cut 'em up ... Remember one time I said I wanted me some ribs. Did that make me a cannibal?*

*Lucas: You wasn't a cannibal. It's the force of the devil, something forced on us that we can't change.*

*Toole: One time you filleted some of them bodies and I did too. That cutting them up like meat, you know?*

*Lucas: I've seen bodies cut up worser than you ever seen bodies cut up.*

*Toole: I know that. I even took fire and burnt the bodies. Some tastes like real meat when it's got barbecue sauce on it.*

*Lucas: Ottis, you know everything you say is going on tape here.*

*Toole: I know.*

*Lucas: Personally, I'd have preferred you not talk about that. I don't want people to look at us as that kind of person.*

*Toole: Remember how I liked to pour some blood out of them?*

*Lucas: Otis, you and I have become something people look at as an animal. There's no way of changing what we done but we can stop it and not allow other people to become what we have.*

Lucas was eventually to confess to 600 of these "free lunches", as he referred to them. Toole claimed to have accompanied Lucas in over 1,000 murders. But the stories attached to many of the confessions varied depending upon *who* told them, and *when*. The descriptions of the methods of dispatch were varied; sometimes the victims were shot, sometimes beaten to death; other times they were strangled. The only known facts were that people were murdered. Lucas was later to explain that the differing *modi operandi* were key to the pair never being caught during their murder spree. He had learned in prison that by varying the method of killing the authorities would fail to connect the crimes. Moreover, he made sure the killings were done in remote areas, without witnesses.

It was on the open road that the pair wreaked the most mayhem. On some occasions they would pick up hitchhikers to kill. On other occasions they would pretend to be hitchhikers, with Toole dressing in drag as a lure. Virtually everyone that they picked up, they claimed, ended up dead.

As if Lucas and Toole's aberrations weren't outlandish enough, their claims were to become even weirder. They independently claimed that Toole had known a man by the name of Meteric, who was involved with a cult called the Hand of Death, and who may or may not have been part of his grandmother's Satanic devil worshipping ring. According to Lucas and Toole, Meteric invited them to carry out executions for the cult, paying them $10,000 per assignment. The two were more than happy to agree, since they were already killing for pleasure.

As an initiation into the group, Lucas and Toole were required to assassinate a man during a black mass celebration. After the unwitting man had been pointed out, Toole reportedly giggled at the prospect of how the body would be used afterwards. Then Lucas and Toole lured the man away from the group with a bottle of whiskey. Due to the ease of conversation between the Toole and the man, Lucas believed that they previously knew each other. Toole enticed the man towards a bench with the promise of a drink of whiskey. As the chosen man tipped his head back for a swig, Lucas stepped forward and deftly slit his throat from ear to ear. Later that night, the man's body parts were used in a flesh-eating ceremony, which provided delicacies that Toole reported finding extremely appetising:

*"Cut off the peter, cut off the balls. It's like put in a little stew pot. The guy who cooks it makes it like a soup of stew.*

*It's a secret recipe from a thousand years ago."*

Sometime in 1981, seven weeks after completing their killing education, the two men trawled the southern states drugging and kidnapping children for use in sacrificial rites within the cult or to be sold onwards to wealthy families. Older children or teenagers were filmed for pornography that was distributed within the cult. For some unknown reason, the cult then told the two men to take a break and go on a holiday.

Regardless of this request, Toole remained where he was whilst Lucas returned to Florida. His mother died following surgery around this time and the loss hit him like a brick. He haunted the cemetery, sometimes stretching himself out on her grave. Sometime later his sister Drusilla died, probably by a drug-induced suicide. Around this time, on 27 July 1981, a six-year-old boy called Adam Walsh disappeared from a shopping mall in Hollywood, Florida. Two weeks later the boy's head would later be recovered from a Vero Beach, Florida canal.

Lucas rejoined Toole in October 1981, and together the two men planned to spring Toole's 12-year-old niece Becky and her brother, Frank, aged 10, from the children's home where they'd been placed upon the deaths of their parents. It seems that Lucas took the children westward for a while whilst the authorities were looking for the children in Florida. Lucas, now spending more time with Becky, allegedly began to find her snappish and challenging. Eventually, he returned to join Toole again, bringing along Becky and Frank.

Having two children in tow did not slow down the pair of murderers. Indeed, the two men reported that the children went with them on many of the killings, not participating in the murders but certainly witnessing them at times. Becky, dressing scantily, was used as a lure for truckers, or she was used as a decoy to gain access to strangers' home. Frank was a lookout for law enforcement. On their travels from state to state, the murdering duo would often commit their crimes whilst the two children waited in the car.[7] Afterwards, the men would get back in and drive off as if nothing had happened. Lucas particularly enjoyed murdering women they found by the side of the road. On one occasion, the victim was found in a field, naked, stabbed 35 times in the best, back and neck. She had deep cuts around her arms and pubis area. Both nipples had been cut off and apparently removed from the scene. Police, piecing together the pair's destructive trail from discarded cars and payslips, were able to conclude that they murdered around four or five times in each state before crossing the border in order to avoid detection.

There were brief respites in the criminal odyssey during which the pair would work odd jobs. But these wouldn't last long. Soon the lust for blood would overtake them and they'd be back on their road, drinking, robbing, raping and murdering once again, and the crimes would become more and more brutal, to the point that the slightest resistance resulted in the victims being slaughtered and left in a pool of blood. Occasionally, the pair committed several murders in the space of a single day.

As the trip continued, Lucas reportedly contacted Meteric seeking another victim. According to Lucas, he was given the job of killing a lawyer who was about to give evidence to the police about the cult. A similar ruse was used to kill him – luring him to a quiet spot with the promise of a drink of alcohol. As the lawyer tipped his head back for a drink Lucas slit the man's throat from ear to ear so deeply that, as Lucas would later brag to police, "the liquor just ran out the bottom of his head". The story has a familiar but implausible ring to it. Then, according to Lucas, he buried the body in a shallow grave out of town, picked up Becky, returned to the body, disinterred it, decapitated it and reburied the parts separately, leaving the feet

---

[7] After his uncle's arrest in 1983, Frank checked himself into a psychiatric facility, the sights he had witness evidently having taken their toll on his mental state. He later took his own life.

projecting from the ground so that they might be easily found. His reasoning was that Meteric would then hear of the murder and issue payment for the job done. Lucas maintained that this murder so enflamed Becky's lust that for the first time he relented and let her sexually fondle him later that night.

Now that the relationship was more than platonic, according to Lucas, Becky became more demanding of sex. On one occasion, after he refused to make love to the pretty pre-teen girl, she accused him of being a homosexual, which he denied. Enraged, whilst she was asleep, he left the motel, drove to a truck stop where he picked up a woman. He drove the unnamed woman to a remote spot where he raped her and slit her throat.

Eventually, Lucas and Becky arrived in California. The cash for the "hit" didn't materialise and so they drifted aimlessly through the state, tired and broke. They robbed and worked odd jobs for money in order to eat. Their truck broke down and they resorted to hitchhiking. Becky, now disillusioned with life on the road, began to complain unremittingly, wanting to return to Florida.

Instead they went northwards to Oregon and Washington, where Lucas alleged that he committed murders in the same vein as the current Green River Killer so that the police would blame *that* murderer for the crimes.[8]

The pair were picked up by a kindly businessman, Jack Smart, who felt sorry for the bedraggled wanderers. He drove them back to his house and put them up for a while, giving Lucas work in his store in exchange for lodgings. Lucas stayed for around four months, during which time he would occasionally take himself off for a couple of days – in order, presumably, to quench his homicidal cravings.

Around this time, it transpired that Jack Smart's old and ailing

---

[8] Police later disproved these claims after it was shown that Lucas was elsewhere at the time.

mother-in-law, Kate "Granny" Rich, was in need to some help around the house. As a solution, Lucas and Becky travelled to Ringgold, Texas to help. The plan was that they would stay there rent-free in exchange for maintenance work.

At first the arrangement went well. Granny Rich took to Becky immediately and Lucas quickly earned her trust. Soon, however, Lucas was squandering Granny's money on drink and cigarettes and began to forge her signature on cheques, leading the local store-holder to become suspicious. The clerk contacted Granny's relatives, the Smarts, and they drove to Ringgold to check for themselves. What they found incensed them. Granny Rich was sitting at the kitchen table in a house that was filthy, with no dishes washed and rooms that had not been cleaned in months. The Smarts demanded that Lucas and Becky leave, even giving them money for the bus journey out of town.

Instead, they were picked up by a well-intentioned man called Reuben Moore, a preacher from nearby Stoneburg, Texas, who offered to put them up in his religious community, the House of Prayer.

The "community", it transpired, was little more than a converted chicken coop on a rundown ranch. Nevertheless, Lucas and Becky settled down for a while. Unbeknownst to Lucas, whilst he worked, Becky was beginning to learn Christian values and mend her ways. She rekindled her relationship with Granny Rich. In order to put her life back in order, Becky felt she needed to return to Florida, give herself up and confess.

When Lucas heard this he became enraged, demanding to know if Becky had said anything about their crimes to Granny Rich. Becky said she hadn't, so Lucas told her get packing, that they were returning to Florida the next day.

On the road, the two found it more difficult to catch a ride. For some reason, as soon as drivers saw Lucas, a dirty, one-eyed tramp-like man, they sped off again.

The two trekked eastward, sometimes staying in cheap motels, other times bedding down in open fields alongside the road. Then, one evening, Lucas lay down and started to drink. He became argumentative with Becky, berating her for the decision to go back to Jacksonville. He told her that he'd changed his mind – the next morning they'd be returning to Stoneburg. Becky's response was to clout him on the head.

> *"That was it, [Lucas recalled]. I just stabbed her with my knife. I just picked it up, brought it around, and hit her right in the chest with it. She sort of sat there for a little bit and then dropped on over. I took her bra and panties off and had sex with her. That's one of those things I guess that got to be a part of my life – having sexual intercourse with the dead."*

After he removed a ring from Becky's finger, cut her body into pieces and stuffed it into pillowcases, Lucas, for the first time, became remorseful. He was overcome with the feeling that he'd destroyed something special in his life.[9]

Needing to build an alibi, Lucas now returned to Stoneburg where he broke down in front of Reuben Moore, telling him that Becky had run off with a truck driver. Word spread about Lucas' return ... *without* Becky.[10] None was more concerned than Granny Rich. She contacted Lucas and he agreed to drive her to her evening church service and talk to her then.

During the drive, Granny Rich pressed Lucas for details about Becky's "disappearance". He became more and more angry at her persistent questions until he finally had enough. He stopped

---

[9] In 1994, a woman came forward claiming to be "Becky". She refuted Lucas' versions of events, saying that she had not been involved in any murders, and that she had disappeared simply in order to move on with her life. She sounded convincing, but it turned out to be a deception concocted by Lucas and a woman 13 years older than Becky would've been.

[10] Frieda "Becky" Powell's skeletal remains were located in a field where Lucas had said they would be. She had been 15-years-old when killed.

the car over, pulled out a knife and plunged it into the elderly lady's body. He dragged the corpse from the car and carved an inverted cross across her chest, had sex with the body and dumped it in a culvert.

Lucas returned to Moore's ranch and told the owner that Granny Rich had been too ill to go to church. Later that night, he returned to the body, dismembered it, packed it up, brought the pieces of Moore's ranch and burned them in a woodstove. Satisfied, he then took Moore's car and put some distance between him and the scene of the crime.

Inevitably, he was caught. Granny Rich's relatives had become suspicious and made their own enquiries. They reported her missing and the investigative trail led them straight to the "House of Prayer". A trace was put on Moore's stolen vehicle, which was later found outside Hemet, California, bloodstains covering the seat. Lucas was picked up (he had been heading back to Jack Smart's antique store), but, as he had informed the police that the blood was his own, and the police having no body by which to compare it, they were obliged to let him go.

In October 1982, Lucas abducted a woman getting into her car in Decatur, Illinois, ordered her to drive south, then took over the driving as she slept. Whilst he drove he felt a chill overcome him and knew that he would kill the woman. He did so, stopping the car outside Magnolia, North Carolina and then instantly stabbing her in the throat before cutting off her clothes, having sex with the body and dumping it nearby. He drove the car to Fredericksburg, Texas where he abandoned it and then, in an attempt to cover his tracks, hitchhiked back north to Bloomington, Indiana.

Lucas, now penniless and desperate, then contacted Reuben Moore. Moore agreed to send him some money. Lucas returned to the "House of Prayer" where he was arrested for the much-earlier theft of his brother-in-law's truck in Maryland. During the arrest he was questioned about the murders. Maryland Police declined to request extradition for something so petty as a stolen truck and Lucas was eventually released. However, he later returned to the "House of Prayer" where he gave Moore a gun, which led to his arrest for the final time.

Meanwhile, months earlier in January 1982, Ottis had felt that he'd been betrayed by his lover and his lover's lover (Henry and Becky). He'd lapsed into a world of his own, muttering about Henry's disloyalty as he paced the floor, his mental state appearing to break down rapidly. He took to wandering to try to forget, passing through six states on a murderous rampage of slaughter and arson between January 1981 and February 1982. Ironically, despite Toole's name being forever linked to that of Henry Lee Lucas, little is known about his own crime spree, despite his independent confessions to hundreds of arsons and murders. On 23 May 1983, two houses were set afire in Jacksonville, Toole's home neighbourhood. Toole was fingered by teenage accomplices on 6 June and he was arrested shortly afterwards. He immediately began to sing like a canary, admitting to over 40 arson attacks over the past two decades.

One of these fires, on 4 January 1982, led to the death of 64-year-old George Sonnenberg, who succumbed to the injuries he sustained in the fire. Toole had barricaded the man inside the boarding house before setting fire to it.

There were no depravities that Toole would not admit to. He readily confessed to abducting young boys, gagging them, sodomising them, stringing them up, killing them, dicing up the flesh to stew and eat. Some of the confessions sounded simply fantastical. He told one reporter, Billy Bob Barton:

> *"A girl 8 or 9 years old, her pussy ain't able to take a big dick. She can take it up her butt same as a boy. I prefer a boy. I make his peter get hard, a boy maybe 12-years-old, I can make him shoot jizz every time while I'm up his ass. A girl, she doesn't do nothing. Ain't much fun."*

He would kill by strangulation, by shooting, by stabbing or disembowelling. He recalled killing a girl called Shelley:

*"I got her when she was hitch hiking in Colorado. I had me an old pick-up truck. I picked her up, took her up into the Rocky Mountains and killed her. She was naked when I killed her. A pretty one. It was the summertime in 1974 and what was funny is that the police blamed the killing on Ted Bundy but Ted didn't get that one, I got her."*

He spoke about the ritual slayings of virgins in rituals within the Hand of Death cult:

*Barton: "What's a human sacrifice like?"*
*Toole: "Secret rituals. I can't reveal it to anyone."*
*Barton: "Generally. Tell me generally."*
*Toole: "Put them on the altar and cut their throat, then make a burnt offering to the Devil. Like that generally."*
*Barton: "Who? Women? Kids?"*
*Toole: "Virgins were preferred. Girls of teenage years."*
*Barton: "Virgins sacrifice?"*
*Toole: "Yeah, slit the throat, collect the blood in a goblet, pass it around and drink it hot. Do chants. It's secret stuff. You aren't supposed to reveal it. They make you take an oath for secrecy."*
*Barton: "You drank human blood from a cup?"*
*Toole: "Yeah, it's in the ritual."*
*Barton: "What's it taste like?"*
*Toole: "Kinda salty. Not so good. I like cooked meat. I didn't mind eating the cooked parts."*
*Barton: "Is eating human flesh part of the rituals?"*
*Toole: "Sometimes."*
*Barton: "What parts are ritually eaten?"*
*Toole: "Well, I'm not allowed to tell about it."*

He revelled in the delights of eating human flesh, especially the intimate parts:

*"The part of the woman around the pussy hole is like lips.*

*Sort of chewy and rubbery. The balls are damned good when fried. Use a little batter and a fryer and it's a real treat. Crisp. Like crispy chestnuts. Fresh fried balls is one of my favourites."*

He admitted to picking up hitchhiking women for use in human sacrifices, but the stories were becoming more and more far-fetched:

*"Certain times of the year the priests wanted virgins for the human sacrifices. They'd say to me and Henry to go up to Texas and collect some. We'd drive on up, get girls hitchhiking, pick up vans at bars. There are a lot of women just walking down the road in South Texas. Migrant workers. We'd get them, tie them up, gag them, put them in the trunk. We fill the trunk, six or eight girls, then go back to Mexico. "*

And all the while he kept telling of the "secret things I can't tell about", chanting, cutting off heads with a guillotine, sacrificing virgins to the Prince of Darkness, killing 13 virgins in one night, using the non-virgins for snuff movies.

By this time, Lucas was also admitting to crimes aplenty. However, despite some inconsistencies and improbabilities (and some definite impossibilities), many of the confessions seemed to back up Ottis' gruesome tales, and the statements "cleared up" a number of unsolved crimes in 11 states. Both men were able to give details that only the committer of the crimes could have known about.

One of the mysteries that Toole's admissions cleared up was that of the murder of Adam Walsh. On 21 October 1983, Toole startled Police Chief Leroy Hessler with details that were "grisly beyond belief". He claimed to have enticed the six-year-old boy from the parking lot of a mall in Hollywood, Florida with the offer of candy and that Walsh had gone with him willingly. He drove off with Walsh but the boy began to cry, saying that he wanted to go home. Toole said that he punched Walsh in the face, causing him to cry more, and this induced Toole to punch Walsh hard enough to knock him out. He drove around for a while, eventually stopping at a rural canal where he decapitated the child using a machete.

Unbelievably, Toole drove around for several days with the head in the boot of his car, eventually forgetting about it. Upon rediscovering the severed head later, he tossed it into a drainage canal around 130 miles from where Walsh had been taken. It was found over two weeks after the boy's disappearance. The coroner ruled that death had been by asphyxiation. The rest of the Adam Walsh's body has never been found.

Toole, already sentenced to death for the murder of George Sonnenberg in the boarding house fire, was found guilty also of the murder of 19-year-old Ada Johnson in Tallahassee, Florida and received a second death sentence. Both sentences were later commuted to life in prison. There wasn't enough evidence to charge Toole for the murder of Adam Walsh; inexplicably, police had misplaced vital evidence. The Walsh family were denied proper justice for Adam's death as Toole died of cirrhosis on 15 September 1996.

Henry Lee Lucas was convicted for the murders of 11 people and sentenced to death for the murder of "Orange Socks", who was identified in 2019 as Debra Louise Jackson, a 23-year-old woman from Abilene, Texas who'd left home in 1977 only to be murdered in 1979. She'd been working at an assisted living unit at the time of her disappearance. She was found only hours after being strangled to death. In addition to the bruising around her neck, there were marks caused by being dragged through grass and dropped from an overpass into a culvert on the I-35. When found, she was naked apart from the orange socks from which her tragic epithet was derived for over 40 years.

In June 1999, after 13 years on death row, just as it appeared that the sentence was about to be carried out, it was reduced to life in prison. Lucas was found dead from heart failure in his prison at the age of 64 on 12 March 2001. Because of ongoing problems with vandalism and theft, his grave is unmarked.

Lucas' credibility is severely damaged by the outrageousness of his "admissions". He began by admitting to 60 murders, then raised this to over 100, then increasing the death toll to a staggering 3,000. Conservative estimates put the number at around 40 killings. It was obvious by the end that Lucas was an inveterate liar. Some of his confessions would have meant he would have had to travel several thousand miles in the space of a few hours in a clapped-out banger of a car, an unlikely feat. It can be surmised that Lucas was simply being fed information by investigators and, because he was given special treatment and favours whilst in custody, he became a compliant fabulist of gargantuan proportions.

However, he *did* have specific knowledge about many crimes that only the perpetrator could have known. His and Toole's involvement with the curious Hand of Death cult is suspect. There is no evidence that the cult actually existed. However, it was mentioned independently by other noted transgressors, Charles Manson and David Berkowitz ("Son of Sam"). The dates of Lucas and Toole's involvement with any cult are unverifiable, but they told interviewers that they severed ties with the group sometime around 1981. If the men had ever been paid for their work for the cult, there is no evidence that either man flaunted any unexplained newfound wealth before or after 1981.

Lucas claimed not to have known the reason why he murdered and raped. He believed he was possessed by a demon that drove him to perform evil, and the influence of his devil-worshipping grandmother may have been key to his self-labelling. He was diagnosed as schizophrenic several times by psychiatrists and psychologists over the span of his life. However, in each of his three murder trials his sanity was questioned, and in each case he was found legally sane.

Toole was declared mentally retarded at a young age. It is probable that he found a perfect companion in the shape of Lucas and he was pushed towards deviance from the time of their meeting and onwards. Because of Toole's low IQ, criminologists theorise that Lucas called the shots and, in an attempt to prove himself worthy, Toole followed along blithely. *He* was the merciless gun that committed many crimes, but from the day he was born, his atrociously brutal upbringing, along with the malignant influence of his twisted companion, certainly had their hand in helping to pull the trigger.

The story of the twisted star-crossed lovers who raped, murdered and cannibalised their way across America is bizarre, astounding and unnerving. Whether they killed 10 or 1,000, the true number is unverifiable. In the worst-case scenario, some of the *actual* murderers, whose crimes Lucas and Toole so eagerly confessed to, are still out there. There can be no closure for the families of those left behind. Those scars will never heal.

# William MacDonald
(active 1962-1962)


A CURIOUS INCIDENT was the undoing of the first recognised serial killer to make an appearance in Australian history. The incident came to be known as "The Case of the Walking Corpse", and it was this freak encounter that eventually brought an elusive serial killer to justice.

The man who would later become internationally known as the "Mutilator" – going by the name of William MacDonald – was brought into the world in Liverpool, England on 17 June 1924, and his name was registered at birth as Allan Ginsberg.

The middle of three children, Allan's early life was solitary and lonely. Short, thin and shy, the boy was almost friendless and unable to form lasting relationships. He never sought out company. The loner was disposed to going out late at night on long walks, and on many occasions his mother resorted to calling the police to search for him. In his mid- to late-teens, the boy displayed "discipline issues" at school, and still he was reluctant to make friends. He was diagnosed at this time as an "erratic schizophrenic".

During the second world war, when he was aged 19, Ginsberg joined the army, serving with the Lancashire Fusiliers. Sometime in 1943 he was raped by a corporal in an air-raid shelter. The attacker threatened to have Ginsberg killed if he told anyone. After initially complaining that the event had traumatised him, Ginsberg later admitted that he had enjoyed it. The incident was to have a profound influence on the direction of Ginsberg's life; it laid bare his latent homosexuality, which he believed would bring him nothing but misery, rejection and humiliation.

After his discharge from army service in 1947, Ginsberg's mother and brother committed him to a mental asylum in Scotland where conditions were medieval, with cells chock-full of raving lunatics and freezing cold rooms. Under these conditions Ginsberg was once again diagnosed with schizophrenia and treated with daily doses of electroconvulsive therapy. He was discharged from this establishment after six months, and the effectiveness (or otherwise) of the treatment he underwent can only be imagined. The rape, meanwhile, played constantly on his mind now and throughout his life, and would be the stimulus influencing the shocking events ahead of him.

Ginsberg was now an active homosexual, openly cottaging[1] and engaging in encounters in public bars. As he had feared, his activities earned him ridicule and taunts. Those were unenlightened, conservative times, and others were disinclined to accept such outlandish behaviours. Ginsberg found this difficult to deal with and moved from job to job. He began to worry about his mental stability, complaining of the persecution and hallucinations that plagued him. He spent another three months in a psychiatric facility but it changed little.

In 1949, convinced that his surroundings were the cause of his mental deterioration, Ginsberg emigrated to Canada and encountered trouble with the law there. Six years later, deciding that he needed a completely new life again, he relocated to Adelaide, the capital of South Australia, in 1955.

By now he was calling himself William MacDonald. The change of name or location did not suppress any unhealthy desires, and shortly after his arrival he was arrested for touching the penis of a policeman in a public convenience. For this misdemeanour MacDonald received a two-year conditional discharge. He moved to Ballarat in Victoria, finding work on a construction site. His workmates beat him up and called him a "poofter". In retaliation, MacDonald slashed the tyres of their bicycles.

He moved jobs frequently, and continually seemed to be dogged by trouble. No matter where he went, others, it seemed to

---

[1] Cottaging is a slang term for the practice between male sexual partners of cruising for anonymous sex in public toilets.

him, would persecute him, talking or laughing about him behind his back, and all the while the urge to wreak revenge upon his tormentors grew and grew.

In 1960, MacDonald met and befriended a 55-year-old man called Amos Hurst outside the Roma Street Transit Centre, a Brisbane railway station. The two had a long drinking session together in a nearby hotel, each man vying to drink the other under the table, and in due course Hurst invited MacDonald back to his apartment where they drank yet more alcohol. When Hurst was almost completely incapacitated by inebriation, Mac-Donald began to strangle his newfound friend.

During the throttling, Hurst began to haemorrhage and blood spurted in profusion from his mouth over MacDonald's hands. MacDonald then punched Hurst in the face. Such was the ferociousness of this blow that Hurst to fell to the floor lifeless.

MacDonald proceeded to wash the body and put it to bed. He sat for a while awaiting the knock of the door that would indicate the arrival of the police. When none arrived he let himself out of the apartment and returned to his lodgings. Every day he checked the papers for an announcement of the murder. There was none. Then, five days later, he was surprised to read about the "heart attack" suffered by Amos Hurst in the obituary column. For MacDonald it seemed a close shave.

The coroner's report *did*, in fact, indicate that Hurst's death had been a heart attack. What the papers did not report, however, was that there had been severe bruising on his neck which could have been caused by an altercation or some other drunken misadventure. Nevertheless, MacDonald's urge to kill had been stimulated and his hunt for the next victim commenced with added gusto. He bought himself a sharp knife and began to trawl the dives of Brisbane in search of another "friend", one of whom, a man called Bill, he found in a sleazy wine joint full of people down on their luck,. Bill, it seemed to MacDonald, looked uncannily like the soldier who'd raped him all those years ago.

After a period of drinking, MacDonald and Bill left the saloon and went to a nearby park, bringing with them a couple of bottles of sherry. MacDonald only had one thought on his mind: murder. He bided his time until his new companion had passed out drunk. Then MacDonald unsheathed his knife and held it above the man's chest. Just at the point when he was about to plunge down the knife for some inexplicable reason the urge left him. He sat with the man for a while before going home, leaving his fortunate acquaintance to sleep it off in the park.

By January 1961, MacDonald (now having assumed a new name, Alan Edward Brennan) had made his way to the inner-city locality of East Sydney. Here, he found employment with the Postmaster-General's Department as a letter sorter. He also found diversions in public parks and toilets, becoming well known in the local haunting grounds for closeted gay men.

The voices in his head continued to torment him, urging him to kill again, and for that eventuality he acquired a new long-bladed knife. On 4 June 1961, a Saturday, MacDonald found his next victim. Alfred Reginald Greenfield was a 41-year-old homeless, unemployed blacksmith who was sitting on a bench in Green Park when he had the misfortune to cross paths with his would-be murderer. MacDonald offered Greenfield a drink from his bottle and the two got talking. Under the pretext that he had more bottles in his bag, MacDonald lured Greenfield towards the Andrew "Boy" Charlton Pool complex, a half-hour-walk away on the shore of Woolloomooloo Bay. By day, the pool complex was a popular public swimming pool, but by night, due to its many hidden alcoves, it became a favoured haunt for drinkers and vagrants.

At the pool, the two chatted. Greenfield, willing allowing himself to be plied with drink by MacDonald, eventually became drunk and passed out. MacDonald had come prepared. He removed a plastic raincoat from his bag and put it on. He now unsheathed his new knife and held it over the unconscious man. There was no hesitation this time – he plunged it repeatedly into the man's neck until it was clear that he was dead. Blood spurted freely, drenching the scene about them. MacDonald remained uncontaminated; the plastic coat had served its purpose.

MacDonald then removed the dead man's trousers and underpants. Now, using his sharp knife, he sliced into the genitals, neatly severing the penis and scrotum from the body. He brought the body part to the edge of the harbour and threw it into the waters of the bay. Then he casually packed up his knife and raincoat and walked home, washing his bloodied face and hands under a tap along the way. The voices in his head were silenced. For a while …

This time the newspapers couldn't fail to report the lurid details of the murder, and they dubbed the crazed fiend "The Mutilator".

An almost identical murder occurred six months later on 21 November 1961. This time MacDonald had brought with him a new six-inch bladed knife. The victim again was a vagrant, 41-year-old Ernest William Cobbin, whom MacDonald had spotted staggering along South Dowling Street under the influence of alcohol. It took MacDonald no time at all to tempt the man with the promise of more drink, and they went to nearby Moore Park and entered the public toilets. Whilst Cobbin sat on the toilet seat watching, MacDonald calmly donned his raincoat. Then, with a single brutal slashing motion, MacDonald swiftly swung the unused knife into his new friend's throat, splitting the jugular vein. Blood spurted everywhere, but luckily for the Mutilator the raincoat provided adequate protection.

As MacDonald continued the frenzied attack, Cobbin, severely wounded and in desperate shock, tried to defend himself. To no avail. He shortly fell dead on the toilet floor, mortally injured by around 50 stab wounds on the face, neck, arms and chest. But even as the man lay dead, his assailant continued his slashing knife onslaught until blood spatters completely covered the cubicle walls. Then he removed Cobbin's trousers and pants and sliced off his genitals. He put them into the plastic bag he'd been organised enough to bring with him. His rage abated, the Mutilator then calmly removed his raincoat, put it into his bag along with the murder weapon. Before leaving, he stopped to wash his face and hands.

Back at his apartment, MacDonald washed the genitals in warm water and placed them in a clean plastic bag which he then slept in bed with overnight.

The next morning, he bound the plastic bag and its grisly contents, along with the knife and a brick, tied the package up with string and went to the Sydney Harbour Bridge where he dropped his macabre package into the deepest part of the waters.

The newspapers seized upon rumours that authorities were considering the killer to be female:

> _Police believe a woman might be the killer who hacked a man to death in a Moore Park toilet to-day._
> _Senior detectives have not ruled out the possibility._
> _The woman might be impersonating a man._
> (_Canberra Times_, Canberra, 22 November 1961)

They reported that the police had linked the two murders and, although they did not report the details explicitly, rumours circulated wildly about the mutilation characteristics of the murders:

> _Police believe the killer also murdered Alfred Reginald Greenfield, of Cathedral Street, East Sydney, in Sydney Domain on June 3._
> _They said the circumstances were identical and both bodies had been mutilated after death._
> _Cobbin's body was found after a man telephoned police at 5.35 a.m. and said: "There is the body of a man in the toilet at Moore Park, opposite the Bat and Ball Hotel."_
> (_Idib._)

The unknown tipster – a man with a hoarse voice – was never identified but it's reasonable to assume that it had been the murderer himself. When detectives arrived at the Moore Park toilets they were confronted with a scene of unimaginable horror. The place was awash with blood and the victim had been slashed and mutilated in the vicious, frenzied attack. They quickly identified the dead man, who'd been married with two children, although living apart from his family, and who'd taken somewhat to the bottle, but who nevertheless was a man without any enemies whatsoever … or so they thought.

The investigators were less quick to identify the *murderer*, for he left no fingerprints or other trace of himself at all. He'd wiped the scene clean of evidence and disappeared into thin air.

Soon, however, the police modified the scope of their investigation and issued a warning to potential victims:

*"Any man who is alone in a lonely street or park for more than ten minutes could be murdered and mutilated by this maniac. We believe he is a psychopathic homosexual who is killing to satisfy some twisted urge."*

The message was also a ruse to attempt to flush out the twisted killer. Detectives staked out public toilets and the known haunts of street-drinkers. Undercover officers disguised themselves as down-and-outs and infiltrated their locales. Their efforts proved fruitless and they were no closer to capturing the Mutilator.

Meanwhile, MacDonald (still going by the adopted moniker of Alan Edward Brennan) had gone back to his job in the postal service. He voraciously read about his exploits in the newspapers, but to him it seemed as though it was another person committing these crimes. He joined in discussions with his workmates about Sydney's mysterious Mutilator, and he became secretly dismayed when they referred to the killer in their midst as a "pervert" or "queer". In his paranoia he believed that they suspected him of being the Mutilator, and he even considered giving himself up to the police. It was only a passing thought, however, for MacDonald was already thinking about his next victim.

On Saturday morning, 31 March 1962, the opportunity presented itself. Frank Gladstone McLean, a man of unknown age (estimated to be in his mid-30s), was drinking at the Oxford

Hotel in Darlinghurst, Sydney. At around 10 o'clock, the inebriated man left the establishment. Outside it was raining, so it would've been no surprise when he met a man wearing a plastic raincoat. The man struck up a conversation with him and proposed that they move into nearby Little Bourke Street to share a drink.

As they turned into an unlit lane, the man suddenly plunged a sharp knife into McLean's throat. McLean staggered and fell to the ground and the man stabbed him again in the face, then punched him in the face, forcing him off balance, and then, whilst he was incapacitated on the ground, stabbed him some more in the face, head, neck, throat and chest. McLean crumpled and passed out.

The attack had created some noise and MacDonald became worried. He heard passers-by and withdrew into the shadows, fully expecting the assault to be discovered, but luck was with him again – the passing family had not witnessed the attack. He returned to the dying man, pulled him into the lane and stabbed him again – six stab wounds in total.

By now, saturated in blood, the Mutilator dragged his victim further into the lane. He removed the man's trousers and sliced off his genitals with a single upward slash. He put the severed genitals in a plastic bag and departed from the scene, taking the bag of genitals home with him, only to discard them the next day by throwing the bag and its incriminating contents from the Sydney Harbour Bridge into the waters below – just as he had done before.

According to the next day's newspaper report,

> *A man walking home found the body around 11.30pm. It had been pushed into the gutter against the kerb. The man was about to walk past when he noticed blood still flowing down the gutter and saw that the man's clothing was disarranged.*
>
> (*Sydney Morning Herald*, Sydney, 1 April 1962)

The audacious murder had taken only 200 yards from Darlinghurst police station and the fact that the killer had not been seen left its occupants baffled. Another thing that perplexed them was the manner in which McLean's genitals had been removed, and investigators at one stage considered that the murderer could be an unhinged surgeon. For a while the medical profession itself came under scrutiny. What the papers didn't mention, though, was that Frank McLean had still been alive when he was found, though he was mortally wounded. He died from his injuries shortly afterwards without providing information about his assailant. Once again, MacDonald seemed to have had the luck of the devil.

By now, the people of Sydney were atwitch. This crime, within metres of a busy thoroughfare, felt more audacious than the others, and whilst the Mutilator was still at large it seemed as if the entire city were under siege. With good reason. The killer's bloodlust was up. Two weeks later he was seeking to take another life. Or so it seemed …

On 14 April 1962, an unknown man attacked a young airman in the vicinity of Goulburn Street, near where Frank McLean had been stabbed. The airman, Patrick Royan, reported that his attacker had jumped over a high fence and lunged at him with a long-bladed knife, only to miss his mark. Royan, with incredible luck, escaped with only a nick. He described the man as between 30 and 40 years old, tall and solid, and of "foreign" appearance. He said that the mystery man had hissed as he attacked. However, Royan, it turned out, was an alcoholic psychiatric patient who'd invented the story for attention. He was sentenced to 18 months in prison for wasting police time.

Meanwhile, William MacDonald's life was taking a turn. He was sacked from his job with the postal service and, in the same week, fell out with his landlord. To solve both problems he decided to go into business for himself. Having saved up money over the years, MacDonald (still going by the assumed name Alan Edward Brennan) bought a small delicatessen in Burwood, in the inner western suburb of Sydney, in which he made sandwiches and sold luncheon meats, pies, cakes and ice cream, and from which he was also an agent for a dry-cleaning company. Best of all, MacDonald lived above the shop and so could be left alone to do what he pleased. To him, this meant that he could bring his victims home and kill in private, with little risk of getting caught, and one night in November 1962 this is exactly what he did.

Forty-two-year-old James Hackett was the unfortunate victim. MacDonald met him in a wine saloon in downtown Sydney. Hackett, a petty thief and vagrant who'd only recently been let out of prison, would've been only too glad to take a taxi back to MacDonald's premises for a drink that cold evening. In Mac-Donald's rooms Hackett drank until he passed out on the floor. Then MacDonald struck. Taking one of the sharp knives used in the preparation of the cold meats in his shop, he thrust it straight into Hackett's neck. Incredibly, this woke the man and he began to defend himself, and in the struggle the knife pierced Mac-Donald's own hand. MacDonald, furious, now plunged the knife directly into Hackett's heart, killing him instantly. In his crazed homicidal rage MacDonald continued to stab the already dead man again and again until the walls and ceiling were spattered with blood. Pools of blood oozed from the body and formed large puddles which then seeped through the floorboards.

So ferocious had the attack been that the knife was bent and blunt. MacDonald attempted to remove the genitals from the body but the knife was now inadequate for the task. He made a few desultory stabs at the penis and cut around the scrotum before giving up and falling asleep beside the body.

MacDonald had a huge clean-up job ahead of him when he awoke the next day. He himself was covered in dried blood. Hackett's blood had soaked through the floorboards and there was danger it would drip onto the produce of the shop below.

He had a bath and washed away the congealed blood, and then took himself off to the hospital where he had the wound in his hand stitched. Scrubbing his flat clean took most of the rest of the day. The flooring could not be cleaned and so he had to remove it and dispose of it in parts.

Next, MacDonald had to get rid of the corpse itself. He removed the clothes (except for the socks) and dragged the body down the stairs and into the foundations of the building, jamming it into a far corner of the brickwork until it was entirely out of sight. He bundled all of Hackett's clothes alongside the man's remains.

However, MacDonald didn't yet feel he was safe. The taxi driver who'd transported the two men back to the delicatessen the previous evening was a witness. There was blood all over the walls of the flat upstairs and on the floorboards. Panicked and paranoid, MacDonald decided his only option was to run. He packed his bags and deserted the shop, catching a northbound train to Brisbane, New South Wales. There, he moved into a boarding house, dyed his hair, began to grow a moustache and started calling himself Allan MacDonald. Every day he scoured the papers for news of the Sydney murder but there was no mention of it. He worried that police had set a trap and were waiting for him should he return to the scene of the crime.

Back in Sydney, however, there were developments aplenty. Customers of Alan Brennan's dry-cleaning business arrived to pick up their laundry and were concerned to find it closed. After three weeks a stench began to emanate from the premises and a week later it became so overpowering that neighbours called the Health Department. Enquiries revealed that the owner had not been seen since 4 November. The police broke in and their noses led them to the cause of the smell – a putrefying body in such a state of decomposition its identity was unrecognisable.

The foul-smelling remains were taken to the morgue where the medical examiner could only determine that they belonged to a male in his forties, a description similar to the missing proprietor of the delicatessen, Mr Alan Brennan. The police thought that for some unknown reason Brennan had crawled beneath his shop and suffered an accidental electrocution. The body's fingerprints did not match any on record, and it had suffered no broken bones. There was no reason for them to suspect foul play. In due course the body of "Alan Edward Brennan" was buried in a pauper's grave, his old postal worker colleagues held a memorial service for him, and no one thought any more about it.

No one, that is, except for the coroner, Mr F.E. Cox. Mr Cox could not fathom why a man, naked except for his socks, should be underneath a shop with the rest of his clothes piled beside him. Mr Cox returned an open verdict on the death. He declared, apparently with more than a degree of dissatisfaction:

> "It seems extraordinary that the body of Mr Brennan should have been found in the position and in the condition in which it was found.
>
> According to the evidence, the deceased had neither his trousers on, nor his boots, or shoes, or singlet [sleeveless shirt]. He was clad only in his socks, with his coat and trousers alongside him. Nothing was found to indicate to any degree of certainty that the deceased had taken his own life, even if it were intention to do so.
>
> It seems to me an extraordinary thing that the deceased should have gone under the house to commit and act that would result in his death. It could have been that the deceased was the victim of foul play, although the police report said that there was nothing to indicate foul play. But I cannot altogether exclude that possibility."

If Mr Cox had been appraised of the bloodstains in the shop, or of the knife slashes in the dead man's shirt, his suspicions would've been raised alarmingly. However, he had _not_ been, and so a man living freely in Brisbane seemed to be literally getting away with murder. The man needn't have worried. Unbeknownst to him, William Allan MacDonald had been officially declared dead. His body, after all, had been found in his own shop. No one at all was looking for him.

If only he hadn't returned to Sydney ...

MacDonald, ignorant of the fact that he had been declared

legally dead, was becoming increasingly paranoid and skittish. He stayed only a short time in Brisbane before moving on to New Zealand, convinced that the police were looking for him. Here, he changed his name yet again, this time to David Ernest Allan. The compulsion to kill was still upon him and he actively sought out men to murder. If he hadn't been overcome with this renewed urge MacDonald would've got away with his crimes. However, the compulsions were getting stronger by the day, and in order to satisfy them he needed to return to the anonymity of a large city such as Sydney.

Six months after the "death" of Alan Brennan, on 22 April 1963, MacDonald was walking along Sydney's crowded George Street. There he bumped – literally – into an old post office colleague, John McCarthy. McCarthy, understandably, was shocked. Standing before was "Alan Bennet", who was supposedly dead and buried.

"I believed you had died," he told the apparition before him.

"What do you mean?" the confused MacDonald asked.

"They found your body underneath your shop," McCarthy replied. "We went to your funeral service."

The realisation of what had happened immediately dawned upon MacDonald. "Leave me alone," he shouted, and then ran away down the street.

McCarthy went to the police but they did not believe his story and so he rang it through to the *Daily Mirror*. The reporter knew a good story when he saw it and filed it under the headline "Case of the Walking Corpse". Police, now forced by the publication of the story, exhumed the body of "Alan Bennet". They re-examined what was left of the fingerprints, noted 41 "signature" stabs wounds on the penis and testicles, and determined that the body actually belonged to James Hackett. They produced an identikit picture of MacDonald, which was circulated widely and eventually recognised by MacDonald's work colleagues in Melbourne who dobbed him in to the authorities.

Meanwhile, immediately after the startling encounter in Sydney, MacDonald returned to Melbourne. The police swooped. A month after bumping into an old work colleague, MacDonald – or "David Allen" – was arrested as he called to collect his weekly pay. He straightaway admitted his identity and confessed to four counts of murder. Referring to the attack he suffered whilst in the army, he told police:

> _"I thought when the corporal attacked me he took my life away. So I thought I'd destroy his sex the same way."_

At Sydney airport, the crowd awaiting a glimpse of the perpetrator of the grotesque and barbaric Mutilator murders were disappointed; the short, thin, nervous MacDonald was nothing like the monstrous beast that they'd imagined.

At his sensational trial before Mr Justice McLennan, MacDonald pleaded not guilty by reason of insanity and testified to stabbing one of his victims in the neck 30 times and removing the testicles with a knife. A female jurist fainted upon hearing the grisly evidence and had to be removed from court. MacDonald went into great detail in recounting how blood had spattered over his raincoat as he attacked his victims. The gallery listened in shock and repulsion as he told of putting the genitals in a plastic bag and taking them home with him, speaking about the incident without a tremor of emotion or remorse and stating that if let loose he would commit the same crimes again, as and when the urge took him.

MacDonald was found guilty, the jury, to the shock of psychiatrists, choosing to ignore overwhelming evidence of insanity. He was sentenced to five life terms with the recommendation that he never be released. However, after nearly beating another prisoner to death with a slops bucket, he was certified insane and transferred to a secure psychiatric unit. In 1980, he was found sane enough to be sent to join the mainstream prison community at Cessnock Prison, 100 miles north of Sydney, where he lived a reclusive existence in protective custody, reading and listening to classical music.

In 2000 he declined to attend a court hearing arranged to set down a date when he would be eligible for parole. He said:

> *"I am institutionalised now. I have no desire to go and live on the outside. I wouldn't last five minutes. I am too old, and besides, I have everything I could ever want where I am."*

That same year, MacDonald gave an interview to a journalist[2] and it became clear that in prison, as he had been on the outside, he remained friendless:

> *"I don't associate with anyone else within the prison system. I never have. I have never had a friend in my life. I keep very much to myself. I prefer it that way."*

When asked *why* he had killed his victims he claimed he hadn't murdered them, reasoning that:

> *"[It] is the other person who lives inside me that actually killed them. As a young boy I was diagnosed as schizophrenic and I still am today. Schizophrenia means split personality and it was my other personality that killed those men as an act of revenge on the soldier who raped me. I then mutilated each one in a manner so that he couldn't rape anyone ever again."*

He didn't want to leave the prison. The thought frightened him and he feared if let out he'd kill again:

> *"They say a leopard never changes his spots. There is something in me and it's in-built. It is something I can't*

---

[2] The journalist Paul B. Kidd, author of *Never to be Released*, Pan Macmillan. Sydney: 1993.

_change."_

MacDonald died (for the second time) at the age of 90 on 12 May 2015 whilst still imprisoned. The cause of death was complications arising from a gastrointestinal perforation. He'd spent a total of 52 years of his life behind bars.

# Jürgen Bartsch
(active 1962-1966)

ON 21 JUNE 1966, a West German teenager had an eye-wateringly lucky escape from death. Fifteen-year-old Peter Frese had been tied up and held by his captor in an underground former air-raid shelter. The tunnel was located a few miles outside the town of Langenberg[1] in West German. Frese had been lured into the pit by an older teenage male. Once there, the older boy suddenly attacked and beat Frese about the head until he lost consciousness. When he awoke some time later, Frese looked around. The cave was lit by the flicker of a couple of candles, but Frese's attacker was nowhere to be seen. Realising the precariousness of his predicament, Frese quickly recognised he needed to escape and he worked out the means by which to do so, using the lit candles to his advantage: incredibly, he exploited the flames and managed to burn through the binds on his feet, securing his release. It was an extraordinarily fortunate piece of luck, for Frese would later learn what his abductor's plans had been for him – to slowly and painfully skin him alive.

On 6 November 1946, a baby was delivered in a hospital in Essen, Germany. The mother, a woman of the surname Sadrozinsky, abandoned her new-born son at the hospital immediately after the birth. She died of tuberculosis a few weeks later. The baby's father was an unknown Dutch itinerant worker. It was left to hospital staff to name the baby: Karl-Heinz. Karl-Heinz remained in the hospital nursey for most of the first year of his life, and in these formative months his cries for food, touch and affection were routinely disregarded, unless they coincided with the regime of the ward.

A month before the child's first birthday, a well-to-do butcher

---

[1] Now called Velbert-Langenberg.

and his wife, Gerhard and Gertrud Bartsch, adopted him and gave him a new name: Jürgen.[2]

Jürgen's adoptive mother allegedly treated him badly from the outset. He was kept isolated from his peers upon the moment he arrived at his new home. According to the writings of Jürgen himself, this was to avoid him finding out that he'd been adopted. Herr Bartsch decided to open a new butcher shop whilst Jürgen was still young so that his adopted son would have a business to look after when he was of age. This meant that Frau Bartsch needed to work more hours, and so young Jürgen was entrusted to the care of his adoptive grandmother. Unhappily for Jürgen, his grandmother's stance was much the same as his mother's; when she was occasioned to "chaperone" him, usually around twice per week, she would lock him underground in the cellar in solitary confinement for many hours at time. Her rationale appeared to be that she did not want Jürgen to get his clothes dirty by playing with other children. The single friendship he did manage to cultivate was with a boy he liked a lot, although this soon developed homosexual overtones and play that included ejaculation.

In addition to ensuring the ongoing isolation of her adoptive child, Frau Bartsch physically abused him. He always seemed to be black and blue with bruises, family acquaintances noticed. Herr Bartsch was also concerned. He once confessed to a friend that he was considering divorce as he couldn't stand his wife beating the child anymore. On another occasion, as he made his excuses to leave, he said, "I have to return home before she beats the child to death."

Frau Bartsch's punishments were both harsh and inconsistent. She was a woman for whom cleanness, neatness and accuracy

---

[2] The adoption of Karl-Heinz by the Bartsch couple did not occur for seven years due to the reservations of officials. Whether these uncertainties were about the adopters or the adoptee has not been explained.

had become pathological obsessions. She continued to person-ally bath Jürgen until he was 19 years of age. Clothing had to be folded perfectly and stored military-style on the shelf. She would charge towards Jürgen for a trifling misdemeanour and slap him about the face – hard and frequently. Sometimes she would use a clothes-hanger as the instrument of punishment. Then she would suddenly change and soon she'd be hugging and kissing the boy ... and yet he loved his mother and would not hear a bad word against her. He simply couldn't believe that she was a bad person or that she could be wrong, accepting the brutal consequences of her whims without question.

As a result, when Jürgen *did* have infrequent contact with his adoptive parents it seemed to him that his presence was an im-position upon them. He learned to suppress his feelings of vic-timisation and powerlessness and resigned himself to his fate. And so, in order to remain emotionally and psychologically se-cure, his developing psyche inevitably paid the price.

At the age of 12, Jürgen was sent to a repressive Catholic boarding school in the German municipality of Marienhausen, an eventuality he had not wanted. Here, along with 300 other boys, he was subjected to the whims and inconsistent punish-ments of his instructors. His educators hoped – unsuccessfully – to teach their charges that homosexuality was an intolerably evil sin, and that physical closeness between boys would result in unnatural sexual desires. Hence the boys were discouraged from forming close friendships with each other. Upon awaken-ing, they were required to dress in silence, to march to mass in silence, to return from mass in silence. Personal contact was strictly prohibited lest homosexual passions be inflamed.

One of the most fervent opponents of homosexuality was a priest called Pater Pütz, whose self-appointed task was to ha-rangue the schoolboys under his care about the evils of sexual-ity, dealing regular, brutal punishments even for *suspected* ho-mosexual behaviour. Pater Pütz himself, however, was capable of giving into the temptations of the flesh on occasion. Jürgen described an occurrence when he and Pater Pütz were convalescing alone in the school infirmary. Pater Pütz, Jürgen remembered, ordered him to get into bed with him, whereupon he began to masturbate the boy. Afterwards he told the boy that there would be dire consequences – hinting at a death-threat – if he should talk about the encounter. Pater Pütz would also expose the boys to details, including photographs, of the terrible atrocities of the Nazis, apparently relishing this. As a means of extracting information from the boys, he would also physically torture them by forcing them to run around a courtyard until the point that they reached breaking point or collapsed to the ground from exhaustion.

For Jürgen, the lessons learned only reinforced what he'd absorbed at home: physical closeness and emotional relationships were forbidden, whilst coercive homosexual acts committed by authority figures were carried out with impunity. Also, punishments could be swift, harsh and irrational. Trauma, anguish, repression and psychological violence can cause scarring to any child's developing psyche. In the psychosexual development of Jürgen Bartsch the scarring would prove to have profoundly catastrophic consequences.

Jürgen's crimes only came to light after the escape from his clutches of Peter Frese. By this stage Jürgen had already killed four young boys and what he had envisaged for the 15-year-old youth was brutal and sadistic. His aim had been to skin the boy alive over a prolonged period, all the while revelling in the agonies such torture would cause.

Jürgen's killings followed a pattern. He would spend many hours scouring local arcades in the search for the right victim. Once he had found the ideal prey – always a boy under the age of 10 – he would invite the child to an out-of-town tavern for a drink of apple juice, where he would give the boy a few Deutschmarks to earn his trust. Occasionally, he would hang around at travelling fairs, hoping to attract the attention of poor children without arousing suspicion. He took to carrying with him a large suitcase in which to transport the child's body, but soon ceased this ploy after he was asked why he was carrying a "children's coffin".[3] he would tell those who asked that he was a detective, or that he worked for an insurance company, and that he needed help in the recovery of a stash of diamonds from a tunnel. He is believed to have attempted this over a hundred times. Fortunately, many of the boys didn't believe this fanciful tale.

However, some did, and Jürgen was able to entice them into the disused air-raid shelter. Upon arriving there, he would beat the boy into submission with a hammer, force them to undress, and bind him tightly with butchers' string, a means of securement of which he had easy access from his father's shops. He would manipulate the boy's genitals whilst masturbating himself. Then, Jürgen would kill the boy by either beating him to death or strangling him. After death, he would kiss the body tenderly with his lips and then proceed to cut open the chest and stomach cavities. After this, the body would be dismembered, decapitated, disembowelled, emasculated and the eyes would be pricked from their sockets. Jürgen would then slice portions of flesh from the corpse's thighs and buttocks. He had literally *butchered* the body. Finally, he would make an attempt at sodomy, apparently without success.

During Jürgen's detailed confessions he described a good degree of stimulation from the sexual fondling of his bound victims. He was aroused by the panic and fright he witnessed in the boys' eyes. However, the peak of his arousal occurred in the butchery of the bodies. By the time of his fourth murder, he finally reached his ultimate goal: the dismemberment of an incapacitated, screaming boy ... whilst he was still alive.

Incredibly, it was Jürgen's affection for Peter Frese, the surviving victim, that was his undoing. As Jürgen was about to depart from the tunnel, to go home for dinner, he remembered that

---

[3] In German, the expression for a large suitcase, *Kinder-Sarg*, literally translates as "child's coffin".

Frese had told him that he was afraid of the dark. Jürgen had wanted Frese to feel comfortable and, as he always carried a few candles with him, he decided to leave two of them burning so that his tied-up captive wouldn't feel fearful once he regained consciousness. Frese, upon awakening and finding himself alone, used the candles to his advantage. The first candle he accidentally extinguished. However, he was able to use the second to burn through the ties that bound his ankles.

Once he was arrested, Jürgen confessed freely to his crimes. He admitted to killing his first victim, eight-year-old Klaus Jung, in 1962. Four years later he killed 13-year-old Peter Fuchs. Next, he killed Ulrich Kahlweiss and Manfred Grassmann, both aged 12. He was sentenced to life imprisonment on 15 December 1967 after a sensational trial that gripped the whole of Germany and the wider world. The sentence was upheld on appeal. However, Germany's federal court reduced the sentence to 10 years juvenile detention followed by psychiatric care at a facility in Eickelborn.

There, Jürgen received little treatment due to staff shortages. He married a woman who had written letters to him and he entertained fellow patients with semi-professional magic tricks. Forensic psychiatrics, in an attempt to manage their patient, considered various treatments, both psychological and surgical.

Jürgen initially refused brain surgery and castration, but eventually voluntarily agreed to castration in order to avoid a lifetime in psychiatric care and also because he came to believe that the procedure would diminish his impulses. He died on the operating table on 28 April 1976 at the age of 29 following an accidental overdose associated with the castration procedure.[4]

For his part in bringing Jürgen Bartsch to justice, Frese received the reward of a considerable amount of money. Jürgen,

---

[4] Curiously, the surgeon who caused Jürgen's accidental death had also killed other patients this way too and he was put on nine months' probation.

whilst in prison, had inscribed a message to Frese on a wall, asking him to give some of the reward to the parents of one of his other victims, as they were very poor. In the German style used for personal friends he wrote:

*Please believe me, Peter, it would mean a lot to me. That is to say, I truthfully began to develop a very strong fondness for you. The fact that I would have killed you is the proof that my impulses controlled over me.*

The words show the complicated thought processes of a highly disturbed man. His desire to dominate and control a victim in the bizarre pursuit of friendship and sexual gratification could only be the strategies of a traumatised and psychologically ruined individual. A foundling child. An inappropriate adoptive family. Emotional detachment coupled with severe and irrational punishment. Sexual abuse and punishment by a hated authority figure. Employment in a butchery. The disparate ingredients that came together to form Jürgen's developing mind were diverse indeed. Perhaps it was little wonder that the boy grew up to become a sadosexual serial killer.

# Patrick Wayne Kearney

(active 1965-1977)

ON THE NOTICEBOARD in the reception of the Riverside County Sheriff's Department was a bulletin. Two photos were printed on the poster. The first image was of a white, close-cropped, dark-haired man with a receding hairline. He was smiling and wearing black horn-rim spectacles. His countenance gave the impression that this was a trustworthy man, an intellectual man. He could've been mistaken for a college professor. The second image was a dark-haired, moustachioed man with warm eyes and the remnants of a slight smile. He had an open, direct look, but he didn't seem as scholarly as his colleague. Dated Tuesday, 14 June 1977, above the two photos was printed the purpose of the bulletin: ARREST FOR MURDER. Although the poster didn't announce it, the police were on the lookout for these two men for the unlawful killing of eight young men. They didn't need to look far – because at half-past one in the afternoon of 1 July 1977 the two men they sought simply walked into the reception area of the police station and pointed to the wanted posted, telling the dumbfounded deputy, "We're them." It marked the end of a 15-year campaign of murder. The two men were the necrophilic murderer Patrick Wayne Kearney and his toady and lover, David Hill, who between them were responsible for the murder of between 28 and 40 young males.

Patrick Wayne Kearney was born in Los Angeles, California on 24 September 1949, the first-born son of Eunice and George Kearney. He was raised in a fairly stable household. His mother was a homemaker and his father a police officer in the Los Angeles Police Department. They lived in the tough east-side of the city where rival gangs were constantly at loggerheads with each other and violence often spilled onto the streets.

Patrick attended elementary school in Montebello from the age of five. As a short, thin, sickly boy he was subjected to bullying from his classmates, and the fact that he wore spectacles with thick lenses didn't help matters. In 1950, when he was aged 11, the family moved across the city to Reseda, California, where Patrick was sent to Reseda Elementary School. He was bullied here too, being an easy target for his fellow pupils who called him "queer boy" and "little faggot". The humiliation would stay with him and have a lasting effect on his personality. The wimpy boy made no friends at his new school and he'd remember his time there as miserable. He began to become withdrawn and fantasize about killing the people who relentlessly tormented him.

By the time Patrick reached his teens he'd become even more withdrawn. His father, taking the slightly effeminate boy in hand, decided he needed to toughen him up a little. He bought a .22 calibre rifle and showed him some hunting tips. The ideal place to shoot a pig, George Kearney informed his eldest son, was behind the left ear. Unsupervised, Patrick practised his skills in slaughtering pigs and became proficient in this method of dispatch. After the killing he found pleasure in rolling around in the blood and guts of the dead animals. There was further pleasure to be found with animals closer to home: the adolescent boy's first sexual experience was to penetrate the family dog.

At the age of 14, Patrick was sent to junior high school at Diane S. Leichman Special Education Center in Reseda. He was bullied at this school also, but it didn't last long; before he'd reached his 15th birthday he was on the move again. This time the Kearney family were relocating to a different city in a different state – Wilcox, Arizona – and Patrick was enrolled into yet another school, the Wilcox Middle School. The records do not indicate whether or not the shy and awkward boy was bullied at this school also, but it would not be surprising if he had been. Nonetheless, he didn't stay long, for the family relocated yet again, this time back to California, to Redondo Beach, and Patrick had to start afresh at yet another new school.,

Academically, Kearney was a very gifted pupil. It was said that he had the remarkably high IQ of 180 and excelled in his studies. He had a flair for languages. He learned to speak

Chinese, Japanese and Spanish, and he would use his fluency in the latter, along with a keen interest in Latin American culture, to further his future criminal career.

In 1957, Kearney graduated from high school. He and his family moved again, this time to Houston, Texas. However, Kearney returned California shortly afterwards, where he attended El Camino Community College in Torrance. The next year, he joined the US Air Force. He'd hoped to see the world but instead he traversed the country yet again when he was stationed in Texas to undertake basic training. Whilst in the Air Force Kearney met David Hill, a younger man who'd joined the Army only to be discharged shortly afterwards for an unspecified medical condition. Hill, it is reasonable to say, was one of life's freeloaders and loafers. He and Kearney became friends and then lovers.

They made an odd-looking couple. Hill was tall and muscular with bland good looks and a rough demeanour. Kearney was short and skinny and, wearing his suit and spectacles, could easily have passed for a college professor. But they must've seen something in each other, for opposites attracted, and their meeting ignited a tumultuous affair.

Kearney did not remain in the USAF long; he was honourably discharged in 1961. Now he moved to Long Beach, California, where he took a job as an electrical engineer with the Hughes Aircraft Corporation, despite never having earned a university degree. Kearney was earning a good wage by now; Hill was scratching a living from various jobs, mostly working as an attendant in gay saunas. Hill's lack of upward mobility caused some friction between the pair, and when they moved to Culver City the relationship cooled somewhat. Nevertheless, they remained in their on-off homosexual relationship for the next 15 years, during which Hill would leave to marry a woman called Linda Gayle, have a child with her, and then return to Kearney, before becoming restless and leaving to hitchhike around the country, eventually going back to his wife in Lubbock, Texas again – over and over. Meanwhile, Kearney relocated *yet again* to the familiar area of Redondo Beach and exercised an option to buy his house. He appeared to be putting down roots at last.

During the spring 1962 hiatus of their relationship in, after the disappearance of his lover Kearney found himself somewhat at a loss. He began to take history classes at California State University but these did not dampen his pent-up feelings of rejection and rage. For a man accustomed to being friendless and bullied for most of his life, this rejection hurt particularly hard and it unleashed a torrent of rage that would last a decade. He began to kill.

His first victim, he would later claim, was a 19-year-old white male hitchhiker who made the mistake of accepting a ride from Kearney on his motorcycle. Kearney drove the young man from Orange County, California to a secluded place, somewhere in Indo, California, and murdered him by shooting him in the head behind the left ear, just as his father had taught him to do with the pigs. Then he sodomised the still-warm corpse and mutilated the body before disposing it somewhere along State Route 86.

His second victim was a matter of expediency. Kearney knew that the younger cousin of the first victim had seen him picking the young man up. He realised that he'd have to silence this potential witness and so he used the same method; he lured the victim to the same secluded area and shot him in the head. Then he sexually assaulted the corpse. The act of necessity allowed him to indulge his dual need for killing and necrophilia. It was pointless to waste the opportunity!

Kearney claimed to have killed another man that year, an 18-year-old called "Mike". It's not known if any of the bodies of Kearney's first three victims – John Does nos. 1 and 2 and "Mike" – were ever found.

By 1966, Hill and his wife had divorced, and he and Kearney met up and reignited their relationship. Soon they were living together in Kearney's smart apartment in Redondo Beach. According to Kearney, another murder took place in December 1968, about a year after Hill had moved in. Whilst they were on a trip to Tijuana, Mexico, they bumped into "George", a friend of Hill, who invited them to stay at his place for the duration of their stay.

Instead of showing his appreciation for the kind gesture, Kearney entered the master bedroom whilst "George" lay sleeping and shot and killed him. Then he dragged the body into the bathroom, had sex with it as it lay in the bathtub, dismembered it and skinned it. In order to reduce the chances of getting caught he painstakingly extracted the bullet with a craft knife. Finally, he buried the remains of "George" in the backyard behind the garage.[1]

Kearney lay low for over a year out of fear that the murder of "George" would be discovered and law enforcement come making enquiries. John Demichik, a 13-year-old hitchhiker, was the next victim. Kearney shot him in the side of the head. His body lay undiscovered for over two years.

Then he murdered a 17-year-old hitchhiker called James Barwick, killing him by the same means with a bullet to the head.

Ronald Dean Smith Jr., a five-year-old child, had been playing with a friend in a local Lennox, California park with his friend. Ronnie and his friend got into a "sand fight". Ronnie and went home to clean himself, leaving his friend crying in the sandpit. Ronnie never made it home. When he failed to return for dinner his grandmother, who'd been babysitting, became concerned.

Eventually, she filed a missing person report and police searched the park and knocked on doors in the local area. To no avail. There was no sign of young Ronnie.

A week later, his mother, Joann, made an emotional appeal to her son's abductor:

---

[1] In his later confession to the authorities Kearney denied that Hill had known anything about the murder, a circumstance which would have been difficult to believe given the amount of time Kearney must've spent with the body. The skeletal remains of "George" were eventually found nearly a decade later, just where Kearney had said they would be. He alone was convicted for the crime.

*"We definitely do feel in our hearts that he's alive and OK and that he's safe. I just want to tell whoever he's with now that he's very important to me, that he's ... he's all I've got. And that I love him so very much. I know that whoever took Ronnie took him because they wanted a little boy to love, and I know you took him because he's so beautiful and that you won't hurt him."*

More than likely Ronnie was already dead. Kearney admitted to torturing the boy for two days before smothering him and dumping his semi-naked body in Riverside County, California.

On 13 October 1974, a group of youngsters discovered a badly decomposed body alongside Ortega Highway. Ronnie Smith had been the first of Kearney's victims to die by means of suffocation. He would also turn out to be Kearney's *youngest* victim, and it can be assumed that the boy's extreme youth meant that the diminutive serial killer had had confidence in his ability to overpower the child.

On 13 April 1975, mutilated remains were found along Highway 74, near San Juan Capistrano, California. The body parts of the unidentified male were stuffed into black plastic garbage bags, and it was because of this means of disposal that the burgeoning killer eventually came to be known as the "Trash Bag Killer". The victim turned out to be Albert Rivera, who had been a 21-year-old San Diegan sex worker, and Kearney would eventually confess to the murder. He told police that after he'd shot Rivera in the head he took the body back to his house. There, he sodomised it, cut it into pieces and stuffed the parts into industrial trash bags. It was this discovery that led police to believe that they had a serial killer on their patch.

Their fears were to be warranted. Hill had left, and Kearney, waking up one morning to find his lover gone, this time leaving only a note left behind, was sent into a tailspin. The only way he found to vent his rage was to kill. In the next year-and-a-half, Kearney was killing victims at the staggering rate of about one per month, and 17 more bodies would eventually be found.

All but one of them had been shot in the temple with a .22 calibre pistol. Most of them were sodomised _post mortem_. Some of the victims were dismembered, with their body parts put into trash bags and dumped; others were disposed of "whole" at the side of the road, thrown into landfill sites or down ravines or canyons. The victims were: Larry Gene Walters (aged 20), Kenneth Eugene Buchanan (aged 17), Oliver Peter Molitor (aged 13), Larry Armedariz (aged 15), Michael Craig McGhee (aged 13), John "Woody" Woods (aged 23), Larry Epsy (aged 17), Wilfred Lawrence Faherty (aged 20), Randall "Randy" Lawrence Moore (aged 16), Robert "Billy" Benniefiel (aged 17), David Allen (aged 27), Mark Andrew Orach (aged 20), Timothy B. Ingham (aged 19), Nicholas "Nicky" Hermamdez-Jimenez (aged 28), Arturo Romos Marquez (aged 24), John Otis LaMay (aged 17) and Merle "Hondo" Chance.

At the age of just eight, Merle Chance, the 25th in the Trash Bag Killer's canon was only the second victim to be strangled to death. Family and schoolmates described him as a sweet-natured boy who was known to have protected others from local bullies. Merle vanished on 6 April 1977 whilst riding his bicycle. Supposedly, Merle's bike broke down, tragically in the vicinity of Kearney's place of work. Kearney, spotting the ill-fated boy, asked him if he'd like a life home, which the trusting boy duly accepted. Once in the car Kearney smothered him with a sweater and took the body back to his Redondo Beach home overnight, only to dump the body later in the Angeles National Forest. The remains were found a few weeks later on 26 May. Merle was the last known victim of the serial murderer.

Kearney's unchanging _modus operandi_ was to pick up his victims at gay bars or whilst driving along the freeway in his Volkswagen Beetle or truck. Typically he would shoot his victim with the gun held in his right hand whilst he steered his vehicle using this left. In doing so he would make sure to monitor his driving speed and direction so that it would not cause undue attention to himself. Often he would drive with the now-dead man or boy slumped upright in the passenger seat whilst he drove to a desolate area where he could molest the body. Sometimes he would beat the corpse after he'd had sex with it. He told investigators that pummelling the dead bodies was a cathartic act for him, effectively allowing him to vent his pent-up rage and acquire a sense of power, saving this treatment for the victims who looked like those who'd tormented him in his childhood.

Kearney's victims, found by trawling gay bars or saunas, or in picking up hitchhikers by the side of the road, were in all senses *random victims* who'd just happened to cross paths with a serial killer. The fact that this serial killer was a nerdy-looking man in a suit and tie made him seem innocuous and safe. Frequently he chose men that were larger and taller than he was. However, once they were in his vehicle they stood little chance of leaving alive. Whilst they were distracted – or asleep – Kearney aimed his pistol behind the ear and shot. This act satisfied his need to be in control. It thrilled him to be able to do what he wanted to the victim's dead body. Raping them when they were dead meant that they could not reject him. To Kearney, a corpse was the ultimate submissive partner. This satisfied his lust for ultimate power and dominance after all those years when, as a child, he had none.

In addition to the accounted-for victims, police also believed that Kearney had killed numerous times in Mexico. He made frequent trips to Tijuana where he would stay for a few days. Sometimes Hill accompanied him. Many crimes that occurred in Mexico around this time were consistent with the *M.O.* and victim type of Kearney's deeds. It is supposed that he made the trip across the border, trawled for victims, quickly subdued, abducted and killed them, undressed and raped the bodies, mutilated them, before dumping the remains and returning to the US.

By this time, Kearney was himself obsessed with serial killers. There were so many of them operating in California in the '70s that it would seem the state was awash with blood. William Bonin, the "Freeway Killer"; Angelo Buono Jr. and Kenneth Bianchi, the "Hillside Stranglers"; the unidentified "Zodiac Killer";

Randy Kraft, the "Scorecard Killer". Kearney developed a particular fascination with one specific madman: Dean Corll, the Texan "Candy Man Killer". He read about this gay serial killer extensively, revelling in the sick atrocities, and he kept as many newspaper clippings about him as he could find. As the web later closed in upon him, Kearney was dejected at having to dispose of his beloved collection of clippings.

Police already had an inkling that a new serial killer was on the loose and on their patch with the discovery of the mutilated body of Albert Rivera in April 1975. Rivera's remains had been packaged neatly and disposed of in a manner different from other murders. The body, in a foetal position, had been secured using heavy-duty nylon fibre tape, placed into two heavy-duty commercial waste bin liners, and then enclosed in a green plastic trash bag which was also secured by tape.

On 24 January 1977, a worker in the Lennox tunnel of the San Diego Freeway stumbled over a carefully-wrapped trash bag. The weighty contents of the bag had been treated to the same level of "care" as the bag found in April 1975. The contents were Nicolas Hernandez-Jimenez. Other bags turned up with depressing regularity, and by now law enforcement officers _knew_ they were seeking a new serial killer.

Michael Craig McGhee was a 13-year-old boy who lived in Redondo Beach. He was well known to local cops. A handsome youngster with brown hair and a pleasant smile, Michael was already a "rebellious teenager". He'd recently dropped out of school and was engaging in criminal activities including burglary, the theft of cars and sexual offences. When Michael went missing on 11 June 1976 the police initially didn't think much of it: Michael was prone to go hitchhiking and they simply assumed he'd done so again.

In fact, Michael _had_ done so in the week before he went missing. During this time he met Kearney, and Kearney had invited him to go on a camping trip to Lake Elsinore, California. Michael declined to go on that occasion, but invited his new friend to ask him again in a week.

Kearney told investigators that he and Michael had done just that: a week later he'd gone to Michael's residence with a view to taking him on a camping trip. As Michael's mother was working, his older sister was in charge. She told Kearney that her brother was grounded and that he'd be going nowhere. Michael, however, had other ideas, and he snuck out of the house whilst his sister's back was turned. He caught up with Kearney and the two left together. Kearney reported that he took the boy back to his house to collect camping equipment. It's easy to guess what happened next: Kearney killed Michael by shooting him in the back of the head, sodomised the body and dismembered it. The body parts have never been found.

Seventeen-year-old John Otis LaMay went missing on 13 March 1977. On the day he went missing, John had cheerfully told a neighbour that he'd recently met a guy called "Dave" at a downtown L.A. gym. He was going to meet this "Dave" at his home in Retondo Beach. That was the last time John was known to have been seen alive.

By the next day, when John hadn't returned home, his mother became highly anxious and completed a missing person form at the police station. Her son, she insisted, would not have just wandered off without letting her know in advance. Police believed that that was exactly what the teenager had done and they chalked the disappearance up as a runaway case.

John's remains were discovered four days later amongst the scrub and brush near Temescal Canyon in Orange County. The exsanguinated, sliced-up body parts – minus the head – had been stuffed into five transparent waste bags, three of which had been crammed into an oil-drum, the remaining two dumped on the ground alongside. Crime scene investigators were able to pluck some evidential items from the body – foreign pubic hair and a few stray carpet fibres, coloured green.

Now the police understood why John hadn't returned home and they began to investigate his earlier movements. They quickly realised that John LaMay had been gay and that he had been a regular visitor of an L.A. gay sauna called the Midtowne

Spa. The Midtowne was one of L.A.'s oldest meat markets. There was no pretence about its purpose. A sign on the door announced that it was a "gay-oriented business". Inside, new clientele were questioned about their sexual orientation. Upstairs, within the "business" area, patrons were free to walk around dressed in nothing but a towel and to use any of the establishment's equipment and facilities ... which included small private rooms in which newly-introduced individuals could become better acquainted. All manner of people were clientele of the Midtowne – businessmen, lawyers, actors, hustlers. (The gay sauna scene can be a great leveller of status.)

The police acquired a list of the Midtowne's client list, and they soon discovered a name on it that perked their interest: Arturo Ramos Marquez.

On 3 March 1977, 15 days before LaMay's remains were discovered, a pair of roadworkers were about their business along the I-10 near Palm Springs, California. Seeing buzzards circling a distance off, the two men drove their truck to inspect the area, fully expecting to see a fallen animal. Instead they found the body of a dark-skinned male, naked but for a ring with the letters A.R.M. engraved upon it. The victim had been shot once in the head and stabbed once in the abdomen. The body was complete (not dismembered) and had not been placed into trash bags. It was identified as 24-year-old hustler, Arturo Marquez. No forensic leads could be taken from the body; nevertheless, it was this discovery that pointed detectives in the direction of a lawyer with whom Marquez had been known to associate at the Midtowne.

Detectives questioned this lawyer. Unsurprisingly, he denied killing Marquez, and even denied having met Marquez on or before the day he died. However, despite this, the lawyer became the prime suspect in Marquez's murder, and this led detectives to closely examine the sign-in sheets at the Midtowne.

Then the body of LaMay was discovered. Investigators took another look at the sauna's sign-in sheet and their attention was drawn to the names of David Hill and Patrick Kearney. Deputies

Larry Miller and Dan Wilson went to Kearney's property at 1906 Robinson Avenue and knocked on the door. The residents allowed them in, invited them to wait, and then left the room to make themselves presentable. In the back of Deputy Miller's mind were the green carpet fibres plucked from the body of John LaMay. Whilst Kearney and Hill were out of the room, the Miller stooped to the floor, scooped up a few carpet fibres and pocketed them. The carpet was green.

Upon returning to the room, Kearney and Hill listened to the deputies keenly. They proffered the information that they were two gay men, and admitted that they were as worried about being raped and murdered as any gay man in Los Angeles would be right now. They were aware of the shocking details of the recent gay slayings in the press and they were "living on their nerves", they said. However, the two gay men couldn't help the police with their enquiries. They knew nothing about the murder of LaMay, they asserted, and they were able to offer alibis for the time when he disappeared.

The next day brought a much-needed development. The green carpet fibres matched those taken from the body of LaMay. Furthermore, some items – waste bags and nylon tape – found at Kearney's workplace matched the bags used to dispose of LaMay's body.

Now the detectives knew they had their man … or men. However, the green carpet fibres had been collected illegally and could not be used in court. So the two deputies returned to 1906 Robinson Avenue and again knocked on the door. Without a search warrant, they fully expected to be told to go away, but instead the occupants invited them in. They granted the deputies permission to collect a sample of carpet fibres, and they even obliged the deputies by allowing them to collect samples of pubic hair.

Under the microscope, the samples matched those taken from the LaMay crime scene. Miller and Wilson began to prepare their move. Meanwhile, however, Kearney and Hill were making plans of their own. By the time the deputies turned up with their search warrant, the two erstwhile lovers had already made their move and arrived in El Paso, Texas, and a resignation letter was duly in the post to Kearney's employers, informing them of his resignation.

At the same time, forensics operatives had moved into 1906 Robinson Avenue and were in the midst of their inspection. The search turned up many damning items including gay pornography, newspaper clippings about a string of murders in Houston, Texas, handcuffs and rubber gloves. Most damning of all were the spots of dried blood that showed up under black light and a hacksaw with human flesh embedded within its parts. On 1 June 1977, the District Attorney's Office issued arrest warrants for the long-gone occupants of the Robinson Avenue residence, and it was two weeks later that Kearney and Hill walked into the Riverdale County Sheriff's Department and pointed at their own images on the ARREST FOR MURDER bulletin, turning themselves in. Their murderous reign of terror was over.

"When I was eight years old I had a feeling I was going to do these things," Kearney told detectives that same day. And once he started talking it seemed like he couldn't stop. He recounted that his first murder (that of the man called "George") set the pattern for most of the ones that followed: a bullet to the brain, *post mortem* sodomy, ejaculation and disposal of the victim. He said that he'd got started on this path after Hill walked out and he'd become lonely. He simply went out cruising in San Diego and picked up this guy, taking him back to his home in Culver City. As soon as they arrived at his home, Kearney shot "George" in the back of the head. It was a much cleaner method of dispatch than stabbing; he already knew this from his childhood memories of killing pigs. Then he dismembered him, skinned the body and buried it behind the garage of some houses on a residential street. Some date! Appalled at what he had done, he waited over a year, fully expecting a knock on the door from someone making enquiries about "George". When none came he realised he'd literally *got away with murder* and so his thoughts turned to repeating the crime, and this set in motion a crime spree that was to last, on and off, for the next eight years. Kearney drew a map to show investigators exactly where the remains could be found. As Kearney progressed he saved himself the effort of digging a hole; he simply packaged the body parts and drove them into the desert and dumped them.

He talked about venting his built-up rage by pummelling the bodies of his victims, only *after* death. He seemed quite piqued when investigators brought up the subject of torture. They asked if he'd ever rammed anything into his victims' anuses or impaled them. "I am *not* the Wooden Stake,"[2] Kearney said pointedly, seeming to understand what the detectives were suggesting. *Did he associate with anyone else who killed people?* his interrogators wanted to know. "Inadvertently," replied Kearney, enigmatically telling them that he lived in Long Beach and corresponded with people in the *Free Press*. He would say no more on this matter.

He admitted to slicing open his victims after death, however, only beginning to do this many years after "George". He did it out of curiosity. "Cutting somebody open does tend to sound a little bit exciting," he told astonished detectives, "but it didn't give me any thrill when I did it."

There were close calls, Kearney remembered. On one occasion, which must have dismayed him mightily, he got a flat tyre whilst making one of his desert disposals. Even more horrifyingly, his spare tyre was also flat. He resorted to calling a tow truck, which hauled his Beetle to a service station where an attendant put the vehicle to rights. All the while, two neatly wrapped trash bags containing body parts rested on the back seat of his car.

On another occasion, he parked his car along the side of the

---

[2] Randy Kraft was a serial torture killer of boys and men committing his crimes in California between 1972 and 1983. He was known to have jabbed sticks into his victim's sexual orifices and eyes. He lived in Long Beach, California.

highway in the search for a suitable dump site. In doing so, he managed to lock himself out of the car, his keys and a couple of bags of body parts remaining frustratingly inside. It took him the best part of the afternoon to jimmy open the lock whilst doing his best to look inconspicuous and avoid the unhelpful attention of any passing good Samaritans.

Kearney talked with pride about the _cleanness_ of his kills. The men were always taken so suddenly that their faces didn't even register surprise. When the act was done as he drove one-handedly along the freeway, he was often able to continue driving with the body propped up in the passenger seat. Kearney never confronted his victims prior to killing them. He preferred to save his domination of them until after their deaths when he could indulge in his necrophilic ministrations uninterrupted. It was the satisfaction, he said, of the fantasies which had ignited and developed within him in his early childhood, ever since he had become the target of bullies who called him queer.

As for the man who'd walked alongside him into the Riverdale Sheriff's Office, Kearney denied that his lover Hill had had anything to do with any of the murders. According to Kearney, the unreliable Hill had been away on a bender or away hitchhiking, putting Kearney into the black mood which brought about yet another urge to kill. It had been on just such an occasion with Kearney's last victim, John LaMay. Hill was not at home when the boy came to visit. The two sat watching TV, awaiting the return of Kearney's housemate. When LaMay reached over to change the TV channel, Kearney, without provocation and on impulse, casually placed his gun at the back of the boy's skull and pressed the trigger. It was another clean killing, but it would ultimately lead to the murderer's arrest and conviction. He would only kill once more before he gave himself up.

The claim that Hill knew nothing of the serial murders seemed astonishing to the investigators. How could he have known and lived with his lover for so many years and yet been ignorant of the crimes? Nevertheless, with no evidence of go on, the District Attorney was obliged to believe Kearney's claims and Hill was released after a week. He skulked back to Lubbock and never returned to the Sunshine State.

Kearney's full confession spared the state of California a lengthy and expensive trial. It also spared Kearney the death penalty. In December 1977, he was charged with the first-degree murders of Albert Rivera, Arturo Marquez and John LaMay; and two months later he pleaded guilty to a further 18 counts of first-degree murder. He was given 21 life sentences in a plea bargain deal that depended upon his full cooperation with the investigators. Authorities are convinced that he is responsible for at least eight further murders that he admitted to, but for which they lack the evidence to bring about any charges. After his sentence, Kearney said, "I can't allow myself to think much about it. It's too painful."

After Kearney's imprisonment, a survivor revealed himself. Tony Stewart reported that for four years as a child he used to do some yard work for Kearney to earn extra pocket-money. Stewart remembered that their paths crossed some years later when he was aged 19. On that occasion, Stewart had been cruising along the Pacific Highway in a newly-acquired car, the engine of which quickly gave out, obliging him to resort of hitch-hiking as a means of getting about.

One evening, Stewart was at a convenience store, hoping that he would meet someone who he could talk into buying beer for him. Unsuccessful in that mission, he headed towards the highway and stuck out his thumb. A man with a familiar face stopped his pick-up truck. It was Patrick Kearney. Stewart told Kearney that he used to mow his lawn, and then pressed his luck, asking him if he would buy him some beer.

Kearney agreed – on one proviso. "You have to drink it at my house," he said. As the boy was a minor, Kearney didn't want to get into trouble. It seemed reasonable enough.

Stewart agreed, and after the beer was bought, Kearney drove the two of them back to his Redondo Beach residence.

Then things started to get strange, Stewart recalled. Once inside the apartment, Kearney reached into a doctor's bag and removed a stethoscope. He wanted to listen to Stewart's heart-beat, Kearney remembered.

Slightly nonplussed, Stewart agreed.

Then Kearney placed the listening mechanism on Stewart's chest, outside the clothing, and moved it up and down, searching for a heartbeat.

"Could you lift up your shirt?" Kearney then asked. "I can't hear anything."

Without thinking, Stewart obliged, lifting his shirt to accommodate Kearney's request.

Suddenly Kearney slid the device lower, moving towards Stewart's naval. Unsurprisingly, Stewart grew uncomfortable with this and told Kearney that he needed to get going. If he arrived home too late, he said, his parents might lock him out.

Just then, the two heard the sound of a key being inserted into the lock of the front door. At this point, Kearney suddenly jumped away from the boy as if he didn't want to be discovered doing what he'd been in the midst of doing.

"Do you remember Tony?" Kearney asked the man who entered. "He used to mow our yard."

The newcomer, David Hill, walked straight past, into the bedroom. Seizing the moment, Stewart said loudly enough for Hill to hear, "Well, I really have to get going now."

The drive home was uncomfortable. Kearney barely said a word, leaving Stewart to fill the void with idle chatter. As they came closer to his house, Stewart asked Kearney to pull over. Because of Kearney's earlier strange behaviour, Stewart didn't wish to disclose the true location of his house. Kearney asked Stewart to come by and visit him the next day. Stewart, keen to get out of the car, promised that he would. He remembered that Kearney had a "strange look in his eyes" that was "almost hypnotic". Kearney said that it would be good to see him tomorrow. Then Stewart got out and his strange chauffeur drove off.

At this point, Stewart ran at full speed around the corner towards his house. He guessed that Kearney must have observed this, for when he looked over his shoulder he saw that Kearney had turned his car and was driving back towards him.

Stewart hid behind a fence and waited as his tracker slowly drove past, apparently looking for him. Only when he was sure that Kearney had finally gone did Stewart decide it was safe to go return home.

Months later, Stewart turned on the news and discovered that the man he'd accepted a lift home with had been charged with killing 32 people. He almost passed out with the shock.

*My God*, he thought, *I was alone with a serial killer drinking beer in the middle of the night.* For weeks afterwards, he had nightmares, reliving the events over and over again in his sleep. If Kearney's roommate hadn't come home at the exact moment he had done, Stewart realised, the outcome would probably have been very different. It looked like he'd escaped certain death by the skin of his teeth.

Kearney is currently incarcerated at Mule Creek State Prison in California. He is kept in a protective housing unit for his own safety. He continues to plead for parole and his hearings occur every six years; however, he has yet to be successful in his quest to be released and it is doubtful that he ever will be.

He is allowed to attend college equivalency classes and, like many serial killers, he sends regular letters to and receives replies from admiring fans and souvenir hunters. In one correspondence with an author,[3] Patrick Kearney was keen to recant his confession that he had molested the family dog.

---

[3] Denis McDougal (1991), *Angel of Darkness*. Warner Books: New York.

# Dean Arnold Corll

[active 1970-1973]

IN THE EARLY HOURS of 8 August 1973, the lives of three teenagers hung precariously in the balance. It started at around three o'clock in the morning when Elmer Wayne Henley, aged 17 at the time, arrived at the door of his friend Dean Corll, an older man aged 33. Wayne Henley was planning to party, and he'd brought along a casual acquaintance, 19-year-old Timothy Kerley. Tim also wanted to join the party.

Wayne had been to Corll's house before and he knew the score. Usually there was drinking and the smoking of dope. Sometimes they would sniff paint fumes – "bagging", they called it – until they hallucinated and passed out. Occasionally, Wayne would bring a good-looking teenage friend – always a male – and he would party too. Mostly, however, the good-looking teenage friend wouldn't make it out alive. If things had gone to plan that was probably what would've happened that same August night. Luckily for Tim, they got the munchies …

At some point in the early hours of the morning, Wayne and Tim decided to leave the house to buy sandwiches. During the excursion, Wayne decided to return to his own house. Getting out of the vehicle he heard a commotion. Across the street his 15-year friend, Rhonda Williams, was in the midst of an argument with her father. She had been beaten by him and, instead of returning home, she decided to tag along with the two boys who were returning to Corll's house.

Rhonda, however, was not made to feel welcome at the older man's residence. From the moment Corll laid eyes on her he bubbled with infuriation. Nevertheless, he let the three teenagers inside.

Still seething, Corll shortly pulled Wayne to one side and told him, "You've ruined everything." Wayne explained that his girlfriend had argued with her father earlier and didn't wish to return home. At this point Corll appeared to calm down. He offered the trio of teenagers some beer and marijuana where-upon they quickly settled down to drink and get high. Corll's relaxation was a pretence. None of them yet knew it, but from that moment on, a series of events was soon to unfold that would change all of their lives forever. The story, when it came to light, would shock and horrify the nation.

Dean Arnold Corll was born in Fort Wayne, Indiana on Christmas Eve 1939, the first-born son of Mary Emma Robinson and Arnold Edwin Corll. The marriage was a stormy one, marred by frequent bickering. Four years after Dean was born came a younger brother, Stanley. The boys were disciplined harshly for the smallest infractions by their father, who seemed to view them with thinly-veiled distaste. Their mother provided a more protective and stabilising influence. Nevertheless, the two boys appeared to have polarised personalities: whereas Stanley was an amiable and outgoing boy, forever playing with his many friends, Dean was a loner, preferring to stay indoors, away from other children.

Arnold and Mary divorced in 1946 and Arnold shortly after joined the Air Force. Mary, saddened by the loss, and also feeling that her two young sons should continue to have contact with their father, drove herself and the boys in a horse-trailer to Tennessee so that they could be closer to the base where her ex-husband was posted. They remarried in 1950. Whilst Mary went to work, the two youngsters were left with an elderly couple, which whom it appears they spent the majority of their time.

The reconciliation was short-lived. Arguments between the boys' parents continued and they decided to give up on the relationship, separating permanently for a second time. Mary retained custody of the boys and altogether they moved to Pasadena, Texas when Dean was aged 11. After the separation, the parents' relationship remained on amicable grounds.

In 1953, Mary remarried. Her new husband, Jake West, a travelling clock salesman, was extremely protective of his two new charges and worked hard at keeping them out of trouble. Soon a half-sister, Joyce, came along.

Dean was regarded as a well-behaved student in school who achieved satisfactory grades. Teachers remembered him as a quiet, polite and diligent pupil. At the age of seven, an undiagnosed rheumatic fever left him with a heart condition which was only recognised at the age of 11. When doctors found this out the result was frequent absences from school and he was ordered to keep away from physical education. For Dean, who was not a naturally sporty child, this was good news. In Vidor High School, his only major interest appears to have been the brass band, in which he played the trombone. He tried scuba-diving, but after a fainting spell due to his heart defect he had to give this hobby up.

Upon the advice of a travelling pecan nut salesman, Mary and Jake started a new venture making and distributing candy, operating from their garage. Dean and his brother Stanley were assigned responsibility for the running of the machinery and packaging the product. Almost from the onset, Dean was occupied day and night as he worked both at school and in the business. He soon found himself exhausted, but he never complained.

Following Corll's graduation from high school in 1958, the family moved to the northern suburbs of Houston, Texas, where they could be closer to where the majority of their candy products were sold. Again operating from their garage, they named their new venture Pecan Prince.

In 1960, for a period of two years or so, Corll, at the behest of his mother, went to live in Indiana with his recently widowed grandmother. Whilst there, he developed a close friendship with a girl who later proposed to him. He rejected the proposal and returned to Houston in 1962. By this time his family had moved to the Heights district, a neighbourhood a few miles west of downtown Houston.

Mary's marriage to Jake broke down sometime around 1963 after he felt that his wife was taking too much control of their business, and the pair soon parted company. Jake retained the business, so Mary launched a new business – the Corll Candy Company. Competition between the two firms was fierce. Mary, wanting to keep hers a family business, appointed Corll, now aged 19, vice-president and his younger brother its secretary-treasurer. Ever indulgent, she allowed her elder son to move into the apartment above the business. Now he had a place to call his own. Mary, a woman with a fondness for marriage, later impulsively wed a third man, a merchant seaman, whom she'd met through a computer-dating service.

By now the business was doing well, employing a small number of staff. Corll found himself spending a lot of free time in the company of its young male employees. One of the teenage employees informed Mary that her son had made sexual advances towards him. The response of Corll's overprotective mother was simply to fire the youth who'd made the complaint.

On 10 August 1964, despite his heart condition, Corll was drafted into the US Army. He was assigned to Fort Polk, Louisiana for basic training, but ended up being permanently assigned as a radio repairman in Fort Hood, Texas. It was in the army that the first signs of Corll's flagrant homosexuality emerged. Army life and its inherently masculine milieu seemed to cause a change in his mannerisms and his thoughts became increasingly sexualised. He spent a year enlisted and during this time he came to realise that he was homosexual. He successfully applied for hardship discharge from service, saying that he was needed by his mother back home, and was honourably discharged after an 11-month stint.

Corll now returned to Houston Heights and resumed his position as vice-president of the family candy business, which was doing well. In order to satisfy a swelling public demand for the product, Corll increased the number of hours he devoted to the business. Around this time he began to experience his first homosexual encounters, and he reportedly divulged to close colleagues that it had been during his spell in the army that he'd first realised he was homosexual. In fact, Mary's third husband had already told his wife that he suspected Corll might be homosexual, basing this upon the number of young boys congregating around the factory. Mary wouldn't believe a word of it.

In 1965, the business relocated to 22nd Street, across the road from an elementary school. Corll was known to hand out free candy to the local schoolchildren. The place soon became a magnet for other youths around this time, some of them runaways. Corll had an easy rapport with these troubled boys and befriended them, installing a pool table in a backroom inside the premises where his employees and the teenaged boys could come and hang out. He gave them rides on his motorcycle and outfitted his van with a carpet, cushions and a television set so they could take picnics on the beach. Corll was openly flirtatious with many of the boys, all the while dishing out free treats. For this reason, he earned himself the innocuous-sounding nickname "The Candy Man" (a fact which the media were to roundly seize upon when his secret life later came to light).

By 1968, the candy factory was nearing its end. Mary had seen a psychic who told her that her marriage was over and she needed to get as far away from her husband as possible. So she shut down the factory, divorced husband no. 3 and moved to Manitou Springs, Colorado, where she set up yet another candy factory. No doubt to his mother's surprise, Corll decided to stay in Houston. He got a job at the Houston Lighting and Power Company, working as an electrician. He moved into a smart, pleasant apartment on Yorktown Street and, with his mother out of sight and out of mind, he began to indulge the compulsions he'd kept secret for years, operating with a newfound gusto.

By 1969, Corll had already begun his fateful friendship with David Owen Brooks, who at the time was a shy, bespectacled sixth grader … and one of the boys to whom The Candy Man gave free product. He'd met Brooks in the candy factory when the boy was just 10 or 11 years of age. Like Corll, Brooks' parents were divorced and living many miles apart. His father lived in Houston whilst his mother had relocated 85 miles away to Beaumont, Texas. When Brooks visited his father, he also called in on Corll. Soon Brooks was regarding Corll's apartment as his second home. Brooks had the feeling that his own father didn't really like him all that much because he was skinny and worse large glasses. Brook began to look up to Corll as a father figure and became emotionally dependent upon him. He later commented that Corll was the first adult male who didn't mock his appearance or call him a sissy. He began to spend a lot more time at Corll's place than at his own home.

On Christmas Eve 1969, Corll reached a difficult milestone: he turned 30. Reaching his third decade changed something within Corll and he became morose and introspective. Brooks, however, was often around the cheer him up. Often this would mean Corll paying the boy five dollars in order to allow himself to be fellated. There were other boys too, only too willing to drop their trousers to allow Corll to give them oral sex. In exchange for cold hard cash, of course.

Corll's first known victim was an 18-year-old college freshman, Jeffrey Konen, who'd been hitchhiking with a friend to his parents' home on 25 September 1970. He was dropped off at an intersection nearby Corll's apartment on Westheimer Road. It is likely that Corll offered a lift which the trusting student accepted.

Although Brooks was not involved in the murder of Konen, he was later able to pinpoint the location of his body in August 1973. It had been buried under a large boulder at High Island Beach, Texas. A post mortem uncovered evidence that the victim had died by manual strangulation. A cloth gag had been stuffed into his mouth, presumably in order to dampen the anguished cries. The body was found with still-attached binds to the hands and feet, suggesting that he had been sexually assaulted. The remains were naked, covered with a layer of lime and wrapped in plastic. It would prove to be a consistent part of the killer's disposal *M.O.*

Things took an even darker turn in mid-December 1970. By this stage, Brooks, now aged 15, was allowed to come and go at Corll's apartment whenever he wanted to. On one occasion, Brooks walked unannounced into Corll's apartment only to find Corll naked. He wasn't alone: two naked boys were strapped to a four-poster bed and Corll was in the process of sexually assaulting them. Seeing Brooks, Corll snapped, "What are you doing here?" Brooks turned and left.

The boys were likely to have been Jimmy Glass and Danny Yates, two 14-year-old best friends who'd somehow been persuaded to leave an Evangelical church service in Houston's Heights district. At some point during the service, the two good-looking youngsters got up and walked back down the aisle, towards the exit. It is not known where or when Corll first met Jimmy and Danny, or how he'd managed to lure them away that day. Jimmy, however, had already been to Corll's apartment on a previous occasion – at Brooks' behest – and had taken a shine to the older man. The two boys were also acquaintances of Brooks, and he _would_ have recognised them as such when he walked into the apartment and found them bound to the bed. In a statement given to investigators later, a witness later stated that the boys had once talked about a man matching Corll's description who'd given then a ride, stopping along the way to buy them beer. At the time of the boys' disappearance, the police labelled the two boys runaways and barely investigated their disappearances, a circumstance for which they have since been roundly and rightly criticised.

Sometime later, Corll told Brooks that he was part of a gay pornography ring and that the boys had been posing for photos. He said that he was planning to send the boys to California for more films. He promised Brooks a car for his silence and Brooks accepted the offer. Corll kept his part of the bargain and bought Brooks a green Chevrolet Corvette. After this he modified his story, telling Brooks that he had, in fact, killed the two boys and buried their bodies in a boat shed he had hired for storage.[1] Corll offered Brooks $200 for any boy he could persuade to come

---

[1] This turned out to be accurate: the remains of the two boys were found buried in the boat shed. Alongside the bodies was an electrical cord with alligator clips attached. It seems likely that Corll had tortured his two victims with electricity.

back with him to the apartment. Brooks agreed to this arrangement. It was the start of a deplorable business relationship that would result in the deaths of at least 28 victims.

Six weeks later, two young brothers, Donald and Jerry Waldrop, aged 15 and 13 respectively, were dropped off by their father at a friend's house in the Heights district in order to discuss forming a bowling league. Their friend was not at home and so the brothers began walking home. At some point on their journey, they had the misfortune to catch the eye of Brooks and Corll. They were enticed into Corll's van and driven to Corll's rented apartment on Mangum Road. There, as Brooks later admitted in his confession, he watched as Corll strangled them. Their bodies were found buried side-by-side in the boat shed alongside identification cards which named them. Presumably Brooks had collected a $200 pay cheque for each victim.

In an astonishing revelation, the father of Donald and Jerry complained that shortly after his sons' disappearance he'd informed the police that an acquaintance had observed Corll burying what appeared to be bodies at the boat shed. The police, in response, performed a cursory search of the shed but dismissed the report as a hoax. The father all but camped out at the police station in an effort to find out what had happened to his sons, only to be told, "Why are you here? You know your boys are runaways." At this point, the murderer could have been stopped in his tracks – if only the police had properly investigated the tip-off. Sadly, due to their failure to do so, other boys would die.

The Heights was quickly to lose three more boys. Randell Lee Harvey was reported two days after he disappeared on 11 March 1971. He'd left his house, riding his bike to work at a gas station three miles away. He finished work that evening but never arrived home again. His body turned up two-and-a-half years later in Corll's boat shed. Unusually, the body had been fully clothed when buried. Randell was identified in 2008. He'd been killed by a single gunshot through the eye. The bike was never found.

On 29 May 1971, two friends, 13-year-old David Hilligiest and 16-year-old Gregory Malley Winkle, were on their way to a local swimming pool. When last seen they were climbing into a white van. David's family had been due to go away on a vacation the next day and David had already packed his case for the trip. Twenty dollars he'd saved up for the trip remained where he'd left it, on the dresser in his bedroom. David's mother, Dorothy, who steadfastly refused to believe that her son had run away, badgered the police constantly, whom she believed were doing nothing to locate him. Gregory's mother likewise insisted her son would not have fled from home. "You don't just run away with nothing but a bathing suit and 80 cents," she said.

A frantic search ensued. One of the boys who volunteered to distribute posters offering a reward for the boys' whereabouts was 15-year-old Elmer Wayne Henley. Wayne was a lifelong friend of the supposed "runaway" David, as well as an acquaintance of Corll's now co-conspirator, David Brooks.

Frustrated by police inaction, Dorothy borrowed money and hired a private investigator, who told her that David might have been abducted by a homosexual vice ring. Undaunted, the softly-spoken homemaker began sitting in a car outside downtown gay bars in the hope of spotting her son. In her quest, Dorothy took note of the licence plate number of a car and asked police to follow up on her lead. The car turned out to belong to Corll. Again, another chance to apprehend Houston's serial killer was lost.

The bodies of David and Gregory were just two of the 16 found in Corll's boat shed. The cord used to garrotte Gregory was still knotted around his neck. When the spidery connections to Corll later came to light, it was revealed that David had used to hang around the Corll Candy Company premises and both Gregory and his mother had years before worked there.

By 17 August 1971, Corll had moved house again, to an apartment at 6363 San Felipe. Ruben Watson Haney, aged 17, left his home that afternoon to walk to the cinema. After the movie, he'd been walking home when he was persuaded by a friend to attend a party at his friend Corll's house. That "friend" was David Brooks. Ruben phoned his mother to tell her that he'd be spending the evening with his friend. He was not found until two years had passed, buried within Corll's boat shed. He'd been strangled. Brooks would later admit that this had been the first murder he'd personally witnessed. Despite what must have been the enormity of this pivotal event, Brooks' memory appears to have been quite hazy in his recollections to police, and he minimised his involvement to being a mere observer.

A month later, Corll moved to another Heights apartment. Now, in addition to helping abduct boys, Brooks became an active participant in their murders. He helped to take the lives of two boys here. One of the victims was kept alive for four days before he was killed. Both sets of remains were found in the boat shed. Both victims have yet to be identified.

Wayne Henley was the boy who'd assisted David Hilligiest's mother with the distribution of reward posters. Henley's background was similar to Brooks'. He came from a broken home and had an abusive, alcoholic father. He excelled at school, but upon the breakdown of his parents' marriage he took a variety of menial jobs to support the family. Accordingly, his grades fell and he dropped out of school. Not long after this he acquired an arrest sheet after being charged with burglary in 1972.

Prior to leaving high school, Henley and Brooks had been friends, often playing truant together. Living in the same neighbourhood, the two friends still saw each other regularly. Henley became aware that his friend was spending a lot of time with an older man and in due course Brooks introduced them. In his later confession, Henley said that Brooks had "lured" him to Corll's home with the promise that he could become involved in a money-making scheme. It's possible that Brooks had planned to earn himself another $200 and that Henley was the intended victim.

Nevertheless, Corll must've seen something in Henley and declined to murder him. He told Henley that he worked for a clandestine organisation in Dallas, recruiting young boys for a sex slavery ring. He offered Henley the same deal as Brooks – $200 for the procurement of a boy. A few months would pass before

Henley would take Corll up on his offer.

The trio began spending more time together. Henley began to wonder about the extent of the relationship between Brooks and Corll and suspected that his friend was pimping himself out to the older man. He also had the inkling that something sinister was afoot. The disappearances of eight neighbourhood boys had formed an insidious pattern. Nevertheless, dire straits in February 1972 meant that Henley now accepted Corll's business offer. In Corll's new apartment (at 925 Schuler Street), he and Corll devised a plan to lure a boy off the streets with the enticement of smoking marijuana and drinking beer.

The plan came to fruition. Henley and Corll picked up a boy from the Heights and all three went back to Corll's apartment. There, Henley showed the boy the trick of releasing himself from a pair of handcuffs. It was a ruse – Henley had secreted the key in his back pocket. Now, he duped the boy into attempting the same. As soon as the handcuffs were on Corll pounced and Henley observed him bind and gag the boy. Then Henley, convinced that the boy would be sold to the white slave trade, left him to Corll's dreadful ministrations. The remains of the boy were found in the boat shed. He has not yet been identified.

Now Henley's appetite for death was up. A month later, he, Brooks and Henley encountered Frank Aguirre, a 19-year-old acquaintance of Henley, leaving the Long John Silver restaurant where he worked. Henley called his friend over and invited him to drink beer and smoke marijuana at Corll's. Frank readily agreed and followed the trio in his own vehicle. Once inside Corll's apartment, the four smoked pot. Frank noticed a set of handcuffs on a table and picked item up to inspect it. At that point, Corll suddenly pounced on the youth, overpowered him and cuffed his hands behind his back. Henley sat still and watched as Corll dragged his friend into the bedroom. He later claimed not to have known what Corll's true intentions had been and said that he'd urged Corll not to rape and kill the youth. Henley alleged that at that point Corll informed him he'd raped, tortured and killed the previous boy whom Henley had assisted in bringing back to the apartment, and that he'd no intention of letting Frank go free. He duly fastened Frank to a board by the hands and feet.

This device – known as the "torture board" – was an eight-feet-by-two-feet plyboard slab through which six strategically placed holes had been drilled. Using ropes and handcuffs, Corll was able to subject his victims to hideous, sustained and meticulous torture. The board was used in most of Corll's ritualistic murders, and he took it with him as he moved between his various homes. He kept it stored in black plastic bags in the back rooms of his various properties, alongside various implements of torture. Once a boy was trapped upon the board there was almost no chance of escape. Corll could – and did – spend several days doing what he pleased with them, a twisted combination of molestation and tortures. He would use gags, taping them tightly to the boys' mouths, rending them voiceless and dampening their screams. One favourite means of torture involved shoving a long, thin glass rod into the boy's penis and then snapping off the end. Another involved the forcible insertion of thick instruments into the rectum, and the police would later find an 18-inch double dildo lying casually upon a work bench in Corll's apartment. Corll also enjoyed systematically pulling out pubic hairs, one by one, and burning the captive with cigarettes. In one gruesome incident that was reported by Henley, Corll became so upset by one of the victims that he gnawed at the boy's genitals, eventually ripping them off completely using his teeth. Another boy was castrated using a sharp knife. Sometimes a boy was shot and injured but still allowed to stay alive for several days. According to Henley, the more Corll liked a boy the longer he allowed them to stay alive … and the longer they were subjected to his sadistic cruelties.

Undoubtedly, Frank Aguirre would've been subjected to tortures such as these. His skeletal remains were found buried at High Island Beach. The manner of his death was recorded as asphyxia due to strangulation.

Despite realising by now that Corll was killing the abductees,

Henley and Brooks continued in the procurement of further victims. Seventeen-year-old Mark Scott was a lifelong friend of Henley and an acquaintance of Brooks. He was known as a "problem child" and had been previously charged with carrying a knife. Just before Christmas 1972, Mark told his parents he was going to Mexico for a while, to "forget his troubles". Instead, Mark somehow wound up at Corll's apartment. There he was overpowered. However, he was able to gain access to a knife and fight back, and during the struggle Corll received a slash wound. After that happened, Corll pulled a gun on the youth. According to Brooks, when Mark saw the pistol pointing at him he "just gave up". Mark suffered a similar fate to Frank Aguirre: he was tied to the board and, after he was raped, tortured and strangled, his body was buried at High Island Beach.[2]

His parents received a postcard a week after his supposed trip to Mexico. It had been franked in Austin.

> _How are you doing? [the card read] I am in Austin for a couple of days. I found a good job. I am making $3 an hour. I'll be home when I get enough money to pay my lawyer._

Mark was never heard from again.

There were suggestions that Mark Scott was an early helper and that he also had been instrumental in leading boys to Corll's apartment. Henley reported that Corll had taught him to strangle using Scott, and that after 40 minutes of this treatment Scott had

---

[2] At least Henley and Brooks insisted that Scott had been buried at the beach. In 1993 one of the bodies recovered from the boat shed was identified as Mark Scott. Henley disputed this, insisting that the body had been buried under the beach. The body that had been given back to Scott's parents was re-examined and sure enough, DNA profiling showed the remains to be those of another boy. There are two possibilities: either another body has been misidentified, or Mark's body remains undiscovered. However, Brooks and Henley's accounts have been consistent and there is no doubt that Corll did, in fact, kill Scott.

pointed to his head in a sign of resignation, imploring Corll to shoot him. Perhaps the fact that Scott fought against capture reveals that he already had an inkling of the fate that was in store for him. It's possible that his desperate plea to be shot means he *already knew* that a release by death would be the preferable option. Scott's involvement, however, is conjecture and its basis is purely on the refusal of Henley and Brooks to give more detailed information about that particular murder.

Soon, two more Heights boys were captured and restrained on the torture board. Billy Gene Baulch, aged 17, was a former employee of the Corll Candy Company and Johnny Ray Delome, aged 16, was his friend. They disappeared as they were walking to a local store. Both boys were raped and tortured. At some stage during their captivity Billy was forced to write a letter:

> *Dear Mom and Dad, I am sorry to do this, But Johnny and I found a better Job working for a trucker loading and unloading from Houston to Washington and we'll be back in three to four Weeks. After a week I will send money to help You and Mom out. Love, Billy.*

Mr Baulch received this letter three days after his son's disappearance. As a truckdriver, he knew that no such job as that described in the letter existed. Johnny's family also received a letter, but they were convinced from the perfect spelling that Johnny had had no hand in it. Both letters had been franked in Madisonville, Texas, around 70 miles from Houston, in order, clearly, to add credence to the lies within. Neither family took any comfort from the letters.

The Baulch parents recalled suspicious incidents from Billy's past. Billy had once told Mrs Baulch that he and another boy had been to Corll's apartment and Corll got them to fool around the handcuffs. Billy had said that Corll could never find the key for the cuffs.

The Baulches went looking for Corll. However, when they found him he was polite and respectful, and so insistent that he didn't know where Billy was that the parents went away disappointed.

In reality, Billy and his friend Johnny were already dead, murdered by Henley. He'd manually strangled Billy, shouted, "Here's Johnny,"[3] and then shot Johnny in the forehead, the bullet exiting his ear. Amazingly, Johnny survived the shooting and begged for his life: "Wayne, please don't." He too was strangled to death by Henley. Both bodies were buried at High Island beach.

Billy Ridinger, who was aged 19 at the time, was the only youth to have been released by Corll. The trio had lured Billy to the Schuler Street apartment where he was secured to the torture board and repeatedly abused by Corll. Brooks claimed that he persuaded Corll to release the youth and allow him to leave. Ridinger did not contact the police following this incident. Because of this, there are suspicions that he had been an accomplice in the abduction of boys, only later to become a potential victim himself. No legitimate explanation for the release of Ridinger has ever been offered. The theory of his involvement is purely speculation, however. Nevertheless, what is *not* speculation is that if Ridinger *had* gone to the police earlier then the lives of at least 15 other boys might've been spared.

Corll relocated yet again in the summer of 1972, moving to an apartment at Westcott Towers. He killed at least twice at this new address. Seventeen-year-old Steven Kent Sickman left a party just before midnight on 19 July and somehow fell into the clutches of Corll. The sweet-faced youth was bludgeoned about the chest and then strangled. A month later, another winsome youth, 19-year-old Roy Eugene Bunton, was snatched whilst walking to his job at a shoe store. He was bound, gagged and shot twice in the head. Both youths were buried in Corll's boat

---

[3] "And now … here's Johnny" opened the late-night talk show *The Tonight Show Starring Johnny Carson* (1962-1992) in order to introduce the host.

shed. Neither murder was mentioned by Henley or Brooks, so it's possible that Corll either acted alone or had an unidentified accomplice to help him. The identities of these two victims were only discovered in 2011.

On 2 October 1972, Wally Jay Simoneaux and Richard Edward Hembree, aged 14 and 13 respectively, were spotted walking towards the latter's home. Wally was going to spend the night with his shy friend, Richard. At some stage on their journey Henley and Brooks stopped the boys to entice them to come to a party at Corll's apartment. They were seen by another friend just after dark in a white vehicle, but when the friend attempted to talk to them another boy (presumably Brooks or Henley) got out and said, "Beat it." It was the last time the boys were seen.

At some stage during that evening, Wally managed to phone his mother at home. He shouted, "Mama" into the receiver. Mrs Simoneaux said, "Darlin', where are you?" but there was a shuffling noise and connection was abruptly disconnected. Mrs Simoneaux called the Hembree residence only to discover that neither boy was there.

According to Henley, the next day Corll accidentally shot Richard in the right side of the face whilst tormenting him with a gun. Richard survived the gunshot. Neither boy survived subsequent strangulations. Their bodies were buried in the corner of Corll's boat shed, sharing a common grave with James Glass and Danny Yates (the boys who were being raped when Brooks first walked in on Corll).

Willard Karmon "Rusty" Branch Jr. was the 18-year-old son of a Houston police officer. He went missing sometime the following month whilst hitchhiking. His gagged and emasculated body was later uncovered in the boat shed. Richard Alan Kepner, a 19-year-old youth, went missing over a month later whilst walking to a phone booth to call his fiancée. His remains were found buried at High Island Beach. He'd been killed by strangulation.

Corll moved house on 20 January 1973 and within two weeks he'd murdered again. Joseph Allen Lyles, aged 17, was lured to

Corll's new home and "grabbed". He was buried at Jefferson County Beach and his remains were only found in 1983. It would be over 26 years before they could be identified.

In March 1973, Corll relocated for the final time, this time to 2020 Lamar Drive in Pasadena. It is supposed that the removal of a hydrocele (an accumulation of fluid) and a painful recovery contributed to a hiatus in the slaughter, for Corll did not kill again for four months. By now, however, Corll's blood lust was up and he went on a frenzied killing spree. In the space of two months eight boys were murdered. Henley was later to comment that he and Brooks instinctively _knew_ when to find Corll a new victim and they would head to the streets and trawl for victims.

On 4 June 1973, William Ray Lawrence, aged 15, phoned his father and asked if he could go fishing. _Who was he going fishing with_, his father wanted to know. "Oh, just some friends," young Billy replied. His so-called "friends", however, had less-than-friendly intent. He was kept alive for three days of abuse and torture before being strangled. The ground beneath Corll's boat shed had by now become quite crowded with bodies and so Billy was buried in the woods near Corll's father's vacation cabin at Lake Sam Rayburn. He was the first of at least four victims to end up there.

Billy's father received a letter a few days after his son's disappearance:

> _Dear Daddy,_
> _I have decided to go to Austin because I have had a good job offer, I am sorry that I decided to leave but I just had to go._
> _P.S. I will be back in late Aug. I hope you understand, but I had to go._
> _Daddy, I hope you know I love you. Your son, Billy._

The handwriting was Billy's own. August came and went but Billy did not reappear. During this time, however, someone calling himself "Wayne" phoned and asked where Billy was. His father said Billy was away for the summer and wouldn't be returning until school recommenced. Two days after this call, the Lawrence house was burgled and some of Billy's possessions and mementos were stolen. It was as if someone familiar with the house had broken in.

Meanwhile the killings were continuing apace, although the wider community knew nothing of it.

Raymond Stanley Blackburn was a 20-year-old married man who'd been hitchhiking to the Heights to see his new-born son. He never made it. He was abducted, strangled to death and buried at Lake Sam Rayburn.

In early July 1973, Henley began to take driving lessons. Whilst doing so, he became acquainted with Homer Luis Garcia, aged 15. On 6 July, Luis phoned his grandmother to say he'd be spending the evening with a friend. Instead, he was shot in the head and chest and bled to death in the bath at Corll's apartment. He was also buried at Lake Sam Rayburn.

John Manning Sellars was killed two days before his 18th birthday. For some reason, he was buried fully clothed, one of only two victims left this way. He'd been killed with rifle shots to the chest, whereas all the other victims had either been shot with a pistol or strangled. Nevertheless, John had been bound with rope in a similar fashion to Corll's other victims, and Henley and Brooks led police to the burial site at Lake Sam Rayburn, putting to bed questions that were raised about the ownership of this murder.

Michael Anthony Baulch was the 15-year-old younger brother of Billy, who'd been killed the previous year by Corll. Michael was strangled to death and buried at Lake Sam Rayburn.

Friends Marty Ray Jones, aged 18, and Charles Cary Cobble, aged 17, were last seen walking along the street in the company of Henley on 25 July 1973 by a local resident. The woman reported seeing three boys walking along in "stiff procession". She recalled that Charles had looked over at her with a beseeching look in his eyes, a look that said, *Don't speak to me*, or *For heaven's sake do something*. She said it was as if Charles had tried to plead with her with his eyes.

Marty and Charles lived in their own apartment just a few doors down from the Cobble family. That night neither boy came home. At just after nine o'clock the next morning the phone rang in the Cobble household.

"I'm in serious trouble," came Charles' voice down the line.

His father, Vern, asked what the trouble was.

"I can't tell you." Wherever Charles was calling from, he said that Marty was there with him. "I have to have a thousand dollars," Charles insisted. His father said he didn't have that amount of money. "But I've *got* to have it," Charles insisted.

Vern Cobble said he'd try to raise the money.

"I'll tell you later where you have to have the money," Charles said, and then there were the sounds of mumbling voices and the connection was cut.

To Mr Cobble, Charles' voice had sounded resigned and without hope. He knew something was up, that the boys *really were* in trouble. He contacted the police. They didn't seem interested as they couldn't identify a crime. Vern called Marty's father. Marty, apparently had made a similar phone call, making a similar request for money. If the police weren't going to make a search, Vern decided, he'd do so himself. He went around the Heights ringing doorbells, and he soon discovered an insidious pattern emerging: young male youths were going missing at an alarming rate. He tried to stir the police into action, to galvanise them into taking the disappearances seriously, but little action was taken. Marty and Charles' bodies were later pulled from the ground in Corll's boat shed. The serial sex-torture murderer had managed to find an empty spot for them after all.

There's an obvious explanation for the two garbled telephone calls from Charles and Marty's to their respective families. The two boys had probably been speaking under duress. In all likelihood they were already captive and incapacitated, restrained on Corll's torture board. Their captor might even have been holding the receiver as they talked, threatening them with even greater torments should either of them speak out of turn. The calls had doubtless been made in order to provide the families with an explanation for their sons' disappearances. Marty was known to have been involved in petty drug-dealing. Corll might have used this fact to his advantage, making it look as if a narcotics gang had taken lethal revenge.

The answer would come out in Henley's later confessions. He had lured the two boys to Corll's house. After a period of abuse and torture, the two abductees had been bound to each other, wrist and ankle, on the same side of the torture board. Corll told the two boys that they were to engage in a fight to the death. He promised that the boy who remained alive would be allowed to live. The battle, according to Henley, lasted several excruciating hours. After this, Marty was then forced to watch Charles being raped and tortured before being shot to death with two bullets. Corll, however, was not a man of this word. Marty was himself then strangled to death with the cord from a venetian blind.

The last known victim, no. 28, was James Stanton Dreymala. On 3 August 1973, whilst riding his bike, the 13-year-old boy was abducted under Corll and Brooks' pretence that they had empty bottles to sell. He was lured to Corll's apartment, attached to the torture board and then raped, brutalised and strangled. His remains were disposed of in the boat shed, the last to be buried and the first to be dug up.

Less than a week later, over at the Heights, Rhonda Williams had just had an argument with her father – one that had grown loud and turned physical. It was by now well after midnight on 8 August and Rhonda was in her bedroom in her house in a tearful state, crying almost hysterically. A friend tried to comfort her but she was inconsolable.

Then along came her friend Wayne Henley. He had heard the commotion from outside and he just let himself in and flopped down on Rhonda's bed with his friend, Timothy Kerley, in tow. Rhonda told the two boys what had happened. If she stayed where she was, she insisted, she was "just gonna die". Wayne was a good friend; he invited Rhonda to jump in his car and come join them back at his pal's house.

The trio arrived at Corll's Pasadena house at around three o'clock in the morning. Corll was not happy to see Rhonda. He pulled Wayne aside and raged: "You weren't supposed to bring any girl!" But after furiously remonstrating at Wayne, he appeared to calm down. He allowed the youngsters in and offered them some drink and drugs, and Wayne and Tim began "huffing" at the bag of acrylic paint. Eventually, after a couple of hours, all three teenagers passed out were they lay, sprawled out across the rug.

When Wayne regained consciousness a few hours later he realised he was being manhandled. Corll had already bound his ankles together tightly and was in the process of attaching handcuffs to his wrists. "You blew it bringing that girl," Corll told him. Wayne saw that the floor was covered in plastic sheeting. Tim had been stripped and he and Rhonda were already secured with nylon rope and straps. "I'm going to kill you all," Corll snarled. "But first I'm going to have some fun," and then he turned the radio up loud so that music rang out through the house.

Wayne recognised the signs. He'd been in this position before, but never on the _receiving_ end of the "fun". Corll promised to "teach him a lesson" and began by kicking him repeatedly on the chest. Then he dragged Wayne towards the kitchen. He jammed a pistol into the youngster's stomach. Wayne gasped and began to beg for his life. He promised to "do anything you want me to". He reminded Corll of the good times they'd had together, emphasising their long friendship and repeating that he'd "do anything – _anything_". He offered to join in with the torture of Tim and Rhonda if Corll would only let him go. The frantic bargaining went on for half-an-hour.

He must've cut a persuasive figure. After a while Corll released the binds and shoved him into the bedroom. Together they secured Tim and Rhonda to the torture board. "Cut off her clothes," Corll ordered Wayne, tossing him a hunting knife.

Wayne used the knife to cut away at Rhonda's clothing. Meanwhile, Corll set the pistol down on a nightstand and began to remove his own clothing. Once naked, he repositioned Tim so that the boy now lay on his back, spread-eagled. He began the process of securing Tim to the torture board.

Then Rhonda opened a bleary eye and groggily lifted her head. "Is this for real?" she asked.

"Yes, this is for real," replied Wayne dispassionately.

"Aren't you going to do anything about it?" she shouted at Wayne.

By now Tim was also awake. He began to struggle against his restraints, screaming for help. Corll put his hands between Tim's legs and when Tim squirmed Corll punched him. Corll straddled him and explained what was about to happen. He told Wayne he could have the girl. "I'll mess with Tim," he said.

Wayne hesitated. He wanted to take Rhonda out of the bed-room. He imagined the upcoming scenes of torture. "She doesn't want to see that," he shouted over the loud music.

Corll ignored him.

Something snapped in Wayne. He knew that this couldn't go on any longer. He grabbed the pistol and pointed it at Corll. "You've gone far enough, Dean. I can't have you kill all my friends."

Corll looked up surprised. He clambered off Tim and then rose suddenly. He lurched towards Wayne.

"Back off now!" the boy shouted.

"Kill me, Wayne," said Corll, still advancing.

The youth backed off, but Corll continued to move towards him. "You won't do it," Corll goaded him.

But Wayne knew it was up. He pulled the trigger – once, hitting Corll in the head. Corll continued to pace. Wayne shot again, hitting Corll twice in the shoulder. Corll turned and ran from the room, barging against a hallway wall and collapsing right there on the floor. Wayne shot him again, unloading the final three bullets into Corll's back. Dean Corll's depravity had finally come to a violent end.

Wayne Henley phoned the police. As the three waited on the step outside Corll's house Wayne told Tim, "I could've got two hundred dollars for you." The police arrived minutes later and Wayne confessed immediately. "I don't care who knows it," he said as they read him his Miranda rights. "I have to get it off my chest." He implicated himself and David Brooks in the procurement and killing of several boys over three years after initially believing that they were to be sold into a child sex ring.

Investigators were initially sceptical of Henley's claims. But when he gave up the names of three boys – David Hilligiest, Charles Cobble and Marty Jones, who'd recently been reported missing – their impressions changed. That same day, they initiated a search of Corll's boat shed and it began to reveal its terrible secrets. On 10 August, Henley and Brooks brought police to the shallow graves of further victims at Lake Sam Rayburn, and again accompanied police to High Island Beach were more bodies were disinterred. Twenty-seven sets of remains in total were found, making it the worst murder spree known in American history.

The Houston Mass Murders, as the case was soon to become known, would make worldwide headlines. It wasn't just the number of murders that caught everyone's attention; it was the fact that most of them vanished from a small vicinity of a working-class area. How was it that the vanishings had happened without drawing wider notice?

Tim Kerley and Rhonda Williams testified before the Grand Jury on 13 August 1973. Billy Ridinger, the boy who Corll had allowed to escape, also gave evidence of his experiences at the hands of Corll and his minions. Henley and Brooks were indicted and tried separately for their roles in the murders. In 1974, Henley was found guilty of all six of the murders of which he was accused and he received a life sentence. A year later Brooks got his own life sentence for involvement in the murder of four. Both youths appealed. Separate retrials reaffirmed the verdicts. Henley now serves his life sentence at the Mark W. Michael Unit in Anderson County, Texas. Brooks was incarcerated at the Terrell Unit near Rosharon, Texas, where he died on 28 May 2020 of COVID-19-related complications.

In the Houston area in the early 1970s, at least 42 boys vanished, many of them without trace. In one grave at High Island Beach extra bones were discovered, indicating at least one undiscovered victim. Former workers at the Corll Candy Company later recalled that Corll used to do a lot of digging in the late 1960s under the pretext of burying spoiled candy. The suspicion is that Corll may have murdered boys prior to his first known victims.

In 1975, Houston police discovered a cache of pornographic photographs and films depicting 16 boys, some as young as eight, many of whom were from the Heights. Of these 16 individuals, 11 may have been amongst victims of Corll. Claims made by Corll that he had been involved in a Californian pornographic sex ring may have held a degree of truth.

In February 2012, a photograph was released. The Polaroid image was found amongst the possessions of Henley, which had been stored by his family since 1973. The picture depicts a blond-haired youth handcuffed to a device alongside a toolbox containing many of the implements with which Corll is known to have tortured his victims. The boy is staring into the camera lens in obvious distress. It is a haunting and disturbing image. The boy has never been identified and it is likely that he met his end at the hands of Corll sometime in 1972 or 1973.

It will never be known what drove Dean Corll to torture and murder. He has been described by various people who knew him as "companionable", "a good dude", "a joker". However, as he got older his tolerance of colleagues' repartee appeared to weaken severely. He became moody and hypersensitive about his age; he continued to want to hang around with younger boys. People knew that he was gay but he didn't go especially out of his way to hide the fact. In those years many people thought that homosexuality was wrong. Perhaps Corll himself was one of those who thought that way. Did he feel shame about his own desires? Is that the reason why he felt an overwhelming need to unleash his fury? Is that why he ended up loathing the objects of his desires and turned to torturing and killing them?

Dean Corll's father was a strict disciplinarian who resorted to harsh punishments, but that does not explain the origin of his son's future brutality. Corll Jr. showed a complete lack of empathy for his victims. He simply killed for kicks. He may have qualified as a paedophile – or, as most of his known victims were adolescents, a hebephile. However, what colours Corll's twisted personality traits most is his *sadism*. He became aroused at the pain, suffering and anguish of others – specifically, youthful males – and as his "blood lust" escalated it became more savage and more irresistible.

On the surface, he was also a "nice guy". With great skill he was able to manipulate two teenage accomplices into the procurement of their own friends and acquaintances. These toadies did so in the full knowledge that they were luring their friends to torture and death, but Dean Corll was capable of killing alone, and he had done so many times. Undoubtedly, he was an evil psychopath who chose to put his own needs and desires above and beyond those of anyone else. He was an organised lust killer. If he himself had not been killed it is likely that his murderous campaign would've become more and more brutal and extreme.

# Randy Steven Kraft
(active 1971-1983)


AT TEN-PAST-ONE, during the early hours of 14 May 1983, two
Californian police officers were patrolling a remote stretch of
the San Diego Freeway round 50 miles south of Los Angeles.
This was the "graveyard shift", when drunks were most likely
to be roaming the desolate Interstate 5. For several minutes
Officers Michael Sterling and Michael Howard observed an er-
ratically-driven brown Toyota Celica which was cruising at
around 45-miles-per-hour. As they followed, the car drifted
across the freeway shoulder. The officers had already become
suspicious that the driver was intoxicated. They continued to tail
the Toyota. When its driver made an illegal manoeuvre the
officers decided to investigate further. They switched on their
red light. The car in front slowed to 30-miles-per-hour but didn't
stop. The officers watched. The driver of the Toyota reached
into the backseat of his car, grabbed a jacket and tossed it onto
the passenger seat. Alarmed, Officer Sterling now flashed his
beams and spoke into his vehicle's loudspeaker, ordering the
driver to pull over. Eventually, the driver of the Toyota in front
drew his car onto the hard shoulder and stopped.

A thin, wide-faced, middle-aged man got out of the car and
walked smartly towards the cops. The cops had seen drivers react this way many times before. It usually meant they had something in their car they wished to hide – a joint, perhaps, or an
open beer can. As if to draw attention to the fact, the driver
lobbed a half-empty bottle of beer to the ground as he stalked
towards the patrol car. The fly on the man's jeans was not quite
done up. The cops' suspicions were double aroused.

They went through their routine and got the man's details.
Randy Kraft was a 38-year-old resident of Long Beach, California. Yes, he'd had a few beers, he told the cops, but he was sober. At that point, Officer Sterling noticed that Kraft had not
been travelling alone, a fact he'd neglected to mention. Leaving

his colleague to cuff the driver and read him his rights, Sterling approached the car. Inside was a good-looking young man. He was slumped over with a jacket across his lap. Sterling rapped on the passenger window. To no avail. The passenger seemed to be either asleep or passed out drunk.

The officer called over to Kraft. *Who was the friend?* he wanted to know. When Highway Patrol catch a drunk driver sometimes they'll allow a sober passenger to drive the car – and the drunk driver – home.

*He didn't know who the guy was*, Kraft told the officer. *It was just some hitchhiker he'd picked up a few miles back.*

Sterling knocked the passenger window again. Again, no response. The passenger seemed to be even drunker than Kraft. Sterling walked around the car and leaned through the driver's door. His suspicions appeared to be correct; the footwell of the car was strewn with bottles and pill containers. A folding knife was in plain sight on the driver's seat. Sterling put a hand on the young man's forearm and recoiled suddenly. The flesh was cold, clammy and, now that he looked closer, yellow-coloured. The man wasn't passed out drunk; he was dead. Sterling pulled the jacket from the passenger's lap and saw what the driver had tried in vain to conceal. The young passenger's zipper was down and his genitals were pulled out, supported by the elastic banding of his pants. Urine stained his lap as his bladder had relaxed *post mortem*. His shoes had been removed and tucked neatly under the seat. Disturbingly, the laces had been removed and used to tie the wrists together tightly. And clearly visible were ligature marks around the passenger's neck. Friday the 13th had evidently been an unlucky night for this man ...

Within moments, Sterling and Howard realised what they'd stumbled upon. Over the past decade a trail of mutilated bodies had been turning up alongside the various freeways of southern California. The victims were always good-looking, physically fit, young males. Their killer was clearly a sexual sadist with a twisted *M.O.*: he'd render the men insensate through drugs or alcohol and then subject them to brutalising tortures before killing them. Investigators who later searched the killer's car found beneath a floor mat 47 Polaroids of naked young men, who were posed as if either unconscious or dead. More disturbingly, they were also to find a list of 61 cryptic phrases, each believed to refer to one of his victims. If the coded scorecard were to be given credence, Randy Kraft would turn out to be one of America's most evil killers, and it was only a chance nighttime encounter with two patrol officers cruising a desolate road that was to curtail his murderous reign of terror.

Randy Steven Kraft was born in Long Beach, California on 19 March 1945 He was the youngest child of Opal Lee and Harold Herbert Kraft, who'd moved from Wyoming to the west coast just four years earlier. Randy had three elder sisters who completed doted on him. He was reportedly a very calm, but sometimes active, baby. On one occasion, when he was one year old, he fell off a couch and broke his collar bone. A year later, he had a more serious injury. The Kraft parents were looking at a house they were thinking of buying on Beach Boulevard in Huntington Beach, California. The house had a set of concrete steps. Unfortunately, Randy fell down these steps and hit his head. He was knocked unconscious and remained out cold for some time, only coming to after a spell at the clinic. At the time, however, the Krafts were thankful that their precious toddler appeared to have suffered no lasting damage.

In 1948, the Kraft family relocated to bucolic Westminster, and their new residence was a small, three-bedroom, wood-frame shack positioned about 50 feet from the highway, although theirs was the only inhabited house within a block that was otherwise surrounded by businesses. On one side was a blacksmith's premises; on the other, the Red Garter cocktail lounge, much to the god-fearing Mrs Kraft's chagrin.

The Krafts quickly made themselves at home. The women became active in the First Presbyterian Church. Randy regularly went to church. Harold preferred to keep chickens; a life of religious devotion wasn't for him. By all accounts, the father of the family was a "distant" man. It was clear to outsiders that Mr and Mrs Kraft didn't get along. Neither did Randy get along with his father, and he found himself always surrounded by women. Money was tight, and Opal had to work several jobs to supplement her husband's meagre pay-packet. She still had time for Randy, however; he would always be the apple of her eye.

Randy sailed breezily enough through his early schooldays. He was quiet, affable and well-liked by his peers. He never got into fights and had plenty of friends. Girls found him to be the perfect gentleman. He was a smart fellow and didn't struggle with academia. Politics was an early passion and he leaned towards the conservative Republican side. He was remembered by teachers as a square-faced boy who always sat in the middle of class. And he _always_ received good grades.

High school proved equally trouble-free. Whilst some of his classmates spent their time joking about and playing pranks, Randy preferred to remain with the more sophisticated, intellectual crowd. Sometimes he would wear a smart shirt and tie to school, for a while even becoming a trendsetter in this new "preppy" fashion.[1] Maybe it was because he was much brighter than the others, but peers would certainly remember him having a particularly wry sense of humour.

Randy didn't chase skirt. Sure, he escorted girls to various functions – the Spring Fling, the Senior Prom – but that was the extent of it. During the summer months Randy and his friends would jump into his car and drive to the beach. There they'd ogle at the girls. Randy would even make a half-hearted wolf-whistle. But again, that was the extent of it. For Randy knew even then it wasn't girls he was interested in – it was guys.

Randy had _always_ known it. He instinctively _knew_ that he was different. Sex and sexuality weren't everyday conversations – especially if the subject was homosexuality, which was still

---

[1] A style of smart, neat dress associated with a pupil from an expensive college-preparatory ("prep") school.

viewed as an aberration and treated as a mental illness. In the ultraconservative bubble of Westminster everyone knew every else's business. It wasn't any wonder that Randy kept his inclinations to himself; if he'd said anything, the whole world would've found out about it, and that would certainly have been problematic. Some, however, already had an inkling that Kraft had a propensity for boys. It wasn't openly discussed though, and Kraft's desires, like those of many other men and women of the time, remained half-hidden behind the closet door. Nevertheless, during this time he had his first homosexual affair, a black man called Mike, whom he brought home to meet his parents. *What an awkward meeting that had been*, Kraft would later reminisce.

He graduated in 1963, 10th out of a class of 360 students, and enrolled in the prestigious male-only Claremont Men's College, reading economics. Shortly thereafter, he entered another male-only environment, the Claremont Reserve Officers Training Corps, only to reject it two years later, along with the on-going Vietnam War. This *volte-face* liberalisation seemed perfectly reasonable to him and caused him no undue consternation. However, in the next year, US President J.F. Kennedy was assassinated – an event that devastated Kraft – and his right-leaning attitudes returned for good. Outwardly, the Presbyterian values remained in place, but the knots were slipping; soon Kraft would be embracing atheism, or, at the very least, a firmly-held agnosticism.

Within the next few years, Kraft was also fully embracing his homosexuality. He was now sporting a moustache and a longer, more casual hairstyle. By 1964, he had begun to frequent the gay establishments that centred Laguna Beach, California, where homosexuality flourished without the unwelcome interference of local law enforcement. He found a job in Garden Grove, California as a bartender at a local cocktail lounge that catered to gay clientele. He was also a patron himself of the various gay-friendly establishments in Huntington Beach. It was here, around the pier district, that he had his first brush with the law. It was a place where hustlers roamed the beachfront and men's rooms. Generally it was the older men who were the clients and the younger guys the service-providers. At some point in the early hours of the morning, Kraft offered to have sex with a man and was promptly busted by an undercover vice officer for lewd behaviour. It is not known whether the issue of payment had been discussed. As an apparent first-time offender, charges were dropped. This had not been Kraft's first time hustling for sex. In fact, by now he was an old hand at propositioning males. He would bring male "friends" back home to meet his parents and sisters, who remained oblivious to his homosexual activities.

Kraft's priorities were shifting; his academic life suffered as he indulged himself in late-night drinking and card games. It was said that he didn't like to lose at bridge. He was elected dorm president, and, possibly because of this, he kept the illusion going by dating girls and presenting himself as excessively macho – endlessly rousing, leering and joking. Some said later that their friend Randy had a glint in his eye, and that his humour was strange: "Not funny ha-ha, but strange funny." Rumours were also beginning to circulate that he was into "bondage and discipline" parties, and some of his male colleagues would warn others that Kraft was a man dangerous to know.

When it became necessary to study Kraft crammed. To aid himself he resorted to chemicals – caffeine capsules. He also suffered from medical problems though – dyspepsia, migraines and nerve problems. The clinic prescribed him Valium, and so the use of drugs was to become a major issue for the next years.

Friends recalled that Kraft would sometimes just disappear. Late at night, sometimes during a party or drinking session, he would leave, usually vanishing for several hours at a time. He would never say where he had gone or for what reason. When questioned, he would be vague in his responses: "Don't worry about me. I'll go out and do what I want." Occasionally, there would be glimpses behind the façade. During times of soul-searching – as most young men are wont to engage in at times –

Kraft would intimate that there was a hidden side to his life: "You know, there's a part of me that you will never know." At the time he was right: *no one* knew about Kraft's secret life.

Kraft graduated from Claremont in June 1967 after having to retake his econometrics examination. No doubt his carousing and late-night card games had impacted upon his studies. Four months later, he had joined the US Air Force. He cut a dashing figure in his boot camp graduation photo, having donned leather flight jacket, airman's leather visor hat and scarf. The truth of it was that Kraft was an aeroplane sprayer, not a pilot, and when there were no planes to spray he was sent to give the airbase housing a lick of paint. There was little to do at his southern California station; the nearest town was 30 miles away. Kraft didn't plan to stay long. He wrote to friends and family to tell them he was homosexual. Friends already knew, but the news came as a complete surprise to family. His father raged; his mother quietly disapproved. His sister Kay thought he'd been corrupted having gone to an all-male college. Randy continued to frequent the cruising areas of Laguna Beach, where newly liberated gays were flocking to in droves. He'd heard about the backroom action of the saunas and gymnasia and he thought that he'd have some of that. And he heard about gay couples now openly living together in the increasingly liberal Laguna Beach and Long Beach areas. Again, Kraft was determined that that was something he wanted to be a part of.

So he informed his military superiors about his sexuality. His inevitable discharge on 26 July 1969 was classed as "general", not "honourable". This could be viewed negatively by future employers and Kraft challenged the ruling. He didn't win his appeal. However, he was now released from his military obligations and for a short period he moved back in with his parents.

That didn't last long; he soon had his own apartment on Fir Drive in Huntington Beach, was working as a bartender and spending much of his time on the beach. He was also starting to distance himself from his family and his appearance and attire became much more liberal. Friends who'd known the buttoned-up Randy of school would not have recognised the trendy peacock he'd now become.

Kraft's first known sexual assault occurred at Huntington Beach in March 1970. A 13-year-old boy named Joseph Gerald Fancher had run away from home and was riding his bike along the boardwalk when he chanced to encounter a stranger who was staring at him fixedly. The man, who appeared to be in his mid-20s, shared a cigarette with the boy. He asked Joey if he'd ever slept with a woman (the answer was no), and then invited him to come and live with him. Joey agreed. He hid his bike and hopped aboard the stranger's Honda motorcycle. Together they rode back to the strange man's apartment.

There, the man showed the boy around and offered him some dope. He left the room for a moment and during that time Joey phoned home, boastfully telling his sister that he'd run away. As he hung up, the stranger returned. He offered Joey four pills, which he took. The stranger stood watching and waiting for a few moments. Then he gave the boy four more pills. This time the effect came quickly. Joey was soon drowsy, disoriented and powerless to move. What followed is the stuff of nightmares.

The stranger brought out some gay pornography and asked Joey if he'd ever had sex with a man. Joey's tongue was thick in his mouth and he couldn't respond. The stranger unzipped his pants and began to fondle himself. He ordered Joey to take his clothes off. The boy was helpless to comply. Then the stranger removed his own T-shirt. Whilst Joey lay immobile on the floor, the stranger orally raped him, ejaculating into the boy's mouth and causing him to retch. The stranger told the boy that if he attempted to leave he'd be killed. Then he went into the bathroom.

When he returned, the stranger again ordered Joey to take off his clothes. Joey was still unable to do. Now the man was angry. He pulled down Joey's pants and sodomised him brutally and painfully. Joey was still powerless, the effects of the drugs having rendered him immobile.

After the rape, the stranger announced he was going to work

and departed, leaving Joey alone.

A while later Joey heard knocking. Drowsily, he went to the front door and opened it to two young boys who asked if Randy was in. Joey mumbled a reply and closed the door. With difficulty, he pulled on his clothes and stumbled outside. In his confusion he forgot to put on his shoes. Blinking in the sunshine, he sobbed until a passer-by came to his aid, took one look and then had him rushed to hospital by ambulance where he had to have his stomach pumped. A doctor told him that if he'd taken another two pills he'd have died.

His parents arrived, and they wanted to know what had happened to Joey's new shoes. He could feel the gaze of disapproval beneath their gaze. He was still dazed, but he was able to direct the police to the stranger's apartment. When the officers scoped the place they found Joey's shoes beside the bed. They also found various vials of sedative medications made out to a person called Mrs Doris Lane, some marijuana, some flyers advertising gay businesses, and photographs depicting men engaged in sexual activities – 76 photos in total. The police no longer believed that this apartment belonged to a woman called Doris Lane. Flipping through the Polaroids, Joey was able to point to a man in some of them as the same man who'd assaulted him. This candidate was the more likely resident. The officers soon learned that the property was occupied by a man called Randy Kraft.

Nevertheless, they couldn't ascertain that a crime had been committed. According to the boy, he'd taken the pills voluntarily. What's more, the inspection of the property had been completed without proper authorisation. This boy Joey seemed like any other of the many runaways who ended up at Huntington Beach every year. The cops filed a report, which wasn't to be looked at again for another 13 years.

Meanwhile, when Joey got home he received a beating from his stepfather for truancy, taking drugs and losing his shoes. It wasn't until many years had passed that he was able to tell anyone about the rape by a strange man. Undoubtedly, Joey Fancher suffered physical and psychological damage, but if he hadn't made his escape when he had then the outcome might've been much worse; Randy Kraft didn't leave many living victims ...

By 1971, Kraft had had enough of bartending. He got a job as a forklift truck operator. His IQ, which was tested at this time, gave him a high score of 129. Running a forklift was not going to be overly demanding.

This was Kraft's "surfer" phase. His hair was longer and shaggier; he bleached it blond. The moustache had grown larger. He wore Levi's and loafers. He smoked grass and cruised the beach. When he wasn't trawling for sex he was studying education at Long Beach State University. Here he met a Minnesotan boy four years his junior, Jeff Graves. Though younger than Kraft, Graves was still able to teach him a thing or two about the gay lifestyle, including threesomes and mixing sex with drugs. Soon the two were an item, living together in Graves' tiny apartment at Seal Beach. Theirs was an open relationship; neither man was committed to monogamy.[2] It is thought that soon after the blossoming of their relationship Kraft's taste turned to murder.

The last place 30-year-old Wayne Joseph Dukette was seen was the Stables Bar, a gay establishment in Sunset Beach, where he worked as a bartender. His car sat unmoved in the bar's lot for two weeks. Next door to Stables was another gay bar, Broom Hilda, where Randy Kraft tended the bar. Kraft was a frequent Stables customer. On 5 October 1971, police found a naked, bloated body at the bottom of a ravine off the Ortega Highway in south Orange County. The coroner could not establish a cause of death – the elements had erased all tell-tale marks on the putrefied body – but the body's alcohol level at the time of death

---

[2] In 1976 Kraft ended his relationship with Graves. During the span of their relationship Kraft is known to have killed 16 times. Prosecutors believed that Graves may have been an accomplice to the 1975 abduction and murder of 19-year-old Keith Crotwell. Prior to Grave's AIDS-related death on 27 July 1987 police were preparing to question him further.

was .36; the victim had been acutely intoxicated.

Young men do not normally walk along isolated highways naked, the police figured. They knew they had a body dump on their hands. The victim was quickly identified as Dukette and he'd been found five miles from his Belmont Shore apartment. However, with no clues as to how the young man came to be unclothed so far from home the trail quickly turned cold.

Years later, when police found a mysterious hidden scorecard in Randy Kraft's car, the first entry on the list simply said "STABLE". It is a strong coincidence. Prosecutors connected the details and concluded that Dukette was probably one of Kraft's earliest victims.

The second on the list was known only as "ANGEL". It is not even known if the body has been found. He does not share that indignity alone; there are 20 others on Kraft's list: "ANGEL", "HARI HARI", "MARINE DOWN", "VAN DRIVEWAY", "2 IN 1 MV TO PL", "LB MARINA", "DIABETIC", "PORTLAND", "NAVY WHITE", "USER", "2 IN 1 HITCH", "FRONT OF NIPPLES", "CARPENTER", "MC DUMP HB SHORT", "OXNARD", "MC PLANTS", "ENGLAND", "OIL", and the last entry: "WHAT YOU GOT". Two of the entries (prefixed "2 in 1") suggest double murders, perhaps raising the unidentified victim count to 22. The annotations clearly meant something to Kraft and one can only wonder at the significance of some of them. A New Zealander from Hari Hari? A hitchhiker from Oxnard? An English tourist? The other remarks are scant clues that offer little by way of explanation. All of the supposed victims are either undiscovered or are unidentified and haven't been connected to Kraft's murder spree.

Kraft, however, is known to have killed again 15 months later. Edward Daniel Moore – listed as "EDM" and no. 3 on the scorecard – was a 20-year-old Marine. As a child he'd been removed from his alcoholic parents, only to be molested at his foster home placement. By 1972, he found himself hustling and pulling tricks along the Oceanside seafront. Those who knew him said he was a shy guy who wouldn't do anyone any harm. He was last seen on Christmas Eve 1972, leaving the Camp

Pendleton barracks. His body was found two days later. It had abrasions as if it had been thrown from a moving car. Moore had been bound about the wrists and ankles, bitten on the penis and genital area, beaten about the head and face and then garrotted. A sock had been forced into his rectal cavity.

Six weeks later, a John Doe, estimated to be around 18 years old, was found alongside the Terminal Island Freeway in the Wilmington, Los Angeles area. He'd been strangled and a sock had been stuffed into his anus. No. 11 on Kraft's scorecard was known as "WILMINGTON". Some recognised him as a prostitute who work around Kraft's cruising areas.

Two months later, another body was found. "AIRPLANE HILL", no. 5 on the list, was found naked on Huntington Beach. There were ligature marks around his wrists. The youth been sodomised and his genitals were removed. Eighteen-year-old Kevin Clark Bailey was identified in 1995, 22 years after have gone missing.

In July 1973, two more bodies would turn up in pieces. One man's body parts were found separately in Wilmington, San Pedro, Long Beach and behind the bar in Buoys Shed, a gay bar in Sunset Beach. He'd been emasculated and mutilated in a sustained attack. Shockingly, his eyelids had been removed whilst still alive. No doubt Kraft had performed this grotesque surgery to force his victim to witness every moment of the torture. No. 29 on the list, "HAWTH OFF HEAD", remains a John Doe.

The second body was named as 20-year-old Ronnie Gene Wiebe. He'd been hung upside-down and beaten, suffering a fractured skull. He had bite marks on his penis and torso. A sock was found in his rectum. The scorecard code, "7TH STREET", connected him to the location where his body was found along the San Diego Freeway.

Vincent Cruz Mestas, aged 23, was a bisexual Long Beach State University art student who, it is believed, had been seen hustling around the Belmont Shore area. His body was found on 29 December 1973, down a ravine in the San Bernardino Mountains. Referred to as "VINCE M", he is thought to have been

Kraft's 10th victim. He had been beaten so hard his intestines ruptured, and before he died a wooden implement – a toothpick or a pencil – had been forced into his urethra. He was killed by strangulation. *Post mortem*, his face and head were shaved and his hands were cut off, with the bloody stumps wrapped in plastic sandwich bags. Like other victims, Mestas was left with one of his own socks stuffed into the anus. The hands were never found.

Six victims were conclusively linked to Kraft in 1974. On 2 June, the body of Malcolm Eugene Little, aged 20, was found a week after he'd gone missing. Kraft's list refers to him as "TEEN TRUCKER". He'd just been dropped off on the Garden Grove Freeway by his trucker brother after having recently arrived in California, but his girlfriend was so annoyed that he'd left her behind that he planned to hitchhike home again to Alabama. Only having $10 to his name, he couldn't afford a bus ticket. He accepted a lift from the wrong person. He was found dead, propped up against a tree, posed spread-eagled with his genitals missing and a thick tree branch projecting from his rectum.

On 22 June, Kraft killed 18-year-old Roger E. Dickerson, a Marine, after chewing off his penis and left nipple and sodomising him. The autopsy uncovered Valium and a modest amount of alcohol in his system.

Thomas Paxton Lee, aged 25, from Long Beach, went missing on 3 August. He used to cruise the same beaches that Kraft was known to go seeking one-night stands. He was found strangled near the Long Beach Harbour. Item no. 13 on Kraft's list refers to "PIER 2".

Gary Wayne Cordova, aged 23, would often talk to his friends about the rugged, mountainous section of California called Big Sur. On 12 August, Cordova went missing, only to be found dead down an Orange County embankment. The cause of death was deemed to be acute intoxication. No. 32 on Kraft's list refers to "BIG SUR".

Sometime in November 1974, an 18-year-old Marine called Oral Alfred Stuart Jr. went missing. "Buddy", as he was known to family and friends, was from Des Moines, Iowa but was stationed at Camp Pendleton in North San Diego County, Southern California. When he failed to return from leave he was classed as a deserter. On 10 November 1974, the body of a naked male was found discarded on the 605 Freeway. He'd been beaten to death. Investigators had little to work on other than his physical appearance and some tattoos on his body. John Doe no. 155 was not be identified as Stuart until 37 years had passed. No. 23 on Kraft's mysterious list, "IOWA", is likely to have been Stuart.

James Dale Reeves, aged 19, went missing from Ripples, a gay bar, on 27 November that year. He was found the same day. The list refers to him as "TWIGGY". Like Malcolm Little, Reeves had had a branch thrust forcibly into his anus. He had also been emasculated.

Come the new year, Kraft was murdering again. John William Leras, aged 17, was last seen getting off a bus near Ripples Bar, carrying the roller skates he'd received for Christmas. His body was found floating in the water at Sunset Beach. He'd been tied up and strangled to death. A wooden surveyor's stake had been rammed deep into his rectum. There was speculation that Kraft had had an accomplice; two sets of footprints were found in the sand, suggesting that another person had been involved in carrying the body. Kraft's list referred to this victim as "SKATES".

Two weeks later, another body turned up, found by construction workers next to the Golden Sails Hotel in Long Beach, in a place where it could easily be found. It was identified as Craig Victor Jonaites, aged 24. His blackened tongue protruded obscenely from this mouth, testament to a death by strangulation. Jonaites was clothed when found. In fact, he wore *two* sets of trousers. The connection to Kraft was made based upon reference no. 27 on the scorecard: "GOLDEN SAILS".

The evening of 29 March 1975 could easily have ended up with a double murder. Sometime around midnight, Kraft enticed Keith Daven Crotwell, aged 19, and his friend Kent May, aged 15, into his Ford Mustang, supplied them with alcohol and Valium and drove around aimlessly for a while. May, who'd taken about 10 Valium tablets, passed out. For some reason, however, Kraft drove back to the parking lot where he'd picked the two youths, opened the back door, and pushed the unconscious boy out, unharmed. As the car sped off again, witnesses saw another figure slumped against the driver's shoulder.

Crotwell was shy and bespectacled but, despite a scholarly appearance, the academic life was not for him; he flunked out of high school in his senior year. He was a decent mechanic and an advanced motorcyclist, and liked nothing more than to bum around the beach, catching the waves, watching girls and drinking beer. He could hold his beer, friends said. When he didn't return home a few days later family filed a missing person report.

On 8 May 1975, he turned up ... partially. Three teenagers searching for starfish at the end of a jetty spotted something wedged into rocks at the foreshore. Despite the erosion of the sea and the elements, the object was clearly recognisable as a human head, with disintegrating flesh and hair still attached. No corresponding body could be found in the vicinity. Two days later, the head was identified as Crotwell. The rest of his remains – minus the hands – turned up some months later. At the time the cause of death was recorded as accidental drowning.

Police investigated Kraft for the disappearance. They interviewed him, and despite the fact that he passed their lie detector test they attempted to bring charges. However, the district attorney dismissed the request, citing the autopsy report conclusion that Crotwell had died of accidental drowning. The discovery of Kraft's scorecard, with listing no. 19, "PARKING LOT", suggested otherwise. It seemed to the investigators now holding Kraft that Crotwell had been yet another Kraft murder victim.

By mid-1975, Kraft's relationship with Jeff Graves had cooled considerably and they'd split for good. He found another Jeff – 19-year-old apprentice baker Jeff Selig – and the two fell into an open relationship, regularly picking up hitchhikers for threesomes and attending bathhouses, both together and separately. Kraft's body count fell during their early years together, and it is supposed that some level of stability contributed to this.

The attention of the police over the Crotwell "drowning" was undoubtedly another factor: the incident had rattled Kraft severely and he laid low. He was not known to have killed again until New Year's Eve 1975. The compulsion must have been building up in Kraft over the months, for when he did next kill his victim suffered greatly in the release of Kraft's rage. Prosecutors were to describe the murder as "the worst" of them all.

Mark Howard Hall, aged 22, was a skinny, good-looking young man who wore his dark brown hair parted in the middle. Quiet and self-effacing, he held down a job as a maintenance man at the Emerson Electric Company in Santa Ana, although, like many other young wannabes, he had originally come to California seeking to make his fortune as a rock star. He _lived_ for rock 'n' roll. The drums were his thing. Back home he even made a few demos in his parents' garage, and he played a few gigs with his band, Heavenly Blue. He could've been a lawyer – or a doctor … He certainly had the intelligence, although with his slow drawl and dull wits anyone would think he didn't have much going for him at all. And seeing him put away drink after drink after drink that last day of the year, one would've been forgiven for writing him off as a drunk and a wastrel.

Hall and his two friends found themselves roaming the bars of Santa Ann that night, and they were partying hard. Close to midnight they ended up heading to a house party in Capistrano, near Laguna Beach. When they arrived the party was just about winding down. All three friends were by now completely wasted. Falling down drunk, in fact. Hall curled up and fell asleep on the sofa.

As midnight approached, one of the friends went looking for Hall. He was nowhere to be found.

That same night, the Kraft family had a New Year's Eve party of their own – a much more civilised affair in his sister's house in Huntington Beach. Whilst all the family were gathered together, counting down the hours until the stroke of midnight, Randy was out working overtime at his computer operator job.

He arrived just after ten o'clock and joined in the celebrations. He didn't drink much – just raising a glass with the rest of the family at the midnight hour. It was 00:30 when he left. He was next seen asleep on the sofa in his parents' lounge at around eight o'clock the next morning. He still wore the same clothes that he'd worn to the party the night before. In fact, when Randy awoke, nobody noticed much different about him at all.

Mark Hall's last moments alive were the stuff of nightmares. His killer had stripped him naked, trussed him up like a pig and raped him. Whilst the victim was still alive, the killer had tortured him monstrously. The cigarette lighter from a vehicle was used to brand circular marks deep into Hall's skin – on his cheeks, nose, lips, left nipple and scrotum. The killer didn't stop there. He'd used the lighter to sear the eyeballs themselves, so badly that the colour of the victim's eyes couldn't be distinguished.

Then the killer had set about Hall with a broken bottle, cutting and stabbing at his legs, slicing deep into the muscle so that it nearly touched the bone. He then inserted a plastic cocktail stick into the young man's urethra, pushing it so that it reached the bladder. He hacked off both the penis and testicles and rammed them, along with some leaves and soil, deep into the victim's anus. Hall was alive throughout this ordeal. The torturer's final desecration, the one that finally killed Hall, was to stuff soil and leaves down his throat, packing it so deeply that loam reached the young man's lungs.

The body was found by off-duty policemen in an isolated spot in a canyon in the Cleveland Forest. The site was several miles from the nearest house; no one would have heard the agonised screams. The body had been posed *post mortem*, lying backward with legs wrapped around a sapling to maximally expose the grotesque tableau. The pathologist reported that death had come by alcohol intoxication and asphyxiation. Kraft's perverse scorecard referred to this killing simply as "NEW YEAR'S EVE".

It was around this time that other serial killers were patrolling the Californian highways. In fact, there were so many bodies turning up that the ink wasn't even dry on one report sheet before another body was discovered. For a while the cops couldn't distinguish between the cases. Then, a development – some of the victims had been molested *after* death, and the bodies came wrapped up in tidy bundles. This was a completely different *M.O.* Now investigators knew there were *at least two* serial murderers haunting the highways.[3]

There was another hiatus throughout most of 1976 and then, in mid-December, Kraft began his murder campaign afresh.

Paul Joseph Fuchs, 19, left his house after Sunday lunch on 10 December, dashing off so quickly he forgot his wallet. He had ambitions to be an artist and there was no reason for him to run away from home. Fuchs was last seen at Ripples Bar. In the weeks that followed his bank account remained touched. His disappearance had remained a complete mystery until investigators noted a reference on Kraft's scorecard: "EXPLETIVE DELETED". It seems likely that Kraft killed the youth and referenced his surname with a sick pun.

There were no known killings in 1977. By this time Kraft and Selig had moved into a condo in Molino in Long Beach, domestic bliss seemingly keeping them both occupied. Kraft was still working as a data-processing operator and during his free time he enjoyed playing cards. He was still a keen and competitive poker- and bridge-player … and he didn't like to lose. He still picked up hitchhikers for casual sex and he didn't hide the fact from his friends. However, the urge to strike again became stronger and, on 16 April 1976, he gave in to his compulsions.

That day, 18-year-old Marine Scott Michael Hughes was abducted and strangled with his own shoelaces, but Kraft went further. He pulled down Hughes' pants, sliced right through the penis and then removed a testicle. Hughes' body was found

---

[3] The "Trash Bag Killer" turned out to be Patrick Wayne Kearney, who surrendered himself to police on 1 July 1977.

discarded on Euclid Avenue near a freeway ramp. No. 28 on the scorecard reads "EUCLID". Now the murders were to resume at a greater rate.

Roland Gerald Young, 23, was an alcoholic who'd just been released from an overnight spell in jail after he'd got drunk and rowdy the previous night. When allowed to go his head was throbbing. His day was about to get worse. On 11 June, Young's body was found near the San Diego Freeway. Abrasions indicated that he'd been thrown from a vehicle moving at considerable speed. His testicles and the head of his penis had been cut off. Death had come by stabbing. Two days later, a woman reported having heard screaming on the night Hughes was killed. He'd clearly been alive throughout the ordeal. He was logged as "JAIL OUT" on the scorecard.

Just over a week later, a Marine named Richard Keith Allen, 20, visited his girlfriend in Carson, California. He decided to hitchhike from there back to his base in Camp Pendleton and left just after 11 o'clock at night. Allen's naked body was found the next day at the side of road. It appeared to have been thrown from a moving vehicle – a 90-foot smear of blood and skin attested to that. Allen had been strangled. However, his death was probably exacerbated by being slowly drowned as a result of the ingestion of alcohol and prescription sleeping tablets. Kraft's list marks the death as "MARINE CARSON".

Three weeks later, a 23-year-old hiker named Keith Arthur Klingbeil was found in the traffic lane of the I-5. He'd been thrown from a moving vehicle. A lace was missing from his hiking boots. He'd been strangled – however, *he was still alive*. He was brought to hospital where he died shortly afterwards. A subsequent autopsy would reveal that Klingbeil's left nipple had been burned using a vehicle cigarette lighter. In his pocket was found a Long Beach matchbook. No. 57 on Kraft's list is "HIKE OUT LB BOOTS".

On the night he was murdered, 29 September, 20-year-old Richard Anthony Crosby had been to see a movie in Torrance, near Redondo Beach. He'd been hitchhiking home when he was abducted. His body was found on Highway 71. It had been subjected to searing with a vehicle cigarette lighter. Death had come by strangulation. Kraft listed the murder as "TORRANCE".

Twenty-one-year-old truck driver Michael Joseph Inderbeiten had the great misfortune to cross paths with Kraft sometime in mid-November 1978, for the brutality was ratcheted up yet another notch. Inderbeiten had been to a nightclub with friends about three miles from his home. One of the friends met a girl at the club and took her home, leaving Inderbeiten stranded. His body was found on 18 November beside the San Diego Freeway, next to the 405-freeway ramp, naked except that his pants were pulled down below the waist. He had been sodomised. Cause of death was suffocation. However, whilst still alive, Inderbeiten's testicles were removed and his penis had been skinned. Like many of the other victims, his nipples were burned. Moreover, the killer had also tortured the youth by burning his eyelids. Recorded as "DART 405" on the scorecard, prosecutors were not able to determine a meaning to the word "dart".

After this, there was a lull of seven months before the killings restarted in June 1976. Kraft took five victims before the year was out. Gregory Wallace Jolley ("LAKES MC"), aged 20, was a Marine found in the Lake Arrowhead-Big Bear area. His body was found without head, legs or genitals.

A young man, John Doe No. 299, ("76") was found in a dumpster at Union 76 station. A sock had been stuffed into his rectum.

Jeffrey Bryan Sayre ("WESTMINSTER DATE"), aged 15, disappeared after a date with his girlfriend. He remains missing.

Twenty-year-old Donnie Harold Crisel ("MARINE DRUNK OVERNIGHT SHORTS") was found dead wearing only his shorts. He had been burned on the left nipple, strangled and then dumped.

The turn of the year did not bring relief; the killings continued unabated. Mark Alan Marsh ("MARINE HEAD BP"), aged 20, was known to have been hitchhiking to Buena Park. His body was found decapitated with the hands cut off. An unspecified object had been stuffed into his rectal passage.

Kraft was deployed by his employers to Portland, Oregon in summer 1980. Six victims in total are listed on the scorecard which suggest that he killed there also. The first was Michael Shawn O'Fallon, ("PORTLAND DENVER"), aged 17, who'd been plied with alcohol and Valium, hogtied and strangled to death.

The next day, an unidentified man ("PORTLAND ELK"), aged 35-45, was also believed to have been killed by Kraft.

The slaughter continued after Kraft's return to California in August 1980. Robert Wyatt Loggins ("MC HB TATTOO"), aged 19, a Marine, had a tattoo on the arm of Merlin the Magician, complete with the words "Dazed and Confused". He was last seen at the Huntington Beach pier. His bound body was found in a trash bag in an El Tor housing development. Cause of death was acute intoxication. Photographs of Loggins – both fully clothed and naked – were found in Kraft's car. In all the photos he was slumped over with his eyes closed, apparently having been posed after death.

In 1982, Kraft returned to Oregon again, where it is supposed he killed Michael Duane Cluck ("PORTLAND BLOOD"), aged 17. Cluck had been sodomised and viciously beaten about the back of the head. The murder scene was extensively covered in blood. On the same day that Cluck's body was found, Kraft attended hospital; he'd somehow bruised his foot. After Kraft's arrest, police found a shaving kit bearing the name of Mike Cluck during a search of his property.

Christopher Allen Williams ("HOLLYWOOD BUS"), aged 17, was a known prostitute who operated around bus stops of Hollywood. His partially clothed body was found in the San Bernardino Mountains. Death had been caused by pneumonia and aspiration. An autopsy found paper stuffed deep into his anus, as well into his nostrils, causing him to choke on his own mucus.

In 1982, Kraft's life, at least ostensibly to those who knew him, appeared good. He lived in a nice house that he and Selig were doing up, he ate good food and exercised regularly, and he socialised with good friends. Behind the façade though, things weren't so rosy. He felt underappreciated by his employers and he'd received a poor report card that seemed to confirm the fact. At home, his relationship with Selig was marred by increasingly bitter and acrimonious arguments. In true Californian style, the two attended counselling. It didn't seem to help matters; Randy felt that the sessions only underlined that he was the mature, responsibly partner whilst Jeff was the unreliable, feckless one. Kraft needed someone to take his frustrations out on.

Raymond Davis ("DOG"), aged 13, who was visiting Los Angeles for the day, had been out looking for his lost dog. Local residents, led by their noses, discovered his disintegrating body. His wrists had been bound and death was caused by strangulation.

Near to the spot where Raymond was found was another body. Robert Avila ("DEODORANT"), aged 16, was known for his excessive use of deodorisers. His severely decomposed body gave off the unmistakable stench of death. Raymond had been strangled.

After a four-month break, Kraft killed again. The unclothed, skeletal remains of 24-year-old Arne Mikeal Laine were found in San Diego a year after Kraft's arrest. Kraft had referred to him as "SD DOPE".

Brian Harold Witcher (PORTLAND HEAD"), aged 26, was found near the I-5 after having apparently been thrown from a moving vehicle. The "head" reference could not be explained by prosecutors.

Dennis Patrick Alt and Alan Schoenborn, both aged 20, were cousins. Their bodies were found in a field in Grand Rapids, Michigan on 28 November 1982. It is believed that the term "GR 2" refers to them. Both had been choked to death. A pen from the Amway Grand Hotel was found inside Schoenborn's rectum. Both men had been attending a horticultural convention, and recently unsealed prosecution evidence suggests that they had been in the company of Kraft at the hotel. After Kraft vacated his room, Alt's car keys were found inside. A later search of Kraft's Long Beach home uncovered Schoenborn's jacket.

When Lance Trenton Taggs ("PORTLAND HAWAII"), aged 19,

went missing he'd been wearing a shirt with the word "Hawaii" printed on it. He also had a bag bearing the same legend. His body was found near Wilsonville, Oregon. Cause of death is unknown. A sock had been stuffed inside his rectum. A bag with "Hawaii" printed on it was found in a later search of Kraft's home.

Anthony Jose Silveira ("PORTLAND RESERVE"), aged 29, had recently completed his National Guard service. His body was found a week before Christmas 1982 near Medford, Oregon. He'd been sodomised, a toothbrush had been inserted into his anus and he'd been manually strangled to death.

On 27 January 1983, a 21-year-old hitchhiker named Eric Church was abducted. His body was found alongside the I-605. He had high levels of alcohol and Valium in his system. An autopsy determined that he'd been sodomised, and that he'd struggled greatly against the restraints around his wrists. A combination of ligature strangulation and blunt force trauma to the head ended his life. Church appears to be unlisted on Kraft's scorecard.

Geoffrey Allan Nelson, aged 18, and Rodger James DeVaul Jr., aged 20, had only met each other a couple of weeks before and it seemed that they had much in common, including a love for the music of Journey and Kansas, and a passion for marijuana. Sometimes they did a little acid. DeVaul had been in the navy but was discharged on medical grounds. He was enrolled in an auto mechanics class. Nelson, the younger of the two, worked as a waiter. He didn't know what he wanted to do with his life, but this didn't seem to bother him. He liked to just hang out. His mantra for life (to the exasperation of his parents) was "Don't worry about it."

On the night of 12 February 1983, Nelson and DeVaul were hanging out outside the house of their friend, Bryce. They told him that they were going to go get something to eat.

Nelson was found close to the Garden Grove Freeway the next day. He was naked and where his genitals had once been was now a gory gash of blood. He had been thrown – still alive –

from a fast-moving vehicle, and a trail of skin and blood on the asphalt showed where he had bounced along. He didn't survive long after being found.

The following day, DeVaul's body was found, 15-feet down a ravine close to Mount Baldy in San Bernardine County. DeVaul had been bound and sodomised. His black denim jeans and underwear were pulled down so that his genitals hung out. His body was dusted with a light coating of beach sand. Autopsies on both men showed that they had large amounts of alcohol and propranolol[4] in their system. They'd both also ingested potato skins and grapes before their killer had taken their lives.

It's possible that Kraft met the two either on Beach Boulevard in Buena Park or on a beach. The double murder is believed to have been listed as "2 IN 1 BEACH" on the scorecard. A photo of DeVaul, in which he appeared to be dead, was later found in Kraft's apartment by police.

The next time Randy Kraft ventured out to kill he'd be caught by the two California Highway Patrol officers who were *just too late* to save the last victim, a 25-year-old Marine later identified as Terry Lee Gambrel. He'd been strangled to death by a ligature. Haemorrhages in the neck indicated that Kraft had repeatedly tightened and loosened the ligature. There was a bruise on the victim's lip. Toxicology results also revealed that he had high levels of alcohol and lorazepam[5] in his blood.

Kraft was charged with driving under the influence and held in custody whilst detectives made a thorough search of his vehicle. The evidence they uncovered was damning. A belt matching the marks around Gambrel's neck was found in the backseat of the car. Various tranquilising prescription medications were found also. And a well-thumbed paperback, *The Essential*

---

[4] Propranolol is used to treat high blood pressure and anxiety, amongst other conditions.

[5] Lorazepam is used to treat severe anxiety and sleep disorders.

*Guide to Prescription Drugs: What You Need to Know for Safe Drug Use*, provided a moment of ironic reflection. The passenger seat and carpet were heavily bloodstained. Beneath the carpet was found an envelope containing numerous photos of young men, posed, apparently incapacitated or dead, many of them in sexual positions. Most damning of all, in the boot of the car, detectives found a list, a coded *aide-mémoire* containing 61 references, written neatly and precisely in block-letters in pen on a yellow legal pad.

Kraft explained away the scorecard as a list of nicknames he'd given to his gay friends but it didn't wash with his interrogators. On 16 May 1983, he was charged with the murder of Gambrel and 15 other victims in addition to two counts of sodomy and one of emasculation.

The trial, which lasted 13 months, was the most expensive in Orange County history. Kraft's primary defence strategy was to offer alibis and alternate suspects and to attempt to dismiss the evidence against him as circumstantial. His lawyers didn't succeed. On 12 May 1989, Kraft was found guilty on all counts apart from one, the sodomy of Rodger DeVaul. He was sentenced to death, and Judge Donald A. McCartin, upon passing the sentence, commented that "if anyone ever deserved the death penalty, he's got it coming".

Randy Kraft still "has it coming". He remains on Death Row at San Quentin State Prison. Despite being found with a corpse in his car, he continues to deny guilt for any of the crimes of which he was convicted or suspected of committing.

Some suspect that Kraft had an accomplice in the murders, conjecturing that he could not have committed the crimes on his own. Certainly, lifting a 200lb corpse alone would be difficult for a slightly-built person alone, and throwing it from a moving vehicle would also, presumably, require some assistance. Two sets of footprints found in the sand at Sunset Beach, close to where to body of John Leras was found, give cause for speculation.

In addition, Kraft did not have access to photo developing

equipment. His photographs were developed _somewhere_, but no reports were made to police by any photo processing agents concerning morbid photographic images having been submitted by Kraft.

There was also DNA evidence found at some crime scenes which is incompatible with Kraft's profile. What this evidence is has not been released.

Jeff Graves, Kraft's former lover, may have assisted in several of the murders, prosecutors contended. When questioned by police about the abduction and murder of Keith Crotwell, he allegedly brushed it off: "I'm not going to pay for it, you know." He succumbed to his illness before he could say anything more incriminating. At the time of his death in 1987, he was still in the minds of the police, who were preparing to question him further.

Denis McDougal, author of an authoritative book on Kraft,[6] has written about his conversations with a petty-criminal called Bob Jackson. McDougal alleges that Jackson knew specific details of some of Kraft's murders for a very good reason ... because he was a part of them. Jackson reportedly knew about other, unreported murders, he knew how Kraft moved the bodies, and he knew how the incriminating films were developed. He stated that he used to work in a photo processing lab in Long Beach and that he would work on the films delivered by his friend and drinking partner, Randy Kraft. He said that he would go on regular night-time excursions with Kraft, but on one occasion the two of them had nearly got pulled over by police. He decided after this incident that it was time to pull out before his luck ran out.

_Were the stories made up?_ The police were unsure. They sounded as though they could've been concocted by the mind of an attention-seeking fantasist. _Why was the witness coming forward now?_ Because his lover had recently died of AIDS and he

---

[6] Dennis McDougal (1991), _Angel of Darkness_. Warner Books: NY.

felt alone. This didn't sound like the most plausible of reasons. Nevertheless, they investigated the man's claims, but ultimately didn't make any arrest. They do, however, still keep him in mind.

Randy Kraft once told a close friend that he'd once heard that the "ultimate orgasm is death". In his case, however, this involved the deaths of others. It *pleased* Kraft to torture and kill young men and so that is what he did. His sole motivation was self-gratification. His internal fantasies involved total control over another. Seduction, followed by pain, was completely rational to him.

However, there was nothing wrong with Kraft's mind other than that he liked to kill for sexual satisfaction. He was not "groomed" for brutality from an early age. He grew up in an average household and excelled at school. When he realised he was homosexual he struggled with the fact, but ultimately he accepted and even embraced it. Right up until the moment he was caught Kraft held surface-level normalcy. There is little to account for the origins of his psychopathic lusts. It's true, Kraft *did* experience a head injury in early childhood, and it's possible that this *may* have inflicted sufficient damage to his brain's amygdala region that it interfered with his decision-making and emotional responses, or left him devoid of empathy. However, this explanation does not seem plausible, for no one appears to have noticed any lack of compassion or humanity throughout his childhood. The roots to his murderous rage continue to mystify us.

Kraft was convicted of 16 murders. Investigators think that he is accountable for at least 51 more, making him one of history's worst serial killers. The alarming thing is, if his spree hadn't been interrupted by a chance encounter with the police, he would more than likely have continued to kill and kill again, and his crimes would probably have become more brutal and more frequent.

# John Wayne Gacy
(active 1972-1978)

TIMOTHY JACK MCCOY was a boy just passing through. On the first day of 1972, Jack found himself standing at the Chicago Greyhound bus terminal. The 16-year-old youth had been on a Christmas vacation, visiting an aunt in Michigan, and he was now heading back to his home in Glenwood, Iowa. He'd been waiting a while, but the connecting bus hadn't yet arrived. Jack was tired, bored and impatient for his bus to turn up.

At some point, a stranger, a pudgy man in his early-30s, stopped his car at the layover next to where Jack stood waiting. He struck up a conversation with Jack. The man said that he was on his way to the Chicago Loop to look at the display of ice sculptures that were on show there. He invited Jack to tag along. It didn't look like the bus would be arriving any time soon. The man had a kindly face, a warm smile and an easy line in patter. He seemed so friendly and harmless that Jack decided to take the man up on his suggestion. The two new friends went and saw the ice sculptures, and afterwards they went on a sightseeing tour of the city.

By now it was getting late, and when the man suggested that Jack come back home with him, the boy readily agreed. The onward journey home involved a seven-hour drive by bus. Grateful to have found a diversion to break the long return journey, Jack accompanied the man back to his detached house in Norridge, in the pleasant, suburban north-east corner of Chicago, Illinois.

Although Jack didn't know it, his new acquaintance had a history of picking up boys at the very same Greyhound bus terminal. Just under a year earlier, the man had been charged with sexually assaulting a teenage boy after having offered to give him a lift home. During the drive, the man had attempted to force the boy into having sex. The case had gone to trial, and if the man's accuser hadn't failed to show up to court then the following series of events may have turned out very differently. However, because the boy *did* decline to attend the hearing, the court was obliged to dismiss his complaint. This was good news for the alleged perpetrator, for he'd only recently been released from prison for *another* crime –the sexual assault of a 15-year-old boy – and at the time he'd still been under parole.

If Jack McCoy had known about the chubby man's criminal history he would've thought twice about going home with him. Nevertheless, he did. The man had promised he'd have Jack back at the bus station early the next morning, in good time to catch his bus home. The man's plan made good sense to Jack.

Nothing is known about what happened that night other than what the man later reported. The man, who was engaged to be married, claimed that that night his fiancée was away. He said that he and Jack had sex (*maybe they did a little S&M*, the man would later say). Soon after this, the two fell asleep. The man claimed that when he awoke early the following morning the first thing he saw upon opening his eyes was Jack coming through the bedroom doorway, a sharp kitchen knife in his hand.

Surprised, the man immediately jumped up and attempted to seize the knife from Jack's hand, in the process injuring his own hand. He couldn't stop looking at the blood pouring from the wound. He felt a "surge of power from my toes to my brains". He sensed that he'd become stronger, a feeling that became overwhelming. He grabbed Jack and they wrestled in a one-sided sort of fight. The man twisted the knife from Jack's hand, banged the boy's head against the bedroom wall and kicked him in the stomach. Jack fought back hard, kicking the man in his ample stomach in return, causing him to double over, winded. In self-defence, the man tore at the boy, grabbed the knife and stabbed him repeatedly in the chest. Jack fell to the floor, gasping for breath.

As the boy lay dying on the floor, the man took the knife to the bathroom to clean it. Then he went into the kitchen. There, on the kitchen table, he noticed a carton of eggs and a side of unsliced bacon. The table had been set for two.

According to the man's later admission, he immediately recognised his mistake. Jack, absentmindedly holding the knife, had merely come into the bedroom to ask the man how he liked his eggs. Nevertheless, the man now had a body on his hands, and he'd only recently come off parole for the sodomisation of another teenager. To say that this was a problem was an understatement indeed. He could only see one solution …

It was the start of a small-town American nightmare.

John Wayne Gacy was born was born on 17 March 1942 in Chicago, the middle child and only son of John Stanley Gacy, a World War I veteran who now worked as an auto repair machinist, and Marion, a homemaker. John Jr. had an older sister, Joanna, and a younger sister, Karen. The family were of Danish and Polish stock, from paternal grandparents whose name was spelled "Gatza" or "Gaca" and who'd immigrated to the USA from Prussia.

John was born a large baby, prone to being overweight, and this didn't change as he grew. The ungainly boy was close to his mother and two sisters. He was eager to please and helpful around the house. He also enjoyed helping his mother out in the garden. But the relationship with his father wasn't so agreeable. For some reason John Sr. took a disliking to the boy from the start, and John Jr. would later recall that no matter what he achieved his father would belittle him, calling him "dumb" and comparing him unfavourably with his sisters.

The elder Gacy male was a good provider for his family. He worked hard and was generous. He was a perfectionist, in the manner that nothing could be done well enough for him. His son certainly felt so. In his father's eyes, he would later say, he was "never good enough". His father's standards were simply too high and his meticulous craftsmanship could never be matched. When John Jr. attempted to please his father he inevitably failed, and for his efforts he'd be called "stupid".

It appears that Mr Gacy was also a pathologically undemonstrative man who simply *could not* show his feelings. At least, not when he was sober. For the man was also an alcoholic – one whose short temper and physical aggression quickly rose to the surface when under the influence. No one in the house escaped his brutality. On one occasion, Mrs Gacy hadn't long returned from hospital after giving birth to Karen. Her husband came home drunk and knocked out several of her teeth. Mrs Gacy fled into the street whilst the two older children screamed in terror. Mr Gacy stormed after his wife and for good measure attacked her again, punching her so that she fell onto the sidewalk. On that occasion the police interceded. As he got older, young John would try to intervene on his mother's behalf. For his efforts he was verbally assaulted by his father, who frequently called a him a "mama's boy" and a "sissy" who'd probably grow up to be a "queer". Often John would be beaten with a whipped with a razor strop (a leather strap used for sharpening razor blades), and on one occasion he was beaten so hard upon the head with a broomstick that he was rendered unconscious. One of John's friends would recall that Mr Gacy would beat and ridicule his son for no reason. He witnessed one incident at the Gacy household when the father began to shout at John and then attack him without provocation. The friend recalled that John simply raised his hands to defend himself and didn't ever attempt to strike his father back. John, it seems, had become emotionally hardened to the beatings.

John recalled incidents when his father would get drunk and start swinging his fists at Marion. John would try to intervene, only to find his father's fury turned upon him. Mr Gacy would roughhouse John, shouting at him and pinning him against the wall. They would stand face-to-face for several long moments, in a terrible sort of rough embrace. John felt the rage burning in his father's eyes along with the smell of alcohol coming from his breath, as he was pressed tightly against the wall. And during those intense moments John felt something else – he could feel himself become slightly aroused …

The children loved their father, however, but the household lived in fear. Each night they would wait patiently in the kitchen until the drunken man finished his endless rantings in the basement. Only when he emerged and sat down at the table could the meal proceed. It's possible that Mr Gacy had undiagnosed mental health problems of his own, although the elevated level of his cruelty and control were more likely caused by circumstantial factors than pathological.

John's sexual awakening began early. Once, his mother found under the porch where her son used to play a bag full of her underwear. He liked the feeling of silk or nylon, he would later admit. He recalled that his mother made him wear a pair of her drawers to embarrass him. When his father found out about this John was beaten with the razor strop.

When he reached around 11 years of age, John later recalled, the teenage daughter of a neighbour would undress him and fondle him. John also said that at the age of eight or nine a family friend would take him for rides in his truck. The man, who was a contractor, liked to play-wrestle with John, pinning the young boy's head between his legs and sexually touching him. John never told his father about these incidents for fear that he'd be blamed and punished for them. Between the ages of 10 and 12, he did get a whipping from his father after a girl reported that he, along with the girl's brother, had taken off her underwear.

John was ordered to avoid all sports at school because of a heart condition. For the plump and unathletic teenager this was not considered a problem. He was often breathless and experienced pain in his chest. At the age of 14 he began to experience blackouts. During one seizure at a friend's house the young Gacy was given the last rites by a hastily summoned priest. Luckily (for John) he survived this apparent brush with death. Over the next few years he was periodically hospitalised as a result of these episodes, as well as for a ruptured appendix. His father reckoned his son was malingering in order to gain attention and sympathy and openly told him so from the bed-side. However, it turned out that John actually _did_ have a burst appendix and he'd nearly died. It seemed as if John Jr. had scored a point over his father that one time. The problem with his health, however, was never conclusively diagnosed and in adult life it would be referred to vaguely as "heart trouble".

John finished eighth grade, getting above average marks in English and mathematics and scoring excellently in general science. His conduct and attitude were favourably received.

He transferred to high school and it was during this time that he appeared to develop a "hang-up" with uniforms. When Gacy turned 18, his father bought him a car and he joined a Civil Defence organisation, which allowed him to "blue light" towards accidents and fires. He became obsessive about "playing cop". His father retained ownership of the car, however, whilst Gacy made monthly payments, and if Gacy ever stepped out of line his father would confiscate the keys. One day, Gacy obtained his own set of replacement keys and drove the car even though it had been denied him. At finding out about this, his father removed the distributor cap and kept it for three days. In response, Gacy felt "sick" and "drained". When the distributor cap was replaced, Gacy simply got in the car and drove off, disappearing for three months.

No one in the family knew where he was. It turned out that Gacy had gone to Las Vegas. He'd got a transient job – in a mortuary, of all places. Some of the bodies that were brought in belonged to young men, with smooth, muscular bodies. Gacy felt an odd mixture of jealousy and lust. As an attendant he got to sleep on a cot in the embalming room. One evening, whilst alone, Gacy clambered into one of the coffins. Its occupant was a deceased teenage male. Gacy caressed the body, manoeuvring it until it lay on top of him. He wanted to feel the weight of a dead body upon him. Then he was jolted with a profound sense of astonishment and fright. The next morning he called his mother. John Wayne Gacy wanted to come home again.

He was already involved in politics. By 1960, he'd joined the Democratic Party. It may have been an attempt to gain the acceptance from others that his father had never given him. Upon his return to Illinois, after his brief sojourn in Nevada, Gacy joined the Northwestern Business College. In 1963, he graduated. He took a trainee management position with a shoe company, became a salesman, was duly promoted to manager of his department. Then, in March 1964, he became engaged to a co-worker, Marlynn Myers. They married in September.

Gacy was by now involved in the Jaycees, a leadership training organisation, which at the time catered only for young men. He became a tireless worker, often organising parades – an activity that allowed him to race around with a red light on his car, just like a TV detective. Fellow Jaycees would snigger at Gacy behind his back, but they had to admit – Gacy was a success at what he did. He revelled in being in charge and in control.

Marlynn became pregnant. Her father owned three Kentucky Fried Chicken restaurants and in order to keep her close to home he chose his son-in-law to manage the restaurants. Gacy accepted with gusto. The pay-packet was excellent.[1] He insisted that family and friends alike called him "Colonel".

Marlynn gave birth to a son in February 1966 and Gacy was rising rapidly through the ranks of the Jaycees. Things were looking up. Gacy himself knew it – he was achieving the success that his father had said he would never achieve. When Gacy's parents came to visit six months later, John Jr. and his father talked together as adults, man to man. It almost seemed to him as if his father were making an apology for the abuse he'd dished out. "I was wrong about you, son," he said, and the two shook hands.

In March 1967, Marlynn gave birth to a daughter and life now seemed to Gacy to be "perfect". These were the days, he would later recall, when he was at his happiest. He'd earned his father's approval, and he was a success in his business and personal life. But it wasn't to last …

On a late summer evening in August 1967, Gacy was driving his car along the highway, in typical fashion – fast, with the window down. Standing by the side of the road was a boy with his

---

[1] The equivalent of $115,000 per annum in 2020, plus 20% of the profits.

thumb out. Gacy didn't normally pick up hitchhikers, but on this occasion something made his change that policy. The boy was short, with long blond hair and a muscular body. Gacy drew his car to a halt and reversed. He realised it was Donald Voorhees, the son of a fellow Jaycee. Tonight Marlynn was out of town and Gacy had the house to himself.

The two struck up a conversation. Voorhees was having trouble with his father, he said. Perhaps inevitably, the talk turned to pornography, and Gacy invited the boy to come back to his house and watch a stag movie. The offer had been an act of compassion, Gacy would later insist. He'd only wanted to further the boy's education ...

He brought the boy back home. He made him a sandwich and gave him some alcohol. Then he put a blue movie on the projector. Whilst Voorhees watched the film, Gacy began to talk. He asked the boy if he'd ever got his rocks off, if he'd ever had sex with a girl ... if he'd ever had a guy go down on him. It's what two guys do when they get horny, Gacy insisted. Soon he was doing just that. It was a *practical* "education" ...

Over the next few months, Gacy continued to sexually assault Voorhees, and Voorhees kept coming back. There were other victims too, for Gacy had opened a sort of club in his basement where his employees could come to drink and play pool. Needless to say, Gacy only ever invited his male employees to this club. When they got there he tricked them into thinking he was undertaking "scientific research", using the recently published Kinsey Report as a means to initiate the ruse. He gave them up to $5 each for their part in the *practical* "research".

This was Gacy's highly manipulative side. He would tell one of the youths that he was writing a book of scientific research. His work was going to revise the "antiquated sex laws" of Illinois. He said that because the law applies to everyone, no matter what their sexual orientation, some of his experiments had to be homosexual in nature. His experiments, Gacy told them, had to be done in the utmost of secrecy, insisting that this was the state governor's wish. Amazingly, some of Gacy's invitees fell for this story. He did his "research" either in his club or he brought them to a motel. Gacy – a thorough scientist, it would seem – duly asked questions of the youths before, during and after sex.

Gacy wasn't above using blackmail. As a joke, he would offer one of his employees his wife's sexual favours. He told the youth, "If I ever catch you in bed with my wife you'll owe me a blow job." One night, the employee was invited to sleep in the guest bedroom. After he got into bed the door opened and Marlynn entered, climbing into bed beside him. Immediately after they'd had sex the door swung opened and Gacy switched on the light. "Now you owe me a blow job," he said. A few days later Gacy collected.

Meanwhile, Voorhees was asking for more money, and it was only later that Gacy realised he was himself being blackmailed. Then, in March 1968, Voorhees informed his father what Gacy had been doing. Voorhees Sr. informed the police and Gacy was subsequently arrested and charged with sodomy.

Gacy raged. He blamed Voorhees for the predicament he was in. He didn't want Voorhees to testify. He came up with a plan. He approached a young man who was employed in one of his restaurants, 18-year-old Russell Schroeder. He persuaded Schroeder to discourage Voorhees from testifying against him. Schroeder, persuaded by a $300 fee, lured Voorhees to a secluded spot, sprayed his face with Mace and beat him up. Voorhees, however, also reported *this* crime to the police. Schroeder was soon picked up. He admitted his part in the assault, indicating that he had done so at Gacy's behest. For this, Gacy earned himself a second charge. He was sent to a psychiatric hospital for 17 days for mental examination, where two doctors concluded that he was mentally competent to stand trial.[2]

---

[2] Gacy scored 118 on an IQ test, and was described by one doctor as "extremely intelligent". They felt that he was pleasant and talkative, but he could be ingratiating with authority figures and domineering towards those weaker than himself. He was capable of twisting the truth to put himself in a better

Gacy was convicted of sodomy on 3 December 1968 and sentenced to 10 years behind bars. The same day, his wife initiated divorce proceedings and demanded that she be awarded the house and full custody of the two children. Her demands were met. Gacy was never to see Marlynn or his two children again. In typical fashion, he saw himself as the victim of injustice rather than a perpetrator.

In a way, Gacy made himself at home in prison. He made friends with the other prisoners and staff. He ingratiated himself with the inmate Jaycee chapter, increasing its membership 12-fold. He secured the prisoners a pay-rise; he supervised the building of a miniature golf course. He got a prized job in the kitchen and from that position he was able to exercise considerable power, rewarding certain prisoners with extra portions or treats. Occasionally, when Gacy got into an argument with someone, suddenly his heart would play up. He'd have to be rushed to the infirmary. This happened more than once. Gacy's dicky ticker was still proving useful.

On Christmas Day 1969, John Gacy Sr. died from cirrhosis of the liver. John Jr. collapsed to the floor sobbing upon hearing the news. He asked to go to the funeral but this was denied.

After serving a mere 18 months of his 10-year sentence, Gacy was granted parole. He walked out the prison doors on 18 June 1970, moving back in with his mother for a while. Eight months later, he was charged with sexually assaulting a teenage boy he'd met outside the Greyhound bus terminal. When the boy failed to appear in court the charges were dismissed. The parole board never learned of the incident; if they had done, he would

---

light, and indeed could produce an "alibi" for everything, often presenting himself as a victim of circumstances or other people. One of his primary objectives was to outwit others. The doctors' diagnostic impression was that Gacy had a sociopathic personality disturbance, antisocial reaction. They could find no evidence of heart disease or organic brain damage. Besides being overweight, he was in robust good health.

most likely have been returned to prison.

Gacy bought a house in Norridge and he and his mother moved in on 15 August 1971. Shortly after, he became engaged to a _divorcée_, Carole Hoff, whom he'd briefly dated in high school. She and her daughters then moved in with Gacy. In October 1971, Gacy's parole ended. He started to become active in the local community – shovelling snow for neighbours, lending them tools. Gacy was settling down.

Two months were to pass before he met another youth at the Greyhound terminal. Timothy McCoy would become the first to die at Gacy's hands. An accidental death, Gacy would later explain. He hadn't been to blame at all ...

By now Gacy had established a part-time painting, decorating and maintenance business, naming it PDM Contractors. The venture was expanding rapidly, and by 1975 he was working 16-hour days and working on many projects simultaneously. He and Carole were now married, but Gacy's interests were less than connubial. Most of the PDM workforce were youths and young men and sex was on Gacy's mind constantly. He'd insist on sexual favours in return for financial assistance or promotions – even for the use of a vehicle. In 1973, he travelled to Florida with a teenage employee. On their first night there he raped the youth in their hotel room. Upon their return from Florida, the boy drove to Gacy's and beat him up. Gacy explained to his wife that he'd refused to pay the employee for shoddy decorating handiwork. He didn't mention Florida at all.

Gacy was working flat-out by now. He spent most of his waking hours working and Carole felt neglected. Their sex life fell by the wayside. He was always "too tired". No wonder. Her husband would often leave the house at three o'clock in the morning to do "business deals". He explained that it was convenient, and that there was less traffic on the roads at that time. One time, Carole watched him as he left on one of his supposed business meetings. She spied him with a young, blond boy, who got into Gacy's car before it drove off.

In May 1975, Gacy met, and then hired, 15-year-old Tony

Antonucci. Two months later, he and Gacy were working on a property late at night. Gacy asked Tony for a blow-job; Tony told him no. Gacy produced a bottle of whiskey and encouraged Tony to drink some. Then Gacy started to talk about homosexual activity, and offered Tony money for sex. Again, Tony said he wasn't interested. Gacy applied pressure: "What if it meant your job?" but Tony repeatedly said no. Later, Gacy told Tony he'd been testing his morals, to see how he'd handle the pressure, and made some derogatory comments about "fags".

But then, after the two had returned to work, Gacy suddenly began to grab at Tony's crotch and buttocks. Finally, Tony picked up a chair and threatened to swing it at his boss. "Why didn't you just say no?" said Gacy. "It was just horseplay."

A month later, Tony was alone in the Antonucci house whilst his parents were away on vacation. He'd stepped on a nail the day before and hadn't been able to work. Then, a knock on the door. Gacy had come to see if Tony was all right. It was after midnight, and Gacy was clutching a bottle of wine. Tony invited him in and the two had a couple of glasses. Then Gacy persistently said he had some stag movies, and he went to retrieve a projector and some films from his car.

After the films were over, Gacy grabbed Tony and began to wrestling him, putting him in armlocks and headlocks. Tony, who was a high school wrestler, didn't take the horseplay seriously, but after a moment or two he felt Gacy slip a handcuff onto his wrist, attaching it and then securing the other wrist. Tony stood up, his arms now fastened behind his back. Gacy pushed him to the ground.

Tony was now lying face-up. Gacy bent down and started to unbutton the youth's shirt, and then unbuckle his pants. He pulled the pants to below the knee in silence. Then he went into the kitchen. From there, Tony could hear rummaging around. He kept his eyes on the door, wondering what Gacy was looking for. He felt that the right cuff was on wrist loosely and he managed to work his hand free.

When Gacy returned, Tony flung himself towards him in a

football tackle. Now he was fighting seriously. He got Gacy on his back and somehow retrieved the key for the cuffs. He removed them and now cuffed Gacy, locking both hands behind his back.

Gacy lay on the floor for a few minutes. He and Tony had a quiet conversation during which it was agreed that Gacy would leave. During this, Gacy said, "Not only are you the only one that got out of the cuffs, you got them on me." A week later, another of Gacy's employees would not get out of the cuffs.

Eighteen-year-old John Butkovitch was peeved. His boss, John Wayne Gacy, had unfairly withheld two weeks' wages. Butkovitch complained to Gacy about it, but Gacy was adamant: Butkovitch had charged materials to the Gacy account for items that'd been used to decorate the Butkovitch's apartment – no money was due. After talking it over, the two came to an agreement and seemed to satisfy them both. Not for long ...

Later, Gacy awoke from a pot- and alcohol-induced slumber. He left his house and drove the streets. Somehow he ended up cruising through the area where Butkovitch lived. He spied the youth getting out of a car. Butkovitch was also drunk. Gacy persuaded him to come for a drive with him so they could sort out the money issue. They ended up back at Gacy's.

There, Gacy began to tell Butkovitch a story. Before picking Butkovitch up Gacy had seen the police arrest someone. The cop had thrown the guy against a car and cuffed him. Gacy wanted to demonstrate what he'd seen. He had in his hands the same cuffs that he'd used on Tony Antonucci just a week before.

Once the cuffs were on Gacy's demeanour changed. No longer was he the friendly employer. He became sarcastic and insulting. Butkovitch told him to take off the cuffs. When Gacy refused, Butkovitch threatened him: "Motherfucker, I'll kill you when I get these off." Gacy was unimpressed: "You ain't gonna get them off. If anyone gets killed it's you."

The next morning, Gacy woke up with a hangover. He was in his own bed, but he couldn't remember much of what had gone on the night before. He went into the kitchen to make himself some breakfast, then remembered that Butkovitch was in the house. He went looking for him.

The sight that greeted him caused him some surprise. Butkovitch was lying in the living room, his hand cuffed behind his back. The front of his pants was wet and there was a rope tied tightly around his neck. His eyes were wide open, his mouth gaped open and his face was a blue-red colour. *Rigor mortis* hadn't yet set in, and from his work in the mortuary Gacy knew that the youth hadn't been dead long.

He dragged the body into the garage, intending to bury it alongside Timothy McCoy in the crawlspace under his house. However, when Carole and her daughters returned home earlier than expected he found his options severely limited. Anyone standing at the kitchen sink would look out directly at the garage door, and Carole was frequently busy at the sink. Gacy had to dispose of the body where it was. He dug a deep hole inside the garage, dumped the body in it and covered it over with concrete. It was really a matter of logistics, and those who knew John Wayne Gacy had always said that he was a good organiser.

Once the body was dealt with, Gacy intended not to think about it anymore. However, inevitably the police came looking for Butkovitch. Gacy told them that his employee had come around, they'd argued about money for a while, and then Butkovitch left. The police told the boy's family that he'd probably run off but his parents didn't believe it. They repeatedly urged the police to speak to Gacy again about the matter. After two years of this the police stopped taking their calls.

At some stage in 1975, during their betrothal, Gacy told Carole that he was bisexual. She didn't understand; she didn't even know what the term meant. Gacy explained. Carole still didn't understand. Her husband had seemed so "straight". In fact, he seemed to loathe flagrant homosexuals – and he'd swept her off her feet in his courtship of her.

Now, after they'd been married a while, Carole began to wonder about the man she'd committed herself to. On one occasion, when cleaning under the sink, she discovered some magazines.

Looking through them, Carole noticed that they contained pictures of nude men. And then there were the silk panties that John owned. She found a pair of them in the bed, crusted with semen. When she confronted him with the evidence he told her that they'd been a gift. The explanation didn't wash with her. It was clear that her husband didn't like sex – not with her anyway. That fact became all too clear on Mother's Day in 1975, when Gacy took his wife to bed to celebrate. Afterwards he announced that that was the last time they would have sex. He was deadly serious.

In October 1975, after a heated argument about an unbalanced chequebook, Carole asked Gacy for a divorce. He agreed to the request. By March 1976, the divorce was finalised[3] and Gacy was living alone at the West Summerdale house

Now the gay _divorcé_ enjoyed a free rein in which to indulge in his pleasures. These were the "cruising years", when Gacy would take his car on midnight jaunts, trawling for young males. He knew the look he was searching for – blond- or brown-haired youths, young and clean-cut. "Queers" were nothing but fake innocence, with their slight, muscular build and tight butts. They were easy to spot. This was Gacy's theory anyway. He knew how to spot the hustlers and he knew where to go to find them. The gay bars of the New Town were always a draw. Likewise the local park. He was down at the park two or three times a week in those days. During these excursions John Gacy called himself "Jack", and he had an alternate personality to match – one that he found it as easy to compartmentalise as the psychopathic killing side of his personality.

Sometimes he would have sex in his car along a dark road. But "Jack" preferred to take them home. There, he could act the father figure – looking after them and tending to their needs, _before_ having sex with them, that is. Neighbours had certainly

---

[3] The false ground for the divorce was Gacy's infidelity with women.

started to notice Gacy's comings-and-goings during the night, often with a young man in tow. They saw lights on and heard car doors slam shut. Several years later, one neighbour spoke about hearing muffled noises emanating from one of the houses adjacent to her Summerdale house. These noises were high-pitched screaming and shouting. The cries had woken her and her son up during the night. In time, she, her neighbours, and indeed the world, would come to realise the cause of these desperate noises, for Gacy, as well as having a solicitous side to his nature, also had the meanest of mean streaks. And when this side showed itself, it came without warning and it was vicious and pitiless.

In 1976, just one month after the formal dissolution of his marriage, Gacy began his killing spree in earnest, in his typical business-like fashion. Gacy had lured 18-year-old Darrell Julius Samson to his home under the pretext of undertaking a construction job. Darrell was Gacy's type – young, blond, good-looking with a slight body. He was last seen in Chicago on 6 April that year. His mother burned up four cars and got blistered feet in the search for Darrell. It was all in vain. The mystery of his disappearance was solved in November 1978. When dug up from beneath the dirt of Gacy's crawlspace, Darrell's remains showed that a section of cloth had been forced into his throat. After subjecting him to unspeakable ministrations, Gacy had permanently silenced the youth's tortured screams.

One youth narrowly escaped Gacy's murderous intentions, it seems. On 26 July 1976, 18-year-old David Cram was hitchhiking on Elston Avenue when he was picked up by Gacy. Gacy bigged himself up for the benefit of the boy and then offered him a job at PDM, at double the hourly rates that would've been considered normal. Cram delightedly began work that same evening. Four weeks later, he moved into Gacy's house.

John Wayne Gacy liked clowns. He had paintings of them on the wall of his front room and he regularly performed at fund-raisers dressed in clown costume, his fat face coated in garish white makeup, with deep blue eye patches and a jagged red smile painted on. He called this character "Pogo the Clown" or "Patches the Clown". He designed his own costumes and applied his own makeup. At functions he would remain in costume for the entire event. After his crimes were uncovered, Gacy became stuck with the moniker the "Killer Clown".

And so it happened that the day after David Cram moved into the Summerdale house Gacy confronted his new houseguest whilst wearing his Pogo the Clown outfit.

It was the day of Cram's 19th birthday and he'd been out with friends. By the time he returned to the house he was drunk. All of a sudden, Gacy was standing there before him wearing a clown suit. Gacy brought Cram into the barroom and poured him a drink. Soon the two were popping pills and knocking them back with stiff shots of alcohol. At some point, Gacy got out the handcuffs. He demonstrated how easy it was to escape from them. Pretty soon Gacy had tricked Cram into donning the handcuffs himself, with his wrists in front of his body. The only thing was, Cram didn't find it so easy to get out of the cuffs.

Then Gacy grabbed him and swung him around. Cram screamed, "Get these off me!" but Gacy had other ideas.

"I'm going to rape you," he said. He pushed Cram to the floor and crawled towards him. Gacy came closer. Luckily, Cram had had experience of close combat in the army. A kick to the face quickly stopped Gacy in his tracks. Cram, sobering up abruptly, stood up. He and Gacy stared at each other for a while, then Cram went to this bedroom and locked the door behind him.

A month later Gacy tried again. He appeared at the door of Cram's room and said in a sing-song voice, "Dave, you know what I want." Cram knew _exactly_ what his employer wanted and had no intention of giving it to him. "Dave, you don't really know who I am," Gacy said. "Maybe it would be good if you give me what I want." He came into the bedroom, growling like an animal and attempted to straddle Cram. Cram again resisted Gacy's advances. He pulled back his fist to strike Gacy, but the man just passed out. It was a fainting spell of convenience. After a while, Gacy regained consciousness and got up. He smiled a bit and left, saying over his shoulder, "You ain't no fun." A short while after, Cram moved out and quit his job.

But Gacy was not to be stopped. Before the year was out, he would kill at least 13 more times. Randall Wayne Reffett, aged 15, and Samuel Stapleton, aged 14, were both abducted on 14 May, only a few hours separating their disappearances. They were found buried in the same grave and were probably murdered during the same evening. One may even have been killed in front of the alarmed eyes of the other. If that is the case, it's also probable that Gacy was by now exploiting his handcuffs trick with chillingly efficient success.

Michael Bonnin, a blond 17-year-old youth who fitted Gacy's preferred victim type, disappeared just over two weeks later. He'd been on his way to visit a uncle, for whom he was helping to refurbish an old jukebox. He died by use of a ligature.

Blond William Huey "Billy" Carroll Jr., aged 16, fell victim to Gacy 10 days later. Three other victims were killed in short shrift following this. They remain unidentified.

James Haakenson has only been recently identified by DNA profiling. The good-natured 16-year-old boy from Minnesota had run away from home to have some fun. What he found was death. Like half-a-dozen before him, Jimmy was interred in Gacy's increasingly full crawlspace.

Another good-looking blond youth, Rick Louis Johnston, aged 17, went missing on 6 August. He'd been to a concert at the Aragon Ballroom in the Uptown area but never made it home. His body was pulled from the earth beneath Gacy's house where it'd been buried alongside two more unidentified youths who'd been murdered around the same time.

On 24 October, Kenneth Ray Parker, 19, and Michael Marino, 14, went missing after having last been seen outside a restaurant. They are officially listed as victims of Gacy. However, the family of Marino refuse to believe that the remains found beneath Gacy's house belong to their son.

Two days later, William George "Bill" Bundy informed his family he was going to a party. Instead he disappeared. He'd been an accomplished gymnast and diver.

Gregory John Godzik – aged 17, blond, slight, muscular – had an unfortunate and ironic connection with Gacy. Gacy chanced upon Greg at a timber store and on the spot offered the youth a job at twice his current wage. Of course, Greg jumped at it. On the night he'd planned to go on a date with this girlfriend he vanished without trace. He'd been at Gacy's PDM merely two weeks, during which time he'd mentioned to his family that his employer had had him dig some trenches – supposedly for a drain – in the crawlspace beneath Gacy's Summerdale home.

After Greg's disappearance, his parents contacted Gacy, who told them that the youth had run away, and in fact had talked to Gacy about doing so. He said that since his disappearance, Greg had phoned Gacy and that Gacy had a message saved on his answering machine. When Greg's parents asked to listen to the message, Gacy told them that he'd since erased it.

Gacy later confessed the truth. One day he'd overheard Greg talking about marijuana. He took the boy to one side and asked if he could get him some. According to Gacy, Greg said he'd be able to drop some off on Saturday.

The next Saturday (the day of Greg's date with his girlfriend), there was some confusion about driving arrangements. Greg rang, sometime around midnight, and asked Gacy to pick him up. Gacy did. They ended up back at Gacy's house, where they drank and smoked pot. Gacy stated that he didn't remember much more than that, other than that he was annoyed that Greg didn't have the dope he'd promised.

Gacy _did_ remember waking up the next morning to find Greg in the living room, sitting on a chair in his underwear, his arms handcuffed behind his back and a rope around his neck. He'd been dead for some time; _rigor mortis_ had set in.

Gacy buried Greg beneath his house – in a hole that the victim had more than likely dug himself – his body lying on its side, contracted into the sitting position in which it had frozen.

As the weeks passed and Greg failed to return home, his parents became increasing frantic. His beloved 1966 Pontiac had been found abandoned in a northern suburb. He had no reason to leave home. He had been planning a future for himself. The whole situation seemed suspect to say the least. Mrs Godzik contacted the police and begged them to interview Gacy about her son's disappearance. Her request came to nothing. Greg was written off as a runaway and forgotten about.

Gacy met John Alan Szyc on 20 January 1977. He was cruising through the rainy night when he saw the 19-year-old walking along. He struck up a conversation. It turned out that Szyc was selling his car, a Plymouth Satellite. Gacy was interested. They ended up back at Gacy's place to discuss a deal. They got to drinking, and at some stage one of Gacy's employees, an 18-year-old called Michael Rossi, joined them. (Rossi had moved in shortly after David Cram had moved out.)

The next day, Szyc was dead, lying in the spare bedroom with a rope around his neck. Gacy quietly hauled Szyc's body out to the crawlspace and dumped it.

Gacy felt that Rossi had slept through the whole thing; however, he such was the state of his inebriation he wasn't exactly sure *what* had gone on the night before. Certainly, Rossi never mentioned anything about any murder the next day, and he later bought Szyc's car from Gacy for $300, with Gacy making sure he collected payment from Rossi's wages. Gacy even kept some of the items that he'd found in the trunk of the car: a clock-radio and a TV. Nearly a year later, when Gacy's crimes were uncovered, the TV still in Gacy's house would be identified as having belonged to Szyc.

In the intervening year, however, Szyn's mother repeatedly contacted the police stating that she did not believe her son had run away. In February 1977, she was to receive a letter from the police informing her that her son's car had been bought by a man. The man, Michael Rossi, had told the police that the owner of the car had needed money to leave town. She would only learn the truth of the matter a year later when police investigators began to dig beneath Gacy's house.

At least 11 youths and young men were killed in 1977. One of them was Robert Edward Gilroy, the 18-year-old son of a police sergeant, last seen alive on 15 September. He lived just four blocks from Gacy. His remains were pulled from the ground beneath Gacy's house. However, at the time of Gilroy's last known sighting, Gacy had been supervising a job in Pittsburgh, Pennsylvania and did not return to Chicago until 16 September. During questioning, Gacy maintained that he'd had accomplices in some of his murders. The fact that he was in another state at the time of Gilroy's disappearance gives credence to this claim.

On 6 January 1978, a police car pulled up near no. 8213 Summerdale Avenue. The driver, police investigator Ted Janus, watched as an overweight man left the house and got into his car. Janus drove his own car and blocked the driveway. He opened the resident's car door and told him he was under arrest for kidnapping and sexual assault. The alleged victim was Robert Donnelly, who had been abducted a little after midnight on 31 December.

On that night, Gacy had stopped alongside the 19-year-old youth and offered him a lift home. He admitted to having had a consensual sexual relationship with the boy, and that he hadn't paid for the sex. That was the way that Gacy told it. The victim himself told a different story. He told law-enforcement officials that Gacy had impersonated a police officer and pulled a gun on him, telling him to get into the car. Once in, Gacy had handcuffed him. He drove the abductee to his Summerdale house, and, once there, Gacy threw a drink in his face and poured another down his throat. Donnelly recalled that Gacy raped him in various ways and tied something around his throat, choking him. Gacy showed Donnelly a gun, telling him there was a bullet in the chamber. He pointed the gun at Donnelly and pulled the trigger – once, twice, a dozen times. Finally the blank bullet discharged with a loud crack. Then Gacy throttled Donnelly until he passed out.

When Donnelly came to he was in the bathroom. Donnelly recalled that Gacy repeatedly pushed his head beneath a bathful of water, taking him to the point of near drowning each time.

This continued all night until Donnelly eventually begged Gacy to kill him.

In the end, the police thought Gacy to be the better witness, and that Donnelly wasn't mentally stable. What's more, Gacy was politically active, an upstanding member of his community and the owner of a successful business. No charges were filed. Gacy was freed, and the following month he killed again. Nineteen-year-old William Wayne "Billy" Kindred, a tough, muscular youth who'd only recently got engaged, turned out the be the last victim buried in Gacy's crawlspace. The murderer had simply run out of space.

On 21 March, Jeffrey Rignall, then aged 26, was walking towards a local gay bar in Rosemont, Illinois. A car pulled up in front of him and blocked his path. The window came down and the driver opened a brief dialogue by saying, "Hey, where'd you get such a good tan?" The driver offered him a ride and a joint. Once Rignall was in the car, the driver pushed a chloroform-soaked rag over his mouth until he passed out. Rignall began to regained his senses several times during the ensuing journey, but each time the driver smothered him again with chloroform, sending him back into unconsciousness.

When he awoke properly, Rignall was inside a house. The man was fixing himself a drink and Rignall asked, "Why did you do that to me?"

"There's a gun under the bar and I'd just as soon kill you as look at you," was the unfriendly reply.

The man, who seemed quite relaxed, came forward seeming to offer his "guest" a joint. Instead, he slapped the wet dishrag over Rignall's mouth again until he passed out again.

When he finally woke up he had been stripped naked, fastened by chains to a wooden board and in front of him was a naked fat man standing alongside an array of large dildos. The man then proceeded to describe to his captive exactly what he intended to do with the items, making sure to let Rignall know that he was under his total control, that the man could do whatever he wanted with him. He forced Rignall to perform oral sex, ordering him to say, "I love it, I love it." The man repeatedly chloro-formed Rignall to the point of unconsciousness each time. During periods when Rignall was lucid, the man forcibly inserted dildos into Rignall's anus, continually telling him to say he loved it. During the ordeal he was raped and whipped often.

Rignall felt that during this experience there had been another man there. The accomplice, who had long brown hair, parted in the middle, was on his knees in front of Rignall. As soon as this man realised that Rignall was regaining consciousness, the chloroform would be reapplied, knocking him out again.

But in a way Rignall was lucky – he survived his torment. As Gacy's crawlspace was now full, Rignall's survival might've depended purely upon the lack of a place to bury the body. Instead Gacy dumped him on the snowy ground in the park near where he'd been abducted. When he came round his flies were undone and his face was burned and scarred. He spent a week in hospital being treated for facial burns and rectal bleeding. There, he discovered that the chloroform had caused irreparable damage to his liver. He reported the attack to the police but they did not investigate due to a lack of identifiable suspect. Rignall eventually saw and recognised the Oldsmobile he'd been taken in and later identified Gacy from a mugshot. He might've expected his accusation to be taken seriously. Instead, Gacy denied that he'd used chloroform, or that any anal sex had taken place, or that he had a "torture rack". He denied that there'd been a third man at his house at the time. He in turn accused Rignall of being a two-bit hustler who'd cooked up a cock-and-bull story for whatever reason. Gacy got away with it again.[4]

There were at least four further murders. Gacy initially considered storing the bodies in his attic, but discounted this plan due to worry about possible "leakage". Instead, he threw the

---

[4] Rignall died of AIDS-related causes on 24 December 2000. The book, _29 Below_, published in 1979, is his account of his quest for justice.

bodies off a bridge into the Des Plaines River. One of the bodies, Gacy believed, landed on a barge passing down the river.

The last victim proved to be 15-year-old Robert Jerome Piest, by all accounts a thoroughly decent, hardworking, reliable, attentive son – not the sort of boy to run away from home.

On the afternoon of 11 December 1978, Gacy was in a Des Plaines pharmacy to discuss contracting work when he chanced upon Robert. Within earshot of the pharmacy owner, Gacy offered the boy work at $5 per hour – double the rate he earned at the pharmacy. Robert's mother came to collect him around nine o'clock. Robert asked her to wait for a while; he wanted to talk to a contractor about a job. He promised to return shortly. Just after ten o'clock that evening Robert was dead.

Suspecting that Gacy might be holding Robert against his will, Des Plaines investigators obtained a search warrant for the Summerdale house. In it they found a raft of disagreeable evidence, including several large dildos encrusted with faecal matter, gay pornographic magazines, a lurid paperback book entitled *Pretty Boys Must Die*, several pairs of handcuffs and police badges, a large rectangular board with holes drilled into each end, a hypodermic needle, and, hidden in the attic, some wallets that belonged to young men. It was said that investigators also found Gacy's skittish dog inside the house, its anus showing signs of having been unnaturally enlarged. However, they didn't find Robert Piest.

Two days later, news came in concerning the battery charge against Gacy brought by Jeffrey Rignall. Now the investigators' suspicions were doubly raised. They put a close tail on him, ensuring their presence was well known. Initially, Gacy appeared to go along with the surveillance, talking affably with his followers, even inviting them for meals in restaurants. At one point during breakfast Gacy make a half-cryptic remark: "You know, clowns can get away with murder."

But, as the days passed by, the visible strain of being continually followed got to Gacy. He began to look anxious. He didn't shave and it was clear that he was drinking heavily. Then his chest pains conveniently resurfaced. "These guys are going to kill me," he said. He was rushed to hospital. His sister arrived and she encouraged him to tell the police everything. Meanwhile, on the same day, new evidence came to light: a receipt found in Gacy's kitchen matched the pharmacy where the youth Piest had worked. Its existence contradicted Gacy's claims that he'd never had contact with Piest. Police obtained a search warrant and began to pick over their suspect's house. In Gacy's bedroom they found a television which they suspected had belonged to missing person John Szyc. One officer also noticed, lingering in the air and unmistakable to anyone accustomed in serious crime, the pervasive stench of death ... It was the start of the end for Gacy. The team inspected the crawlspace and then began to dig. It wasn't long before they found the first human bone ...

When he got discharged from hospital, Gacy consulted his lawyers in preparation for throwing a civil suit at the Des Plaines police. Immediately upon arriving, he asked for an alcoholic drink. Then he noticed on his lawyer's desk a newspaper article referring to the disappearance of Piest. Now Gacy seemed to resign himself to that fact that the game was up. "This boy is dead," Gacy said. "He's in a river." And then he began his confession. *Or rather, his excuses.* The boys were "hustlers" and "liars". Due to the amount of alcohol he'd drunk he fell asleep during the long and rambling statement. Against his lawyers' advice he then left, ostensibly to say his goodbyes to family and friends. "I've been a bad boy," he told one work colleague. "I killed thirty people ... give or take."

Upon hearing about Gacy's movements, the police, concerned that Gacy might be about to commit suicide, arrested him on possession of drugs charges. Now Gacy began to talk freely. "I just want to clear the air," he said.

But still he blamed the victims. "They sold their bodies for twenty dollars," he said. "They killed themselves." It might've seemed justification enough to a psychopathic serial killer but it wasn't what the cops wanted to hear. One of the officers reminded Gacy of the time in prison when he had been told too late about his father's death. *Didn't he want to give the relatives closure, just like he'd wanted himself all those years ago?* Within hours Gacy was naming names.

In total, 29 bodies were pulled from Gacy's crawlspace or under the garage, many of them still with rope around their necks and some with foreign objects lodged into the pelvic region as if they'd been inserted into the victims' anus. Four were found in the Des Plaines River. One of these, found on 9 April 1979, was Robert Piest. Wads of paper had been shoved down his throat whilst he was still alive causing death by suffocation. Of the 33 found, 27 have been identified; six remain without name. It's thought that Gacy killed up to 12 more youths and young men, the remains of whom have not been found. Gacy's reply, when asked if there were any more victims, was terse: "That's for you guys to find out."

Psychiatrists determined Gacy fit to be tried. His defence strategy centred on the premise that he'd been compelled to commit murder and that a study of his criminal behaviours would be of benefit to science. The jury were not convinced; they deliberated for a mere two hours before finding him guilty of the murder of 33 males by unanimous verdict. For the sentencing phase of the trial Gacy's defence team chose to have the decision made by the jury. A single dissenter would've meant a reprieve from the electric chair. The jury deliberated for two further hours before giving the death sentence for each of the 33 murders – again, a unanimous decision.

Gacy was incarcerated for 14 years in the Menard Correctional Center in Chester, Illinois before the sentence was carried out. From the isolation of his prison cell he found a new love for painting. Many of his artworks included subjects as diverse as birds, flowers, skulls and clowns.

For his last meal he ordered a bucket of KFC, a dozen fried shrimp, french fries, strawberries and a Diet Coke. His life was ended by means of a lethal injection. Reportedly, his final words to his lawyer before the execution were a complaint that the state was about to commit murder. The Killer Clown's final spoken words were brusque: "Kiss my ass." After his execution, many of Gacy's pieces of art were publicly burned.

Speculation about the involvement of accomplices remains just that. After his arrest, Gacy had asked if his "associates" had also been arrested. When asked by police if they'd participated directly or indirectly in the murders, Gacy replied, "Directly."

Suspiciously, before his arrest, when Gacy was being followed by the police, he'd met up with two of his employees and officers overheard hushed parts of a conversation which sounded like, "Buried like the other five?" Speculation continues.

"There is overwhelming evidence that Gacy worked with an accomplice," a criminal defence attorney publicly proclaimed. Others, however, feel that Gacy got away with it for six years and that there was no reason for him to jeopardise that by involving anyone else. Certainly, though, no one has since been charged with involvement in his dreadful series of crimes.

# Dennis Andrew Nilsen

(active 1978-1983)

CARL STOTTOR WAS UNEMPLOYED and depressed that particular
evening sometime in April or May 1982. Carl, a good-looking
21-year-old homosexual, was drinking to forget his troubles. A
love affair had recently gone wrong and he was still hurting in
the aftermath. Shy and effeminate, there was something rather
pathetic about the young man as he sat alone, drowning his sor-
rows in the Black Cap bar in London's Camden Town.

When a seemingly friendly man approached seeking to comfort him, Carl was grateful. The man, tall and thin, wearing
large, silver-rimmed glasses, was sympathetic. With a clipped
Scottish accent, he nevertheless talked to Carl gently, telling
him how pretty he was, and he even paid for the drinks all night.
And there were *a lot* of drinks …

Eventually, the man suggested that he and Carl go back to his
place, promising that there'd be no funny business. In the back
of the taxi, on the way to the man's flat in Cranley Gardens, a
four-mile journey, the two held hands; but back at the man's flat
the sympathetic stranger was true to his word – he made no attempt to initiate sexual activity. A small black-and-white mongrel pup called Bleep was wandering around. Her intervention
would later save Carl's life.

The kindly Scottish man gave Carl a drink – probably a rum
and coke, for that was his own favourite tipple. And then he gave
him another. He might've introduced himself as "Des", but Carl
at the time probably wouldn't have remembered it; he was getting more and more drunk by the minute. At some point he said
he wished he were dead. Des told him not to be so silly, that he
had a whole future to look forward to.

At another point, Des might've put on a record. One of his
favourites was Laurie Anderson's *O Superman*, a strange, hypnotic art pop song. Or he may have put on something by Rick
Wakeman, a keyboard instrumentalist whose solo projects were

known for their mythical influences. It may even have been Barber's _Adagio for Strings_, or Aaron Copland's _Fanfare for the Common Man_. Whatever – the combination of music and alcohol soon banished Des' inhibitions, rendering him relaxed and feeling happy. Carl, on the other hand, had by this stage been rendered unconscious under the influence of copious amounts of alcohol.

He remembered waking up without being able to breathe. There was something wrapped around his neck, and it seemed as though Des, who was behind him, were trying to untangle it. "Stay still, stay still," Des kept saying, but the thing around Carl's neck got tighter. Now he was fighting for breath, his tongue felt swollen and he lapsed in and out of consciousness.

Then he felt himself being carried and heard the sound of running water. Now he was in the bath, submerged in cold water, and his head kept going under. He tried to push himself up, only to find himself being thrust back down again. This happened several times. His lungs were taking in water and he was in excruciating pain. He managed to gasp a final plea: "No more, please stop." At last he could take the struggle no longer; he gave up and relaxed, passing out into a deathlike blackout.

The next he knew there was something touching his face. When he opened his eyes, Carl saw that he was on the bed and the small black and white dog was licking him on the cheek.

Carl spent a long time in Des' flat, periodically rousing, sleeping for longer periods. When he eventually caught sight of his face in the mirror he was shocked. There was a red mark around his neck and his eyes were shot with broken capillaries. His host explained that Carl had become entangled in the zipper of the sleeping bag and nearly strangled himself; Des had saved him by splashing water in his face, he explained. He'd kept him warm and comfortable. Carl felt inclined to believe this version of events, even attributing his frightening memories of the water as being part of a nightmare.

Some while later, Des accompanied Carl to the underground station. He gave Carl his contact details, telling him he hoped they would meet again soon. Carl had other ideas. He went to the emergency department of the London Hospital, only to be told that his injuries were consistent with having been strangled. A part of Carl wondered at this. Nevertheless, he decided not to go to the police. Due to heavy intoxication, his recollection of events was foggy to say the least. And he had no witnesses, other than Des himself. And Bleep, the pup who'd recognised the ember of life still within him. Bleep, who'd saved his life ... although, in some sense, Carl's life was already over, for he was never to be the same again ...

Dennis Andrew Nilsen's surname was inherited from his Norwegian father; his mother was a Scot. He was born on 23 November 1945 in Fraserburgh, back then still a small fishing village on the blustery coast of Scotland. Des was the middle child of the family, between older brother, Olav Jr., and younger sister, Sylvia. The parents' marriage was difficult, with father Olav spending much time away in the Free Norwegian Forces, leaving Betty behind to look after the children. Betty's parents didn't approve of the frequently-absent husband, and Betty herself would say that she'd "rushed into marriage without thinking". Inevitably, perhaps, in 1948 the marriage failed. Betty, however, was well supported by her own parents, whilst grandfather Andrew became a sort of surrogate father for young Des, and the two became particularly close. Des thought of Andrew as his "great hero and protector". The elder had brought up his own family well, despite meagre funds, and now helped to raise his daughter's children also. Although known for his hair-raising stories, no doubt designed to impress, he was well respected in the village. And Des worshiped him, drinking in the overblown stories enthusiastically, and he would later describe his childhood as being one of contentment.

Even as a toddler he loved to wander, his mother even having to resort to tying him to the garden gate with a length of string to prevent him from disappearing without a word. As he got older, he enjoyed long walks by the harbour, through the sanddunes and along seafront with his beloved grandfather. Indeed, the sea, with its power and menace, was an omnipresent force for most of Fraserburgh's inhabitants, for many made their living from the sea, or were close to someone who did. Des Nilsen was no different. He knew as well as anyone that when the fishermen pushed out to sea on another expedition there was a real danger they might be swallowed up by the unpredictable waters; they might never come back alive. And so it happened. On 31 October 1951, Andrew, Des' grandfather, at the age of 62, died of a heart attack whilst out at sea. Des was not yet six.

The body was brought ashore at Yarmouth. After the inquest it was laid out in the tiny family home at 47 Academy Road in Fraserburgh, a house that was now filled with continuous weeping and loudly expressed grief. Visitors came and went all day, but no one thought to tell young Des what had happened.

Eventually his mother asked him if he wanted to see his grandad. Des said yes. He was brought upstairs where he was held aloft to look inside the coffin. Inside lay his much-loved grandfather, looking as if he were sleeping quietly. And indeed, that's exactly what Des' mother told him that his grandad was doing.

At the time, Des didn't understand why he was feeling such fear and excitement, but the occasion was to have profound consequences for the youngster, now and in the future. When he returned to the bedroom the next day, his grandfather was gone. No one mentioned his name or where he'd gone, and it was to be another six months later before Des would come to understand that his grandfather wouldn't be returning home. It had no doubt been a well-intentioned misdirection, yet its repercussions would echo down the years, coming to touch and destroy the lives of many young men in its wake. As Nilsen would later conjecture:

> _My troubles started there. It blighted my personality permanently. I have spent all my emotional life searching for my grandfather and in my formative years no one was there to take his place ... Relatives would pretend that he had gone to a "better place". "Why," I thought, "should he go_

*to a better place and not take me with him?" "So death was a nice thing," I thought. "Then why does it make me miserable?" ... What storms of reasoning fury must have gone through my mind at that age.*[1]

Already a quiet and shy boy, Des withdrew into himself, becoming more sombre and introspective, often spending long hours standing at the harbour, watching the herring boats sailing in and out. He began to resent the time his mother spent with his siblings, and he also came to envy his older brother Olav's popularity with others at home and abroad.

Then, around 1955, there occurred a strange incident. On one of his solitary walks along the shore, Des was feeling miserable. He stopped and took off his shoes and socks. He looked out to sea and became "hypnotised by its power and enormity". He walked in, slowly and steadily, ever further from the shore. He slipped and felt himself become submerged beneath the tide. He panicked and waved his arms, gasping for air which wouldn't come. Then he entered a dreamlike state, suspended at the edge of reality, feeling that his grandad would come and save him.

It wasn't his grandfather who saved him; it was a teenage boy, who, according to Nilsen, waded in and dragged him from the depths and back onto the beach. When he regained consciousness he realised he was naked, lying on the sand beneath the warm sun, looking up at the blue sky. He covered his nakedness with his hands, only to realised that there was a white sticky mess on his thighs. The recollection may have been as fanciful as his grandfather's tales, but the essentials are true – Nilsen *did* nearly drown after walking into the sea.

Shortly after this episode, the family moved out of the tiny Academy Road flat and into a larger property. Mrs Nilsen later

---

[1] Written by Nilsen in prison in 1993, quoted in Masters, Brian (1985). *Killing for Company: The Case of Dennis Nilsen.* New York City: Random House

acquired a new husband, Andrew, a builder, which whom she would have four more children. Des initially resented Andrew, but in later years he came to respect him.

Adolescence delivered a confusing and shaming discovery to Des: he realised that he was homosexual. He kept this from those who knew him, but some were soon to guess his secret. His older brother, for one, whose body Des caressed as he slept. Olav Jr., after becoming aware of his younger brother's sexuality, began to taunt him, calling him "hen", a Scottish dialect term for "girl". In what must've been perplexing for Des, he found that he was attracted to boys with facial features similar to his sister, Sylvia, although he never made any attempts to initiate sexual contact with them. He did, however, on one occasion, fondle Sylvia herself, leading him to consider for a while that he was bisexual.

Des joined the Army Cadet Force at the age of 14, and in 1961, at the age of 16, he moved to the Army Catering Corp. He was posted to Aldershot, where inevitably his close proximity to around 20 other young adolescent boys tipped his leanings a little further towards the homosexual. His time spent at Aldershot made Des keenly aware that the was attracted to boys, but as a necessity he kept this self-knowledge hidden. Anyone finding out about it would surely have subjected him to intense derision and scorn. When "queers" were mentioned, Nilsen also joined in the ribald laughter, all the while knowing that he was deceiving his colleagues and scorning what he was himself.

Although he was able to excel well enough at drills, exercise and technical training, there was one area in which Nilsen struggled – the shower rooms. Here, his secret ran the risk of becoming cruelly exposed. Fearful of taking a shower in the company of others – he was afraid that he'd get an erection – he opted to take baths alone, using the opportunity to masturbate in privacy without being discovered.

In 1964, now aged 18, Nilsen passed his catering exam and was assigned to the Royal Fusiliers in Osnabrück in West German, serving as a private. His colleagues here were a "hardworking boozy lot", and Nilsen did his best to fit in. Now, he began to drink to excess, using alcohol to mask his underlying shyness. On one occasion, he and a German youth found themselves drinking themselves into oblivion. When he awoke, Nilsen found himself lying naked on the floor of the other youth's flat. Whatever fantasy had lain dormant now stirred into life. Nilsen began to fantasise about having his own unconscious, prostate body interfered with by his army colleagues. He would feign intoxication in the hope that one of them would fondle him sexually whilst he lay supposedly unconscious. They never did.

A posting in the State of Aden (soon to become part of Yemen) in 1967, proved to be less pleasant. Nilsen saw many disturbing sights here, including multiple dead and mutilated bodies, both friend and foe. He claimed even to have nearly been the victim of an attempted assassination himself when he was abducted in the boot of a taxi, only escaping by playing dead. The story may have been the fanciful imaginations of a fantasist, but it is telling that he should have told the story.

The summer of 1967 brought Nilsen to the Trucial Oman Scouts Mess at Sharjah near the Persian Gulf, a much more relaxing posting, where alcohol flowed freely and easily. Alcohol led to the death of one of his colleagues, who was buried in a simple grave in the desert sand. Nilsen remembered seeing the sand blow over the young man's grave, making it disappear.

It was at Sharjah that Nilsen became a non-commissioned officer, which came with the added benefit of a private room. This afforded him the opportunity to masturbate in privacy, which he did whilst staring at his own naked, prostate body in a mirror. His masturbatory fantasies evolved during this time, and he gradually became more fascinated by the dichotomy of being both the passive and the domineering partner. Here, also, Nilsen had his first consensual sexual experience with another, an Arab boy who declared his undying love for Nilsen and begged to be taken back to England with him. Nilsen never gave the proposal a second thought, and in the coming months he was transferred (without the Arab boy) to Plymouth, Cyprus, Berlin (where he had unremarkable sex with a German prostitute, which he made sure to brag about to this colleagues), Bavaria (where he honed his butchery skills, cutting up the carcasses of animals), and Inverness, later ending up in the Shetland Islands.

At this final deployment, Nilsen met an 18-year-old private, for whom he fell head over heels. Nilsen would later write that "he had the effect upon me of an electric shock". The two took long walks together, and when they met in social gatherings Nilsen would take furtive glances at his friend, knowing he couldn't risk the other men observing him. One of the private's duties was to awaken Nilsen in the morning. Nilsen would already be awake in anticipation, waiting for the young man's hand to gently rouse him with a shake. Nilsen, we can conjecture, would've been happier had the youth woken him in a more intimate manner. It's unlikely that idea ever crossed the private's mind, for he himself was not homosexual.

The private shared Nilsen's love of photography and filmmaking. During some of their private shootings, Nilsen would encourage the private to "play dead". Later, after the films were developed, Nilsen would privately masturbate to them.

On a couple of occasions, the relationship crossed professional boundaries further. The private, struggling with homesickness, lapsed into tearfulness. Nilsen was there to comfort him, hugging him and clasping his hand for a short moment. These were Nilsen's recollections, yet it's hard to know if they weren't merely the whimsies of one-sided love affair. When the private eventually left for good, Nilsen was distraught. He considered throwing himself off the overhang at Fitful Head. Instead he threw all of his films into the incinerator in an attempt to erase all memory of his first true love. In the event, it would take Nilsen two years before he could call himself recovered from the loss.

He completed his 11-year military career at the rank of corporal in October 1972, now aged 26. Throughout Nilsen's time in the army, alcohol had been his constant and (considering the parting of the young private) his most reliable friend. Now, back at his mother's house, he found himself wondering what to do next. The answer didn't come immediately.

One night whilst at the house, Nilsen was watching a film on TV. *Victim* was the story of a man who was being blackmailed due to the discovery that he had been having an affair with another man. Olav, who'd already suspected that his brother Dennis was homosexual, noisily derided the film. That was it. Their relationship broke down irreparably and Dennis never spoke to his tormentor again.

In December 1972, Nilsen elected to become a police officer and joined the Metropolitan Police's Training School in Hendon, North London. After 16-weeks of preparation, he was posted to Willesden Green Police Station, where he was to remain for the next year. He was liked reasonably well by his colleagues, and he seemed to pass himself admirably enough there, but there always clung to him a sense of dissatisfaction. He felt lonely in the large city, and left to his own devices he did what he had become accustomed to doing – drinking.

The Sexual Offences Act 1967 was a landmark piece of legislation: it decriminalised homosexuality in England and Wales. Nevertheless, sexual relations between men were not yet readily accepted by society, and the pubs that Nilsen chose to frequent were dark and clandestine places. Here – in the seedy Coleherne in Earl's Court, or at the more urbane King William IV pub in Hampstead – Nilsen met men, engaging with them in a series of transient sexual dalliances that he would later describe as "soul-destroying". Once, he thought he'd found himself a permanent partner, even trying anal sex for the first and last time, but this lover made no bones about it – he was not going to commit to an exclusive relationship, and he too left Nilsen – just as the others had done. Eventually, realising that his personal and professional lives were incompatible with each other, Nilsen resigned from the police force after only a year, a decision which astounded his colleagues.

For a few months in 1974, he found intermittent work as a security guard (which he found interminably boring) before finding permanent employment in May 1974 as a civil servant at a Jobcentre. The job suited him and at the beginning he was known to be quiet and conscientious, if sometimes a little boring. He was active in the trade union movement, keen to do overtime. Matching the unemployed with job vacancies gave him feelings of achievement and job satisfaction. However, his mannerisms became more officious and direct with his fellow employees, a possible throwback to his army training. (Later, in 1979, he was to be promoted to executive officer at the Jobcentre, and in June 1982 he was transferred to the Kentish Town branch, where he would remain employed until his criminal career eventually caught up with him.)

By night, he was as promiscuous as ever. Indeed, his landlady took exception to the nocturnal comings and goings and asked him to leave. His habit of entertaining strangers did lead to one alarming incident. By chance, he picked up an unemployed 17-year-old youth who'd earlier come into the Jobcentre. After striking up a conversation, Nilsen invited him back to his room. There, they drank and the youth eventually fell asleep. He later awoke to find Nilsen pointing a camera at him. The two then scuffled until Nilsen lost control. At this point the youth left and called the police. Nilsen was interrogated at the same police station he'd worked at in 1973, but in the end no charges were brought. The episode with the camera, however, with Nilsen taking photographs of a sleeping youth, shows that absolute passivity and objectification continued to be twin features of his inner fantasy life.

In November 1975, Nilsen received news that his father – still a virtual stranger – had died, leaving him a legacy of £1,000. Shortly afterwards, he chanced to meet an effeminate, slender 20-year-old man named David Gallichan, who was being hassled by two men in the street. Nilsen intervened and ended up inviting the young man back to his room. He stayed the night, and the next morning Nilsen asked him to move in permanently. The two men then looked around for a ground floor flat with a garden, finding one that met their requirements at 195 Melrose

Avenue in Cricklewood. In due course the pair moved in.

As he was unemployed, Gallichan (whom Nilsen had rechristened "Twinkle") spent his time decorating the flat whilst Nilsen worked. It soon became a cosy home, complete with armchairs, furnishings and wall art. Nilsen began to expand his record collection. In his spare time, he tended to the garden, transforming it from a patch of wasteland to a pleasant area with trees and a vegetable-growing patch. Now that it was more attractive the upstairs neighbours wanted to use the garden; however, Nilsen blocked off the side entrance, prohibiting them access. Then he installed a garden pond, replete with fish. Next he bought a tiny black and white puppy from a Willesden Green pet shop. Hearing the dog yip from beneath Twinkle's jacket on the journey home, Nilsen named the animal "Bleep". A budgerigar called "Hamish" was next. The only words it learned to speak would be "piss off". Finally, to complete their home, the pair adopted a stray kitten, calling her "D.D.", presumably after her owners' initials.

The normalcy was only skin deep, however. A chasm soon formed, founded on the fact that the two men were completely unsuited to each other. They started to look outside their relationship for sex, bringing strangers home, causing resentment to build and tension to hang in the air. After two years, in May 1977, Twinkle moved out. Nilsen later claimed that the two had had an argument and he'd ordered him to leave. Gallichan refuted this, saying he'd left on his own account. Whatever the reason, Nilsen's attempt at a relationship was over and he was now alone with Bleep and the neck of a bottle. He threw himself into his work. When at home, he watched TV and listened to music. He walked the dog and tended to the garden. And he drank. There was one final attempt to form a lasting relationship after he picked up a rent boy at the Golden Lion pub. The boy came to live with Nilsen for four months, but the relationship didn't endure, and in the end this boy left … just like all the others had done. By this stage, Bleep, the scruffy black-and-white mongrel, was the only constant in Nilsen's life, and he came to love her as if she were his own child.

The loneliness, however, was a constant companion. By the last days of 1978, Nilsen was drinking heavily. He would've drunk himself to death, he thought, but for the fact that Bleep would have no one to care for her. There was plenty of social drinking, but afterwards he was left with nothing but desolation and a hangover. As Christmas passed and the New Year beckoned he wallowed in self-pity. He needed to get out. He left the flat and walked to a local bar, the Cricklewood Arms. There, he met a teenaged boy who was on his way home after a pop concert. If they exchanged names, by the end of the night Nilsen had forgotten it. The boy evidently felt comfortable enough with Nilsen to agree to return with him to the Melrose Avenue flat.

They stayed up late, drinking themselves into oblivion. Eventually, the pair stripped off, climbed into bed together and passed out. There had been no sexual contact.

A couple of hours later, Nilsen awoke, stared at the sleeping boy, and then snuggled up to him. In his own recollection, Nilsen then slipped the blanket down so that his eyes could take in both of their bodies. He ran his hands over the teenager, exploring the skin, and becoming aroused himself. At that point, he became afraid that the boy would leave him, just like all the others had done. He glanced down at the pile of clothes beside his bed and his eyes alighted on his tie. Nilsen remembered thinking that he only wanted the boy to stay with him to see in the New Year, whether he wanted to or not. He picked up the tie and slipped it around the boy's neck. He straddled him. Then he pulled the tie tight.

The boy immediately awoke and in the struggle both fell off the bed. The boy pushed out with his legs, moving across the floor, overtopping the coffee table. Now he was jammed against the wall. Nilsen continued to pull the ligature tight, and after about a minute the boy became limp. Nilsen stood over him, trembling.

After a while, he noticed the boy drawing in a raspy breath, although still unconscious. Nilsen quickly went into the kitchen, filled a bucket with water and returned. There, he manoeuvred the boy over a dining chair, placing the bucket beneath. He pushed the boy's head into the water and held it there until the bubbles stopped coming. Then he sat down with a cup of coffee and smoked silently, looking at the boy and wondering about what he'd done.

Next came the ritual that would accompany all his future murders. He transported the body to the bathroom, lowered it into the bath and tenderly washed it. Afterwards, he towelled it dry and removed it back to the bedroom. He placed it carefully into the bed and pulled the blanket over it, right up to the chin. He half expected a knock on the door, but none came. His next thoughts turned to how to disposed of the body. He went for a walk down Willesden High Road to think it over. Whilst out, he must've come up with the solution, for he called into an ironmongers and bought a large cooking pot and an electric knife, but when he returned home he put the items away.

Now he dressed the body, putting on underwear and a pair of new socks whilst it was still in bed. He had a bath himself, and afterwards climbed in beside the body and explored it with his hands. During this, Nilsen was erect, and he made a half-hearted attempted to enter the body, but it was cooling rapidly by now and then his erection deflated. He got up, took the body from the bed and laid it on the floor, covering it with an old curtain. Then he got into bed and fell asleep until the evening.

A plan had come to him. It was more of a halfway measure. He prised up some floorboards with the idea of placing the body on the earth beneath. However, by now *rigor mortis* had rendered it stiff and it wouldn't fit into the hole. He stood the body up against the wall whilst awaiting the *rigor* to pass. The next day, the body was pliable enough for the limbs to be moved. Nilsen spent some time exploring the body before placing it into the hole, covering it with some soil and bricks from the garden. During the process, D.D. the cat also made her way in, and the murderer had to spend 10 minutes coaxing her out. Then he replaced the flooring and disposed of his own clothes.

A week later, Nilsen unearthed the remains. The skin was dirty but intact, so he drew a bath and washed it. He placed the body on the floor and became aroused, kneeling and masturbating over it. Before going to bed, he suspended the body by the ankles so that it was upside-down, the fingers brushing the floor. The next morning, he masturbated again whilst looking at the body. He took it down and briefly considered dismembering it, but he thought that would spoil the perfectness of the body and so he stopped himself. He put the remains back under the floorboards where it remained for the next seven months.

On 10 August 1979, Nilsen set up a bonfire in the back garden. The next day, he disinterred the body, wrapped it in bags tied with string, and placed it into the kindling, along with some rubber tyres to mask the smell of burning flesh. The fire burned brightly. After the blaze died, he raked the ashes into the ground, obliterating all trace of the teenager whose name he didn't even remember.[2] No one had come to look for the boy, and during the intervening months between the murder and the cremation Nilsen was able to forget what lay beneath his floorboards. He put it down as a one-off incident, never to be repeated.

It was to be repeated less than a year later, only this time the victim's unexplained vanishing would make it to the national papers. Kenneth Ockenden was a 23-year-old Canadian student on a tour of England whilst visiting relatives. It was his last day in the country as he was due to fly home the following day. That morning, he took breakfast at the Central Hotel near London's King's Cross and then left with his camera to go sightseeing. He ended up at a West End bar where he must've felt fortunate to

---

[2] In November 2006, Nilsen identified Stephen Dean Holmes as his first victim after police showed him a photo during a review of missing person cases. Nilsen had told police that his first victim was Irish. Stephen's parents had emigrated from Dublin to London, where Stephen was born. He'd been 14 years of age at the time of his death. His family corroborated Nilsen's report that the boy had been returning home after a pop concert.

cross paths with a friendly Scot called Des. The two chatted the lunchtime hours away merrily before leaving together to see what London had to offer. They went to Trafalgar Square, down Whitehall, past Downing Street, along Parliament Street and onwards to Westminster Abbey. Later in the afternoon, Ockenden agreed to return to his new friend Des's flat for something to eat and then to go out for a drink in the evening. On the way home, they stopped at an off-licence near the Underground where Nilsen bought alcohol. Ockenden insisted upon splitting the bill.

They had a relaxing time back at the flat, settling down to drink, watch television and listen to music, each appearing to enjoy the other's company. For Nilsen especially it was a very pleasant evening, but he couldn't get rid of the thought that his new friend was due to fly back to Canada the next day. Describing the incident as he recalled it, at an hour or so after midnight, Nilsen went into a kind of trance. Whilst Ockenden was listening to music with the headphones on, Nilsen suddenly wrapped the flex tightly around the young man's neck and pulled tightly. He claimed there was no struggle,[3] but after the man was dead Nilsen undressed him and saw that he'd messed himself. He wiped the mess away with kitchen paper and, as he'd done with the Irish teenager a year ago, transported him to the bath where he washed him tenderly.

After this, Nilsen laid the body on his bed and slept alongside it. In the morning, Nilsen disposed of Ockenden's clothes and property, put the body in a cupboard and went to work as normal. When he returned, the body was stiff with *rigor mortis*. The next day, Nilsen bought a Polaroid camera. Back at home, he straightened out the body (it was now more malleable), posed it and took photographs of it. Then he set the body on a kitchen

---

[3] This is belied by Nilsen's recollection that Bleep had been barking so frantically at the kitchen door that he had to put her into the garden with a chastisement: "Get out, this is fuck all to do with you."

chair, dressed it in underwear, and painted makeup on the face. Later, he lay on the bed beneath Ockenden's spread-eagled body and watched television. He chatted to the lifeless body; he had nonpenetrative sex between its thighs. Eventually, he wrapped the body before placing it beneath the floorboards in the space only recently vacated by his first victim.

During the following fortnight, Nilsen removed the body four times. The cold underfloor conditions preserved the body ("he was still very fresh"), and Nilsen would strip it, put it in a chair beside him and, like an old married couple, the two would sit and watch television together, with Nilsen engaging the other in a necessarily one-sided conversation of whispered sweet nothings.

The killing of Ockenden haunted Nilsen. He spoke of his "shock, grief and horror", which had "hit [him] like an 'A' bomb". He could never listen again to the music that Ockenden had been listening to (a classical rock arrangement played by the London Symphony Orchestra) and he smashed the record with a spade and put it in the bin. Sitting in his armchair with a knife, he contemplated suicide, only to be interrupted by Bleep's approach with wagging tail. At this, Nilsen sank down beside her, sobbing.

The death of Ockenden filled Nilsen with a particularly strong sense of remorse ... _because he had known him._ The two had spent almost a full day together; they'd felt comfortable in each other's company. Ockenden had had family ties, whereas Nilsen's other victims were homeless or estranged from their loved ones. He'd felt protective of Ockenden and (without irony) of the young man's family. In another sense, however, Nilsen _must also have known_ that Ockenden (who was due to return to Canada the next day) would inevitably leave him. Despite this, he invited the young man back to his flat to spend the night. Perhaps he'd had murder on his mind all along ... And yet the risk of him being caught after the murder was high: numerous people would've seen them together during the day – at the pub or wandering around Trafalgar Square. Perhaps the murder had been, as Nilsen claimed, an irrational, impulsive act borne of the looming threat of a crushing loneliness. Nilsen himself certainly didn't have the answers.

He met Martyn on 17 May 1980 on a return journey from a union conference in Southport. Martyn Duffey was an attractive, dark-haired 16-year-old catering student with a troubled past. Originally from Birkenhead near Merseyside, he'd had a brush with the law for theft and threatening behaviour. He was also a product of the care system, had been seen more than once by psychiatrists, and along the way had picked up a dependency on diazepam. He seemed to be on the verge of turning his life around when he joined catering college. However, four days before meeting Nilsen, he simply picked up his chef knives, left his home without saying where he was going and hitchhiked his way to London. Since then he'd been sleeping rough near Euston Station. By the time he crossed paths with the kindly stranger he was cold, tired and hungry and only too glad to accept the offer of some food and a warm bed for the night.

After two beers, Martyn crept into bed. Nilsen remembered sitting on the youth's chest and pulling a ligature tightly around his neck at the same time until the youth wet himself. Whilst the boy was unconscious but still alive, Nilsen carried him to the kitchen sink where he drowned him, holding his head beneath the water for around four minutes until he was certain that his guest was dead. Then he laid the body onto the floor and, like his two previous victims, dressed it in underwear. He took it into the bedroom and put it on the bed, complimenting it and kissing it all over. Then he sat astride the body and masturbated over it. After being stowed in the cupboard for two days it started to bloat, so Nilsen placed it under the floorboards. The aspiring chef's cherished set of knives eventually started to rust, at which point Nilsen threw them away.

Following this, the rate of murders began to accelerate. Before the year was out, five more bodies would trade places beneath the floorboards, and a further three would come in 1981. The next to die was 26-year-old William David Sutherland, an occasional sex-worker who slept with men out of necessity. He met Nilsen in a Piccadilly pub and the two began a pub-crawl togeth-er. Eventually, Nilsen decided to return home and bought a train ticket at Leicester Square Underground Station. When he turned around Sutherland was behind him, saying he'd nowhere to go. Reluctantly, Nilsen said the man could come home with him.

Nilsen couldn't recall the exact details of the death (suggesting that he'd been intensely intoxicated) other than when he'd woken up the next morning the other man was dead – strangled. Sutherland had been a father-of-one with a girlfriend. He was reported missing by his mother (who lived in Scotland) when he abruptly stopped contacting her.

The repetitive murderer couldn't recall the names of the next seven victims, but he remembered their deaths in great detail. One was a tall Irish labourer with rough hands, around 30 years of age;[4] the next was a slender male prostitute with a swarthy, gypsy-like appearance, aged between 20 and 30. A pale, emaciated English vagrant in his 20s was next to die. He had several missing teeth and Nilsen believed the man had had a particularly hard life. As he died, the victim moved his legs in circular fashion, as if riding a bicycle. Nilsen viewed the death as putting him out of his misery. Sometime around November or December, Nilsen killed a "long-haired hippy" in his late 20s[5] whom he'd met in the West End after the pubs had shut. This was the first victim to be dismembered. The remains remained under the floorboards before being burned in bonfires in the garden along with the body parts of several of the previous victims. At one bonfire, three local children stood around to watch the flames. After the fire had died down, Nilsen noticed a skull which had not been reduced to ash and he smashed it to smithereens with

---

[4] Nilsen later claimed to have fabricated this victim.

[5] Nilsen also later claimed to have fabricated this victim.

his rake.

In early January 1981, Nilsen killed an "18-year-old blue-eyed Scot", with whom he'd had a drinking contest in the Melrose Avenue flat. The body was dissected, the organs removed, and the remains stored beneath the floorboards. The next month he strangled a slim man in his early 20s who was originally from Belfast. His 11th victim was an English skinhead, aged around 20,[6] who had a tattoo on his neck which read "CUT HERE". Nilsen had different plans for that neck. After luring the man back to his flat with the promise of alcohol and a meal, Nilsen instead chose to strangle him. He hung the unfortunate victim's body upside-down in his flat for 24 hours before cutting it down and placing it beneath the floorboards.

To date, none of these eight victims has been identified.

The last victim to die at Melrose Avenue was Malcolm Barlow, aged 23 but looking much younger. The young man had spent most of his life in care. His parents were dead and he had no one. Living in hostels, he signed on the dole, but would do anything for money, including sleeping with men. He was an epileptic who wasn't above feigning symptoms in order to draw the sympathy of others. On 17 September 1981, as Nilsen left his flat to go to work, he spotted Barlow leaning against a wall. If it was a ploy to gain Nilsen's concern it worked. Nilsen allowed Barlow to stay in his flat whilst he went to a telephone kiosk to ring for an ambulance.

The next day, upon his return from work, Nilsen found Barlow sitting on his doorstep. He'd come back to thank the kindly stranger for helping him. Nilsen wasn't overly pleased about the man's return. "Well, you'd better come in then," Nilsen told him coolly.

Nilsen cooked him a meal and then the two sat down to watch television. When Nilsen began to drink Barlow asked for one.

---

[6] This was the third victim Nilsen later claimed to have fabricated.

Nilsen initially refused, telling him that alcohol and medication shouldn't be mixed, but Barlow was insistent and in the end Nilsen relented. "Be it on your own head," he said ominously.

After a couple of rum and cokes, Barlow fell into a deep sleep where he sat. Nilsen attempted to revive him by slapping him around the face. Without success. He felt he might need to call for another ambulance and sat for around 20 minutes, trying to decide what to do. He decided to fall back into old habits. Placing his hands around Barlow's neck he squeezed, holding the grip for about three minutes until he was sure the young man was dead. Then he switched off the television and went to bed. The next morning, reluctant to prise up the floorboards, he dragged the body into the kitchen and stowed it in the cupboard under the sink. This murder, it seemed, had been a matter of convenience. Barlow was murdered simply because he'd been in the way. For Nilsen, however, it was back to the quotidian routine: he left the house for work as normal.

Nilsen was compelled to vacate his Melrose Avenue flat in early October 1981 after his landlord decided to commence renovation work. The day before he left, he built a large bonfire in the garden and disposed of five dissected bodies which had been allowed to build up. Again, he threw on a rubber tyre to disguise the smell of cooking flesh. The next day he moved into an attic flat at no. 23 Cranley Gardens in Muswell Hill. In comparison to pleasant Melrose Avenue, the new apartment was squalid, barely furnished, and drably decorated. But with no access to a garden and unable to stow any bodies beneath the floorboards, any visitors to the flat were relatively safe ... for a while ...

During the December after his move, Nilsen met a man who claimed to be an ex-Grenadier (Nilsen called him "John the Guardsman") in a West End pub. After meeting him a second time in March 1982, Nilsen and the man went back to the Cranley Gardens flat (stopping to buy alcohol on the way), where Nilsen cooked them both a meal. After this, they settled down to watch television and drink. Sometime around midnight, John said he wanted to get a little rest. An hour later, Nilsen found the man asleep in his bed with his clothes removed. "I thought you were getting your head down. I didn't know you were moving in," he said in annoyance. He attempted the awaken John, intending to call him a taxi, but the man was unarousable.

Nilsen then poured himself a rum and coke and sat at the edge of the bed. Not wanting to get into bed with John, Nilsen instead when to the armchair, removed a length of upholstery strap and wrapped it around the sleeping man's neck, pulling it tight and shouting, "It's about time you went!" Now John *did* rouse, and he fought back so furiously that Nilsen thought he'd be overpowered. After a few minutes, though, the struggle was over and there was blood on the bedspread. Bleep was barking in the next room. Nilsen went to comfort her. When he returned to the bedroom he was shocked to notice that John had started breathing again. Nilsen now tried to throttle him again. After two or three minutes, he was amazed to find the heart still beating. This time he finished John off by drowning him in the bath. Afterwards, he fell asleep in his armchair with Bleep curled up on his feet.

"John the Guardsman" turned out to be John Howlett, originally from High Wycombe, a 23-year-old petty criminal who'd become estranged from his family. His body was later dismembered by Nilsen. Large body parts were put out with the rubbish; small pieces were flushed down the toilet.

Ten years before meeting Nilsen, Graham Archibald Allen, a good-looking, brown-haired 27-year-old Scot had made his way to London to find work. Instead he found the capital's seamy underbelly of drugs, alcohol, pickpocketing and possibly sex work. Becoming a father did little to straighten out his act. His relationship with the mother of his child was stormy and violent, fuelled, it seemed, by an unquenchable appetite for heroin. The last words his girlfriend said to him were, "Fuck off, and never come back!"

He didn't.

Allen had the misfortune to bump into Dennis Nilsen, a fellow Scot, sometime in September 1982 whilst making his way home in a drunkenly befuddled state. He was spotted by Nilsen who tried his luck. Accepting the offer of a warm meal and warm bed, he and Nilsen got a taxi back to Cranley Gardens. Allen got his meal, a large omelette prepared by Nilsen. Nilsen later gave a vague recollection to police investigators:

> "He started to eat the omelette. He must have eaten three-quarters of the omelette. I noticed he was sitting there and suddenly he appeared to be asleep or unconscious with a large piece of omelette hanging out of his mouth. I thought he must have been choking on it but I didn't hear him choking. He was indeed deeply unconscious. I sat down and had a drink. I approached him. I can't remember what I had in my hands now. I don't remember whether he was breathing or not, but the omelette was still protruding from his mouth. The plate was still on his lap. I removed that. I bent forward and I think I strangled him. I can't remember at this moment what I used ... I remember going forward and I remember he was dead ... If the omelette killed him I don't know, but anyway in going forward I intended to kill him. An omelette doesn't leave red marks on a neck. I suppose it must have been me."

Nilsen then stripped the body and masturbated over it. He moved it to the bathroom where it lay in the bath for three days, during which time Nilsen would continue to wash, brush his teeth use the toilet, all in the presence of the corpse.

On day four, he laid the body on a plastic sheet, decapitated, eviscerated and dismembered it. He sliced off the flesh in pieces and flushed them down the toilet. To deflesh the head, he boiled it for hours in a large pot on the stove. The remaining bones were placed into two large plastic bin bags and stored in the wardrobe. He never got around to properly disposing of them.

Nilsen's last victim was also a Scot. Originally from Perth, Stephen Sinclair, aged 20, had somehow made his way to London. A heroin addict, he also engaged in deliberate self-harming behaviours. On 26 January 1983, the blond-haired (dyed, originally ginger) young man encountered a kindly stranger on London's main shopping thoroughfare, Oxford Street. The man offered to buy him a hamburger. Sinclair accepted. Eventually, they ended back at Nilsen's Cranley Garden's flat, where they drank alcohol before Sinclair disappeared into the bathroom to inject heroin. Nilsen wrote in detail about what happened next. According to his description, it was the premeditated killing of a deeply intoxicated man, and the manner of it was very similar to the previous murders. After performing his *post mortem* rituals, Nilsen gazed at the body in admiration, feeling "at one" with it, not wishing to spoil it with everyday sex. He dressed it in his own clothes and kept it for several days before commencing the process of disposal. He never got to finish …

On Friday, 4 February 1983, Nilsen's neighbours contacted their letting agency, complaining that the drains at Cranley Gardens were blocked. In response, on Monday 7 February, a Dyno-Rod employee was despatched to the address to sort out the plumbing problem, only to find the drain packed with a flesh-like substance. Nilsen went down to speak with the worker and mentioned that it "looks like someone's been flushing down their Kentucky Fried Chicken". Later than evening, someone – presumably one of Nilsen's neighbours – knocked at the door of his flat. Nilsen was at home but he turned down the television and waited in silence until the visitor went away. He had a valid reason: the half-dismembered body of Stephen Sinclair lay on a plastic sheet on his kitchen floor; the head was simmering in a pot on the stove.

The next day, two Dyno-Rod employees arrived to deal with the blockage, only to find that it had been cleared overnight. This aroused their suspicions and they contacted the police. A few remaining pieces of flesh were analysed by a pathologist who declared them human.

When Nilsen returned home from work that evening the police were waiting for him. Three officers followed him into his flat where they immediately smelled the distinctive odour of decomposing flesh. One of the officers informed Nilsen that the blockage had been caused by human remains. Nilsen replied, "Good grief, how awful!" – at which the officer immediately responded: "Don't mess about. Where's the rest of the body?"

At this, Nilsen calmly led the officers to the two plastic bags in the wardrobe containing some of the remains of Graham Allen. He was arrested and brought to Hornsey Police State where he made a full confession. Asked how many bodies lay beneath the floor at any one time, he replied, "I'm not sure. I didn't do a stock-check." It was grim humour indeed. He admitted to having killed "twelve to thirteen" men at Melrose Avenue, three at Cranley Gardens, and to having attempted to kill approximately seven others, who'd either escaped or been brought to the brink of death by strangulation before being allowed to leave. He spoke about marvelling at the beauty of some of his victims' body, and that the sight of the skin of Kenneth Ockenden "almost brought me to tears". He cut a sad, lonely figure – a friendless man who took no pleasure from killing, only doing so in order to prevent his guests from leaving him.

Later that evening, detectives removed the plastic bags from Nilsen's flat and took them to Hornsey mortuary. Inside, they found parts of two dissected torsos and a plastic carrier-bag containing various internal organs. The second bag contain a human skull almost completed defleshed and a partial torso with the arms intact but the hands missing. A further search of the premises revealed a partial torso and a pair of legs stowed under the bath, and a skull and some bones in a tea chest in the living room.

The headlines splashed on the tabloid frontpages were lurid: "A CUT-UP CORPSE FOUND IN DRAIN", "16 MURDERS AT HOUSES OF HORROR", "NILSEN, THE EVIL BUTCHER WHO LOST COUNT OF HIS VICTIMS". Inevitably, a photo of Nilsen in uniform from his policing days made it into the papers, causing the Met not a little embarrassment.

But what became of Bleep? Some considered Nilsen's faithful dog, to have been his last victim. At the age of eight she was transferred to Battersea Dogs' Home where, rather than being rehoused to a new loving family, she was humanely destroyed by lethal injection. A newspaper reported that the small, scruffy, endlessly faithful mongrel bitch – bought for £1 from a pet shop in the mid-seventies – had "pined to death". Nilsen had fed, water, walked and comforted her. In custody, he'd asked about her welfare continually until being told of her eventual fate. She was mourned by Nilsen at least.

He stood trial in October 1983 for six counts of murder and one attempted murder, these being the victims who could be identified. The prosecution argued that Nilsen had been sane at the time of the murders, citing premeditation; his defence pleaded diminished responsibility rendering him incapable of murder, hoping for convictions only of manslaughter.

Several surviving victims testified for the prosecution. They cut pathetic figures and their accounts were damning. Only two psychiatrists testified on behalf of the defence, describing narcissistic and schizoid personality disorders. It mattered little. On 3 November, the jury retired to consider their verdict. The following day they returned: guilty of all charges.

He was transferred to Woodwood Scrubs. He didn't appeal the sentence of life imprisonment. In 1994, the sentence was replaced by a whole-life tariff. Nilsen accepted the ruling. He spent his time inside reading, writing, painting and composing music on a keyboard. His 400-page autobiography, *The History of a Drowning Boy*, remains unpublished. To the public, he became known as the "Kindly Killer", an epithet at which his victims' families must surely have raised a dubious eyebrow.

During his incarceration, Nilsen brought a judicial review against the prison service after complaining that some of the soft-corn gay pornographic magazines he subscribed to, *Vulcan* and *Him*, had had explicit photographs removed before being given to him. The legal case was dismissed after he couldn't establish that his human rights had been breached.

He died in great pain on 12 May 2018 after complaining of stomach problems. Cause of death was a blood clot on the lung and internal bleeding following surgery to repair a ruptured abdominal aortic aneurysm. Like many of his victims, his body was cremated.

# Jeffery Lionel Dahmer

(active 1978-1991)

IN THE EARLY HOURS of the morning of 27 May 1991, two black
teenage girls chanced upon an Asian boy on a Milwaukeean
street. He was naked and disoriented, lurching across the street
in front of them. Shocked, they approached him. Although he
was fluent in English, such was the boy's dazed state that he
could only mumble a few broken phrases. Then another girl
came along. Upon closer inspection, the three girls noticed that
the boy had scrapes on his knees, buttocks and shoulders, and a
thin rivulet of blood ran from his rectum down his inner thigh.
Clearly something horribly untoward was going on here. The
girls called the police and waited with the boy until they arrived.

Whilst they waited, a tall, blond man appeared carrying some
beers. He calmly approached the trio and attempted to resolve
the situation. The Asian youth, the blond newcomer said, was
his boyfriend, Jim. He explained that at weekends Jim was in
the habit of drinking too much. The blond man tried to convince
them that the youth was under his care, and he tried physically
to manoeuvre him away from the girls by taking his arm, yank-
ing and twisting it aggressively. The boy appeared to be struggling against the man. "This is nothing to do with you," the man
told the girls, but the girls were unconvinced of the older man's
good intentions. They told the man – who appeared to be in his
30s – that the police were on their way.

Then the police did arrive at the scene. The older man's demeanour visibly relaxed. He told the three officers – and the
teenage girls – that he and his boyfriend had had an earlier argument and that he always acted like this when he got upset. He
informed the officers that Jim was actually his 19-year-old lover
and that they were in a consensual relationship. He said that he
should take Jim back to his apartment.

The two teenage girls insisted that the youth was in danger.
However, to the police the incident looked like a domestic

squabble that had spilled out onto the street. One of the officers told the girls to "butt out", telling them that this was a domestic incident, and that they shouldn't interfere. They covered the youth's modesty with a towel, and then, after brief consideration, they decided to return with the youth to the man's apartment.

However, the youth didn't seem to want to return. He mumbled in protest and even reached out to the teenage girls for help. Nevertheless, the police had made up their mind that the youth should be returned to the older man's apartment and they decided to help bring him there by force. The three teenage girls looked on in horror. They couldn't understand why the police couldn't see what _they_ were seeing, but they were powerless to intervene and could only watch as the youth was physically dragged towards the nearby apartment block.

Once at his apartment, the man showed the police some photographs of the youth in his underwear to prove that the two were lovers. The police took a cursory look around, one of them peeking his head into the bedroom for a quick look. The place looked clean and tidy, they noticed. Sure, there was a strange smell – it seemed like excrement – but they decided not to investigate any further. Had they decided to take a closer look, the police would have found the three-day-old decomposing body of a man in the bedroom. Had they conducted a background check of the tall blond man they would've discovered he was a convicted child molester still under probation. Had they looked closer they would've realised that the man's "19-year-old lover" was in fact a 14-year-old boy who'd gone missing the day before. Instead, the police had walked them both back and personally delivered a serial killer's next victim straight into his clutches.

Lionel Herbert Dahmer and his wife Joyce Annette were not exactly made for each other, having polar opposite personalities and temperaments. Lionel was a quiet, introspective man, apparently incapable of demonstrating outward emotions, whilst Joyce, seemingly, was a tense, attention-needing seeker of arguments, frequently prone to outbursts of passionate hysteria. Nevertheless, the ostensibly mismatched couple married and their first son, Jeffrey Lionel Dahmer, entered the world on the afternoon of 21 May 1960 at the Evangelical Deconess Hospital in Milwaukee, Wisconsin. He was an eye-catching infant with bright blue eyes, a thick head of blond hair, full lips and even features, and he retained these good looks throughout his childhood and into his adult years.

The household that Jeffrey was born into was noisy with bickering and argument. Joyce, who'd herself been born into an environment of indifference and neglect (her father was a chronic alcohol), resolved that in adulthood she'd never to be the object of abandonment. The measure of her success, in her own eyes at least, was the level of response she was able to elicit from others. Hence, Joyce would pick fights and needle her husband with ceaseless regularity.

Lionel, on the other hand, was reserved and measured and seemed only to have interest in his studies.[1] His temper was difficult to rouse, but when it was awoken he could be just as fiery as his wife.

The birth of the infant Jeffrey, however, momentarily united the two delighted parents, and Joyce immediately began a scrapbook in which she recorded every milestone and development. In his early years, young Jeff's advance was as remarkable and unremarkable as those of most other children. He began to walk and talk, and was potty-trained – all at the appropriate times. He appeared to be on-track to becoming a well-adjusted normal toddler with every prospect of enjoying a happy childhood.

He showed an early interest in animals and owned goldfish

---

[1] Lionel began studying for a Bachelor of Science degree in Chemistry at Marquette University at the age of 23, and later studied for his Masters and Doctorate, and in doing so spent more time in laboratories than at home. Whether this was to fulfil his study and work obligations or to escape the scolding tongue of his wife is debatable.

and a turtle at the ripe age of 18 months, all of which he cared for solicitously. In order to accommodate Lionel's postgraduate work a house move brought the young family to Ames, Ohio. This also brought opportunities for Jeff to observe animals in their natural environment. He quickly made friends with a squirrel which he called Jiffy, which became tame enough to be fed from the windowsill. Soon Jeff was observing all different kinds of small wild animals.

At the age of two-and-a-half, Jeff went into hospital to have a double hernia treated, an operation that involved the sectioning of the boy's body. After his recovery from the effects of anaesthesia, he complained of a great pain in his groin area, an ordeal which lasted for a week. Indeed, he wondered aloud to his mother if his genitals had been cut off. The probing around by surgeons inside Jeff's body might possibly have had a more lasting effect than anyone could've envisaged at the time. Certainly, it was an intensely intimate act, the reverberations of which may have echoed down the years of Dahmer's lifespan.

At school, Jeff was a shy boy, and he remained shy throughout his life. All seemed normal, however, for the youngster was capable of getting into trouble for such childhood demeanours as stealing apples and coming home covered in dirt, which earned him a scolding from his mother. Near his house on the outskirts of Ames there was a scientific research centre. It enthralled Jeff to stand and watch the activities going on there. On one occasion, he saw a man don a long plastic glove and then thrust his arm, right up to the armpit, into the anus of a cow. On another occasion, he wandered up to a long shed, the steps of which were littered with the corpses of rats and mice. Upon opening the door of this building, Jeffery witnessed a massive multitude of rats and mice suddenly scurrying towards the corners.

His fascination with animals grew. He was given many pets – mice, snakes, rabbits, a toad, a kitten – which captivated him enormously. One day he found an injured nighthawk and he took it home and nursed it to health. Around the same time, Jeff found some tiny bones beneath the crawlspace of his house. He called these bones "fiddlesticks" and in his endless play with them his imagination grew. He began to feel the "fiddlesticks" inside his own pets, and he wondered at the workings within.

Lionel then got a new job and this involved another move of house – to Doylestown, Ohio. For Jeff it was another move to another school. Buffy the kitten was sold in the process. Buffy wasn't the only casualty of the relocation. Inevitably, perhaps, Jeff's problems were only exacerbated; the shy boy's ability to make friends – already poor – now became worse, and he retreated into himself, becoming withdrawn, remote and aloof – "darkening his mood considerably", according to his father.[2]

When Jeff was six years old, Joyce was delivered of her second son. Jeff named him David. Joyce, however, was laid low with postnatal depression and a gloom pervaded the house. In compensation, Jeff was given a dog, which he called Frisky, and it was Frisky – not Davy – that had the boy's heart.

Joyce had always been a complainer. In each of the previous residences where the family had lived she complained about the noisy neighbours. Now she did so again. As a compromise, Lionel agreed to another move – the sixth – and the family relocated *yet again* to Bath Township, Ohio. This time no pet was left behind; Frisky came too. However, yet another relocation meant yet another change of school for Jeff, which meant having to make new friends. It's little wonder that now he retreated even further into himself.

Jeff did not take to the new school easily. He had difficulty developing trust and a couple of incidents at the new school seriously challenged and eroded his ability to open up to others. The first incident involved an oft-played childhood game when one child would pretend to choke another. Jeff, however, took his part too far and ended up half-strangling his playmate, who in turn went and told the teacher, resulting in Jeff being

---

[2] In Dahmer, Dr. L (1994) *A Father's Story*. William Morrow: New York

punished. In another incident, Jeff presented a favourite teacher with some tadpoles in a jar. The teacher acted delighted, thanking Jeff profusely. However, Jeff was later to discover that the teacher had given the tadpoles to another pupil. When he realised this, Jeff poured motor oil into the jar, killing the tadpoles. His thinking was that if the teacher didn't want them then no one could have them. These events were not the *source* of Dahmer's difficulty with trust, but they certainly point to the consequences.

Jeff's fascination with animals and their inner workings remained unabated. At home, he collected insects and kept them in jars. He collected roadkills and brought them home to study, dismembering them and keeping their constituent parts in jars. On one occasion, he decapitated a dog and put its head on a stick in the forest. The body he nailed to a tree. His explanation for these activities was that he wanted to see how animals "fitted together". Despite all this, if one discounts the childish incident with the tadpoles, it's not thought that Dahmer showed cruelty to live animals. In fact, he was later to recall his relationship with another boy, a friend from school. The friend owned a car, and he would take Jeff out driving. The friend had a pleasure which Jeff did not approve of: if he spotted a dog on the road he would accelerate towards it and deliberately run it over. In one day, Jeff recalled, the friend drove over four dogs. Jeff remembered one incident when the friend hit a beagle puppy which flipped over the hood of the car and ended up behind them. Jeff recalled seeing the dog run off with a terrified look upon its face. The incident sickened him and he would never forget the reproachful look in the injured animal's eyes.

At school, Jeff continued to be quiet and introspective. He had a small group of friends and seemed to have been quite popular. This may have been in part to the fact that others saw him as a joker. Occasionally in class, Jeff would let out loud, unprompted yelps for the amusement of his peers. He also staged pranks, such as feigning a seizure or simulating cerebral palsy at the local mall. To other pupils, however, he was seen as an outcast and he rarely spoke to them. To cope with his crippling shyness, Jeff began drinking alcohol. By the time he was 14, he would come to school already drunk, often taking swigs from a bottle of hard liquor throughout the day. It was his "medicine" he told a classmate. Teachers, nevertheless, saw him as polite and intelligent, and he certainly had the abilities to succeed. However, he only managed average grades, but as he progressed through the school years even these declined.

Jeff realised he was gay when he reached puberty. He had a tentative exploratory relationship with a neighbour at the age of around 13, but by the age of 17 he was still sexually inexperienced. Then he discovered gay pornography and masturbated regularly to the images of the athletic bodies of young men on display. He wanted to meet such a man and explore that man's body, but he didn't know how he could contrive any such encounter. Anyway, he didn't want to have a personal interaction with the man; he simply wanted to have the man's body *there*, for Jeff to do with as he pleased. He wanted a completely available, passive partner.

What seemed an impossibility to Jeff in real life then became a fertile source for his imagination. Internally, his fantasy life was running riot, and soon the ideas in his head started to take on a sinister and ominous overtone. The kernel of an idea began to take seed in Jeff's head. A jogger used to run past the Dahmer residence on West Bath Road every morning, and this man had the sort of physique which interested Jeff. He planned to attack the man from behind, to render him unconscious and capture him so that he'd have the man's unresisting body completely under his control. His strategy reached the stage where he lay in wait for the man to jog past. However, on that occasion, when Jeff intended to carry out his plan, the jogger, by happy happenstance, had decided to go another route. Instead, Jeff left the bushes, took his baseball bat and returned home disappointed. The fantasies, however – well, they persisted …

By now, the Dahmer parents' marriage had stalled and was on the brink of dissolution. Lionel had discovered that Joyce had

had an affair and the two were barely on speaking terms. In 1978, when Dahmer was 18, his parents finally divorced. Lionel was living temporarily in a nearby motel and Joyce had loaded the car and moved herself and David to Wisconsin. Consequently, Dahmer now had the house in Bath all to himself.

On 18 June 1978, he asked his father if he could borrow the car, saying that he wanted to go to the cinema. Lionel agreed. Dahmer collected the car from his father and later that sunny afternoon he was driving along the highway. Then he saw him – a young man walking towards him along the side of the road, wearing pale blue jeans and white tennis shoes, and, because of the heat of the day, his shirt was off. He had his thumb stuck out in the universal signal of the hitchhiker.

Immediately, Dahmer's attention was aroused. The young man had dark, shoulder-length hair and looked quite young – _his_ age, in fact. Dahmer passed the young man by and drove on for a moment. The fantasises reared up in his head as he drove. It was the bare chest. To him, this seemed like an invitation. After a while, Dahmer turned his car around and came back again. As he reached the hitchhiker he pulled over. The two got talking. Dahmer told the hitchhiker he wasn't going anywhere in particular and he invited the young man back to his house. He had the place to himself, he said. They could have beer and marijuana and listen to music. The young man agreed and jumped in the car. Dahmer drove off. The man introduced himself as Steve.

Steven Mark Hicks was three days off his 19th birthday. He was from Cuyahoga Falls, Summit County, Ohio and he was on his way to a rock concert in nearby Lockwood Corners. Hicks was white and, unfortunately for Dahmer, straight. This much became apparent during their drinking session together for the subject of girlfriends and moving on was very much on Hicks's mind. Eventually, Hicks' conversation turned to his more imminent departure. This scared Dahmer. All _he_ wanted to do was ask his new friend to stay, take off his shirt and allow Dahmer to indulge his homosexual caprices.

After a few hours of drinking, Hicks told his host that it was getting late and he should be going. Dahmer couldn't allow that. The frustration within him was overwhelming. He went down to the cellar and when he returned he had the heavy bar from a dumb-bell in his hand. As Hicks sat on a chair, Dahmer approached from behind. With a wide swing, he struck his guest on the back of the head with the weighty bar. Hicks jolted, momentarily stunned, but then he got up in astonishment. They fell into a scuffle. Dahmer struck Hicks again and this time the youth went down permanently. To complete the act Dahmer strangled Hicks until he was dead. Then he stripped the clothes from Hicks' body and kissed and caressed it. And then, as he stood above the corpse, he masturbated over it.

After climaxing, he realised what he'd done. He dragged the body down to the basement. Then panic set in. He spent a sleepless night wondering how he could get away with it. He came up with an answer. In the morning, he cut the corpse open – just as he'd done with his roadkill finds – and dismembered the body, placing the parts into trash bags and storing them in the crawlspace beneath the house. He burned any of Hicks' personal identifiers in a fire some distance away from the house.

All through the following day, Dahmer wondered how to properly dispose of the body. In the end, he decided to dump it in a ravine several miles away. To do this he got drunk and loaded the car with the plastic bags. In the early hours of the morning, he began his 10-mile journey.

At around 03:00 he was stopped by a police car. Dahmer had been crossing the middle line of the motorway and the cop thought he might've been drunk. The cop called for backup and a second officer arrived. Meanwhile, Dahmer was asked to tap the end of his nose with his finger. In the days before breathalysers this was considered a reliable indicator of intoxication. Dahmer apparently did this to the officer's satisfaction. However, just before they left, one of the officers shone his torch into the back of Dahmer's car. *What was in the bags?* he wanted to know. Just some trash, Dahmer told him. *Why was he out so late?* Because his parents had been arguing and he couldn't sleep. Again, this seemed to satisfy the officer and Dahmer was given a ticket for erratic driving and allowed to leave.

What happened next took Dahmer over the final step towards madness. Back home, he removed Hicks' head from the bag, brought it upstairs to his bedroom, set it on the floor in front of him and masturbated, whilst all the time looking at it.

Over the next days, Dahmer disposed of the limbs and torso by dissolving the flesh in acid and flushing the solution down the toilet. He crushed Hicks' "fiddlesticks" with a sledgehammer and scattered the fragments in the woods behind his house. The knife used for the dismemberment was thrown into a river. He kept the head for a while, only disposing of it when it began to become putrid. His life would be forever changed after that impulsive act and he knew it. "Nothing's been normal since then," he was later to say, with not a little understated irony. "It taints your whole life."

Dahmer enrolled at Ohio State University in August 1978, hoping to major in business. On a first visit by Lionel, his son appeared to be doing well. But it was an illusion. On a second surprise visit, Lionel found the room strewn with empty alcohol bottles. Dahmer's alcohol use was uncontained. His grades had slipped from mediocre to terrible, and inevitably he dropped out of college before the end of the first term.

His choices were limited. Either he get a job or he join one of the armed services. He resignedly chose the latter, urged along by his father, joining the United States Army in January 1979 with a view to train as a medical specialist.

Lionel wrote of his astonishment at the transformation in Jeff after his initial six-month spell away from home:

*This new, completely refurbished Jeff was a handsome, broad-shouldered young man who smiled brightly when he stepped off the bus. His hair was close-cropped, his clothes neat and orderly. More importantly, perhaps, there was not so much as a hint of liquor on his breath.*

It didn't last long. Dahmer was then sent to Germany. Whilst stationed at Baumholder, it later emerged, Dahmer drugged, raped and tortured two fellow servicemen. But it was due to his chronic alcohol abuse that his superiors felt that a life in the forces was not for Dahmer and he was honourably discharged on 24 March 1981. His personal effects ended up back at the house in Ohio but Dahmer himself did not. He'd been provided with a plane ticket to anywhere in the country: he'd chosen Miami Beach, Florida, having felt "tired of the cold".

There, Dahmer found work in a sandwich and pizza place and rented a room in a motel. However, most of his money was spent on alcohol and soon he lost the room after defaulting on the rent payments. He briefly toyed with the idea of marrying Mary, an English illegal immigrant, so that she could obtain a green card, but his father convinced him not to do so. Now homeless, Dahmer slept on the beach for a while, although still continuing to work at the shop. Soon, however, he tired of his experiment with freedom; he called his father and asked to return home.

When Jeff stepped off the plane, his father immediately recognised that his son was drunk. Independence had not dampened his thirst and the drinking continued, leading to arrests and charges for being drunk and disorderly. In due course, after some discussion, Lionel and his new fiancée decided it would do Jeff some good to spend some time with his paternal grandmother in West Allis, Wisconsin. He'd always had a good relationship with the elderly lady and it was hoped that a change of scenery might persuade him to live more responsibly.

Dahmer quickly realised that life at his grandmother's house suited him. The relationships between the pair was harmonious, and for a while the elderly woman's influence proved stabilising. Dahmer did work around the house and garden; he accompanied his grandmother to church; he even got a job as a phlebotomist at the Milwaukee Blood Plasma Center.

Dahmer was attempting to live a normal life. However, two striking incidents now occurred that showed the difficulties he was facing in suppressing his inner compulsions. The first occurred during his employment at the blood plasma centre, he recalled, when he secreted a phial of freshly donated blood, took it onto the roof and drank it. He did not like the taste and spat it out, but all the same, he'd now taken that first tentative step towards the consumption of another one's body matter. Not long after this, Dahmer was arrested for indecent exposure. On 7 August 1982, at a local park, he flashed his genitals at a crowd of over 20 women and children. He was given probation and fined $50 for the crime.

The second incident occurred in January 1985 and was perhaps the more disruptive. By now Dahmer had lost his phlebotomy job and was working the night shift at the Milwaukee Ambrosia Chocolate Factory. Shortly after commencing this employment, he was sitting in a public library when a man walked past Dahmer and tossed a note into his lap. The note invited Dahmer to "meet me in the second-floor bathroom" with the offer of a blow-job. Dahmer, by now aged 25, was still a virgin. The note had surprised him and he did not take up the proposition of a sexual dalliance. However, the incident stirred and re-ignited the sexual fantasies he'd long repressed, and soon he was masturbating more than ever, which in turn led to attendance at local gay bars and gay saunas. At the saunas, he became frustrated by the movements of his partners' during sex and so he took to covertly sedating them with sleeping medication. After around 12 such incidents of "spiking", the bathhouse workers started to become wise to it. It reached a head when one of Dahmer's "dates" became unrevivable and had to be removed to hospital, where he lay sleeping for a week. At this point the bathhouse revoked Dahmer's membership.

Shortly after this, he read about the death of an 18-year-old youth in a newspaper obituary column. He attended the funeral and then began to fantasise about disinterring the body and taking it home for sexual experimentation. He was later to tell various psychiatrists that he'd even got as far as attempting to dig up the grave but found that the ground was too frozen to continue. Also, in a vivid illustration of his fantasies of control and dominance, he stole a plastic male mannequin from a store, using the item as a sexual stimulus until his grandmother became so anxious that he removed it from the house.

Dahmer's urges were becoming more irresistible. On one occasion, David, now 18, came to stay at his grandmother's house for two nights and the two brothers were obliged to share a bed. During the night, Jeff felt the need to interact with an unconscious, prostate body and here, right beside him, was one. His hands began to wander over David's body. The next morning David let Jeff know in no uncertain terms that he was not happy about what had happened. The incident was not repeated.

Becoming more and more fascinated with the lifeless, Dahmer bought a copy of the video-nasty *Faces of Death*, which purportedly showed documentary footage of death and how it is viewed in various cultures. One of its shock-exploitation features included footage of the autopsy of a young man who'd been killed in war. In the detailed footage, the victim's skull was opened and the brain removed. Dahmer rewound and watched this scene many times, not understanding why he'd become so intrigued by it.

After being banned from the bathhouses, Dahmer resorted to taking sexual partners to hotels. On 20 November 1987, he encountered a blond, 24-year-old restaurant worker at a local bar and invited him to come back to the Ambassador Hotel. The next morning, Steven Tuomi was lying dead on the bed of the rented room, his body "black and blue", chest "crushed in" and blood leaking from the mouth. Dahmer claimed that he had no recollection of having harmed Tuomi, that he'd planned only to drug and rape his date, but his own extensively bruised fists and forearm gave testament to a violent assault.

A newly slain corpse in a hotel room caused Dahmer "shock, horror, panic" – and also somewhat of a problem. To deal with it, he purchased a large suitcase and transported the body to his grandmother's house. A week later, he decapitated and dismembered the body, filleted the flesh from the bones, cut it into small chunks and placed it into plastic bags which he later disposed of in the trash. The head he kept for two weeks before boiling it in an industrial detergent. It was an attempt to preserve the skull, but it became brittle in the process and in the end he pulverised it and disposed of the pieces. Tuomi's relatives only discovered what had happened to him after Dahmer's later arrest and subsequent confession.

Both of Dahmer's murders, according to him, had been "accidental", but he was soon to cross the point of no return. From now on he would actively seek victims, most of whom he'd encounter in or around gay bars.

Two months after killing Tuomi, on 17 January 1988, Dahmer lured 14-year-old James "Jamie" Doxtator, a Native American sex worker, back to his grandmother's house with the offer of $50 to pose as a nude model and spend the night with him. Mrs Dahmer was a sound sleeper and never awoke during the night, so Jeff felt it safe to bring a stranger back. After well over an hour of touching, undressing, mutually masturbating and then fellating each other, the teenager told his new friend that he must be getting home. Dahmer couldn't allow that to happen. He mixed a drink laden with sleeping tablets and tranquillisers and gave it to Jamie. The two then kissed repeatedly, but half-an-hour later the youth was asleep in Dahmer's lap. Dahmer then carried the teenager down to the basement, and it's probable that he'd already had prior ideas of what was going to happen there.

In the basement, Dahmer laid the deeply sleeping boy's body down on a sheet on the floor and caressed and kissed it. Then, because he did not want the boy to leave, Dahmer strangled him. He continued to hold and caress the body until the sun came up. Then he hid it in the fruit-cellar where it stayed for several days.

Dahmer visited Jamie's body several times, but after about four days it'd begun to smell, and his grandmother had begun to comment upon the odour. He had to wait until the following Sunday, the day his grandmother went to church, until he found the opportunity to dismember the body and dispose of it, treating it in a manner similar to which he'd treated Tuomi.

Two months later, in an almost identically replicated murder,

Dahmer met Richard Guerrero, aged 23-24, outside a local gay bar and lured him back to his grandmother's house with an offer of $50. There, the Hispanic bisexual man was drugged with sleeping tablets and strangled with a leather belt. Dahmer performed oral sex on the dead body, which was disposed of the next day in similar fashion to the two previous murders. Dahmer's victim pattern was now established. Most of his prey from this point onwards would continue to be young, good-looking males with dark skin whom he'd meet in local gay bars.

The next weekend, a young man had a lucky escape. Like his previous victims, Dahmer met Ronald Flowers, a handsome, 24-year-old black man, outside a gay club. The two got talking and during the conversation Flowers mentioned that his car battery was flat. Dahmer invited Flowers to get a cab with him back to his grandmother's house, the plan being that Jeff could retrieve his own car and then return with Flowers to his own vehicle and help him jumpstart it. This Flowers agreed to.

We have an insight into the state of mind of Dahmer preceding his murderous forays, for in this case the potential victim survived to tell his tale. Flowers reported that during the cab ride to West Allis he quickly formed the opinion that Dahmer had a gloomy disposition, the focus of his conversation being about how much he hated his job and how he didn't get along with his family. He noticed that Dahmer instructed the cab driver to drop them off two blocks from his grandmother's house. This, Dahmer explained, was to avoid awakening his grandmother. Flowers' suspicions, he remembered, were further aroused when he didn't notice a car outside Dahmer's house.

As they entered the house a voice came from upstairs. Mrs Dahmer called out "Is that you, Jeff?" and, although Dahmer replied in a manner that suggested he was alone ("I'm just going to make myself a cup of coffee"), he couldn't ascertain whether or not his grandmother had observed that Dahmer actually did have company. Flowers' nervousness increased as he sat in the kitchen with his host. Dahmer's hands shook and he studiously avoided his guest' eyes. His demeanour wasn't that of a relaxed man. As they had coffee, Flowers wondered how soon he could get away from this house, but soon he was becoming sleepy …

He woke up in hospital two days later. There, he was told that he'd been found in a field and brought by ambulance to the emergency department. Some of his items were missing – some jewellery and $200 in cash – but there was no sign of sexual assault. When he got home, Flowers noticed bruising around his neck, and that his underpants were on inside-out.

Flowers made a complaint to the police but a denial from Dahmer and a dearth of evidence thwarted any case against him. Flowers saw Dahmer three months later at a gay club and was prevented from punching him by the intervention of his friends. Later, when Flowers saw Dahmer and a black man about to get into a cab, he shouted, "Don't go with him, he's fucking crazy," whereupon the unknown black man withdrew from the scene, more than likely having just escaped a narrow brush with death.

At last, probably as a result of being questioned by the police in the Flowers investigation, Mrs Dahmer became discontent with her grandson's drinking and bringing home strange men. Although she could scarcely have been aware of its cause, the old lady was also unhappy with the strange odour emanating from the basement. She asked Jeff to leave.

Dahmer then took on the lease of a small apartment on North 25th Street and moved in on 25 September 1988. It was a high crime area (which Dahmer's arrival did little to change), and the predominant characteristic of the local populace was that they were black. Living in the area, Dahmer was an uncommon Caucasian, a fact which concerned him little. The apartment was close to his workplace and it was reasonably priced. He quickly settled in. A little *too* quickly. Within one day of moving into his apartment, Dahmer was arrested for drugging and sexually molesting a 13-year-old boy he'd lured there … and, four months later, there followed a similar offence, along with a subsequent conviction.

After two months, during a 10-day absence from work, Dahmer moved temporarily back to this grandmother's house.

There, he strangled his fifth victim, a 24-year-old mixed-race aspiring model called Anthony Lee Sears whom Dahmer had met outside a gay bar. The following morning, Dahmer decapitated Sears' body in his grandmother's bathtub before skinning the corpse. This was the first victim whose body parts Dahmer permanently retained: he kept the head and genitalia preserved in a jar which he stored in his work locker.

In January 1989, Dahmer was sentenced to five years' probation and one year in a house of correction for second-degree sexual offence crimes after having enticed a child, 14-year-old Somsack Sinthasomophone, to his apartment for a nude photography session. He was also required to sign the sex register. Crucially, however, he was permitted work release so that he could keep his job. He spent a period of only six days in custody following this misdemeanour. Had he served a longer jail sentence, it's probable that this would've led to the discovery of the body parts in his work locker, which would've curtailed his murderous career. However, again, luck was on Dahmer's side.

This was Dahmer's *second* close brush with the law, and it could easily have led to his undoing. During his anxiety-ridden six-day period of incarceration his apartment was searched by the police. They found and removed the Polaroid camera and two nude photos, along with some male pornography and sleeping tablets, but they failed to find the skull of Richard Guerrero.

Upon his release from work camp, Dahmer returned briefly to his grandmother's house before moving, on 14 May 1990, into another apartment on North 25th Street, taking Sears' body parts along with him. It was yet another step in Dahmer's decline. Within a week, another victim was dead.

Aged 33, Raymond Lamont "Ray" Smith, for some inexplicable reason, also went by the moniker "Ricky Beeks". By his own admission, he was a hustler who, although not homosexual himself, was amenable to providing men with sex for money. His reputation was such that he was already known to clients by the name "Cash D", a name which he'd had tattooed on his chest. He was black, muscular and good-looking. Dahmer spotted him immediately. On 20 May 1990, he followed his well-established *M.O.* and by the end of the night "Cash D" was dead.

The next morning, Dahmer rushed out to purchase a new Polaroid camera with which he took several suggestively posed photographs of "Cash D", retaining this macabre pornography as keepsakes. His home-made pornography of posed, naked men with smooth, muscular bodies became integral to his sexual fantasies and enabled him to reach satisfactory masturbatory climax. Living in a second-floor apartment with neighbours close by, smashing his dead victim's bones wasn't an option. After he dismembered "Cash D's" body, Dahmer boiled the arms, legs and torso in a large steel kettle, and then dissolved the remainder – minus the skull – in a barrel filled with acid. He spray-painted the skull and placed it alongside Sears' in a metal cabinet. The rest of the body, once it had degraded into a slushy morass, got flushed down the toilet.

A week after killing "Cash D", Dahmer invited another man back to his apartment. This time, however, Dahmer inadvertently drank the wrong cup of coffee and *he himself* fell into a deep sleep. When he awoke the next day he was poorer by $300 and missing some clothes and a watch. Dahmer didn't report the crime and his potential victim has never come forward.

Now the rate of murder escalated. Edward "Eddie" Warren "Sheikh" Smith, aged 27, was next; but rather than bleach the bones, Dahmer instead kept the body in his freezer for several months in the hope that the skeleton would retain moisture, but when he placed the skull in the oven to dry it exploded, and Dahmer later complained to the police that he felt "rotten" for not having been able to retain any body parts. By now, however, he'd given up all hope and pretence of dislodging his intrusive thoughts, which had become stronger and more urgent, and he welcomed them. He was now embracing his "dark side", and it was *this* part of himself that dominated the quiet, mild-mannered man he outwardly presented to others. He was later to tell his psychiatrist, Dr Kenneth Smail:

*"These thoughts are very powerful, very destructive, and they do not leave. They're not the kind of thoughts you can just shake your head and they're gone. They do not leave ... After the fear and the terror of what I'd done [at the Ambassador Hotel], which took about a month or two, I started it all over again. From time to time there was a craving, a hunger. I don't know how to describe it – a compulsion – and I just kept doing it, doing it and doing it, whenever the opportunity presented itself."[3]*

The crimes, if possible, turned even darker. Twenty-two-year-old Ernest Marquez Miller had the misfortune to meet Dahmer on 2 September 1990. Dahmer was especially attracted to the dance student's physique, and Miller in turn agreed to allow this handsome stranger to listen to his heart and stomach for $50.

Back at his apartment, Dahmer also attempted to perform oral sex. Miller informed him, "That'll cost you extra." Dahmer laced Miller's drink with the only two sedative pills he had left. On this occasion, he was obliged to kill his prey by severing the carotid artery. Miller bled to death, after which Dahmer photographed the body, dismembered it in the bath, and kissed and talked to the severed head. He flayed parts of the flesh from the body and kept it in the freezer for later consumption. The head was later denuded of flesh and coated with enamel. By now, Dahmer had amassed a considerable collection of skeletons and skulls, which he planned to display in a private "shrine".

Three weeks later, he met and enticed back to his apartment 22-year-old David Courtney Thomas with the promise of money for posing nude for photos. After lacing Thomas' drink with sedatives, Dahmer decided he "wasn't my type". However, he was afraid to allow his victim to awaken lest he become angry

---

[3] In: Masters, B. (1993) *The Shrine of Jeffrey Dahmer*. London: Hodder and Stroughton Ltd.

at having been drugged and so he strangled and dismembered him, photographing the process but keeping no body parts afterwards.

Although he tried at least five times, five months were to pass before Dahmer was able to lure his next victim back to his apartment. Now, as Dahmer descended further in madness and unreason, the rate of his crimes escalated. Accepting an offer of money in exchange for posing nude and sex, Curtis Durrell Straughter, aged 17, accompanied Dahmer back to his apartment in February 1991. Dahmer strangled him with a black leather strap (which he'd bought for this specific purpose) and then dismembered the body, taking many photographs of the process and retaining the skull, hands and genitals.

On 7 April 1991, Dahmer drugged 19-year-old Errol Lindsey, who was heterosexual, rending him unconscious. Now beyond repair, Dahmer drilled a hole into the back of Lindsey's skull in order to inject hydrochloric acid directly into the brain, hoping to induce a permanently unresisting state. Lindsey, however, awoke and said, "I have a headache. What time is it?" Dahmer duly strangled Lindsey again, this time killing him. He decapitated the body and flayed the skin off in one piece, reluctantly discarding it when it became too "musky". He kept the skull.

Dahmer actually "dated" a 31-year-old deaf-mute man, Tony Hughes, for around four days during the start of May 1991. The pair went out together and hung around the mall. It was the closest Dahmer ever got to a normal relationship. When Hughes told Jeff he had to go he seemed genuinely sad. They arranged to meet up again the next week. However, Dahmer felt unable to trust that he'd ever see his lover again and so strangled him on the Sunday evening before leaving for work. As Dahmer later told police, he wished he _had_ waited to see if Hughes would return. Hughes was Dahmer's 12th victim.

This had not been the first time that Dahmer toyed unsuccessfully with "dating", however. Shortly after having killed Eddie Smith, he met a 15-year-old part-time bus boy, Luis Pinet, who worked at a gay bar. In order to pique the youth's interest,

Dahmer offered him $200 to come back to his apartment for some nude photography. Luis, already drunk, agreed. Dahmer had already decided to kill him. However, he'd now run out of sleeping tablets and couldn't afford another prescription. Luis had a lucky escape. Instead, Dahmer went to an army surplus store and bought a rubber mallet with which he planned to subdue the boy. He had agreed to meet the youth at 12 o'clock. However, noon came and went and Luis did not arrive. It was his *second* close brush with death.

By chance, Dahmer met Luis again later that night at a gay bar. Luis explained the misunderstanding. He thought Dahmer had meant 12 o'clock *midnight*, and Luis had had every intention of meeting up. He went back to Dahmer's apartment for a second time. Whilst the boy was lying on his front, posing for photos, Dahmer struck him with the rubber mallet. "Obviously, he got upset about that," Dahmer would later mention. The two argued and Luis left. Ten minutes later he was back, asking Dahmer to lend him a few dollars for the bus home. Dahmer, now panicking over the thought of losing Luis again, grabbed him with the intent of strangling him. Luis, however, was too strong.

Bewilderingly, Luis and Dahmer both calmed down and sat down to discuss the evening's events. During this, Dahmer convinced Luis to let him tie his arms behind his back. Luis, however, was able to wriggle free of his binding, at which point Dahmer produced a large knife. Again, the two fell to talking things over until around seven o'clock in the morning, by which point Luis had promised he would not tell anyone about what had happened between them. Dahmer then walked the boy to the bus stop.

Luis *did* report the incident to the police and a false imprisonment report was filed. Unfortunately, it was not properly investigated. Had police made a search of Dahmer's apartment at this time they'd have found evidence of serious crimes and they could've put an end to them. Dahmer's luck was holding out.

Eventually, Dahmer's neighbours began to complain about the foul odours emanating from his apartment. Additionally, they were also perturbed by the sounds of objects falling and occasional noises of a chainsaw. The building manager approached his troublesome tenant about the smell, which Dahmer explained away as spoiled food from a faulty freezer and dead fish from his tropical fish tank. He didn't mention the putrefying body of Tony Hughes, a contributing factor to the miasma.

It was into this fetid atmosphere that Dahmer invited 14-year-old Konerak Sinthasomphone.[4] Dahmer lured Konerak to his apartment, photographed him in his underwear, and drugged and fellated him. Whilst the boy was still conscious, Dahmer drilled a hole in his skull and injected hydrochloric acid into the frontal lobe. To complete this nightmarish scenario, Dahmer led him into the bedroom where the bloated, naked body of Tony Hughes still lay. Probably due to the effects of the ad-hoc lobotomy and the sedatives he'd ingested Konerak didn't react to seeing this. Instead he lapsed into unconsciousness. Dahmer sat alongside the youth for a while, drinking several beers before deciding to go out for a drink at a bar. Whilst out, he also dropped into a store to buy some beers.

As he was returning to his apartment, Dahmer became annoyed to find Konerak in the street, naked and bleeding, in the company of three distressed teenage girls. He was further disconcerted to discover that the police were on their way. When they arrived, Dahmer managed to keep his cool and explained that the youth – he called him "Jim" – was his boyfriend and they'd had a domestic tiff.

It would be Dahmer's final run of luck with the police. They escorted the pair back to Dahmer's apartment, took a cursory look around, noted the strange smell reminiscent of excrement (caused by Hughes' decomposing body), and then, before

---

[4] By dreadful coincidence, Konerak was the younger brother of Somsack Sinthasomphone, the sexual assault of whom had nearly sent Dahmer to jail in January the previous year.

departing, told the older man to "take good care" of his apparently drunk friend.

Dahmer "took good care" of his friend all right – by injecting a fatal dose of acid into his skull. The following morning, he took a day's leave from work and dismantled both of the bodies he now had in his possession, retaining two skulls.

Twenty-year-old black man Matt Cleveland Turner was next, drugged and strangled to death on 30 June 1991. Parts of his body were retained in plastic bags in the freezer. Then, five days, later Jeremiah B. Weinberger, aged 23, was invited to spend the weekend with Dahmer at his apartment. There, his host drugged him and injected boiling water into his skull. Unsurprisingly, this grim experiment to turn a man into a zombie also failed. Weinberger fell into a coma, dying two days later with his eyes still open. Dahmer dealt with the body by placing it into a 57-gallon drum filled with acid.

Within a week, Oliver Joseph Lacy, 24, was next to die. Dahmer drugged and strangled the black body-building enthusiast, sodomising his toned form *during* the dismemberment process. He then stored the heart in the refrigerator.

Joseph Arthur Bradehoft, 25, suffered a similar fate on 19 July 1991. The father-of-three had been looking for work in Milwaukee when he fell victim to Dahmer after agreeing to pose nude for money. He would turn out to be Dahmer's final murder victim. His head was placed in the fridge whilst his torso was stored in the drum alongside Weinberger.

By 22 July 1991, Dahmer's unhingement was complete. He'd just finished dismembering his latest victim and was wandering the streets outside, approaching men he found attractive and offering them money in exchange for posing nude. Rebuffed several times, he now went to the Grand Avenue Mall. There, he approached a group of three men, one of whom he'd casually spoken to previously. He invited them to join him for a nude photography session, offering them $100 as a procurement. *Does it involve sex?* one of them asked. *Just handcuffs*, came the reply. Dahmer told them he lived at the Ambassador Hotel.

The four wandered towards a liquor store, which Dahmer entered in order to buy some rum and coke.

After he returned, there was a brief conversation. Two of the friends decided to go off to find their girlfriends, but one of the men, Tracy Edwards, aged 23, decided go along with the stranger. They got into a cab and drove off. Meanwhile, Edward's two friends returned in order to warn him not to do anything foolhardy. Not finding him, the two friends went to the Ambassador Hotel and waited there for one-and-a-half hours for Edwards to turn up.

They were right to be worried. Their friend had instead gone with Dahmer to his Oxford Apartments residence. There, Edwards couldn't fail to notice the sickening stench. Whilst Edwards' back was turned as he looked at the tropical fish tank, Dahmer approached him from behind and slammed a handcuff on his wrist. He attempted to cuff the second wrist but failed. The failure probably saved Edwards' life. Dahmer told him to accompany him to the bedroom, which he did. In the bedroom, Dahmer produced a knife, telling Edwards' he intended to take some nude photos of him. With incredible presence of mind, Edwards attempted to appease Dahmer by saying he *would* do so, but only if Dahmer put down the knife. In order to show his compliance, Edwards removed his shirt. When Dahmer was momentarily distracted, Edwards kicked the knife beneath the bed.

Dahmer then turned his attention to the television – a favourite video, *The Exorcist II*, was playing. He rocked back and forth at the edge of the bed whilst chanting to himself as if in a deep trance. After a moment, his attention returned to Edwards. He placed his head on his guest's chest and listened to the heartbeat. It soon became clear to Edwards that he was in the company of a madman. The next words his host spoke confirmed it: "I'm going to eat your heart."

Then there were some very tense moments for Edwards as he attempted to placate Dahmer by insisting he was his friend, that he would stay with him, whilst looking for any opportunity to escape. He asked to use the bathroom; he asked to sit in the living room where there was air-conditioning. And he asked to use the bathroom a second time. When Dahmer arose from the couch, Edwards noticed he wasn't holding the handcuffs. Suddenly, he punched Dahmer and rushed for the front door. Dahmer pursued and caught him by the wrist, but Edwards was able to make his escape and dashed onto the street. There, he flagged down two policemen, told them that some "freak" had handcuffed him and asked them to remove it. The officers' key failed to unlock the cuffs, so Edwards led them back to apartment no. 213.

Dahmer appeared now to have come back to his senses. He invited the trio at his door inside. At this point, Edwards told the story of what had just happened to him, including the fact that this madman had brandished a knife. One of the officers, Rolf Mueller, went towards the bedroom to look for the knife but Dahmer attempted to intercept him. "Back off," Mueller told him, and went into the bedroom. He looked under the bed and found the knife. Upon standing up again, he noticed an open drawer. Inside the drawer were some Polaroid photos. A closer inspection revealed the gruesome subjects of the photos – severed heads and dismembered human bodies, in different stages of decomposition, all of which appeared to have been taken in the apartment in which he now stood. In shock, he went back to his partner, taking some on the Polaroids with him. "These are for real," Mueller said.

Dahmer immediately fought to resist arrest but he was quickly overpowered and cuffed. For him it was the end of a murderous campaign claiming 17 lives.

Tracy Edwards then informed the officers of something that Dahmer had told him earlier, as he'd approached the fridge to get a beer – that there was something inside that he'd not believe. Intrigued, Mueller went to the fridge and looked inside. Dahmer hadn't been exaggerating; the officer could scarcely believe it himself. On the bottom shelf, in a box, was the head of a black man. He quickly closed the door and returned to the living room. Dahmer, still detained on the floor, turned his head and muttered to himself: "For what I did I should be dead."

A more detailed search of the property revealed four severed heads in the kitchen and seven skulls in the bedroom. Body parts, including two human hearts, were wrapped in plastic bags in the refrigerator. Blood drippings had collected in the tray at the bottom of the fridge. In the freezer was an entire torso, plus further bags of human organs. Elsewhere in the apartment were severed hands, preserved penises, scalps and, in the 57-gallon drum, three dismembered torsos. A number of Polaroid photos – total 74 – illustrated the posing and dismemberment of several male individuals, the majority of them black or Hispanic in appearance.

Dahmer's confession would be complete and detailed. He even admitted to having killed victims for which the investigators didn't have bodies, beginning with Steven Hicks in Ohio (easily recalling the name because "you don't forget your first one"), and also including Steven Tuomi, whom Dahmer could not remember killing, and David Thomas, the remains of whom would never be found.

He spoke about going out with the intention of killing already in his head. He would sit in bars alone, watching different individuals, choosing one whom he found attractive. He said that it didn't matter the ethnic heritage of the man, as long as they met his preferred profile – mid-teen to mid-20s, slender build with smooth skin. He admitted to killing them by strangulation, posing the dead bodies with the torsos typically thrust upwards to display the chest. He confessed to necrophilic activities with his victims, including fondling and sexually engaging with the viscera, raping the dead bodies and cannibalising some parts, including the heart, livers and biceps.

The black table upon which he had kept his fish tank, Dahmer also explained, was to have been used as a shrine. He'd planned to decorate it with painted skulls and incense sticks and adorn it at each side with complete skeletons. He'd wanted to place it directly in front of his black leather chair so that he could sit and look at it and draw power from it. It was to be "a place for meditation".

The trial lasted two weeks. Dahmer pleaded guilty to 15 counts of first-degree murder. His defence argued that he'd been driven insane due to necrophilic compulsions, mitigated by borderline and schizotypal personality disorders, alcohol dependence and psychotic disorder. Perhaps the very summation of his bizarre acts would provide evidence enough!

Predictably, the prosecution rejected the argument of insanity, pointing to a pattern of cunning premeditation and preparedness, reasoning that the use of alcohol prior to killing contraindicated compulsion: "If he had a compulsion to kill he would not have to drink alcohol."

On 15 February 1992, the jury ruled that Dahmer was sane and gave a verdict of guilty on all charges, although two jurors signified their dissent. A capital punishment was off the cards in Wisconsin. He was sentenced to life in prison.

Three months later, Dahmer was extradited to Ohio and tried for the murder of Steven Hicks. He pleaded guilty to the crime and was sentenced to a further life sentence.

For the first year of his incarceration at the Columbia Correctional Institution, Dahmer was held in solitary confinement following concerns that he'd be attacked by fellow inmates. Then he was transferred to a less secure unit. Here, he was assigned toilet-cleaning duties. He turned to religion and was baptised as a born-again Christian.

> *"If a person doesn't think that there is a God to be accountable to, then what's the point of trying to modify your behaviour to keep it within acceptable ranges? That's how I thought anyway."*

He questioned whether being allowed to live was an affront to God, and it was said that he was remorseful and longed for his own death.

He survived an attempt on his life in July 1994 when a prisoner slashed his throat with a makeshift knife fashioned from a toothbrush. A second attempt on his life succeeded on 28 November 1994. He was bludgeoned with a 20-inch metal bar whilst in the showers of the prison gym. He was dead within the hour. Christopher Scarver, a schizophrenic inmate, reportedly said that, "God told me to do it," and that the attack had been unplanned. He also said that Dahmer had taunted both him and prison staff by shaping his food into the shapes of severed limbs, decorated with tomato ketchup to represent blood. He alleged that Dahmer had been so disliked by prisoners and staff alike that he'd been left deliberately unsupervised so that he could be killed. Upon hearing of her son's death, Joyce said, "Now is everybody happy?" Some were.

Dahmer's remains were cremated, but not before the brain was removed. His parents received half each of the ashes but that wasn't the end of the matter. Joyce petitioned that the brain be given over to science and research into antisocial personality disorder. Lionel, on the other hand wanted it all over and done with and for the brain to be cremated in line with Dahmer's last will and testament. After a bitter court battle, the matter was resolved in December 1995 in favour of Jeffrey's own wishes: the brain was cremated.

Jeffery Dahmer's childhood showed many of the red flags that would signal a life going off the rails. A hernia operation, early alcohol use and homosexuality when it wasn't accepted can't be entirely to blame. The breakup of his parents' dysfunctional marriage may have contributed. Extreme shyness and a pathological inability to be intimate were certainly a part of it. His feelings of loneliness and sense of rejection grew until they aggravated his compulsion to keep his lovers with him at all costs, even if it resulted in their deaths. Cannibalism – the actual _consumption_ of the body of his lovers – proved to be the ultimate method by which to do this. The "Milwaukee Cannibal", as Dahmer came to be known, felt that the only way he could fill the pathetic void left by loneliness was to depersonalise the objects of his desires and view them as that – objects. It was a process, and it didn't happen overnight. But for Dahmer it was an *irresistible* and perhaps *inevitable* compulsion. As he put it himself:

> *"I was completely swept along with my own compulsion. I don't know how else to put it. It didn't satisfy me completely, so maybe I was thinking, 'Maybe another one will. Maybe this one will.' And the numbers started growing and growing and just got out of control, as you can see."*

# William George Bonin
(active 1979-1980)

SOME SERIAL KILLERS SELECT the knife as their weapon; others prefer the rope. In a very specific sense, the chosen tool of the trade
of one evil serial killer was his camper van. It was an olive-green
coloured second-generation Ford Econoline model. It had a side
door which opened into a rear compartment and a small window
which provided inner illumination. Outwardly, it was an ordinary workaday vehicle, used and driven across America's highways thousands of time daily. It was old, rusty and dented; it
wouldn't have attracted much attention to the casual eye.

However, for some, once they saw the inside of this van, it
was a nightmare come true. Inside the van all the inner handles
had been removed. The rationale for the curtain on the small
window – innocuous-looking from the outside – would quickly
have revealed its malignant purpose: to provide the killer with
privacy. Various tools, weapons, ligatures and other instruments
were stashed away for easy access. These were used to restrain
the victims, allowing their killer to drive countless miles across
American freeways before stopping to rape, torture and then
kill. And it was in this same camper van, shortly before midnight
on 11 June 1980, that police eventually caught up with the man
they'd named the "Freeway Killer".[1] When arrested by the police – not a moment too soon – the pale and podgy 33-year-old
man with the Tom Selleck moustache was already in the act of
sodomising the anus of an unwitting teenage hitchhiker who'd
been cuffed and restrained by rope. The youth told the police
that the sex act had been voluntary and that the handcuffs were
merely part of an older man's fantasy. He was later to learn that

---

[1] He was the third southern California serial killer to share the epithet, along
with Patrick Kearney and Randy Kraft.

if the police hadn't interrupted the impromptu sex party the older man's next move would probably have been murder ...

William George Bonin was born on 8 January 1947 in Willimantic, Connecticut, the second of three sons to Robert and Alice Bonin. Although Robert was an alcoholic who regularly beat his wife and the three boys, it was the middle child who bore the brunt of his father's wrath. Their father was also a compulsive gambler who eventually lost the family home due to gambling debts. His insatiable rage seemed to stem from having more mouths to feed, and Bill felt the fists of his father's wrath early on, even whilst still a toddler. Alice, the boys' mother, was said to be overbearing and overprotective. However, the years of abuse she suffered took their toll on her, and eventually she too fell into alcoholism. Bill and his brothers, when they weren't being beaten by their father, were neglected by their mother and she would fail in even the most basic of maternal duties, such as feeling and clothing the boys. Sympathetic neighbours often had to step in to provide food, clothes and even some positive attention. But it wasn't enough to shelter the boys from the horrors they faced back home. Alice, in desperation, sent the boys to their grandfather to protect them from their father. However, the grandfather was a convicted serial child molester with a history of sexually assaulting his own daughter (Alice) when she'd been a child and adolescent. The boys' mother either ignored or repressed the fact. She later admitted that she'd been the attempted subject of her father's unnatural attention *even after* she was married. Unsurprisingly, when he had them in his care, he also sexually abused his three grandsons. This twisted imprint of the male role model – of a carer who gave attention only at the point of abuse – was instilled in William Bonin from a lamentably early age. Inevitably, he'd become conditioned to believe that behaviours such as these were acceptable amongst men.

In 1953, when Bill was aged six, Alice Bonin placed her three sons in an orphanage, again in the misguided hope that it would protect them. Unfortunately, the orphanage was known to severely discipline its unruly charges for offences both major and minor. As well as beatings, the punishments involved placing the children in borderline-torturous stress positions and subjecting them to partial drowning in water-filled sinks. At the orphanage, Bill "consented" to the sexual advances of older boys, doing so only if they would first tie his hands behind his back. Quite why Bill made this request is unknown, for in his later years he would habitually refuse to discuss many of his memories of the orphanage where he spent three formative years. Something about the experience was so horrific that he couldn't allow himself to dwell upon it.

In 1956, Bill returned to live with his parents, now in Mansfield, Connecticut. The new home didn't change any old behaviours, and Robert's mistreatment of his sons showed no sign of slowing down; his drinking and gambling also continued unabated. There were suggestions that the father was also sexually assaulting young Bill. Soon Bill himself was fondling his younger brother and other boys from the neighbourhood.

By the age of 10, Bill was engaged in petty criminality and had already been arrested for the first time. Initially, his misdemeanours were minor robberies and burglaries, but they soon escalated to more serious felonies such as grand theft. In 1955, he served time in a juvenile detention centre for stealing license plates and here also he became the sexual plaything of older boys, and even of one of the adult counsellors. Right up until he reached his teenage years, Bill never experienced a normal relationship with an adult male. Abuse had been persistent and unremitting. It would now seem more likely than not that he'd perpetuate the cycle.

After leaving the detention centre, Bill _did_ continue the cycle. He lured boys – always boys younger than himself – into the Bonin family home, often with the promise of alcohol. There, he'd engage in the molestation activities he'd learned as a child himself, carrying on the tradition he'd learned from his father and grandfather.

In 1961, the foreclosure of their home brought the Bonin parents the dilemma of remaining where they were in Connecticut or relocating. They decided the latter, and opted to move to California, settling in Downey, a small city southeast of Los Angeles. Within weeks, Robert Bonin was dead. A lifetime of alcohol abuse had taken its toll on his liver and he died of cirrhosis.

Straight after graduating from high school in 1965, Bonin was coaxed into doing his patriotic duty and he joined the US Air Force. Also that year, he became engaged to be married. The proposal was at the behest of Alice, who believed that the prospect of marriage would suppress her son's evident homosexual urges. It wouldn't. Soon after, Bonin left to serve as a helicopter gunner in the Vietnam War, clocking up five months of active duty and logging over 700 hours of combat and patrol time. On one occasion, he risked his life under enemy fire to save a wounded colleague and was awarded a medal in honour of his gallantry. After three years in the Air Force Bonin was honourably discharged. The homosexual urges *had not* been suppressed, as his mother had hoped; Bonin later admitted to having raped two fellow soldiers at gunpoint. Evidently this dishonourable conduct had not been reported by his victims. The army experience left him dejected. He claimed that it had instilled in him a belief that human life was overvalued.

After returning home from service, Bonin moved back in with his mother in Downey. Shortly thereafter, aged 21, he married his long-waiting fiancée. The marriage didn't last. His wife soon caught wind of Bonin's dark past and wanted out. Within weeks the couple were divorced. The two brothers also moved on, leaving Alice Bonin alone with her troubled son.

William Bonin began his crime spree in earnest on 17 November 1968, at the age of 21, when he sexually assaulted a youngster. Bonin lured the 12-year-old boy into his car. He then drove the terrified boy to a secluded area. There, he pounced, forcing the boy into oral copulation. When the boy fought back, Bonin bludgeoned him about the face and head with a tyre iron, forcing him into submission, upon which he then restrained the boy by the hands and feet with cord. At this point, Bonin repeatedly anally raped his prey. When this ordeal was over, the boy was released and Bonin allowed him to flee into the night.

It was the beginning of a pattern. Over the next four months, three other boys between the ages of 12 and 14 were abducted and assaulted in similar fashion. A vile *M.O.* had now been established. Added to the torture was the squeezing of the victims' testicles. A fifth rape attempt was interrupted when the boy, a 16-year-old youth, managed to break free of the restraints and escape. Bonin was subsequently indicted on five counts of kidnapping, four counts of sodomy, and one each of oral copulation and child molestation. He pleaded guilty and was sentenced to be detained at the Atascadero State Hospital as a mentally disordered sex offender.

During his time at the hospital, it was revealed that Bonin had a higher than average IQ, scoring at 121. Personality profiling indicated an unhelpful internalised struggle in dealing with his mother. She kept him close by – emotionally tethered to the apron-strings, as it were – whilst also castigating him as a worthless human being. Scans revealed damage to the prefrontal cortex, the impulse-regulating and decision-making region of the brain. In addition, physical examinations showed evidence of extensive scarring to the head and buttocks.

Whilst in hospital, Bonin engaged in forceful sexual activity with other male inmates. Despite this, he was declared unsuitable for further treatment and released on 11 June 1974, a doctor noting on the release form that Bonin was "no longer a danger to the health and safety of others". That expert opinion was to be proved inaccurate over a year later.

On 8 September 1975, 14-year-old David McVicker was thumbing for a lift in Garden Grove, California, hoping to catch a ride to his parents' home in Huntington Beach, around 10 miles distant. A red Ford Pinto stopped alongside him. The driver – a swarthy, dark-eyed man with a shock of black hair and a handlebar moustache – spoke to him through the open window and agreed to help the young hitchhiker. Instead, he took a detour. David turned to ask the man where they going and found himself looking down the barrel of a revolver. The man drove David to an open field, parked, undressed and ordered David to also disrobe. He then beat and raped the youth, tying the boy's own t-shirt around his neck, using a tyre iron to tighten the ligature. "The look in his eye when he raped me scared the hell out of me," David would tell a reporter later. As the attack continued, with his last breath David managed to gasp, "God help ...", whereupon Bonin stopped what he was doing and became immediately apologetic. He then drove David home before casually telling him, "We'll meet again."

Back home, David sat by himself as his parents both happened to be out at work. After several hours, he phoned a child abuse helpline and informed them of what had happened. His mother came home, picked him up and brought him to the police station where he filed a complaint.

Two days later, Bonin attempted to lure a 15-year-old youth into his car by propositioning him for sex with the offer of $35. The boy declined the offer, whereupon Bonin attempted to run him down with his vehicle.

Three weeks later, Bonin was picked up and charged with the rape and forcible oral copulation of a minor and the attempted abduction of a 15-year-old. He pleaded guilty to the charge, and on New Year's Eve 1975 he was given a sentence of 1-15 years' imprisonment. He was released from the California Men's Facility in San Luis Obispo on 11 October 1978, the parole board having ordered 18 months' supervised probation, admonishing him to "start his life afresh".

Ostensibly, this is what he did. But to William Bonin, "starting afresh" meant only one thing – never getting caught again. Upon his release, Bonin moved into an apartment at the Kingswood Village complex within a mile of his mother's home, got a job as a truck driver for a delivery firm and, unfathomably, acquired a girlfriend, whom he liked to take skating each Sunday. He also joined the party circuit and acquired a curiously diverse circle of friends, including a man 12 years older than himself named Everett "Scott" Fraser.

Fraser lived in the same complex as Bonin. He was an ex-bank worker who enjoyed throwing parties nearly every night of the week, inviting people whether he knew them or not, and mixing freely the druggies, hippies, bikers, rootless youths and ex-cons of the area. It was perhaps inevitable that Bonin would find himself at one of Fraser's wild soirées.

They enjoyed each other's company. They also shared a preferential lust for the bodies of boys and young men, taking pleasure in regaling each other with tales of their sensual exploits. However, whilst Fraser's stories were mostly fantastical musings, Bonin's urges were real, voracious and unremitting.

Ten months after his release from prison, Bonin phoned his friend Fraser. He was back inside, in the Orange County Jail, after having molested a 17-year-old boy at Dana Point, near the coastal town of San Juan Capistrano, California. Still under parole, the violation should've activated an automatic return to jail. However, an administrative error meant that Bonin would soon be back on the streets again. This time, he vowed, he *really would never* be caught again. "No one's going to testify again. This is never going to happen to me again," he told his friend. Fraser interpreted this as a sign of remorse. However, in Bonin's mind he meant there could be no witnesses. The decision to kill had apparently already been made.

Through his acquaintance with Fraser, Bonin also met and made friends with two other individuals. Twenty-one-year-old Vernon Butts was a porcelain-factory worker by day. At other times, he was a self-styled magician with a fondness for dressing up as Darth Vader (complete with cape and light sabre). His apartment contained a coffin for a coffee table, plastic spiders hanging from the ceiling and weird strobing lights. Gregory Miley, aged 18, was an illiterate Texan odd-jobber with an IQ of 56 who followed Bonin around like a puppy. Both men, at various stages, became active toadies involved in the murder spree which Bonin was soon to commence. Both men willingly became worshipful hangers-on at the altar of Bonin's influence. Butts, in particular, freely admitted to taking great delight in viewing the spectacle of abuse and torture inflicted by Bonin.

There must've been something in Bonin's Pied Piper influence that seemed attractive to these two impressionable weirdos, and Bonin, tragically, had clearly been able to recognise this.

Butts is thought to have been with Bonin on 28 May 1979 when a murder took place.[2] Thomas Glen Lundgren, a 13-year-old hitchhiker, accepted a lift at around 11 o'clock in the morning that day. By now Bonin had acquired his camper van, and if the boy had got into it he would've stood no chance. If he'd attempted to make an escape, he'd have quickly discovered the measures had been taken to prevent him from doing so. The inner handles had been removed from the rear and passenger-side doors of the van. Weapons had been hidden away, but were stowed for the easy access of the captor. The windows had curtains draped across them, so no one outside the van could've observed the scene occurring within. And although no one knows exactly what *did* happen, it's likely that the van was driven to a quiet, secluded area where the torture-sex slaying could take place in privacy, without any fear of discovery.

When Thomas' body was found later that afternoon, clad only in T-shirt and footwear, it'd been subjected to unspeakable horrors. He'd been bludgeoned about the face and head, slashed across the throat and body, stabbed extensively and strangled to death. And, providing clear evidence that the attack had been sexually motivated, the boys genitals had been sliced off. In his 1981-1982 trial, Bonin strenuously denied committing this crime and he was found not guilty. Thomas Lundgren's name does, however, remain attached to the canon of Bonin's list of victims.

Mark Duane Shelton was another apparent victim of homicide at the hands of Bonin and his accomplice Butts. Mark, aged 17,

---

[2] It's possible that Bonin had already killed by now. Two teenagers, Danny Jordan and Mark Proctor, were travelling to Laguna Beach in April 1979 when they disappeared. Both of their bodies were found off a Palmdale hiking trail, and subsequent autopsies found amounts of sedatives in their systems.

went missing on 4 August 1979 around the time that desperate screams were heard by his neighbours. He'd been walking from his home in Westminster to a local movie theatre. His dumped body was found a week later. He'd died of shock after various foreign objects were inserted into his body.

The day after Mark Shelton went missing, Markus Alexander Grabs, also aged 17, vanished. The West German student was kidnapped, bound with wire and taken to Bonin's home. There, he was sodomised, bludgeoned and stabbed 77 times before his body was dumped alongside a Malibu freeway where he was found by a rancher. His clothes were strewn across the open field. Butts had also played an active role in this murder and in at least six of the following.

Around three weeks later, on 27 August, Bonin and Butts abducted 15-year-old Donald Ray Hyden in Hollywood, Los Angeles as he walked along Santa Monica Boulevard at around one o'clock in the morning. By now a dreadful *M.O.* had solidified. Hyden's body was found in a dumpster the next day by construction men. He'd been subjected to binding, sodomy, ligature strangulation, bludgeoning, stabbing, slashing and an attempted emasculation.

On 9 September, David Murillo, aged 17, suffered a similar fate. His remains were found in ivy, dumped at the side of Highway 101. The back of his head had been smashed to smithereens, and his throats was completely crushed, such was the tightness of the ligature compression. On 17 September, Robert Wirostek, aged 18, was kidnapped on his way to work at a grocery store. His body was found discarded on the I-10.

In November 1979, Bonin and Butts killed twice. The identity of the first victim remains unknown, although Bonin estimated his age to have been around 23. Bonin admitted to savagely beating the young man and inserting an ice pick into his nostrils and ears prior to murdering him. The other victim, whom Bonin found alone, was Frank Dennis Fox, aged 17. He died on the last day of the month. He'd been restrained by the wrists and ankles using wire. His body – naked when found – showed extensive blunt force trauma. He'd evidently been alive and conscious throughout his ordeal.

Ten days later, John Frederick Kilpatrick, aged 15, vanished en route to visit friends. And on New Year's Day 1980, Michael Francis McDonald's fully clothed body was found dumped alongside Highway 71. He'd been 16-years old.

Bonin's victims, the majority of them teenagers, were schoolboys, male hitchhikers or male sex workers. What they had in common was that they were all physically slender with slight frames – boys who could easily be overpowered. Bonin had sought them out purposefully, his excitement surging as he searched for and eventually found them. They were all sexually assaulted, tortured to an extensive degree and stabbed, bludgeoned or strangled to death. The brutality shown to the victims escalated rapidly, over a short period time, with Bonin using new and invented cruelties, showing that he required ever-more violence to stimulate himself to satisfaction. The victims were all killed inside the camper van before being dumped like trash along the various freeway corridors of southern California. Their killer showed them no mercy in life nor dignity in death.

At some stage in early 1980, Bonin recruited his lover Gregory Miley as a twisted minion. On 3 February, the duo drove from Downey to Hollywood, cruising the streets with the active intention of finding a boy to slaughter. On Santa Monica Boulevard, they encountered 15-year-old Charles Dempster Miranda standing outside a nightclub, thumbing for a Hollywood-bound lift. Charles accepted the offer of a lift and, according to Miley, also agreed to have sex with Bonin in the back of the van. As Miley drove the "death van", Bonin whispered in Charles' ear, "Kid's going to die." Bonin then overpowered him, bound him and demanded to know how much money he had in his possession. "About six dollars," was Charles' response. Bonin ordered Miley to take out the boy's wallet and then Bonin orally raped and sodomised the terrified hitchhiker who by now was crying. To shut him up, Bonin struck him repeatedly on the face, knocked him down, bound and gagged him. The evil duo then beat the boy in a vicious onslaught until he passed out. Miley attempted to rape him also but couldn't sustain an erection. Angry and frustrated, he then assaulted Charles with some sharp objects before joining Bonin in physically beating him. Then, as Bonin raped the boy, Miley jumped up and down repeatedly on the boy's chest. When later asked by the prosecutor at his trial what Bonin had been doing at the time, Miley said, "I don't know. I was too busy killing the guy." After this, Bonin garrotted the boy with his own T-shirt tightened with a tyre iron, finally achieving the aim and ending the boy's misery. The naked corpse was then dumped in an alleyway in central Los Angeles.

Minutes after dumping the body, Bonin told Miley, "I'm horny again. Let's go and do another one." They found their prey after driving to Huntington Beach, where they picked up 12-year-old James Michael Macabe, the youngest victim, with the promise of a lift to Disneyland (Macabe's original destination) and an offer to share some dope.

Bonin drove to a grocery store parking lot where he parked the van and got into the rear with the boy. Miley then took over the driving, covering many miles aimlessly as Bonin repeatedly beat and raped his victim. After a while, Bonin forced James to sleep in his arms. Miley parked the van and fell asleep himself for a while. When he awoke, he noticed that Bonin was kissing and cuddling the boy. At this point, however, Bonin's demeanour changed, and he began to punch and pummel James repeatedly. Miley joined in too, also crushing James' neck with a tyre iron. Bonin then strangled James with his own T-shirt before the body was dumped, fully clothed, alongside a dumpster in the city of Walnut, California.

The same day, Bonin was arrested for violation of his parole conditions. The reason: he'd strayed outside his neighbourhood of Kingswood. He was remanded at Orange County Jail and served a month in custody. Within 10 days of his release, he'd killed again.

It was a familiar pattern. On 14 March 1980, he abducted 18-

year-old Ronald Craig Gatlin, whom he tied up, beat, raped and tortured by sticking an ice pick deep into the ears and neck. Gatlin was finally strangled to death with a ligature and dumped in Duarte City, California. The body, still bound by the wrists and ankles, was discovered the next day.

On 21 March, two teenage boys died. Fourteen-year-old Glenn Norman Barker was lured into the "death van" and treated in similar fashion to Bonin's previous victims. Glen, however, was also tortured with a lit cigarette, his body also evidencing numerous burns to the neck, in addition to having foreign objects forcibly inserted into his rectum, distending it unnaturally.

The second boy to die that day was 15-year-old Russell Duane Rugh, who was abducted from a bus stop in Garden Grove. His ordeal lasted eight hours, after which his remains were dumped alongside those of Glenn Barker in Cleveland National Forest.

For Bonin, murder wasn't a solitary activity; it was a group sport. Like drinking or getting high, it was much more fun to do in company. In March 1980, when he met the boy at a party at Fraser's, his eyes lingered. There was something in the look of this boy that Bonin liked. He cast his eyes over him again. The boy was young, blond, slender and very good-looking – what was there not to like! – and so after spending some time with the boy it was perhaps inevitable that Bonin would consider offering him a lift home. He did so. It was late. The boy accepted. They set off.

It wouldn't have taken 17-year-old William Ray Pugh long to wonder what he'd got himself into. Immediately upon setting off, the thick-set driver asked him if he wanted to have sex. Young Billy stammered a reply. *No, he did not want to have sex.* As the driver continued driving, the two sat in silence for several long minutes. At last, the driver came to a stoplight and slowed down. Billy grappled for the door-handle in an attempt to leave but he quickly discovered the van's internal modifications which made this impossible. In any event, the driver, just as quickly, reached over and grabbed him by the scruff of the neck, pulling him back. As the driver drove off, Billy sat in petrified silence.

The driver continued driving. After a moment his irritation seemed to lapse. He began to chat. What he enjoyed doing, the driver mentioned in an offhand way, was going out on Fridays and Saturdays, picking up young hitchhikers, getting his rocks off with them and then strangling them to death with their own T-shirts. Billy was dumbfounded. The blasé manner in which the driver spoke had literally left him speechless.

"If you want to kill someone," the driver went on, "you should make a plan and find a place to dump the body before you pick a victim."

Bonin was apparently weighing up the teenager. The two of them had been seen leaving the party together. That fact alone precluded the murder of the boy. It was simply too risky, and Bonin remembered his old promise to himself: _no one's going to testify again_. Perhaps he believed that his attempt to recruit the boy had been successful. When the time came, he drew his van up outside the teenager's house and let him out.

Except it wasn't Billy Pugh's house. There was no way that the youth was going to let this weirdo know where he lived. He'd told the driver to stop the van a few blocks from his residence and after getting out he walked up the nearest driveway. He waited a while until the driver had gone before running quickly back to his actual address. He kept the details of the strange encounter to himself for two months, only coming forward later to tell a counsellor of his suspicions about the heavy-set man with the deep eyes. Only then did he come to realise how close he'd been to being marked down as the latest statistic of a psychopathic marauder. At least that's what he _wanted_ the authorities to think. In fact, it wasn't quite like that ...

On 24 March, Bonin – accompanied by Billy Pugh, who thought he was only going along for the ride – abducted 15-year-old runaway Harry Todd Turner from a Los Angeles street. Harry had absconded from his boys' home four days earlier and, after he was enticed into Bonin's "death van" with the offer of $20 for sex, he instantly came to regret it. The boy was bound, bitten and anally raped. Bonin ordered Billy Pugh to beat the youth up, which Billy did for several minutes, severely fracturing the skull. On that lift home after the party, Bonin had mentioned to Billy what he liked to do to hitchhikers. Now he got to show him. Bonin strangled Harry Turner with his own T-shirt until he was dead. Harry's naked body was discarded outside a business premises. An autopsy revealed bite marks to the chest and blood around testicles. That grim daytrip was to cost Billy Pugh six years in prison for involuntary manslaughter.

The catalogue of murders continued unabated. On 10 April 1980, Bonin abducted and strangled Steven John Wood. The 16-year-old boy had been returning home from a dental appointment when Bonin chanced upon him. His body was later found in a Long Beach alleyway. He'd been ferociously beaten but death had come by strangulation.

Three weeks later, Bonin and Butts lured 19-year-old Darin Lee Kendrick to the van, bringing him to Butt's apartment under the pretext of selling him drugs. Instead, they overpowered and restrained him with binds, sodomised him and partially strangulated him. In a new twist, Bonin forced Kendrick to drink hydrochloric acid, which caused extensive caustic burns both inside and outside his body. And as if that weren't enough, Butts then drove an ice pick into the young man's ear. It was this that killed him. When Kendrick's body was found, dumped behind a warehouse off State Route 91, the ice pick was still protruding from his ear.

Lawrence Eugene Sharp, aged 17, was an acquaintance of Everett, and for a while, according to Bonin, he'd been Bonin's lover. On 12 May, Bonin woke up and decided to kill him. He later admitted his thought process with cold insouciance: "I just got up one morning and decided I was tired of him. I just got tired of having him around and so I decided that I should kill him." Sharp received no special treatment; he was killed and dumped in similar fashion to most of Bonin's other victims.

One week later, Bonin invited Butts out for another chicken-hawk expedition. Butts declined so Bonin went out alone. He kidnapped 14-year-old Sean P. King from a Downey bus stop, killed him and discarded the body in a canyon near Yucaipa, California. Police were alerted to the location of the body by an anonymous phone call.

Bonin acquired the last of his four accomplices just nine days after the murder of Sean King. James Michael Munro had been thrown out of his family home in Michigan a few months earlier. Nor had his life had not been easy up to this point. He'd been left in a German orphanage by his biological mother and ended up with American adoptive parents. An attractive blond-haired boy who smiled a lot, he'd grown up with various physical and mental handicaps which didn't make things easier. Even so, the boy seemed to have no redeeming qualities and no one seemed to like him, not even his adoptive parents who eventually also rejected him. Now, at the age of 18, Munro found himself home-less and drifting along the streets of Hollywood, and so when Bonin invited him to move into the apartment he shared with his mother the drifter jumped at the chance. He also jumped at the offer of a job at the delivery firm where Bonin worked. A bisex-ual with a preference for females, Munro agreed to a consensual sexual relationship with his benefactor. It was a small price to pay for the much-needed turn in fortune. Munro's initial impres-sion was that Bonin was "a good guy, really normal".

That changed on 1 June, when Bonin abruptly announced that he wanted them both to kidnap, rape and kill a teenage hitch-hiker. It can only be due to the mesmerising effect that Bonin seemed to have on his toadies that Munro agreed to this perverse plan.

However, events were afoot elsewhere. The murders commit-ted by the "Freeway Killer", as the unknown marauder had now become known,[3] had attracted a large amount of attention from the police and media. He was now killing at a rate of once every

---

[3] Randy Kraft, who shared the epithet, was still killing in southern California.

two weeks. Anxious to apprehend the Freeway Killer, gay rights activists offered a reward of $50,000 for information leading to the conviction of the perpetrator. The endgame was on. William Bonin's name had already been given to the police by David McVicker, the teenager who'd been raped by Bonin in 1974. McVicker's suspicions had not been dismissed; the information was added to the growing pile of tipoffs yet to be investigated.

By this stage also, the teenager whom Bonin had given a lift home from the party two months ago, William Pugh, had been arrested for auto theft. Pugh overheard details of the murders on the radio and recognised the killer's *M.O.* He'd seen it enacted with his own eyes during the killing of Harry Turner. Perhaps the offer of the large reward for information had incentivised Pugh – perhaps it was civic duty – nevertheless, he informed a courthouse counsellor of his suspicions, and the counsellor in turn informed the police. Pugh was interviewed and he told investigators that he'd deduced the identity of the killer, giving the name of William Bonin. (He withheld the information that he'd been an active participant alongside Bonin in the killing of Harry Turner.)

The police had enough to commence surveillance of Bonin and began to shadow him on 2 June 1980. The tail began too late in the day to save Steven Jay Wells, an 18-year-old print shop worker who'd been standing at a Downey bus stop a few hours earlier. Bonin, accompanied by James Munro, enticed the light brown-haired, good-looking youth into the camper van. "Hey, what do you think of gays?" Bonin asked him. Wells replied, "Oh, they're okay, because I'm bisexual." That was enough for Bonin. He stopped the van, told Munro to drive home, and got into the rear. As Munro drove, Bonin got Wells to fellate him.

Back at Bonin's apartment, he suggested that Wells could make some money by allowing himself to be tied up for sex. We only have Munro's word for it that Wells agreed to this. In any event, Munro helped to hold Wells down whilst Bonin used a clothesline to restrain him. Bonin got a knife, at which point

Munro asked, "Hey, you ain't going to hurt him, are you?" Bonin replied, "It's too late. I already got him tied up. I'm going to kill him."

As Bonin set about attacking Wells, the boy pleaded for his life. To no avail. Bonin ordered Munro to get the boy's clothes, which he did, thinking that Bonin planned to let the boy dress and leave. However, Bonin instead removed Wells' wallet, raped him and strangled him to death using his own T-shirt. At around nine o'clock that evening, the duo carried the body outside in a cardboard box and loaded it onto the van. Then they drove to Vernon Butts' residence. There, Butts showed Munro the I.D. cards of some of the victims who'd already been killed – some 20 or so cards. Bonin invited Butts to come out to the van to "come look what we did".

Butts did come out for a look. He said, "Oh, how nice. You got another one." Bonin asked him for advice on where best to dispose of the body. Bonin considered dumping it "in the canyons where the other bodies are". Butts, presciently, thought that too risky. There were likely to be police combing the highways on the lookout for nefarious behaviour. He suggested dumping the body somewhere nearby: "Try a gas station, like we dumped the last one."

In the back of the van a malodour had begun to emanate from the body. This didn't stop Bonin and Munro; they simply wound down the windows and drove on. They even stopped at a McDonald's for hamburgers, using cash taken from Wells' wallet to pay for them.

After disposing of the body at a disused Mobil service station, the duo drove back to Bonin's mother's house. There, they sat in front of the TV, flicking through the channels in the hope of finding news about the latest murder. As Bonin bit into his Big Mac he raised his gaze heavenward and gave a grim toast: "Thanks, Steve, wherever you are." As he laughed loudly Munro joined in nervously.

That night in bed, Munro wouldn't let Bonin turn off the lights. He said he was afraid he'd be killed. Bonin told him, "I know a way you can trust me. Let me tie you up so you'll know that I won't kill you." Munro, probably fearful that it wouldn't go well if he refused, allowed himself to be bound with rope. True to his word, Bonin didn't kill his lover.

Steven Wells was Bonin's final murder victim. His naked remains were found five hours after being dumped.

The denouement occurred on 11 June 1980, nine days after the murder of Wells. Police had been observing Bonin driving in an apparent random manner throughout Hollywood, attempting unsuccessfully to lure five different boys into his van. At his sixth attempt, Bonin managed to persuade a youth to accompany him in his van. The police remained in discreet pursuit as Bonin drove to a disused parking lot close to Hollywood Freeway. There he parked up. The police weren't far behind, approaching the vehicle on foot. As they came closer they heard muffled screams and banging sounds from inside the van. They forced their way in and found Bonin in the midst of raping a bound, handcuffed youth.

The youth, 17-year-old runaway Harold Eugene Tate, initially said that the sex had been consensual. However, it was technically the rape of a minor and Bonin was arrested and charged. Inside the van, investigators found the tools of Bonin's wicked trade including lengths of cord, assorted knives, coat hangers, a set of pliers and a tyre iron. They noted the obvious alterations that'd been made to the interior of the van, as well as extensive bloodstains. Damningly, they also discovered in the van glove pocket numerous newspaper clippings related to the Freeway Killer murders.

James Munro escaped to Michigan a few days later. He was soon brought back again, whereupon he agreed to sing in return for a deal with the prosecution. Bonin, by now, was also confessing freely, admitted to 21 murders that were later confirmed with DNA profiling evidence. He showed no remorse for his crimes, only regret and embarrassment that he'd been caught. He gave details about his accomplices' involvement – including William Pugh's participation in one of the murders. Pugh did not receive the reward he'd no doubt been anticipating.

The trial of William Bonin commenced on 5 November 1981. Miley and Munro agreed to testify against him, and the details they gave graphically showed the extent of Bonin's planning and enjoyment of killing, pride in having committed the acts, and his complete disregard for his victims, either before or after death. They spoke of his insatiable sadistic lust which only culminated with a release at the point of murder.

The trial was short but not sweet. The details outlined in court disgusted all those who heard them afresh. The defence argued that Bonin's insanity had been the inevitable result of a childhood of abuse and deprivation, and that early exposure to rape had fused within him the acts of violence and love. It didn't take the prosecution long to poke holes in that argument in their rebuttal: Bonin was a sexual sadist with an antisocial personality disorder. Neither condition, however, would've impeded Bonin's ability to control his actions. He'd acted with malice aforethought.

He was found guilty of 10 of the murders for which he stood trial. The prosecution pressed for the death sentence, and in response to recommendations from the jury he was sentenced to death. Numerous appeals failed, and on 23 February 1996, at the age of 49, after 14 years on death row at San Quentin State Prison, Bonin was eventually executed by lethal injection. By the time of his death, he'd still expressed no remorse for his crimes, merely leaving a note that stated:

*I feel the death penalty is not an answer to the problems at hand. I feel it sends the wrong message to the people of this country. Young people act as they see other people acting instead of as people tell them to act. I would advise that when a person has a thought of doing anything serious against the law, that before they did, they should go to a quiet place and think about it seriously.*

For his part, William Pugh was given six years in prison for voluntary manslaughter. He served less than four, and was released in 1985. James Munro was sentenced to 15 years to life for the second-degree murder of Steven Wells. He will not be eligible for parole until 2029.

Vernon Butts was accused of accompanying Bonin on at least nine murders. He died by hanging whilst awaiting trial on 11 January 1981, When found, a towel was twisted around his neck in the same manner that many of the Freeway Killer's victims were strangled. Sheriff's officers maintained that he'd done this to himself; Butts' own attorney, however, said that he "doubted it".

Gregory Miley was sentenced to 25 years for his part in the murder of Charles Miranda. Later, he was also sentenced to a consecutive term of 25 years for the abduction and murder of James Macabe. Throughout his incarceration he violated prison rules and was reprimanded for possession of contraband drugs and attempting to anally rape fellow inmates. On 25 May 2016, Miley died of injuries sustained two days previously when he was attacked by an inmate at Mule Creek State Prison.

# Wayne Bertram Williams

[active 1979-1981]

OVER A TWO-YEAR PERIOD, between July 1979 and May 1981, at least 28 males – children, adolescents and adults – were killed in the metropolitan area of Atlanta, Georgia. The two-year series of homicides, in which the targeted victims were exclusively blacks, became known as the "Atlanta Child Murders". Although the story is horrific, the American public paid little attention to it at the time. Unfounded allegations of law enforcement apathy have been made. However, the initial apparent indifference of the Press raises other questions. The trial of the killer, after a suspect was eventually found and charged, had enough twists and turns to provide interest, cause for concern and pause for thought. The tale isn't over yet. Many people feel that the man who came to be found guilty of several of the murders is *not* the man who should've been jailed. The evidence is undoubtedly scant, and some say that the conviction may have had more to do with race than evidence. In recent years interest has renewed. Some would suggest that the jury is still out.

It began in mid-1979. On 28 July, a woman was hunting for empty bottles alongside an old dirt road in a remote area of Atlanta. She found the remains of two black boys lying side-by-side in a wooded region. The first victim had a .22 calibre gunshot wound to the upper back. The body was identified after a month as Edward Hope "Teddy" Smith, aged 14, who'd been reported missing on 21 July after parting from his girlfriend at the Greenbriar Skating Rink in town. When found, Teddy's socks and leather sun visor were missing.

The second body remained unidentified for a year. Last seen alive on 25 July 1979, Alfred Evans (also known as "Q"), aged 13, had been on his way to the Coronet Theatre in town. The cause of his death was "probably asphyxiation by strangulation". When found, he was wearing an unfamiliar belt. There were suggestions that both Teddy and "Q" had been going to a "pot" party when they disappeared.

It's fair to comment that at around this time Atlanta had the dubious reputation of being the murder capital of the country. In 1978, there were 731 murders in Georgia. A large amount, assuredly, but at least they were *consistently* terrible. Distrust of the police by the large Africa-American population had already been high, and it would remain so. Nevertheless, law enforcement officers were working overtime, and a popular new black mayor in the shape of Maynard Jackson was making waves in an attempt to usher a new era of domestic peace for the city. The police *did* take the child-murder cases seriously. The trouble was that they'd so little to work with.

On 9 November 1979, the body of nine-year-old Yusuf Bell was found in the crawlspace under a disused school. He'd last been seen getting into a blue car by a witness who'd said that the driver looked like the boy's father. At the time he went missing he hadn't been wearing shirt or shoes; when found, he only had on his cut-off brown shorts. Yusuf had been hit over the head twice. However, the cause of death was asphyxiation by manual strangulation. The death of Yusuf, who lived only four blocks from where his body was found, hit the black community hard. A friend of the family's said: "The whole neighbourhood cried because they loved that child. He was God-gifted." Indeed, with his particular aptitude for history and mathematics it seemed as if Yusuf could've made something of his life.

Then four black youths were all murdered in the span of a few months. Suspicions inevitably became raised amongst the victims' families that the cases were related. The Atlanta police still failed to establish any official connection between the murders.

Four months passed before a female victim was found. Angel Lenair, aged 12-years-old, would be the first of two. Angel disappeared on 4 March 1980. Just under a week later, the comely schoolgirl's body was found in a wooded lot three blocks from her home. Someone else's white panties had been stuffed into her mouth and her hands were bound with an electrical cord. She'd been garrotted to death with a ligature. Her murder is still considered unsolved.

Eleven-year-old Jeffrey Mathis disappeared the day after Angel Lenair's body was found. His body was found in a patch of briar-covered woodland, some 11 months after his vanishing. Such was the condition of the body by this time that a cause of death couldn't be conclusively established.

Whispers circulated suggesting that the victims themselves were to blame for their own demise. They were made out to be "streetwise" or "tough guys", or even homosexual hustlers who'd brought it on themselves. That was nonsense. Jeffrey Mathis sang in two choirs; he was a boy scout. Yusuf Bell had been at the top of his fifth-grade class; he played the drums and trumpet in his school band. He'd also been in the boy scouts. Winsome Angel Lenair had been an ordinary girl who'd not long finished her homework before leaving her apartment. She was _not_ a troublesome sex worker.

Three of the victims' parents, however, were not to be kowtowed. They'd realised there was a pattern and believed that the authorities weren't doing enough to stop the child murders. They formed a committee and named it Stop the Children's Murders –or STOP. They called upon the police department, the mayor's office and the Department of Justice to link and investigate the cases. Their pleas were spurned.

Over the next two months, five further children went missing. The body of Eric Antonio Middlebrooks, aged 14, was found next to his bicycle behind a garage at the rear of the Hope-U-Like-It bar. His pockets had been turned inside-out. He'd suffered slight stab wounds on the arms and chest, but cause of death was blunt trauma to the head.

On 9 June 1980, a local resident approached police (who were looking for the body of a missing youth) with information that his dog had come home smelling bad. The resident thought that his dog may have been nosing in "something". That "something" proved to be the bodies of Christopher Phillipe Richardson, aged 12 (who'd gone missing on 9 June), and Earl Lee Terrell, aged 10 (last seen on 30 July). The two sets of remains were found in a hardscrabble wooded area outside Atlanta. Both bodies were missing items of clothing. Christopher was wearing unfamiliar swimming trunks, and the medical examiner noted that the teeth found with the remains didn't match Christopher Richardson's dental records. Found next to the bodies were shotgun shells, a *Penthouse* magazine, a cigarette butt and recording tape. These items didn't lead to any new leads. Due to the condition of the bodies, cause of death couldn't be established.

By now, large groups of volunteers began to search local wooded, derelict and abandoned areas. They were to have miserably grim success. LaTonya Yovette Wilson, a four-foot tall girl, had gone missing whilst wearing a slip and white panties. When found by the volunteers, four months after going missing, her body was skeletonised and the medical examiner couldn't identify the cause of death. LaTonya would be the youngest of the known victims in the Atlanta Child Murder spree.

Ten-year-old Aaron Darnell Wyche was last seen getting into the front seat of a car with two black men. The witness reported seeing one of them "doing something with his hands in his lap". Other witnesses saw the vehicle's license plate number. It didn't match the car. Aaron's body was found the next day under a bridge, and cause of death was ruled "positional asphyxiation". The fall from the bridge appeared to have broken his neck.

Anthony Bernard Carter, aged nine, was playing hide-and-seek with his cousin outside his house on 6 July. His body – which had suffered multiple stab wounds – was found in the early hours of the next morning. Anthony was the 12th victim in the grim toll of deaths.

Spurred on by the parents of STOP, a new task force was formed headed by an individual of extremely limited experience. This was evident from the fact that his first port of call was psychic Dorothy Allyson. Unsurprisingly, this effort to solve the murders brought no new leads. Eight children had now been found dead, and several others were still missing. Mayor Maynard Jackson, anxious to achieve progress, formed a special task force comprised of various state and local law enforcement agencies. The task force, struggling to make sense of the connection between the victims, produced a running tally of their names – "The List" – which shortly grew so large and so quickly that the pattern fairly slapped them in the face. Though the term had yet to be widely adopted, investigators finally had to admit that they were chasing a serial killer. Although the causes of death varied, there were striking similarities between the cases. Most of the victims were black; most were young black boys. All were slim, with similar physical characteristics. Their remains had been left in quiet locations where they could be easily found. In time, as the case developed, emerging from the data were distinct socioeconomic and geographical patterns that linked many of the victims, including connections to paedophilia, interpersonal homosexual activity and links to Atlanta's Memorial Drive and other streets in the vicinity.

This was all to come, however. Now, on 21 August 1980, 12-year-old Clifford Emanuel Jones turned up dead and his name too was added to the list. Three weeks later, 10-year-old Darron Glass went missing, never to be found. Authorities announced a city-wide curfew to keep the under-15s off the city streets after 11 o'clock at night. It didn't prevent 12-year-old Charles Stephens from turning up dead, dumped in plain sight on a hillock nearby his home. Then, on 2 November, the body of 9-year-old Aaron Jackson Jr. was found on the banks of the South River near a bridge. Bridges would later become a feature of the investigation. The FBI were invited to become involved in the task force. The case would now be referred to as "Major Case 30".

Sixteen-year-old Patrick Rogers ("Pat Man") Pat was a talented singer and performer in local talent shows. On 10 November, he'd been on his way to meet an aspiring talent scout and record producer. For the first time, the name of Wayne Williams comes into the mix. Williams himself had Svengali pretensions, wanting to create the next big boy band. He'd also been known to freelance as a journalist and crime reporter.

"Pat Man" had known Aaron Wyche and Aaron Jackson, both now dead. He was friendly with a white boy from school who knew Wayne Williams. Pat was into music; he wrote his own stuff. A week before Pat went missing, Wayne Williams had been handing out flyers in the housing project where Pat lived. The year 1980 would end with a similar story, depressing in its familiarity: another young, black, male victim was discovered 15 miles from his home in the projects. Pat Rogers had been bludgeoned about the head, death coming from the resulting blunt force trauma. His body was pulled from the Chattahoochee River eight days after having gone missing on 7 December. He was the first victim suspected of having been dropped into the water from the bridge above.

Lubie Geter was the boy that police had been looking for on 9 June 1980 when their attention was diverted (by the disturbing smell which turned out to be the remains of Christopher Richardson and Earl Terrell). The severely decomposed remains of Lubie "Chuck" Geter Jr., aged 14, were eventually found on 9 January 1981, also by a dog. He'd had been missing for over five months. In the intervening time, animals had scavenged the corpse. The body was missing all clothes apart from white jockey shorts. It was considered, quite seriously, that the killings may have been related to the Ku Klux Klan. Subsequently, Geter's case became the focus of a widely publicised appeal. A suspect was brought in for questioning but never charged.

It wasn't the first time that FBI had conjectured that the killer would be white. An earlier profile had also suggested the possibility. Local investigators, wise to local issues, knew that a white man wouldn't easily fit into the neighbourhoods where the murders were happening. Local people would've taken notice of the new face. And multiple murderers were *white*, just like Dean Corll and Ted Bundy; that was the current theory. The thought that their local murderer could be black was unthinkable. To square the circle, the media even suggested that a white policeman could be responsible. The answer would come soon – but not soon enough …

Another "pattern case" was discovered on 23 January. A tip had been phoned in to police, but they never found the body where the caller had said it would be. The unknown caller then made a second call, claiming to have just put a second body in the same place. A passer-by found the body of Terry Lorenzo Pue, aged 15, in a predominantly white neighbourhood, 17 miles from his own project housing residence. Abrasions on his elbows and head suggested that he'd struggled with his assailant. He'd been killed by ligature strangulation. Several years later, the skeletonised body of the second reported victim was found within the same vicinity.

In shockingly quick succession, within the month of March, eight more bodies disappeared. Patrick Wayne Baltazar, 12, was later discovered near an office complex. Curtis Lamar Walker, 13, would be found 18 miles from his home. The body of Joseph "Jo-Jo" Eugene Bell, 15, would be dragged from the South River, whilst the remains of Timothy Lyndale Hill, 13, were to be pulled from the Chattahoochee River. Twenty-four hours later the body of Eddie Lamar "Bubble" Duncan, 21, the first adult victim, would be found in the same river. Its waters were also to be the temporary grave of Michael Cameron "Mickey" McIntosh, 23. William "Billy Star" Barrett, 17, would be found lifeless on a kerb in Dekalb in western Atlanta. Also found dead was "Little" Larry Eugene Rogers, 20, dumped in an abandoned apartment building. All were young, slim, black youths and young men. All had died via strangulation or asphyxiation.

John Harold Porter, 28, was found in the vacant lot on NW Bender Street. He'd been stabbed multiple times, the severity of the wounds causing his death. His name was only added to "The List" _during_ his murderer's trial.

It is thought that Jimmy Ray Payne, 21, had been attempting to assume a new identity in the days before he died. He'd had a troubled life, having only been released from prison in December the previous year, and he may have attempted suicide on at least two occasions. On 27 April 1981, Payne's body was fished from the Chattahoochee River, dressed in nothing but his red-coloured underwear. Although "The List" was to more than treble in length, Payne was the last known victim _officially_ attributed to the Atlanta Child Murderer. However, another body had yet to be found and it would prove to be the long-awaited break in the case.

In the early hours of 22 May 1981, a police surveillance team was staking out the James Jackson Parkway bridge spanning the Chattahoochee River. It was a "Hail Mary" stakeout – when selected sites were put under surveillance with the hope (and a prayer) that something would come of it. At around 03:00, the officers heard a loud splash and then saw a car's headlights turn on before it pulled away. One of the officers radioed an FBI agent nearby. Then they raced to intercept the car before it could depart the scene. They caught up with it half-a-mile away.

Behind the wheel of the white 1970 Chevrolet station wagon was Wayne Bertram Williams, a plump 23-year-old African-America who still lived with his elderly parents. One of the officers asked to check inside Williams' vehicle. Williams consented. Inside the car were gloves and a ski rope.

Williams was already known to police, although there was nothing especially suspicious about his background that matched the FBI profile of the multiple murderer they'd been seeking. On the surface, he was a law-abiding citizen, the son of two schoolteachers who, showing early promise in music, was encouraged to follow his ambitions in promotion, photography and radio broadcasting. And the man himself gave them no grounds to suspect that he was a multiple murderer – other than the fact that the police had just heard a loud splash. Williams was questioned for over an hour. He was a talent-broker, he said. He explained his presence on the bridge, saying that he'd driven to a nightclub in the neighbouring town with the aim of picking up a tape recorder in advance of an audition he was amid organised for a promising young singer. He gave police the name and number of "Cheryl Johnson", the singer he planned to try-out. He said that the address Cheryl Johnson had given him was unclear and that he'd stopped to read it again. He said that he'd been driving to a convenience store to phone her. The whole story sounded vague, the officers felt. However, with nothing concrete to go on, Williams was let go. Two days later, another body turned up.

Nathaniel Cater, 27, would be the last victim found. On 24 May 1981, his body was discovered by two boys, floating in the Chattahoochee River, half-a-mile south of the I-285 bridge. The body was naked. Cause of death was asphyxia. Also found near the body was a safe. Police have not revealed what they found inside. Recalling the suspicious splash heard upstream from the site where the body was found, police brought Williams in for more robust interrogation. Putting two and two together, it seemed possible that the splash had been caused by a body being dumped. They hoped Williams would give them some answers.

He failed three polygraph tests. The name and number of the singer Williams claimed he'd been planning to audition proved to be fictitious. Nevertheless, after a sustained grilling, police were obliged to let Williams go. Now the fame-hungry man's desire for attention came to the fore: he played up for the cameras, staging media interviews and news conferences, loudly proclaiming his innocence, volunteering that he'd failed three polygraphs, whilst also offering various alibis to prove that he could not be responsible for any crime. The alibis proved only to be full of holes.

He was questioned again over a 12-hour period between the 3 and 4 June at FBI headquarters. Once again, investigators were obliged to let him go. However, they now put their number one suspect under 24-hour surveillance as they sought the forensic evidence that would link him to the crimes and nail him. On 21 June, they had enough proof consistent to the crime scenes (carpet and bedspread fibres, dog hair and car mat material) to move in and arrest their man for the murders of Nathaniel Cater and Jimmy Payne.

Wayne Williams was born on 27 May 1958, the only son of Homer and Faye Williams, two schoolteachers of African-American heritage. He was brought up in Dixie Hills, the area where many of the Atlanta murder victims had either lived or from where they'd vanished. His was a modest three-bedroom home in a modest neighbourhood, with well-tended lawns and manicured hedges. Although his parents doted on him, young Wayne frequently quarrelled with them. This was not an early indication of murderous psychopathic behaviour, however; many young boys bicker with their parents. The three generally got on well enough at home. Homer bought his son a toy train, and a bike. He also bought him a combination rifle and shotgun and the pair used to go into the country on hunting trips. Wayne "didn't like to kill very much," Homer was later to say at his son's trial, "so he gave that up."

Wayne schooled at Douglass High School, where he took an early interest in the fields of radio and journalism. In his teens, he even constructed a working radio station in the basement of the family home, and for a while worked as an announcer and reporter for WBJE radio. Friends attested to the fact that Wayne was "brilliant" at science and mathematics, and an especially excellent student at electronics. A teacher described him as "a sensitive boy [who] wasn't extremely outgoing, but would talk with you about topics of interest to him". A bright student, Wayne William's IQ would later be determined as an above-average 118.[1] He graduated in the top ten percent of his class at Frederick Douglass.

Williams had a brush with the law around this time when he was found to have installed red lights behind the grille of his car. At the time, he said this was because he worked for a radio station and he used the lights to help him get to where he needed to cover stories. Working as a crime-scene photographer took him all over the city, and it could be supposed that flashing red lights, as well as his own police scanner, would've facilitated easy movement. He was arrested for impersonating a police officer and unlawfully using emergency equipment. Nonetheless, Williams was never charged for the misdemeanour.

---

[1] This was to happen at prison.

In January 1977, he enrolled at George State University, majoring in business administration and psychology. In August that year, he was charged by police for making a false charge. It's not known what the specifics of this charge were, but it was eventually dismissed.

Williams' parents had indulged their son every step of the way. They'd encouraged his entrepreneurial bent and bought him what he needed to indulge his pursuits. They spent a lot of money on his goals, but got very little in return. His life up until then, however, had been a series of disappointments and failures, and Williams was to disappoint his parents yet again: in March 1979, he dropped out of college. He dipped his toe into automobile racing and freelance television photography before turning his hand to music production. However, in reality it was a "career of limited achievements". Williams was just a struggling huckster, still living at home with his parents and their Alsatian dog, handing out flyers to promote himself. And just four months later, the first two victims would turn up dead.

A grand jury indicted Williams for two counts of first-degree murder. The trial commenced on 6 January 1982. The jury – comprised of three men and nine women, amongst them eight African-Americans – spent six days listening to the evidence.

Williams insisted that he was innocent. During the trial, the jury heard evidence of Williams' "aggressive homosexuality", as two young men testified about the unwanted advances he'd made towards them. Important forensic evidence that upheld the case against Williams included canine hair and fibre analysis linking him to Jimmy Ray Payne and Nathaniel Cater, as well as to 12 other pattern-murder cases. There was little the defence could do other than present Williams himself. He described himself as a "carefree, happy-go-lucky person". Under cross-examination, prosecutors followed a strategy for questioning him: they kept him on the stand for as long as possible, riling him up by focusing upon his failures in life. The tactic worked. Williams' "happy-go-lucky" demeanour was shot to pieces. As was his frankly unbelievable explanation for being in the Ku

Klux Klan haunting ground of Cobb County at three o'clock in the morning. He appeared combative and defensive, unwisely alienating the jury. He was found guilty after the jury deliberated for 11 hours and he was given two consecutive life sentences. As he was hurried out by deputies, dressed in a brown suit, Williams told reporters:

> *"I maintained all along through this trial my innocence. I hold no malice against the jury, the prosecutors or the court ... I hope the person or persons who committed these crimes can be brought to justice. I did not do this."*
> (*The Plain Dealer*, 28 February 1982, Cleveland, Ohio)

Police immediately attributed all by six of the remaining 22 Atlanta Child Murders victims to Williams, unceremoniously shutting down the cases without bringing charges and ending further investigation into them.

Today, Williams continues to maintain his innocence. He believes that law enforcement investigators, desperate to make an arrest in a high-profile case, railroaded the case against him. He says there is a lack of physical evidence against him. He points out that no one has ever testified against him or even claimed to have seen him being violent towards anyone.

Some of the parents of the child victims also maintain that Williams is innocent, including the mother of Yusuf Bell. She considers that the prosecution was political. "I believe that the pressures were so extreme that once Atlanta was provided an out, they took it," she stated. On 21 March 2019, officials announced that evidence from the case would be re-tested. It could be that the authorities simply want closure.

Meanwhile, Wayne Williams is serving two consecutive life sentences at Telfair State Prison in Georgia. On 20 November 2019, he was denied parole. Whether a sociopathic murderer or the victim of a miscarriage of justice, he is described by his custodians as a "model prisoner".

# Herbert Richard "Herb" Baumeister
## (active 1980s-1996)

AFTER THE 1991 ARREST of Jeffrey Dahmer, the necrophilic serial killer known as the Milwaukee Cannibal, his neighbours wished to vacate their properties as quickly as possible. Ghoulish sightseers and thrill-seeking tourists used to come to the site in order to feast their eyes upon the grisly spectacle of the scene of multiple murders. The Oxford Apartments building was demolished within a year, and the former site of Dahmer's crimes remains a vacant lot to this day. When the crimes of John Wayne Gacy, who came to be known as the Killer Clown, were discovered, the quiet Chicago neighbourhood suffered a similar fate, with unwanted visitors arriving by the carload – like moths to a flame – hoping to satisfy their cravings for the macabre. Gacy's home was also, in due course, torn down. When the site was redeveloped by a subsequent owner, he found it necessary to change the property's street address in order to discourage morbid day-trippers.

Fox Hollow Farm is unusual in one specific sense. This property is the 18-acre site where a serial murderer committed numerous despicable deeds – and yet it still stands. It is largely unchanged. The address remains the same, and there have been no attempts made by succeeding owners to change its name; a wooden sign bearing the name of Fox Hollow Farm on both sides still welcomes visitors travelling along East 156th Street in bucolic Westfield, 20 miles north of Indianapolis. The 11,000 square-foot Tudor-style building also remains much the same, sitting proudly, surrounded by lush pastures and standing trees. It is an idyllic site, yet it holds a haunted past.

The area falls within the bounds of the socially conservative swath of the US southeast known as the "Bible Belt". It is a region dominated by evangelical Protestantism, where God-fearing citizens attend church and religion generally informs their thinking and behaviours. The state has moved with the times, and in recent years homosexuality has become more tolerated, if not embraced. It wasn't always like that. Even as recently as the 1980s there were no safe bars in Indianapolis where the local gay population could congregate with like-minded people. The first Pride event, in 1981, was a sit-down dinner at a local hotel to which the attendees arrived wearing masks so that their identities couldn't be seen. Pride the following year was better attended, and better supported by the local gay business community. Attendance the next year doubled again to nearly 1,000 supporters, and the increase continued right through the '80s and into the first years of the next decade. By then the organisers of Indy Pride had extended their invitation more widely, turning it into more of a public event than a private function.

The emergence of gay pride over the span of the 1980s, however, was an *evolutionary* rather than revolutionary process. Homosexuality was not by any means widely accepted, and society still tended to shun gay individuals. In light of this, some preferred to suppress their natural desires and attempted to lead so-called "straight" lifestyles, getting married and having children. Others though, embraced their sexuality, and they sought places where they could go out to meet other like-minded individuals. Gay bars were few and far between, *but they were known* – and to the gay community who supported these downtown establishments they were popular, well-loved lifelines where they could relax and be themselves. That is, until men started to vanish and the missing persons flyers began to get posted around town. And then the gay community of Indianapolis gradually began to suspect that a serial killer was at work …

Herbert Richard Baumeister was born in Indianapolis, Indiana on 7 April 1947, the eldest of Dr Herbert Baumeister and his wife Elizabeth's four children. The family home was in Butler-Tarkington in the city. Herbert Sr. practised anaesthesiology at the nearby Methodist Hospital; Elizabeth was a homemaker. By all accounts, Herb had a perfectly normal, uneventful childhood, and it's difficult to find anything that happened in it to explain what he was to become. Yet, the boy somehow developed a nickname: "Weird Herb". It didn't come without reason. Young Herb had strange hangdog eyes, which gave him an unfortunate appearance, similar to the cartoon dog Droopy. That wasn't all, however. Herb had also developed an early obsession with death and decay. Classmates later recalled that he had a fondness for playing with dead animals. One day, he found a dead crow and he took it into the school classroom where he left it on a teacher's desk in order to elicit a response from her. What isn't clear is whether or not Herb had *killed* the creature in question. On another occasion, he was caught urinating upon a teacher's desk. Acquaintances also recalled that he'd asked what it would be like to drink your own urine. "Weird Herb" was certainly living up to his name.

The anti-social behaviour continued as Herb entered his adolescent years. He developed a macabre sense of humour and his peers began to distance themselves from the odd boy with the morbid bent in their midst. In class, he became disruptive and unpredictable. Teachers, concerned at the deepening of Herb's difficulties, reached out to his parents for help. The Baumeister parents had also become concerned about their eldest son's behaviours. They sent him for a psychiatric evaluation. The results returned – Herb was schizophrenic. There were also suggestions that he had a multiple personality disorder.[1] The details of what steps the Baumeister parents did to treat their son are unclear, but it's believed that they did not seek treatment.

As Herb progressed through high school – he enrolled at North Central in 1961 – the strange behaviours continued unabated. He remained an average student, although one who was never able to fit in and who was failing socially. The school's

---

[1] Nowadays known as dissociative identity disorder, this is a mental disorder characterised by the maintenance of at least two distinct and enduring personality states, often accompanied by memory gaps. It is overwhelmingly associated with childhood trauma or abuse, although there is no suggestion that Herb had suffered from either as a child.

extracurricular focus was sports, and the football team were revered as the most popular pupils. Herb was in awe of this tight-knit group, and he often attempted to gain their acceptance. He failed. Following their rejection, Herb retreated into himself and spent his final years at school in solitude.

He enrolled at Indiana University in 1965, majoring, unsurprisingly, in anatomy. His strange behaviour followed. He remained an outcast and didn't make any new friends. After the first semester he dropped out, but under pressure from his father he re-enrolled in 1967, only to drop out again before the end of the first semester.

Baumeister's brief time at college wasn't a complete write-off, however. It was here that he met Juliana ("Julie") Saiter, a part-time student who also worked as a high school journalism teacher. The two found that they had a lot in common and they began dating. Extremely conservative politically, they had entrepreneurial ambitions and wanted to go into business.

By 1971 the two had married, but the following year, six months into his marriage, Baumeister spent a short period in a local psychiatric institution. Julie said that Herb was "hurting and needed help". The emotional breakdown, it seems, was caused by some difficulty with a car. Upon his release after two months, after his father pulled some strings, Baumeister started working as a copyboy at the *Indianapolis Star*. It was a low-paid, low-level position, but the young rookie dove straight in. As at school and at university, he tried to ingratiate himself with his colleagues. Co-workers later reported that he was efficient and well dressed ... but irritating. His over-eagerness appeared childlike; his displays of pique when his work wasn't recognised also earned him little respect. Once again he'd failed to fit in.

Disillusioned with the low-level work, and sour about his diminished status, Baumeister resigned to take up a position at the Bureau of Motor Vehicles (BMV). He started with a new attitude, coming across as officious and belligerent towards his colleagues, emulating the manner in which he imagined an effective supervisor would behave. Once again he'd got it wrong. His conduct was unpredictable and off-key. As a joke one year he sent a Christmas card to everyone picturing himself dressed as a woman in holiday garb. In conservative Indiana in the early seventies few found amusement in that. "Weird Herb" simply could not escape being thought of as an oddball. He was also labelled a closet homosexual.

Despite all of this, things seemed to be going reasonably well for Baumeister at home. Nine years into their marriage Julie gave to a daughter, Maria. Two years later, in 1981, a son, Erich, followed, and in 1984 Emily arrived. They couple were happy, but it was not a demonstrably physical relationship. Julie was later to comment that the two had only been sexually intimate six times in the 30 years of their marriage.

At work, however, things were to take a turn for the worse. Baumeister had retained his post at BMV for some 14 years. Evidently he'd managed to prove himself an asset to the company, a go-getter able to produce results. He was promoted to programme director, a position he'd long yearned for. Within the year, however, he was out, under circumstances entirely of his own making. In 1985, he urinated on a letter addressed to the then-Indiana Governor, Robert D. Orr. Rumours had already been flying about who'd been responsible for an earlier misdemeanour, in which urine was found on the desk of Baumeister's manager. Given that Baumeister had committed the very same act whilst at school, it's not difficult to surmise that when BMV terminated his employment they'd got the right man. Financial strains gripped the Baumeister marriage and this led to Julie spending weekends at her mother-in-law's condo on Lake Wawasee. Baumeister stayed behind. Now, jobless and with too much time on his hands, he began to drink more. Unbeknownst to his wife and family, he also began to spend time downtown, making secret forays to hang out in Indy's gay bars.

It was also around this time, from the mid-1980s onwards, that unexplained deaths occurred alongside roadways in Indiana. In 1985, the body of Eric Roetiger, a 17-year-old white male, was found abandoned not far from the route between Indianapolis and Columbus. Then the body of 26-year-old Steven Elliot was found, followed by that of 32-year-old Clay Boatman. At least nine other unexplained deaths were discovered along the same I-70 corridor between Indianapolis and Ohio. Although never categorically proven to have been the handiwork of Herbert Baumeister, his wife was later to inform authorities that her husband had travelled this route to Ohio many times for business purposes. Then, from late 1991, the bodies suddenly stopped turning up along that part of the road.

Coincidentally – or perhaps not – in the early 1990s, the gay citizens of Indianapolis began to wonder what had happened to certain young men who appeared to be disappearing unexpectedly. Here today, gone tomorrow – the departures couldn't be explained. But as the baffling disappearances continued, word began to spread within Indy's gay community during 1993 and 1994. Misgivings were aroused; nervousness grew. The perplexing disappearances were reported to the police.

Unfortunately, the police at that time weren't overly interested in the apparently transient lifestyles of a few men from Indy's gay community. The alarm was tentatively raised from a different quarter. The mother of 28-year-old Alan Broussard approached a private detective in June 1994. She told him that her son had gone missing. She'd last seen him before he headed out to see his partner at a popular gay bar called Brothers. A week later, he still hadn't returned.

In Indianapolis, a person is not classed as "missing" until 24 hours have passed. After that, the case goes to a district detective. If the person is not found within 30 days the case is transferred to the Missing Persons Bureau. Alan Broussard's mother, quite understandably, didn't want to wait that long. She told PI Virgil Vandagriff that her son appeared to have evaporated into thin air. She spoke of his trusting demeanour, and of his tendency to drink too much. It started to look like the casual wandering of a wayward party animal.

Despite reservations, Vandagriff took the case. At first he presumed no ill-intent had befallen his client's son. That soon changed. As information quickly tumbled in, Vandagriff learned of other mysterious disappearances of young gay men, all with similar characteristics, all with similar lifestyles. As his exploration of the inexplicable vanishings continued he discovered a pattern: all of the men were gay and they'd all been visiting the area's gay bars at the time they'd gone missing. The men all had a similar look – white, clean-cut, good-looking, of similar weight and height, their ages ranging from the early-20s to mid-30s. Some of them had come from rural communities across Indiana, leaving behind their families to move to the big city where they could express their sexuality more freely. Some of them were male prostitutes who worked the downtown gay bars. Some hadn't even told their families they were moving; they'd just left. Then they went missing. No one knew whether they'd packed up to return home or gone further afield. Vandagriff was perplexed, but he was able to draw one startling conclusion, for the connections were there to be made ... if only someone had looked. He came to believe that a serial killer was haunting Indianapolis' gay district. And with another man vanishing later that month – 34-year-old Roger Allen Goodlet – he became convinced that the disappearances were more than circumstantial. He'd never have discovered the pattern of disappearances if it hadn't been for the misgivings of his concerned client, and of members of the gay community themselves. He knew he had to take these suspicions seriously. The only problem was, there were no bodies to be found.

Tony Harris[2] almost became a "body". In 1992, Harris contacted investigators with the claim that he'd almost been killed by a man he'd met at a gay bar. Harris had been a friend of Roger Goodlet, one of the men who'd vanished without a trace. No one in officialdom seemed to care about Roger's disappearance, but Harris did. He offered to help find Roger. He began posting

---

[2] A pseudonym used to protect the witness's privacy.

flyers around gay scene bars that they'd both frequented. And he was acutely aware that a poster asking for information about Roger Goodlet had been pinned to one of the walls of the 501 Club.

One night, Harris was at the 501 Club when he noticed a man sitting at the bar, staring fixedly at the poster of his friend Roger. There was something odd about the intensity with which this strange man stared at the poster – and about how the man was licking his lips. The man wasn't a regular at that particular establishment, but Harris recalled having seen him a couple of times in other bars. He was a tall, skinny, quiet man with drooping eyes. The eyes were *particularly* memorable. Harris had a feeling about the way the man seemed captivated by the poster of Roger. Intuitively, he knew there was something amiss, that this stranger had some idea about what had happened to Roger. Harris approached him.

"Do you know him?" he asked.

The man denied that he did.

The two fell into conversation. Harris introduced himself, and in return the man gave his name as "Brian Smart". "Brian" was a landscape gardener, he said, and he was in the process of preparing an empty house before the new owners moved in. He invited Harris to come along to the house for cocktails and a swim in the indoor pool. Despite a few reservations, Harris reluctantly agreed.

Outside the bar, "Brian" suggested that the two drive to the house separately, and this also stirred Harris' suspicions. Somehow overcoming his misgivings, Harris got into "Brian's" grey Buick and they set off, driving through the city streets, leaving town, and eventually travelling what seemed to Harris a lengthy journey, turning along many country roads dotted with expensive homes set in bucolic farmland. Eventually, "Brian" made a turnoff at a property with a sign at the gate. The only word Harris could make out was "farm".

The car stopped at the end of a lengthy drive alongside a large Tudor-style farmhouse. There appeared to be no one at home, although an array of other vehicles were parked in the garage. Inside the house several dogs roamed about. Harris was told not to pet them. The place itself was haphazardly appointed, with many items of furniture and boxes strewn about. "Brian's" explanation that he was fixing up the property seemed genuine enough.

"Brian" told Harris that the electricity was off in this part of the house. He led Harris through various darkened rooms and down a stairwell into the basement. There, there was a recreational room. When the lights were turned on Harris was disconcerted to see further clutter down here, amongst it a collection of mannequins, all of them dressed and posed. It sent a shiver down his spine. "Brian's" explanation for this made less sense: "I get lonely down here," he said. "They give me company."

When offered a drink Harris declined. The party mood had all but left him. His host, however, must've felt different, for he left for a while, and when he came back his darkened mood had become more buoyant. Harris later speculated that he'd perked himself up with cocaine; he'd recognised the signs.

"Brian" encouraged Harris to have a naked swim. By the time Harris had undressed, "Brian" had opened the sliding patio doors, allowing the cold night air to drift in, and a fog had formed above the warm water. Harris slipped in.

Immediately, as if the thought had just come into his head, "Brian" asked his guest if he wanted to see a neat trick. He then went on to describe how cutting off the flow of blood to the brain could induce a greater orgasm, demonstrating by pinching the two carotid arteries in his own neck. "You should see how someone looks when you're doing it to them," "Brian" said. "Their lips change colour." By chance (or otherwise), a section of hose was floating on the surface of the water. "Brian" told Harris to perform the trick on him.

"Brian" then stripped and lay down on a foldout couch. He guided Harris into placing the hose around his throat and pulling it ever more tightly. Whilst Harris did this, "Brian" masturbated. Then "Brian" wanted to try the same trick on Harris.

Harris, by now, had become disturbed by his host's behaviour. However, feeling compelled to do whatever "Brian" wanted him to do, he agreed to give it a try. That almost unbelievably irrational decision was driven by fear and apprehension rather than a desire to try an erotic game. The only way to get out of this situation, he rationalised to himself, was to play along. He placed "Brian's" hands around his neck and lay down.

"Brian" himself was keen to play along. Taking the bait, he now wrapped the hose around Harris' neck and began to tighten the noose. Harris felt the garrotte constricting further. The pressure in his head mounted and he felt himself coming closer to passing out. Now, he knew he couldn't wait: he feigned unconsciousness.

As he lay there, his eyes closed, he felt "Brian" release the grip of the hose and get up. He waited. "Brian" shook him, lightly at first, then more vigorously. "Brian" whispered his name. But it didn't sound like concern; it was almost as if he was checking that Harris was actually dead. At this point Harris opened his eyes and grinned. "Brian" suddenly raged. "You scared the shit out of me! You know you can die doing this!"

Harris decided to lay his suspicions bare. "Is that what happened to Roger Goodlet?"

At this, "Brian" stared at him. He acted as if the incident were a joke, an amusing game during which he'd been totally in control. Harris didn't believe it. His only intention now was to get out alive. He played along with "Brian's" charade, all the while thinking about how he could find out the true identity of this man, and also how he could make his escape.

"Brian" showed Harris around the house and what he saw confirmed his suspicions. The house was not unoccupied, as the stranger had claimed. Clothes and children's toys were testament to that. Eventually, "Brian" became tired and feel asleep. Harris took the opportunity to rifle through "Brian's" trousers, looking for an ID, something that would confirm his actual name, for by now Harris was convinced that this strange sleeping man *was not* called "Brian Smart". Unfortunately, whilst he was looking for a wallet, "Brian" gave a snort and stirred and Harris quickly had to abandon his mission.

Harris had to work hard to convince "Brian" to drive him back to town. Nevertheless, he managed to do so. "You're a good sport," "Brian" told him on the way. "You really know how to play." As he dropped Harris off at the 501 Club, "Brian" insisted that Harris promise to return to the bar the next week.

Harris _did_ return the next week. But in the interim he'd also spoken to the private investigator, Virgil Vandagriff. If "Brian" showed up again, there would also be a covert welcoming party awaiting him. The tall, dark-haired stranger with the dropping eyes, however, did not arrive. It appeared that Harris had been stood up.

Undoubtedly, "Brian Smart" was not the true name of the erotic asphyxiation aficionado. It was Herbert Baumeister, and Tony Harris had had a miraculously close shave with death. Quite why Baumeister didn't return to the 501 Club and finish off the job is not known, but it's certainly possible that that had been his plan when he'd made Harris promise to return. Perhaps he'd been spooked. Or maybe he simply felt that he'd already got away with it. We will never know.

We do know, however, that by this stage Baumeister was a wealthy man. His luck had turned in the years following his abrupt dismissal from BMV after urinating on a letter. For a while he'd worked in a thrift store and, although initially feeling that the work was menial, he soon saw the potential. He borrowed money from his now-widowed mother in 1988 and opened a store selling discounted goods, which proved popular and lucrative. The Children's Bureau of Indianapolis invested. The store was neat, clean and only sold quality merchandise, and it became a mecca for those on a budget. No doubt buoyed by Baumeister's management acumen, Sav-A-Lot was a surprising success. A second store was opened, and then another, and soon its owner became rich. The Baumeister family were able to move to Fox Hollow Farm in the fashionable and exclusive district of Westfield ... and then began the disappearances of young men from the Indianapolis gay bar scene ...

Two men disappeared in May 1993 – Michael Andrew Riley, aged 22, and Johnny L. Bayer, aged 20. They were closely followed by Jeffrey Allen Jones (31) and Richard D. Hamilton (20) in July. Allen Lee Livingstone (27) vanished in August. They were all young, good-looking gay men whose lifestyles meant that their disappearances might not have been reported.

The next year brought no respite. Stephen S. Hale (26) disappeared in April 1994. Then, in June, Alan Wayne Broussard (28) disappeared. The following month, Roger Alan Goodlet vanished, leading to his mother hiring a private investigator, which in turn led to posters being placed in gay bars. The killer's house of cards was about to come tumbling down ...

PI Vandagriff, now realising that he was onto a larger case than it had at first seemed, enlisted the help of a no-nonsense police detective called Mary Wilson. She'd been working the case of missing person Jeff Jones and, as it happened, was also investigating the disappearances of other Indianapolis men. After hearing Tony Harris' account, in all its bizarre detail, she recognised the importance of this potential connection. Wilson and Harris prowled the roads of Westfield in an attempt to find the Tudor-style farmhouse, the scene where Harris had been throttled. None of the residences appeared familiar.

Meanwhile, Vandagriff was now working unpaid, feeling the case too important to give up. He dispatched one of his investigators to peer in the windows of homes in the Westfield area that matched Tony Harris' description, hoping to find one that had an indoor pool surrounded by mannequins. Eventually, he came across one on a rambling estate that struck a chord. Its owner was Herbert Baumeister. When shown aerial photos of the farmhouse, Harris was uncertain: from his own recollection the driveway was too short. The case had stalled.

Herb Baumeister, at this stage, was living his life under a cloak of counterfeit normalcy. He was still married to Julie and he was still a successful businessman living in the suburbs. Yet there were changes afoot. People began to wonder at and talk about the strange marriage of their neighbour. Shoppers began staying away from Sav-A-Lot in droves and business began to suffer. Bills started to pile up. Employees were now talking about their boss's dark moods and the behind-the-scenes disarray of the stores. They especially noted his middle-of-the-day drinking.

Baumeister must've assumed after a year that the heat had cooled after his incident with Tony Harris. He went out drinking again. On the evening of 29 August 1995, he stopped by the Varsity Lounge. Also present at the bar that night was Tony Harris, who had all but given up hope of spotting the tall, thin man with the distinctively droopy eyes. Harris could barely contain himself. He approached "Brian Smart" and began a friendly chat with him. Then, at the end of the evening, as the man drove off, Harris took a note of his pickup registration number.

The next morning, the detective Mary Wilson learned that plate number 75237A belonged not to "Brian Smart", but to Herbert Richard Baumeister of Westfield Indiana. She cheered when she learned that his Hollow Fox Farm manor house had a basement swimming pool.

Wilson didn't hang about. On 1 September, a Friday, she and a male colleague went straight to the Washington Street Sav-A-Lot store and walked straight up the counter and told the clerk she was here for Mr Baumeister. The boss came out and greeted the detectives with a friendly handshake. Wilson asked him if he'd ever visited any Indy gay bars. Baumeister quickly and adamantly denied ever having frequented such places. Wilson straightaway responded by saying that several eyewitnesses had given evidence to the contrary, and one had even noted down his vehicle number plate.

Now visibly shaken, Baumeister admitted in a hushed voice that he _had_, in fact, visited such bars occasionally, but that his family weren't aware of it. This seemed a reasonable enough response to Wilson; the man, after all, had a wife and three children. Wilson told him exactly why they were there, that they were investigating the disappearances of several young men in the Indianapolis area, and that she felt he were somehow involved. *Could we search your property?* she enquired of him in a pleasant voice. Baumeister's demeanour immediately changed again. *No,* he said, *if the detectives had any further questions they should speak to his lawyer.*

The detectives tried to do just that. However, the criminal defence attorney whose name Baumeister had given them had no idea who he was. Baffled, the detectives returned to Baumeister's Sav-A-Lot store, only to be given the same response: *Talk to my lawyer.*

The detectives *again* approached the attorney that Baumeister said represented him. *Again,* the lawyer denied any knowledge of him.

For a third time the detectives returned to Baumeister's store, where they got the same response. By now, however, he'd managed to submit a cheque to the law firm. Now Baumeister's newly-retained attorney was able to tell the detectives, *No, you may not search Mr Baumeister's property.* Baumeister informed his wife that a disgruntled employee who had it in for him had been approaching the police with false claims. As a result, she too declined to give consent for a search.

Frustrated but undeterred, the detectives arranged for an aerial surveillance of Fox Hollow Farm. On board the helicopter was also a forensic anthropologist, whose brief it was to search for potential burial sites. Unfortunately, this strategy drew a blank. Either there were no bodies on the property or too much time had lapsed since any burial, they surmised.

Some months later, the Baumeister son, Erich, now aged 14, was playing in the woods behind the house. Hidden within the undergrowth, just 50 feet from the back patio, he found a human skeleton. As any youngster might be wont to do, he decided to put the skull on the end of a stick and use it to scare his sister. Unsurprisingly, their mother got wind of this and wanted to know where Erich had found the macabre item. He told her it had been lying in the woods. Julie demanded that he take her to the exact spot.

Upon being taken there, sure enough, Julie saw in the undergrowth a very-human-looking skeleton. Stunned, she waited until her husband returned home and then let him have it full blast. "What the hell is this?" she demanded.

Initially shocked by having his misdemeanours raised before him, Baumeister quickly recovered. He told his wife that this was one of this father's previous anatomical specimens, a remnant from his medical career. He wasn't sure how it had managed to end up in the woods, but he'd be sure to get rid of it in the morning. So convincing had Herb been in brushing off the find that Julie took his account at face value.

She went out to the same spot again a week later, and true enough, the skeleton was gone. For now, Julie said no more about it.

However, something must've been at the back of Julie's mind when she contacted the police one day. Her husband and son were away at the condo on the lake, and if the police wanted to search their property then this would be an ideal time. Investigators sprung quickly into action. They came to the house and asked Julie where she'd seen the skeleton. She brought them to the spot. At first it seemed as if the site were clear. Then, as the detectives performed a finer search, they began to find small bones. First one ... then another. A number of teeth that appeared to be human. As they continued searching, the volume of bones they found increased. Soon it appeared that here lay the skeletonised remains of several individuals.

The forensic anthropologist arrived to the scene, who was able to confirm with certainty not only that the bones were human, they had only recently been deposited there. They were standing amidst a crime scene.

Julie, already concerned about the state of Herb's mind – and of greater concern, about the safety of her son – asked the police to go to the condo and get her son. She didn't know which way Herb's unbalanced mind would tip once he was confronted with the evidence of a body with the grounds of their home.

Deputies duly arrived at the condo with a story about Mrs

Baumeister wanting her son to be with her due to the divorce action. No mention was made of any bones having been found at Fox Holly Farm. However, Baumeister knew then that the game was up. Nevertheless, he kept his counsel and allowed the boy to go with the deputies whilst he remained at Lake Wawasee.

Now, legal manoeuvrings became pertinent as the state prosecutor had to decide on how to proceed with the case against Baumeister. It wasn't as open and shut as it at first seemed. The man hadn't been in trouble with the law for a while, and the evidence, at this stage, was circumstantial at the very least. The most pressing problem was that Baumeister's attorney might ask for a speedy trial, and in Indiana that meant within just 70 days. And an unprepared prosecution ran the risk that their only suspect might walk free.

Meanwhile, the investigators' examination of the body discovery sites had exposed some unpleasant facts. The murderer had simply left the bodies unburied in the woods, allowing them to rot. Once decomposition had done its work, the remains were then doused with petrol and burned in an act of further concealment. Animals had evidently removed some of the body parts, scattering them throughout the woods. Some of the parts had "self-buried", a process by which the natural movements of earth and decaying foliage, mulch and other debris, helped along by the weather, gradually inters the remains. All of the bones – some 5,500 items – were collected, collated and packed away for removal from the 18-acre graveyard. Amongst them were 11 first metacarpal bones. The unavoidable implication was that a minimum of 11 bodies lay within the woods.

On the day that the forensic team were due to leave, a couple of teenagers from the next-door farm approached them. The youths mentioned a local creek in which there appeared to be a lot of bones. When the forensic team surveyed the creek they were amazed by the sheer volume of human bones within its waters. All types of bone, from all parts of the body. And all of them human. Eventually, the remains of eight individuals were identified. However, from the sheer range of bones and bone fragments, forensics officers estimated that the total number of bodies that had been dumped at the farm ranged somewhere between 17 and 20.

The investigative team consulted an FBI profiler who theorised that the bones in the creek were the killer's original disposal site. Then, as he continued his crimes, succeeding in drawing no attention to himself, he became more arrogant and more lazy. Over time, he began to discard the bodies closer to the house, making less effort to disguise them, until at last he was dumping remains practically on his own doorstep – and, in fact, the most recent victim appeared to have been placed a mere 50-feet distance from his backdoor patio. This complacency is a well-known feature of some serial killers, and it's often their undoing. As they become more emboldened, they begin to take chances that they'd never have even considered at the start of their criminal careers. This complacency can often result in the best – and sometimes *only* – leads that law enforcement have to follow.

Herbert Baumeister no doubt saw news of the unfolding investigation at Fox Hollow Farm on the television. Now he knew with absolute certainty that the game was up. Packing up a few items, he got into his grey Buick and began a long journey north across the Canadian border. On the way, he stopped at a pay-phone and asked his brother to wire him some money.

In Canada, he stopped his car beneath an overpass bridge. Whilst Baumeister was sleeping, a passing Canadian Mounted Police officer rapped on the window to warn him that it wasn't safe to stop there. Baumeister told her that he was just a tourist passing through. The Mountie glanced into the back seat of the vehicles and noticed a large quantity of videotapes. Nothing more was said about this, and the officer, with no reason to detain Baumeister, allowed him move on.

Just what had been recorded on those videos remains pure speculation because they have never been found. However, out of all the items that Baumeister could've brought with him when he left the condo for the last time, he'd chosen to bring a number of videos. Of course, one's first thoughts might be that they contained snuff movies documenting his crimes ... or some evidence that the men whose bodies had been found on his property had been guests there. Perhaps the recordings had been taken using hidden cameras. A strategically hidden video camera was later found at the Fox Hollow Farm estate. Many killers like to keep souvenirs of their victims so that they can use them later in their fantasies. Perhaps in Baumeister's case this had been a collection of snuff movies. Whatever the case, in taking the videos, he may have been spotted in the act of disposing of critical evidence against him.

He found his way to an idyllic spot on the shores of Lake Huron in Pinery Provincial Park. Sitting down at a sandy picnic area close to the shore, he took a few moments to compose a rambling three-page suicide note on yellow notepaper, written in scrawling, almost illegible writing. In the note, he apologised for his family's financial woes and his failing marriage as the reasons for taking his own life, but he made no mention of the crimes for which he was now being investigated. *His* was going to be the last word. He ended his note by mentioning that he was going to eat a peanut sandwich and then go to sleep. He signed the note "*The* Herb Baumeister".

Presumably after having his sandwich, *The* Herb Baumeister then set the paper down carefully beside him, put a .357 magnum revolver to his forehead and pulled the trigger. He died on 3 July 1996 at the age of 50, taking many of his secrets to the grave.

Inevitably, the conspiracy theorists have had their say. Some claim that no gun was found alongside Baumeister's body when it was found, leading to speculation that another person had forced him to write his own suicide note before killing him in order to gain his silence. Others maintain that his body was found at the centre of an "occult symbol", surrounded by several dead birds. All the evidence, however, pointed clearly to death by suicide, and to date no other person is being sought for the murders of the men found on Fox Hollow Farm.

Another interesting theory has arisen. The so-called "I-70 Killer" is the unidentified serial murderer of six store clerks who shot his victims in premises located nearby Interstate 70. The victims were usually young, petite, brunette women. Although one of the victims was male, it's believed that because this individual wore his hair in a ponytail and was kneeling with his back turned, the killer may have *assumed* he was dispatching a woman. The killings occurred in Texas between 1993 and1994. Although money from taken from the stores, robbery was not the motive for the attacks. A witness to one of the assassinations described the killer as a thin man with "lazy eyelids". Could Baumeister have travelled further afield, killing for the sheer enjoyment of it? The victims had not been sexually assaulted, and the spree ended with Baumeister's death. It is certainly a feasible thought.

And of course, as already mentioned, another killer, the "I-70 Strangler", was a prolific killer of men in the early 1970s. After Baumeister's death, witnesses came forward to identify his picture as the same man who gave his friend a lift home one night, and who was never seen alive again. One's suspicions could easily be drawn to a natural conclusion.

Serial killers chiefly fall into one of four categories – the psychotic, the missionary motive type, the thrill killer and the lust killer – and of these categories Herbert Baumeister best fits into the last. It is the most common type, the one that induces most public fear and revulsion. Inevitably, the newspaper headlines were splashed big: "THE 'GAY SLAYINGS' MYSTERY", "PROBE EXPOSES DOUBLE LIFE", "BUSINESSMAN PUZZLED PEOPLE IN LIFE AND DEATH" and "GRISLY INDY". As if public interest in the case were not already aroused!

Julie Baumeister cooperated with the investigation after her husband's death, giving up credit card receipts, phone calls logs and even access to Herb's car. Everything pointed to the victims found on Hollow Fox Farm having disappeared when Julie and the children were away. The police had already concluded that

Baumeister was responsible; they now had enough evidence to close the case. Quite *why* Baumeister engaged in his heinous killing spree will probably never be known. One can only suppose that a deep-seated hatred of his own self and his hidden sexuality led him to kill others who reminded him of this. It is scarcely a great insight. Where the childhood interest in death and decay came from is lost to time. Certainly nothing from his early years has come to light to support any causation. Untreated mental illness may have loosened his impulse-drive, but it's not the answer as to *why* he killed. Superficially, he was the man who had it all – a wife, children, a successful business – and yet he'd begun his murderous campaign well before the decline in his fortunes. Perhaps it really *is* as simple as homosexual self-loathing. The mysteries of the man remain long after his death.

Finally, we have an interesting afterthought. Herb Baumeister had an older brother. During the period when it's believed that Herb was strangling men in his pool, his older brother was found dead in a whirlpool. The cause for the death remains a mystery. Is it possible that one of Herb's victims was closer to home? Again, we may never know.

# Larry William Eyler
(active 1982-1984)

SOME SOCIETIES DO NOT make it easy for those facing challenges –
especially those who find themselves struggling to accept their
sexuality. Sometimes they find themselves living in families
which are extremely conservative or overtly masculine; sometimes their ties are the constraints of fundamentalist religion. It's
sewn into the fabric of their lives; it's ubiquitous. They can feel
demonised and degraded by the intolerance and non-acceptance
of family, friends and colleagues around them. There is nowhere
and no way to express themselves. They begin to experience a
lack of belongingness. They know *what* they are, *what* they
were born to be, but they must suppress their natural inclinations, denying their urgings so profoundly that when the built-
up rage against themselves finally erupts, the resulting explosion
can be unpredictable and have wide-ranging consequences.
When that happens, innocent passers-by can get caught in the
maelstrom and end up paying a mighty price – their lives.

On 21 December 1952, in Crawfordsville, Indiana, Larry William Eyler was born, the youngest of George Howard Eyler and
Shirley Phyllis Kennedy's four children. George Eyler was a
chronic alcoholic who physically and emotionally abused his
wife and children. Shirley divorced George when Larry was
aged two and he remained living with his mother. She married
again when he was aged four, but this marriage also failed and
a year later she divorced. A third marriage was followed by a
third divorce. When he was 10, Larry's mother remarried for the
fourth time. This was also destined to fail. Shirley was a woman
who liked to marry.

In addition to marrying, Shirley also enjoyed several boyfriends, and new men were constantly coming in and going out
of young Larry's life. He didn't enjoy a good relationship with
any of them. One in particular brutally tortured the boy by running scalding hot water over his head. However, it's thought that

much worse was done to Larry by his natural father.

All the same, Shirley tried her best to care for her family. She had various jobs – waitressing and factory-work during the week, and at weekends she did occasionally bussed a bar – but it wasn't enough and she struggled to support her children financially and couldn't care for them sufficiently. As a result, Larry and his sister were regularly taken into foster placements, given over to babysitters or even left in the care of their two pre-teen older siblings. Inevitably, difficulties associated with a lack of early childhood attachment would take their toll on Larry's psychological status and he'd go on to experience the great twin fears of separation and abandonment. School provided little relief; at St Joseph School in Lebanon, Indiana, he was bullied for being from poor family and teased about his parents' divorce, leading to Theresa, his older sister, having to step in to confront those who persecuted him.

Due to his snowballing obstinacy and unpredictable behaviours he was sent to a home for unruly boys. He found the experience depressing and begged his mother to allow him to return home, promising that his behaviour would change. Within a few weeks this wish was granted.

At the age of 10, when he spent a spell at the Riley Child Guidance Clinic at Indiana University Medical Center in Indianapolis, staff noted that Larry felt unloved and insecure in his relationship with his parents. They believed that his home-life was chaotic and unstable, and they recommended he live elsewhere. As a consequence, he was placed in a Catholic boys' home in Fort Wayne, Indiana, where he remained for six months before being allowed to return home.

Puberty brought new challenges when he realised he was homosexual. Although open with his family about his sexual orientation, he was a young man at war with himself: having been somewhat religious since childhood, he struggled with a deep-rooted self-loathing and had great difficulty in accepting his sexual preference. At high school he occasionally dated girls, but none of these became a physical relationship. The thought of sexual activity with a female repulsed him, whilst the idea of same-sex sexual contact also repelled him. Yet it also fascinated him, and Larry Eyler was torn between the conflicting values of so-called societal "norms" and the cravings that threatened to overwhelm him from within.

In 1970, Eyler dropped out of high school in his senior year. He was aged 18. He worked a series of odd jobs – private security guard, a clerk in a shoe store – before earning his General Educational Development certificate. He was going to the gym regularly, and in order to show off his well-developed muscles he took to wearing T-shirts. It was during this time that Eyler began to familiarise himself with Indianapolis' gay lifestyle, frequenting gay bars and engaging in transient sexual liaisons with other gay men. In particular, he seemed to prefer the bars that specialised in leather fetishes. He was noted to be good-looking and laid-back, and the fact that he was now into bodybuilding certainly earned him some affirmative attention. However, another side would come to the fore during some of sexual escapades. He became known as someone with a sadistic streak, whose violent temper would surface during sex. Some of Eyler's casual partners later came forward to reveal that during intercourse he averted his eyes and would shout "bitch" and "whore" at them. Perhaps it was an awkward attempt to pretend his date was female. He was also known to bludgeon his more unwilling partners, and to also inflict light knife wounds upon their torsos, going well beyond the acceptable level of rough play normally tolerated by the BDSM subculture.[1]

Eyler enrolled at the Indiana State University in 1974[2] where his attendance was sporadic. The following year, he was befriended by a Professor Robert David Little, the short, stocky

---

[1] Bondage-discipline sadomasochism sexual activities are often characterised by one of the partners taking on a position of physical or psychological power over another, causing pain, restraint or humiliation.

[2] He left without gaining any qualifications.

white-haired chairman of the library science department. Eyler moved into Little's condominium in Terre Haute, Indiana shortly after meeting. The relationship was platonic, with Eyler viewing the older man (15 years separated the two) as something of a father figure. Little supported Eyler financially, and in exchange Eyler acted as a sort of "wing man" for Little who, because of his appearance, needed help in attracting sexual partners. The pair regularly trawled Indy's gay bar circuit together, the result of which was that Eyler – the better looking of the pair – would bring home men for his socially awkward and unattractive friend to enjoy sexually as well. In their symbiotic relationship, however, Little essentially fit the role of a sugar daddy.

Craig Long was a 19-year-old former Marine in Terre Haute. On 3 August 1978, he was hitchhiking at the side of the road when Eyler's pickup truck stopped beside him and the driver offered a ride. Shortly after Long entered the truck, Eyler propositioned him by motioning towards a shaded patch off the road and saying, "Why don't you come down here with me?" Long reached for the door-handling, intending to leave the vehicle, whereupon Eyler brandished an 8-inch long butcher's knife, held it to the young man's chest and told him to stay where he was. When the light changed green, the driver sped off, eventually arriving at a secluded gravel road which took them to a wooded area in a field. The knife remained aimed at Long throughout the journey. "I don't have any money," Long said, to which his abductor responded, "It's not your money I want."

Once stopped, Eyler ordered Long to undress. "Just cooperate and you won't get hurt," he told him. As the Marine was pulling off his shirt, Eyler suddenly snapped a handcuff around the man's wrist, twisted his other arm behind his back and handcuffed that too. Then he ordered him to climb into the rear of the truck and lie down on the mattress that was already in position there. Eyler tugged off the man's trousers and underwear leaving him naked. Eyler tied the man's legs and ankles together with a clothesline. After a few moments, when the man glanced over his shoulder, he saw that Eyler was also naked.

Eyler then ran the knife up and down the young man's naked body, all the while muttering under his breath. Despite the handcuffs, Long managed to twist himself onto his front and escape Eyler's truck. As he stumbled away he shouted, "You fuckin' queer!" He didn't get far before hearing the sound of Eyler in close pursuit.

Long turned to face his would-be captor. "Get in the truck," he was told. "No," Long replied. Then Eyler stabbed him with the knife – once, in the chest. Long could feel his chest struggling to fill with air. He knew he had a punctured lung.

He collapsed to the ground where he closed his eyes and played dead. Fortunately, his attacker fell for the ruse and walked off. When Eyler was gone, Long managed to bring his arms in front of him and wriggled out of the clothesline that bound his legs. He clasped his hands to his chest, which was now slick with the blood that kept spurting through his fingers. He scrambled to his feet and stumbled towards a house in a nearby trailer park. There, the occupants summoned the assistance of paramedics.

Whilst Long was receiving first aid attention from the paras the sheriff's deputy arrived. So also did Eyler, who had driven up in his pickup truck. He gave the key of the handcuffs to a young boy, telling him that it would open the handcuff around the young man's wrist. He was duly arrested, but he quickly claimed that the knife wound had been caused accidentally. He wasn't believed. He was arrested and taken into custody. His vehicle was searched, revealing various knives, a metal-tipped whip, a sword, another set of handcuffs and some tear gas. He was charged with aggravated battery, to which he pleaded guilty, after having admitted to his lawyer that he had committed the crime. Meanwhile, Craig Long had been brought to hospital and was in a critical condition.

Eyler was released on bail – the bond of $10,000 having been raised by friends – to appear before the judge again on 23 August. Long was ready and willing to give evidence. On the day of the hearing, however, Eyler's attorney stopped Long in a corridor and informed him that a private individual wanted to pay off his $2,500 medical bill – in exchange for Long agreeing not to press charges. Long agreed and he eventually received a cheque signed by Eyler's friend, Robert Little. At this point, Eyler changed his plea to not guilty and on 13 November he was acquitted. He was fined $43 in court costs. However, Eyler took home a lesson from the experience. He learned not to allow victims to live … because then they can't come back to throw accusations. In a way, he'd now learned it's safer to kill.

The killings took place at an astonishing rate, starting with the strangulation murder of 14-year old Delvoyd Baker in March 1982. At least 24 young men died between then and April 1984. During this time there was a hiatus of a month or so between murders; other times there might be a couple of murders within the same week. The age range of the known victims was between 16 and 29. Most of them were plied with alcohol or sedatives before being restrained. Typically, their trousers and underwear were taken down. Several victims were subjected to stabbing and slashing across the chest and abdomen. Some were disembowelled *post mortem*. Many had personal items removed from the crime scene. All were discovered after being discarded in fields nearby rural highways in Indiana or Illinois.

Eyler's first victim, Craig Long, had survived his ordeal. Despite Eyler's worst intentions, so too would the second. After being lured into Eyler's vehicle on 12 October 1982, 21-year-old Craig Townsend was then drugged, stripped, beaten and abandoned in a field. His killer left him for dead, but the young man survived the unprovoked attack. He was taken to hospital in a comatose state, suffering from exposure. Police spoke to him but he discharged himself from the hospital before they could complete their investigation.

The next victim was even less fortunate. On 23 October 1983, the body of Stephen Crockett, aged 19, was discovered in a cornfield in Kankakee County, Illinois, near the Indiana border. He'd been beaten and then stabbed to death, his body and head suffering 32 knife wounds. Even though his clothes had been removed there was no evidence of sexual assault. None of Eyler's attacks would leave a surviving victim from this point onwards. More young men would disappear over the next months, only later to turn up dead. The knife was the killer's weapon of choice; the method of killing was stabbing. Mutilation was often carried out *post mortem*. Sometimes pre-death torture occurred. An outbuilding on an abandoned farm off Indiana State Road 63 was found to have flesh embedded in its plasterwork, leading investigators to speculate that the killer had hung his victim against the wall in order to stabilise the body so as to open it up in the same manner as a deer is dressed. The coroner referenced it as an act of "tremendous rage". Now, for the first time, one of the pathologists performing autopsies noticed similarities between the victims and suggested that a serial killer of unspeakable ruthlessness and barbarity was roaming the highways of North East America. And as the bodies began to pile up, investigators came to suspect that more than one perpetrator was involved in the ongoing series of murders.

Prior to this, in August 1981, Eyler had formed a dalliance with a 20-year-old married man, John Dobrovolskis, only this relationship was sexual. Dobrovolskis lived in Chicago. Whilst Dobrovolskis' wife, Sally, was in one room with their two boys and her mother, Dobrovolskis would be engaging in BDSM sex with Eyler in an adjacent room. Sally tolerated Eyler staying over during weekdays. It was an arrangement that she freely allowed, as it suited her to have her husband perform his sadomasochistic deviancies with someone else, meaning that she didn't have to do them herself.

Eyler would frequently bind his partner, whip him and hurl abuse at him before engaging in penetrative sex. The pair understood their relationship wasn't monogamous – each dated other men – but they *did* consider it permanent. Nonetheless, Eyler continually accused his lover of infidelity, and Dobrovolskis, frustrated by the onslaught of recriminations, would sometimes strike out at Eyler. The other man, however, would never retaliate.

Like a malignant influence in the background was Robert Little, who made no secret of his animosity towards Dobrovolskis, jealously resenting the fact that he and Eyler were in a long-term liaison. Nor was the animosity one-sided: when Little was at home in his Terre Haute apartment, Dobrovolskis wouldn't go to visit Eyler. Eyler by now was working as a house painter in Illinois during the week. On Saturdays, he worked across the border as a liquor store clerk in Greencastle, Indiana whilst living rent-free at Robert Little's residence over the weekend. Between his relationships and employment he made a lot of journeys between Terre Haute, Greencastle and Chicago. Inevitably, that meant a lot of time spent travelling along long rural highways. By the summer of 1983, he was also becoming well known in Indy's burgeoning gay scene, at the same time that other regulars of the scene began to wonder about the unexplained disappearances of young men.

During this time, Larry Eyler was also working at the Equal Economic Opportunities Commission, helping out people who were down on their luck. He was one of their most popular workers and would often go out of his way to make a difference in people's lives. Co-workers liked him too. It was a complete turnabout from how things had been in school. At a Christmas party organised for senior citizens, Eyler dressed up and played the role of an elf. He must've looked a comical sight at six-foot-tall, with muscles bursting from the costume. He played it up though, keeping within the spirit of the event, good-naturedly making fun of the partygoers. No one would've suspected anything was awry with the fun-loving goof in their midst.

By mid-1983, the roll-call of victims was around 13. Bodies were still being found in fields alongside the freeways – all young men, most of them Caucasian, all undressed, all stabbed, some eviscerated. Some attempt had been made to conceal the bodies, although not much: a few had been partially buried in rudimentary graves; others had been placed into plastic bags. A couple of bodies had been dismembered, apparently with a hacksaw. A few were found around the same disposal sites.

Twenty-eight-year-old Ralph Calise was a handsome, dark-haired Hispanic college dropout who came with a record sheet of arrests for arson, violence and drug possession. Living on welfare state benefits, Calise was known to family and friends as a heavy drinker and drugs user who often disappeared from the apartment he shared with his girlfriend. It was no surprise when he left the apartment around midnight on 30 August 1983.

It also came as no surprise when his mutilated body was found the next day close to an I-60 tollway in Illinois, in the same vicinity that the remains of two dead men had been found only six months before. Investigators noted similarities between the victims, and also learned about similar cases being discovered across the state line. The idea of a repetitive killer who crossed the border, possibly in an attempt to thwart detection, now emerged and grew legs. Interstate cooperation led to a case conference to which the FBI were invited. Behaviour profiling agents described a physically strong man who projected a macho image, wore military gear, worked in a menial profession, a "night owl" who patronised rough-and-tumble bars in a bid to seek the approval of other males and to disguise his sexuality, but who was also always on the edge of homosexual panic, fearful of being labelled as "queer". Investigators would eventually turn their eyes to a suspect who fit this description nicely – 31-year-old Larry Eyler.

By late September 1983, Eyler was the prime suspect in the serial murder investigation. A former lover had reported his suspicions about Eyler to the police, also reporting that he'd stabbed someone in 1978. Detectives managed to trace survivor Craig Townsend (the stab victim who'd fled from hospital), who viewed mugshots of Eyler and grudgingly admitted that he was the man who'd attacked him. It was circumstantial evidence – not enough to arrest their man – but it was enough to have Eyler placed under covert surveillance. The police watched as he cruised for dates in an area frequented by male sex-workers. He picked up one young man but then dropped him off a few blocks away. Police descended upon the man to question him, but the witness explained that because he'd only wanted to party (do drugs) he'd rejected Eyler's advances.

Still unaware that he was being tailed, Eyler picked up Darl Haywood, a blow-in from Arkansas. Eyler offered him $100 for sex, stating his preference for bondage, and after a moment's consideration Haywood agreed to the deal.

Eyler drove his date through the Chicago streets, eventually moving onto the I-90, crossing in to Lake County, Indiana where his followers lost track of him. Despite suspicions that a murder was about to be committed, the Illinois team failed to alert their counterparts on the Indiana side of the border that a suspicious car was headed their way.

It was by sheer luck that State Trooper Kenneth Buehrie spotted a Ford F-Series pickup truck parked along the I-65 in Lowell, Indiana. Nearby were two men, both walking towards a stand of trees. One of the men appeared to be bound and so the officer went to investigate. The owner of the truck identified himself as Larry Eyler. The youth who accompanied him alleged that his companion had picked him up for sex before asking permission to tie him up. The officer performed a search of the pickup truck, which revealed nylon clotheslines, handcuffs, surgical tape, two baseball bats, a mallet and a hunting knife which appeared to be stained with blood. The driver was detained for a traffic violation (illegal parking on a freeway) and brought to the police station. There, Eyler was formally questioned about the charge, and he was also informed that he'd become a suspect in the interstate murder spree. Eyler willingly discussed any aspect of his life – but he refused to talk about his sexuality. Unsurprisingly, he denied any involvement in the murders. With little evidence to arrest Eyler, however, he was allowed to leave. It also turned out that the search of his vehicle had been illegal, and this consequence led to a series of police failures which allowed Eyler to remain at liberty. He was also permitted to retain custody of his truck.

Eyler's truck was later impounded in order to obtain tyre impressions. Its owner now allowed himself to be subjected to further questioning but he denied involvement with any murder. For the first time, however, he admitted to being in a love-hate relationship with Dobrovolskis, his secret lover, and to practising bondage with him. It was put to him that after he'd get into a fight with his lover he'd pick up men who looked like Dobrovolskis and then stab them. At this, Eyler visibly winced.

Eyler was released on 4 October 1983. Now he moved in with Dobrovolskis and his wife, and even started paying a third of the rent. Meanwhile, the dead bodies continued to be discovered, including one find of four skeletons, all together, all still wearing pulled-down trousers. One of the bodies had been decapitated.

Fearful that he was about to destroy evidence, however, investigators obtained a warrant authorising the search of the Terre Haute home he shared with Robert Little. The search was conducted at dawn, just a day later. Further circumstantial evidence came to light, including credit card receipts which indicated that Eyler had been in some of the vicinities in which victims ascribed to the Highway Murderer were found. Phone call records showed that he'd made calls to Little at antisocial hours, around the times that victims had gone missing. This discovery led the investigators to remark wryly that if Eyler were not the killer then he had certainly been following him on a regular basis. Several days later, the task force had sufficient evidence in the form of boot impressions, tyre impressions and bloodstain evidence to charge Eyler with the murder of Ralph Calise. The next day, they were able to obtain a further warrant to retrieve samples of Eyler's hair and blood. Meanwhile, a series of legal shenanigans was in place: Eyler had filed a civil suit against the police citing harassment and violation of his Fourteenth Amendment[3] right and civil rights, although the case was eventually

---

[3] Amongst others, the Due Process Clause prohibits the deprivation of life, liberty or property without a fair procedure.

thrown out. Eyler was duly arrested for a second time on 29 October 1983 and charged with the murder of Calise. Bond was set at $1,000,000, a figure that Eyler's attorney contested without success.

A second search of Robert Little's property on 1 November took place specifically in order to look for the victims' missing T-shirts and wallets. No keepsakes were found. However, investigators retrieved a key which was an exact match of a key that had been found beneath the body of one of the victims. This victim was Steven Agan, a youthful-looking 23-year-old (whom the investigators suspected had been suspended against the wall and opened up). It was later determined that the key fit a lock in an office where Eyler had previously worked.

In the meantime, the legalities concerning the admissibility of evidence ground on. Eyler appointed a new criminal defence attorney and his bond was eventually reduced to $10,000. This was paid by Robert Little and, on 6 February 1984, Eyler was released from custody on bail. He promptly moved into an apartment complex in Rogers Park, a pleasant neighbourhood on the shore of Lake Michigan, with Little paying the rent and buying new furniture ... as well as a new set of tyres for Eyler's pickup truck. A pretrial hearing held on 6 February led to the exclusion of all evidence recovered from the pickup truck. Eyler's jubilation was mirrored only by the investigators' despair.

On 21 August, Joe Balla, a building janitor, arrived for work at 1640 West Sherwin in Rogers Park. It was a Tuesday morning, and he'd got there early, in time to collect the garbage to take it out for the usual morning pickup. As he went about his business, Balla's skittish dog drew his attention to some trash bags which had been dumped in an area not intended for tenants' use. Balla became irritated at this act of apparent fly tipping. He was familiar with the bags that the tenants in his building used and he knew that these bags didn't belong to them. He removed them from the garbage receptacle to inspect them. Doing so caused one of the bags to split open. What fell to the ground was a human leg. He called the police.

By the time officers arrived three janitors were standing around the dumpster. One of the janitors gave the officers a description of a man whom he'd seen carrying the bags the day before. The third janitor recognised the description as belonging to one of his tenants, Larry Eyler. A short while later, the officers forced their way into Eyler's apartment, only to catch him and Dobrovolskis in the midst of intercourse. The pair were duly arrested, although Dobrovolskis was released shortly thereafter.

A medical examiner arrived at the scene of the dumpster and the garbage bags were removed, opened, and their contents assembled on the ground. There were eight bags in total. Each contained a body part – two thighs, two lower legs, two arms, a head and a torso. The bags were taken to a lab and subjected to a kind of "superglue" fumes treatment in order to enhance any latent fingerprints. Two of Eyler's prints were found on two of the bags.

Eyler's apartment was searched. Officers later noted that if they'd not been searching for specific evidence of murder they'd have noticed nothing amiss. The place was clean and smelled fresh. Two of the bedroom walls had been given a recent coat of paint. Investigators found a hacksaw, hacksaw blades and an awl. Luminol tests revealed extensive traces of blood spillage, whilst markings on the floor indicated that a largish object had been dragged from the bedroom to the bathroom.

A closer inspection showed blood patches and spattering all over the apartment including on the bed mattress, the seat of a chair and a sofa within the bedroom, on a black belt, and on a pair of blue jeans which belonged to neither Eyler nor Dobrovolskis.

The jeans had instead belonged to 16-year-old Daniel "Danny" H. Bridges, a habitual runaway and already a seasoned hustler. He was the youngest of 13 children and evidently a neglected child. Danny had engaged in sex-work from the age of 12, working the area at Clark Street and Montrose Avenue. Although heterosexual, most of his customers were men.

Coincidentally, a couple of months before the Rogers Park body was found, Danny had given an account to an NBC reporter who was filming a report on child exploitation. In the documentary, Danny had described a "real freak" who was known to the male prostitutes of Uptown Chicago. The description matched that of Larry Eyler.

Danny Bridges had gone missing two days before on the Sunday evening of 19 August. He'd been lured by Eyler to his apartment. There, the older man bound him to a chair with a clothesline, beat him around the face, tortured him and stabbed him to death. Five knife wounds to the abdomen were sufficiently deep to cause the intestine to protrude through the injuries. There were additional stabbings around the sternum and the back, the latter causing perforation of the lungs and heart.

Eyler then dismembered the body, drained each of the eight parts of blood before placing them in separate plastic bags which he put out for disposal in the expectation that they'd duly disappear into landfill. Danny Bridges would be Eyler's 23rd and final known victim.

His trial for the murder of Danny Bridges began on 1 July 1986. He formally pleaded not guilty. The first witness against him was Robert Little. He claimed to have been in Eyler's company between 17 and 19 August, departing for Terre Haute at around 22:15 on the supposed evening of Bridge's murder. He was also able to produce a receipt proving that he'd paid property taxes on 20 August (despite these not being due for two months), also paying in person (when previously he had paid his bills by mail). The defence suggested that Little had done this in order to construct an alibi. Dobrovolskis testified that he'd phoned Eyler several times on the 19 August, on one occasion saying that he was on his way and would be there in 15 minutes, only to be told, "No, don't do that." He stated that Eyler instead drove to the Terre Haute house, after having apparently recently showered, and after arriving declined to have sex, leading Dobrovolskis to conclude that he'd been with another man.

In summing up, the defence long-windedly speculated that

Bridges had known that Eyler had a penchant for bondage and had consented to be restrained, attempting to throw doubt on the validity of the Robert Little's testimony. He attempted to show an "alternative scenario", suggesting that it was "possible" that a "friend" of Eyler had made a killing in his apartment whilst he was out. The prosecution's rebuttal, by contrast, was brief, presenting overwhelming evidence pointing to Eyler's guilt and thereafter rested its case. The jury considered for three hours before delivering their guilty verdict for the aggravated kidnapping, unlawful restraint, murder and concealment of the homicidal death of Daniel Bridges.

At the sentencing phase of the trial, Eyler's mother and sister openly wept as they pleaded with Judge Urso to spare his life. To no avail. On 3 October 1986, Eyler was formally sentenced to death by lethal injection. Judge Urso told the guilty man:

> "The senseless and barbaric murder of a 16-year-old boy,
> a killing which was so brutal it defies description, shows me
> your complete disregard for human life. If there ever was a
> person or a situation for which the death penalty is appro-
> priate, it is you. You are an evil person. You truly deserve
> to die for your acts. I thereby sentence you to death for the
> murder of Danny Bridges, committed during the course of
> his aggravated kidnapping."

At the Pontiac Correctional Centre, Eyler underwent psychiatric evaluation. Tests concluded he suffered from borderline personality disorder with pathological sensitivity to feelings of abandonment and rejection, leading to the acts of rage and murder in order to preserve a sense of control.

In November 1990, whilst Eyler languished on Death Row, the county prosecutor made known its intentions to present evidence before a grand jury to determine whether a case could be brought against him for the murder of Steven Agan. Upon hearing this, Eyler decided to plead confess and agreed to testify against his accomplice upon condition that his death sentence be commuted to a fixed term of imprisonment. His offer was accepted, and on 13 December, Eyler confessed to his culpability in the murder of Agan and in addition testified against Robert Little, claiming that his lover had been a knowing and willing collaborator in this murder. He received a jail term of 60 years for the first-degree murder. It wasn't good enough for Eyler. The following month he agreed to confess to 20 further murders in exchange for a sentence of life imprisonment without parole. The offer was ultimately rejected by the State's Attorney.

On 11 April 1991, Robert Little was brought to trial. He entered a plea of not guilty. Eyler testified that he and Little had jointly killed Steven Agan in December 1982. He stated that he and Little regularly trawled Indianapolis's gay scene, bringing home men to have sex, with Little frequently photographing the acts. He asserted that on 19 December, Little suggested the pair "do a scene", which Eyler understood to mean to create a snuff scene and photograph it with a Polaroid camera. He said that he – along with Little – lured Agan in Little's vehicle with the promise of having a drink together. He said that Agan, although heterosexual, agreed to participate in a bondage photography shooting session for money.

Eyler attested that the three journeyed to an abandoned shed near the I-63, where Agan's hands were tied above a beam and he was bound and gagged. According to Eyler, Little shouted, "Get the knife," whilst Eyler stabbed Agan, and masturbated as he took photos of more stabbing. Eyler maintained that Little also stabbed the young man before saying, "Okay, kill the motherfucker." According to Eyler, Little took Agan's undershirt away the scene as a trophy, and complained later that the murder event had been a little too quick for his liking.

Little's defence cross-examined Eyler, seeking to show that his evidence was in revenge for Little's previous testimony against Eyler. The defence then proceeded to question Eyler about each of his identified victims, upon which the witness persistently exercised his Fifth Amendment right to remain silent.

Little's defence questioned Little's mother, who insisted that her son habitually spent the week before Christmas at her house and so could not have been involved in the murder in Indiana on 19 December 1982. This claim was discredited by the prosecutor, who introduced evidence that put Little at a Terre Haute garage on 21 December of that year. Little himself declined to testify in his own defence, claiming that his sexuality would itself be under trial.

In their closing arguments, the defence proposed that Eyler's claims were fabrications, a "last ditch" attempt to have his death sentence commuted, also pointing to Eyler's repeated exercising of his Fifth Amendment rights. "Would you convict an honourable man [referring to Robert Little] on the word of Larry Eyler?"

The jury would not. Little grinned as the verdict of not guilty was read out. After the trial, he informed reporters that he was "just so happy the ordeal is over", and announced his intention to return to his position at Indiana State University.

Larry Eyler died on 6 March 1994 of AIDS-related complications. Two days later, his attorney, Kathleen Zellner, revealed Eyler's posthumous confession to having personally murdered 17 individuals, as well as the joint murder of four others with the collaboration of Robert Little. Her client had insisted that Little _had_ been responsible for the murder of Daniel Bridges. She revealed that her client had asserted that he and Little _had_ jointly killed Steven Crockett (the second known murder victim), and that Little _had_ actively encouraged, aided and abetted in all subsequent murders. According to Zellner, Eyler confessed to having lured victims – both gay and straight – with a variety of enticements and then torturing them before pressing a knife to their abdomen and telling them to "make peace with God". She affirmed that he took the victims' T-shirts for Little to use as masturbation aids. Eyler's confession, Zellner averred, had been made in the knowledge of his impending death, and that he had wanted the families of his victims to know that he had confessed.

# Robert Andrew Berdella Jr.

(active 1984-1988)

JUST AS SOME GAME HUNTERS take home the heads of their kills
and mount them on their walls, so too do some serial killers collect "trophies" from their victims. Ahmad Suradji believed that
collecting and drinking his victims' saliva would bring him special powers. Ted Bundy removed the heads of some of his victims and put them on display in his apartment. Jerry Brudos stole
his victims' shoes. Charles Albright removed and retained his
victims' eyeballs. Anatoly Onoprienko kept his victims' underwear, giving some of them to his girlfriend to wear. They would
keep these treasured trophies long after the crimes has been
committed so that they could revisit and relive them, taking
pride in their dark achievements, often using the "souvenirs" in
their masturbatory fantasies.

However, it is known that several serial killers have captured
the moments leading up to cold-blooded murder on film, recording their brutal acts in the most depraved variety of *memento
mori*. These photographs document actual images of the victims
and their ordeals – the binds that hold them, their tormented facial expressions, the tortures to which they were subjected – all
up close up and personal. They are the viewpoint of a killer, and
the primary aim of the killer is to capture and preserve it all, in
the most agonisingly lurid detail. Often the victims are alive …
at least for a while. Sometimes they are posed, both in life and
in death. *Always*, they are afraid, and it is that image of terror
that the killer seeks to immortalise on film. It is the ultimate degradation, when the captor has his prisoner under his absolute
control, to do with as he pleases – and at that point the chasm
between the torturer and the tortured becomes immeasurably
vast, greater than any that can ever exist between two humans.

This was the degradation that Robert Berdella sought – and
sought to record for posterity. After his arrest, Berdella's home
was searched and investigators found evidence of his weird

interest in voodoo, black magic and sadomasochistic literature. More disturbing, though, were the 334 diabolical photographs that eventually came to light. Brutal and stark, the Polaroid snaps were a chronicle of the twisted atrocities that had gone on behind a merciless serial killer's closed doors ...

Robert Andrew Berdella Jr. came from a deeply religious household, emerging into the world in Cuyahoga Falls, Ohio on 31 January 1949. His father, Robert, was a tools operator for the Ford Motor Company who came from proud Italian Catholic stock; his mother, Mary, a devoted homemaker. Daniel, a brother seven years Bob's junior, completed the family.

From the onset, he was known as a loner. That was certainly the impression that he left on those who knew him from an early age. He rarely played outside and hardly ever had friends over to visit. Pathologically unathletic, Bob received an early diagnosis of hypertension and took medication to lower his blood pressure. He was highly intelligent and excelled academically. He joined the algebra club; he collected stamps. His peers viewed him as a nerd. But there were other reasons why he made such an impression. Bob was aloof, arrogant and disdainful, particularly towards women. Teachers found him a challenge to teach; his peers didn't like him. A voracious reader, he soaked up knowledge, but he also liked to project the image that he knew more than everyone else. The subjects that interested him were art and cooking; he showed an early aptitude for both.

By his mid-teens, he had already grown tall, standing in stockinged feet at 6'2". With a slight build, having worn thick-lensed spectacles from the age of five and speaking with a slight speech impediment, Bob was never destined to make it into the jock clique. His clothes were conservative and he wore his jet-black hair short. Few wanted to hang out with him and he couldn't have cared less about that. With little interest in sports, girls or making friends, Bob Berdella _was_, in modern parlance, a nerd.

Bob desperately wanted to win his father's approval, but Bob's passion was art – not sports – and Robert Sr. valued athleticism highly and consequently looked disappointedly upon his elder son and his obvious lack of sporting ability. In his view, Bob was a failure. Bob's brother, Danny, was sporty and their father treated his younger son differently. The two would go to Cleveland regularly to view baseball games. Bob was left out. He *tried* to prove himself to his father but it was an uphill struggle, and he was destined never to achieve his aim.

On Christmas Day 1965, whilst the family were visiting relatives, Robert Sr. had a heart attack and died at the age of 39. Bob was aged 16. The loss threw Bob's life into a tailspin and he began to consider his own mortality. He spent even more time alone in his bedroom and began to read extensively about many faiths in an effort to find some meaning to life. It was short-lived; his interest soon lapsed. He stopped going to church services and never again turned to religion for solace.

At some stage in 1965, Berdella watched a film adaptation of *The Collector*, a Gothic-inspired thriller novel about a lonely, psychotic young man who drugs and then abducts a female art student, keeping her captive in his windowless cellar. The themes of domination and social status permeate the book and the film. The work's eponymous protagonist – the co-called "Collector" – is painted as a chilling, emotionally dead character. It struck a resonance with Bob and he'd later claim that the film had left a lasting impression on him. Around the same time, Berdella earned extra money by working at an Ohio restaurant. Allegedly, whilst employed there, he was raped by an older male coworker. It's difficult to imagine that this experience wouldn't have also left a lasting impression on him.

It's untrue to say that Bob Berdella had no friends. His best and only true friend may, in fact, have been close to home. His relationship with his affectionate and doting mother was said to be reciprocal, and so it came as something of a shock when his mother remarried shortly after her husband's death. Bob instantly resented his stepfather, viewing the remarriage as a betrayal of his father, and he wasn't hesitant in showing his dislike for his mother's new husband. He withdrew into himself, immersing himself in solitary activities such as reading, stamp and coin collecting, painting and writing to pen pals, who would post him stamps from foreign countries. He was later to claim that the latter activity sparked his curiosity for historical items, foreign architecture and history, and that this in turn was to ignite an avid interest in antiques. It led to Berdella collecting such artefacts and the generation of a business idea.

Berdella graduated from Cuyahoga Falls High School in 1967 with excellent grades and enrolled in the Kansas City Art Institute. He wasn't particularly liked there either, being viewed by his peers as arrogant and condescending, a man not given to responding with a single word when a string of verbose intellectualisms could be used instead. However, he was initially considered a talented and focused student, although that changed within his first year when he began to drink heavily and got switched on to drugs. He became vocally anti-authoritarian, aligning himself to a clique of students who supplied him with drugs, which he then sold on at a profit, gaining himself something of a reputation as a low-level dealer. He foolishly ended up selling amphetamines to an undercover police officer and was promptly arrested. He pleaded guilty to the offence and was dealt a five-year suspended sentence. Within a month, he was arrested a second time for possession of marijuana and LSD and as a result spent five days in jail, only to be released due to a lack of evidence.

Whilst a student at the Institute, Berdella engaged in at least three acts of animal cruelty. One of these was an art piece during which he tortured a live duck before decapitating it, dancing around the bloody carcass and then cooking it. Another so-called performance involved the destruction of a dog using sedatives, onstage, in front of a crowd. The College Board decided that that was enough. Berdella voluntarily withdrew from the Institute before he could be stripped of his place, a fact which brought him considerable shame and resentment. Following this development, he got work as a short-order cook at various restaurants around the city. Then, in 1969, he moved house. His new address was no. 4315 Charlotte Street, a nondescript detached building in a quiet stretch of residential homes in Kansas City's Hyde Park district. The dull exterior would hide its secrets. This house would later become exposed as the torture dungeon of "The Kansas City Butcher" or "The Collector".

On the surface, though, Berdella was an upstanding American citizen. He joined the neighbourhood crime watch programme; he became a court-appointed advocate for juveniles through the Kansas City justice system. He grew his reputation as a chef; people talked about his food. He also began to deal in the arcane curiosities he'd collected over the years. Gradually, this business took off. After a few years, it'd become well enough established to enable him to give up working as a chef. He opened a booth at the Westport Flea Market, naming it Bob's Bazaar Boutique and selling indigenous art, jewellery and antique items. In time, he'd amass a superb collection of rare ancient and antique items. With this day-to-day expenses, it wasn't enough to sustain him, and as a result he occasionally had to sell items at a loss or steal items to sell. Additional income came from taking in lodgers – invariably young males – at 4315 Charlotte Street.

Berdella had by this stage been living as an openly gay man for many years. Upon reaching puberty, he'd realised he was gay, although this remained a closely guarded secret for some years. In his early teens, he'd briefly had a girlfriend but for obvious reasons this didn't last. He'd first begun to frequent Akron's gay bars in 1967, although he only started to openly embrace the gay lifestyle upon his move to Kansas City. He became involved with a Vietnam veteran, but the man was unstable and the relationship didn't last. Now, he took to picking up young male prostitutes, often ones with drug habits, becoming friendly with them and allowing them to stay at 4315 Charlotte Street until they'd got their lives back in some sort of order.

By all accounts, Berdella exhibited some of the flamboyant and overtly camp mannerisms frequently associated with homosexuality. At the Westport Flea Market, he became acquainted with a fellow trader who operated a neighbouring stand, Paul Howell. Howell's younger son, Jerry, and his friends used to taunt Berdella about his obvious homosexuality. Their encounters would sometimes spill over into heated arguments, but generally it was a casual acquaintance, and Jerry once confided in Berdella that he and his friends earned money as sometime sex-workers. In fact, Berdella had even seen Jerry hustling in town. Berdella occasionally helped the youth when he was in trouble with the law, all the while also supplying him with drugs including Valium and marijuana. At around the same time, Berdella was also procuring drugs, ostensibly for his dog. He obtained these animal tranquillisers – chlorpromazine, acepromazine and ketamine – from a veterinarian supply shop. He began to stockpile them. Perhaps Berdella already had them in mind for another purpose ...

By the time Jerry Howell had reached the age of 19, he and Berdella had become good friends. On 5 July 1984, the two met up. Howell had agreed to go to go with Berdella to Parkwell, Missouri, where he was due to pick up a car that he'd lent another youth. Howell, however, announced that he didn't have time to go pick up the car. Instead, he had plans to go to a dance contest in Merriam, Johnson County, Kansas. But first he wanted to party. Berdella gave him some tranquilisers and bought a six-pack of Coors. They went back to Berdella's house, where Howell took some more drugs. Inside, the older man was seething. In his mind, he was always helping others but getting very little in return. At 18:40 that evening, after ingesting one tablet after another, Jerry Howell passed out on Berdella's bed. At seven o'clock, whilst his guest was still out cold, Berdella injected 1 cubic centimetre of chlorpromazine into Howell's arm. At 7:25, he injected Howell again, then another 3cc at 7:30. At 7:55, he introduced a further 11cc of the tranquiliser, this time into Howell's buttocks. At 8:40, another 11cc was injected, a cumulative dosage of 29cc. Berdella made copious notes in a diary, detailing the drugs he used, dosages and the times of administration. In addition, he made a log of his other deviancies. He wrote down "TIED" and noted down the time: 8:45. This meant that by now Howell had been bound and gagged. Berdella made entries at 9:00 and 10:00: "F". That was the abbreviation for "fuck", indicating his anal rape of the unconscious youth. At 11:30 Howell vomited. "EYES BLANK", he carefully jotted down. At 11:45: "BF": this meant "butt fuck", a third anal sodomy, whilst Howell was snoring. There were yet further entries of "BF", at 12:30, 1:30, 2:30, 4:30 and 6:30. According to his detailed register, Berdella raped his victim eight times that night.

At a quarter-past-eight in the morning, Howell began to rouse from his insensible state. Berdella remedied that with another prompt shot – 6cc of chlorpromazine and 10cc of acepromazine. Fifteen minutes later, after noticing that Howell was still "active", Berdella gave him two further doses of 5cc of each tranquiliser, thereby rendering him insensate again.

At 8:40, Berdella subjected Howell to an anal rape using a carrot, carefully documenting the incident as "CF". The idea had come to him spontaneously after looking around the house for inspiration. He injected Howell once more at 11:00 and then went out to his shop, leaving the drugged youth tied to the bed.

When he returned home sometime around three o'clock, Berdella viewed his victim as he lay in situ. He had two choices at that point: let Howell go or never let him go. If he let Howell go there was every risk that the youth would report him to the police. Reasoning that by now he'd gone beyond the point of turning back, he injected Howell yet again.

Berdella recorded "RP" at 5:15. This was a rape, distinctive from the other attacks because by now Howell was awake and resisting, responding to Berdella's unwelcome advances by saying, "Why are you doing this to me?" and "Let me go." Berdella simply ignored his victim's pleas. However, as the youth was "still fighting restraints", Berdella injected him again, this time with two large doses of tranquilisers totalling 21cc.

Then, at 6:00, Berdella found further inspiration from the kitchen: he subjected Howell to "CUC R", a rape by cucumber. Nearly three hours later, he violated his victim with a metal ruler. Not only was Berdella being methodical in his written documentation of the torture of Howell, he also photographed it, taking numerous Polaroids of his deeds. The reason for this, he was later to admit, was to form trophies. He was also open about their purpose: he wanted to keep a record of the events in order later to be used as a stimulation for masturbation. The photographs are dreadful evidence of systematic and brutal torture, chronicling the carrot and cucumber violations as well as other degradations.

At 9:45, Berdella copulated with Howell face-on, using the area between the legs as a friction point ("FRONT F", or "front fuck"). After this, as Howell struggled against him weakly, Berdella changed the gag and washed the youth's mouth. By 10 o'clock, Howell had stopped moving. Berdella made a brief attempt to perform mouth-to-mouth resuscitation and chest compressions, but it soon became clear that his victim was dead. Berdella drily denoted the fact with a brief notation: "DD". From its chilling beginning to its coldblooded conclusion, the entire episode had lasted 28 hours. And yet, dreadful though it would be to consider it, compared to Berdella's next victims, Howell had got off relatively lightly.

After this, Berdella next had to consider how to deal with the remains. He brought the body down to the basement where he hung it upside-down from a beam, placing a large cooking pot below the head. Then, using a sharp knife, he made incisions on the inside of the elbow and at the jugular vein for the purpose of exsanguination. He took some photographs of the scene and then left the body suspended in that position overnight to allow all the blood to drain out.

In the morning, a Saturday, Berdella went to the Flea Market. There, he reflected upon his options for getting rid of the body. He remembered that Monday was the day that the trash was collected. That would be the solution.

Back home, he donned his apron and gathered his chef's knives ... as well as chainsaw. Then began the process of dismemberment. Once done, he wrapped the body pieces in newspaper and placed them in plastic trash bags.

The next evening, Sunday, Paul Howell came looking for his son. Berdella had to deal with that problem also, adding to his anxieties. He fobbed the father off with a tale about driving Jerry to Merriam as arranged, only to part company afterwards. He claimed not to have seen his friend since. Unable to dispute the story, Jerry's father left dissatisfied.

Early on Monday morning, he left the trash bags out for collection – maybe four or five of them, all filled with human remains. He waited and watched for around three hours until the truck came by to pick up the bags. And the deed was done. Soon, Jerry Howell's constituent parts were en route to the landfill. But at least Robert Berdella had a few photographs to remember him by …

At first he couldn't look at the photos. He was repulsed by what he'd done and locked the Polaroids away. But then, after around four to five months, he developed an urge to view them. It would be another few months before he began to use them for masturbatory purposes. During this time, his mind turned to torture again, for now he went shopping for the tools he planned to use on his next victim …

Robert Sheldon, a moustachioed 23-year-old of Hispanic appearance, was one of Berdella's on-off lodgers. The connection had come about through their mutual use of drugs and a party that Berdella had hosted at his house. Berdella, knowing that drugs and alcohol made him more popular with the gay and bisexual crowd, was still indulging in both. A couple of Berdella's other acquaintances had brought Sheldon to party at his house and somehow the man had inveigled his way into Berdella's life, and his house. From time to time, he would lodge at Berdella's, although often failing to pay him rent. The arrangement was an inconvenience to Berdella. Sheldon was often drunk so no physical contact took place between them. In his typical notetaking habit, Berdella would jot down on dates on his calendar when his lodger was drunk ("RS ON BINGE"). He was *often* drunk.

On 10 April 1985, he turned up unannounced on Berdella's doorstep yet again, looking for a place to stay for a few days.

Berdella let him in. Two days later, when Berdella returned home from work, he found Sheldon sleeping in a drunken stupor. According to his detailed notes, at 9:30 that evening Berdella administered several injections into Sheldon's arm. He'd already made the decision to keep the man captive in his house in order to control him. He didn't find Sheldon attractive, but, as he later explained his motives to detectives:

> *"The best I can interpret what happened was, the impulsive behaviour that started with Jerry Howell became a reality for me. You're looking at what would be some of my darkest fantasies becoming my reality, where I was capturing people, controlling them. You don't necessarily need sexual attractiveness to do that."*[1]

Berdella gave Sheldon another shot at half-past-midnight, but within 10 minutes, whilst Berdella was upstairs, he heard Sheldon up and walking about downstairs. Berdella all but gave up his plans to bind and torture the man.

The next day, Sheldon went to hospital complaining of muscle pain. Berdella figured that it was probably caused by the injections he'd surreptitiously administered. After being given some antibiotics, Sheldon was duly discharged and went home with Berdella.

The next day, a Friday, Berdella went to work at the Flea Market as normal. When he returned home, Sheldon was lying drunk. Berdella got out his notes and recommenced where he'd left off. That evening, he pulled apart one of Sheldon's antibiotic capsules, emptied out the existing medication, and replaced it with five crushed sedative tablets. Not long after Sheldon took the tampered capsule he conked out senseless. Berdella then

---

[1] Quoted in Jackman, Tom & Cole, Troy (1995) *Rites of Burial*. London: Virgin.

rolled him to the floor, stripped him, tied his ankles together and carried him upstairs. By 10 o'clock, he'd administered a shot a ketamine and tied Sheldon to the same bedframe upon which Jerry Howell had spent his last hours.

The level of torture now escalated, all documented in Berdella's notes. Using a cotton swab, he applied Drano[2] into Sheldon's left eye. The victim, understandably, was screaming in agony by this stage. In police interviews, Berdella was up-front about the reason had done this: to cause pain and damage to the eyes, making it easier to control his captive. Despite Sheldon having done nothing against him personally, Berdella had decided that he would be the scapegoat upon whom he'd vent his pent-up anger and frustration. He attempted to tattoo Sheldon, but the unwilling victim resisted. Berdella injected him with ketamine and then branded the word "HOT" on his left shoulder with hot needles. It was a symbolic act of ownership. The word itself had no meaning.

Further experiments were to follow. Berdella injected caulk[3] into Sheldon's ears. It was an attempt to deprive the man of another of his senses, to increase the level of control. He inserted needles beneath Sheldon's fingernails. His aim was to see what kind of reaction this would induce. One can uneasily imagine. He bound piano wire tightly around Sheldon's wrists with the intention of permanently damaging the nerves in his hands. The experimentations were all designed to assert Berdella's domination over the body. That was how he thought of his prisoner by now – a "body" – something "reduced to the level of, say, a blow-up doll or a clay figure you would make as a kid and moving around, having complete control over", as he put it.

Further sodomies took place, one of them with a carrot. When

---

[2] A household drain cleaning product containing strong acids formulated to break down organic matter.

[3] A durable, flexible material used to seal gaps or cracks against leakage.

Sheldon begged to be released Berdella simply hit him on the back of the head with a rubber mallet. The injections continued. Then the electrocutions started. A transformer was one of the items he'd purposefully purchased after the killing of Jerry Howell. He used it to pass 7,700 volts of electrical current through Sheldon's body for several seconds at a time, attaching the connectors to the shoulders and back. The tortures lasted for three pain-filled days over a weekend. Each event was coolly documented by the eye of the camera.

On Monday morning, 15 April 1985, Berdella went to a trade show. When he returned he found someone on his roof. He'd engaged the workman weeks earlier to do some repair work. Now Berdella didn't know what to do. He anticipated the workman might ask to use the toilet at some stage. He spoke briefly with the man before telling him he "had to take care of something". A euphemism indeed! He went inside and checked his stock of drugs. Deciding he hadn't enough to knock Sheldon out in order to avoid any problems should the workman come into the house, he resorted to a more permanent method of silencing him. He put a plastic bag over Sheldon's head and tied it securely with a rope. Then he stood and watched as the life drained out of him. He took a single photo of the murder.

The workman remained at his business for 90 minutes whilst Sheldon's body began cooling inside. After the man left, Berdella dragged the corpse into the bathroom, placed it in the bath and made some deep lacerations in order to drain away the blood. After five hours or so, he disjointed the body using a boning knife and a bow saw. He placed the head in his freezer for a couple of days before removing the skin and then disposing of the skull in a hole in his backyard. The following Monday, the rest of the remains were packed up and set out with the trash.

A couple of months later, Berdella first met his next victim. Mark Wallace (aged 19 when they'd first become acquainted) was friendly with a man whom Berdella had arranged to cut his lawn (the same man who'd also come to work on Berdella's roof the previous year). Through that association, Wallace had been in Berdella's house a few times. During these visits he'd apparently been a taciturn presence. On 22 June 1985, 14 months after the murder of Sheldon, a fearsome thunderstorm was sweeping across the city and Berdella's dogs would not stop barking. Upon investigation, he soon discovered the cause of his dogs' agitation. Twenty-year-old Mark Wallace was sheltering from the rain in Berdella's backyard tool-shed. It was a kindly act; at that stage Berdella possessed no ill-intent towards the young man. He invited him inside to dry off.

Wallace suffered from depression. His mother was out of the country and his sisters didn't want him around because he was so morose. He was also very drunk. Berdella offered to give him some drugs in order to help him "calm down and relax". He told police:

*"He was very uptight, tense, depressed. Even with the alcohol that he had in him he didn't appear that he would be able to sleep that evening I volunteered to give him a shot of chlorpromazine, telling him that it maybe would calm him down and relax him. And he readily accepted."*

But within 30 minutes of administering the injection Berdella had changed his mind. The deciding factor was that there was been nothing to link Wallace to his house; no one would come knocking at the door of 4315 Charlotte Street looking for him. Besides, Berdella had other irritants in his life right then, including being owed money by others, and Wallace was a readily available scapegoat. Noting the man was unconscious on the couch ("OUT LIKE A LIGHT", he recorded), Berdella injected him with more chlorpromazine and some ketamine and took a photo. He undressed him, tied him up and carried him upstairs. There, he sodomised him with a carrot. Occasionally Wallace would rouse and attempt to speak before lapsing back into unconsciousness. Berdella sexually assaulted him a further four times – "BF" and "FF".

As daylight broke, Wallace awoke, realised he was bound and

gagged, and began to struggle. Berdella attached alligator clips to the man's nipples and flicked a switch. Berdella's sadomasochistic tendencies awakened and the association between pain and sex now became blurred for the first time. Now he came to enjoy inflicting pain as part of the sexual act. Occasionally he would strike Wallace with the rubber mallet, to induce disorientation. ("Firm but not overly hard" was how he'd later describe the beating to the police.) Berdella had already planned to leave for work that Sunday, so he clubbed Wallace again, administered further sedatives and headed out.

Returning later that evening, Berdella found Wallace awake, sitting up and struggling to release himself. Berdella injected him with two more hefty doses before beginning to stick needles into the comatose body, giving it an enema, fist-fucking it and anally raping it. He also electrocuted Wallace on the back again, attempting to ruin the muscles there in order to gain dominance over the young man. At some point around seven o'clock, he realised that Wallace was dead, probably as a result of asphyxiation secondary to over-sedation. Berdella treated the body as he had his previous victim – draining the blood in the bath before dismembering it and leaving the parts out with the trash for collection.

Berdella met Walter James Ferris through an acquaintance at the Flea Market and ended up selling him and his friend some drugs. When Berdella was later questioned by police about a drug sale he immediately concluded that he'd been set up by Ferris and his friend. Some months later, on 24 September 1985, he encountered 20-year-old Ferris hitchhiking and picked him up. The pair (along with the friend) hung around with each other for a couple of days, but Berdella started to become annoyed by constant late-night phone calls, unannounced visits and suspicions that the pair were rooting about in his possessions. One evening, Ferris phoned Berdella and invited him to meet him at a downtown gay bar. When he got there, Berdella learned that Ferris wanted to crash out at his place. Berdella agreed, but he already had less charitable ideas. He was still angry about being questioned about the drugs and Ferris having made himself a nuisance over the past two days. He'd already planned to capture, torture and kill Ferris, figuring that he wouldn't be missed by anyone other than his ne're-do-well friend. And so, after they'd collected Ferris' stuff, the two drove to Berdella's.

Berdella then prepared them both something to eat. However, Ferris' portion of microwaved burritos was laced with several crushed sedatives. Within half-an-hour Ferris was out cold. Berdella immediately tested him for consciousness by sticking pins in him. Satisfied, he then removed Ferris' clothes, bound and gagged him and carried him to the torture bed. There, over several hours, he raped Ferris, sodomised him with his fingers, a carrot and a cucumber, and electrocuted him on the buttocks, shoulders and testicles. For this last torture, Berdella had concocted a new method of administering the treatment using two spatulas. In this way, he could switch on the power and leave it on without having to disconnect it, thereby prolonging the suffering. (When later asked by investigators how long this treatment would last for, Berdella said, "Probably no more than two to four minutes, two to five minutes, at one time.")

In addition to this, Berdella performed his acupuncture experiments in the most painful bodily parts imaginable, continuing the sadistic rituals of injection and rape with persistent attentiveness until Ferris was "UNABLE TO SIT UP MORE THAN 10-15 SEC". By now, Ferris was delirious and barely able to beg for reprieve. At 11:45 that night, Berdella made a note of his victim's "VERY DELAYED BREATHING, SNORING". By 12:00, he realised it was all over, notating "86". This was shorthand terminology from the catering business. It simply meant "no longer available". It could refer to a person who wasn't welcome at the premises and should be ejected. And so was Ferris' death recorded by his killer. Typically, however, when asked how that death came about, Berdella's verbal response was long-winded:

*"I'm not in a medical position to make that determination. It was either the drugs in connection with his physical*

*response and also on the basis that his gag had just been retied and in response to that."*

As with his previous victims, Berdella exsanguinated the body, dismembered it, packed it and disposed of it in the trash.

One observation that Berdella was to make was that Ferris had been in a motor vehicle accident which had affected his voice so that he couldn't shout very loudly. This gave him an idea to be used when torturing his next victim.

Tod Stoops, aged 21, was a slim, attractive drug addict who sold his body for money to support his habit. He and Berdella had first met in spring 1984 in an area known for cruising men. Stoops was looking for money for a fix; Berdella had just been stood up and was annoyed as he made his way back to the car. Stoops spotted the man getting into his car and came over. Uninvited, he got in. One thing led to another and in due course Stoops briefly moved into Berdella's house, along with his wife, Rachel. Berdella had the intention of helping the pair to get off drugs and straighten their lives out. He didn't succeed. The pair moved out a short while later and Berdella wasn't to meet Stoops again until a chance encounter in the Liberty Memorial Park on 17 June 1986. Berdella immediately remembered his old friend and the two were soon chatting away. Stoops mentioned that he and Rachel had split. After heading off to buy some drugs, Berdella enticed Stoops back to his place with an offer of a meal and money for sex. Needing the money for drugs, Stoops readily accepted.

As far as Berdella was concerned there was something attractive about Stoops. He was a good-looking young man with a hot body. More especially, he was alone in Kansas City with no one to come looking for him. Berdella had already made the decision to capture his next victim. His reason for doing so – stress-relief. He gave his guest a peanut butter sandwich laced with ground-down tranquilisers and a glass of milk, also spiked. Soon after ingesting this potent meal, Stoops went upstairs and zonked out on the bed. Berdella immediately set about administering the first of many doses of ketamine. Within half-an-hour, the first rape occurred. Just an hour later, the first electrocution. Now Berdella sought to blind his captive by sending jolts of electricity through Stoops' eyeballs, placing his spatulas close to the sockets. At 11 o'clock, he inserted a cucumber into Stoops' rectum, then electrocuted him again. The unfortunate man revived, struggled weakly against his restraints and then lapsed back into oblivion. Further rapes, injections, forcible insertions of vegetables took place right the way through the night – all of it documented by Berdella's pen and camera.

At 11 o'clock in the morning, Berdella left for the Flea Market after having subjected Stoops to 17 hours of incessant torture. By three o'clock, he was back and the torment resumed. Now he resorted to biting Stoops' fingers, forcing them backwards, and ramming his fist into the man's rectum. The latter eventually caused a rupture of the anal wall, leading to heavy bleeding.

The tortures continued into the night. At one point, Stoops began to fight back so Berdella whipped him with a belt. Then came the new experiment he'd had in mind since killing Ferris – Berdella injected Drano into Stoops' neck, aiming for the larynx. His aim, he'd later admit in his confession, was to silence the voice box, to prevent Stoops from screaming. The twisted treatment worked a treat, for Berdella didn't have to resort to gagging him at all.

Then the tortures became psychological. Berdella withheld food and drink for long periods until Stoops was forced to beg for sustenance. Sometimes he would give him a soft drink or a sandwich. Other times he would deny the request. On one occasion, Stoops broke down in tears after being refused food. It was punishment for having resisted an earlier rape. Instead, his tormentor delivered a sermon on "the facts of life", about what Stoops would have to do to avoid being whipped or electrocuted. In between, Berdella would administer treatment – antibiotics to fight infection and fever. He shaved off Stoops' hair. Eventually the brutal regime worked and the broken man's mental state collapsed to the point where he became childlike and cooperative. The entire ordeal had lasted nearly two weeks. Stoops, by now, was emaciated, his formerly toned body now shrunken, his face drawn, his eyes sunken and hollow. Berdella, the copious notetaker, wasn't even bothering to record the minutiae of his exploits by now; he'd given up believing that Stoops could survive any further – yet still he continued the injections, sodomies and electrocutions. And he photographed it all. The Polaroids make difficult viewing; they are studies in abject misery.

On 1 July 1986, at 11 o'clock a.m., Berdella lifted Stoops' wasted form and carried him to the bathroom. After bathing him, he set the man on a chair, dried him off and sat him on a chair, restraining him with a sash. When he returned at half-past-eleven Stoops was dead.[4] Now he made a record: "86". The remains were disposed of by leaving them outside his house, with Berdella watching through his front window to ensure that the bags were collected by the unwitting garbage collectors.

Berdella met and began a casual friendship with 20-year-old Larry Wayne Pearson in the spring of 1987. The young man had fatefully wandered by Berdella's store in the Flea Market and the two struck up a conversation. Pearson informed Berdella that since childhood he'd had an interest in witchcraft and the occult. Before long, Pearson was living at Berdella's, sleeping on the downstairs couch and doing odd jobs such as cleaning in lieu of rent. There was no physical involvement between them.

After two weeks, when it seemed that his lodger had no intention of getting a job, Berdella's irritation began to rise. On 23 June, the pair went to see a movie (_Creepshow II_) and had lunch. Afterwards, as they were driving around, Pearson jokingly began to talk about hustling gay men in Wichita, almost bragging

---

[4] A pathologist would later testify that the fatality had come about by septic shock secondary to the rupturing of the anal wall.

about it. At that point, Berdella formed that opinion that Pearson was a man who'd not be missed.

Then the logbook came out again. Berdella covertly gave Pearson tranquilisers and challenged him to a shot-drinking contest. After an afternoon drinking session, Pearson was out for the count. Berdella injected him and took some photos. Pearson was the largest of Berdella's victims, and so, instead of carrying up to the bedroom, he dragged the limp body down to the basement. There, he tied the man's hands behind his head, secured him with a chain wrapped around a brick column and with an injection of Drano into his throat attempted to destroy Pearson's vocal cords. This was followed by a series of electrocutions.

Pearson quickly learned to be submissive and cooperative, but to make sure there'd be no doubt, Berdella explained it anyway: Pearson was to be kept as a sex slave. If Pearson complained about the pain in his arms, Berdella advised him to compare it to the pain of electrocution. Pearson stopped complaining.

On 8 July, Berdella allowed his prisoner to perform oral sex on him. Pearson had been completely defeated and was utterly compliant. Or so Berdella thought. By 5 August, his only means of restraining Pearson was a dog-collar. The two were upstairs, Berdella lying on the bed reading a magazine, Pearson by his side attending to his master's needs. However, whilst fellating "Master Bob", Pearson suddenly chomped down on Berdella's penis, causing it to bleed. He started to shout about how he wasn't going to be treated this way. Astonishingly, such was the level to which he'd been broken down, he made no attempt to escape and allowed Berdella to reapply the restraints. Berdella went to the hospital emergency department. There, he was told he'd have to come in for a couple of days. Berdella reasoned that he had a few things to attend to at home first, one of which was to make sure the dogs had enough food and water whilst he was gone. He got a cab back home and saw to the dogs' needs. Then he bludgeoned Pearson into unconsciousness with a tree branch, put a bag over his head and suffocated him to death – all whilst the cab awaited him outside for the return journey to the hospital. Pearson had lasted six long weeks in Berdella's clutches. Before leaving, Berdella turned on the air conditioning so that the body wouldn't deteriorate in the heat. Upon his discharge from hospital two days later, he dismembered, eviscerated and disposed of the remains, saving the head and storing it in the freezer for a week before burying it in the backyard.

In the early hours of 29 March 1988, Christopher Bryson, a 22-year-old hustler, was working the streets of downtown Kansas City. Bryson, a high school dropout, was a married man with a wife and son to support; he needed to earn a few extra bucks. And so, when he spotted the brown Toyota Tercel hatchback slowly cruising 9th Street, he stopped. The driver wound down the window and asked him if he wanted to party. Bryson thought the driver looked harmless enough – middle-aged, pudgy, rounded face, receding hairline, softly spoken with a slight lisp and wearing thick glasses. _He had some Valium back at his place_, the man said. He looked to be out of condition. Bryson was muscular and confident; he knew how to look after himself. He got in the passenger side of the car. "I'm Bob," the man said.

Back at the man's house, Bob made him welcome, talked about his dogs, showed him his antiques and artworks. There was more stuff upstairs, Bob told him. Bryson picked up his beer and headed towards the stairs, Bob following closely behind him. He scarcely knew what happened next – a hard knock to the back of the head rendered him unconscious.

The next he became aware of, as he woke up groggily, was Bob taking numerous photos of him. In his dazed state, he realised that he'd been bound fast, was lashed to a bed, and his mouth had been stuffed with a rag. He lapsed back into unconsciousness, only to come to again in the morning.

Bob entered the room and immediately began to jab an index finger repeatedly into Bryson's eye. Bryson, gagged securely, couldn't scream. Bob left, only to return moments later with a soaked cotton swab, which he then jabbed directly into Bryson's eyes. The burning pain was inexorable.

Next, Bob straddled Bryson's chest and, with a two-foot iron bar, began to batter his captor's hands, fracturing bones and causing more intolerable pain.

Worse was to come. Bob then used his transformer on Bryson, electrocuting his testicles. All the while, he took photos of the anguish he was inflicting so callously. This was followed by two injections of a substance which sent Bryson into oblivion.

The tortures continued immediately upon his revival some hours later. Bob coldly informed Bryson of his intentions:

*"You did not choose to be here, but you are. For you to survive being here, and for you to, you know, make it, it could either be rough or it could be easy. If I grow to like you, and to trust you, then I could do special things for you, such as buy you cigarettes, pick up a movie on the way home from work and so forth. Don't try to fight me, or you'll just get more of what you had earlier. You see, what you got, is nothing compared to what you can have."*

He warned Bryson: "The only way you can harm me is with your arms or teeth ... And I can surely take care of your teeth."

Byson made the decision to comply. Meanwhile, however, whilst the tortures and rapes continued, his thoughts were on escape.

The next day, Bob mentioned the other prisoners who'd previously been in Bryson's position: "I've gotten this far with other people before and they're dead now, because of mistakes they made." However, he allowed his captor small leniencies, renting videos for the pair to watch together, leading him around the house by a dog collar. He made Bryson pose for photos. And he raped him. After sex on Friday, the third day of captivity, Bryson asked Bob for permission to speak. Bob allowed it. Bryson then informed Bob that having his arms tied behind him was extremely painful. He asked Bob to instead tie his arms in front of him. This Bob agreed to.

On Saturday, Bryson convinced Bob to allow him to have a remote control in order to watch a baseball game on TV. Later, it seemed as though Bob had left the house, but Bryson couldn't be sure. Yet he took his chance. Bob had dropped a book of matches by the side of the bed. Bryson grabbed them, lit a match and held it beneath one of the binding ropes. All the while, he held a dreadful terror that his captor might walk in at any moment and catch him trying to escape. Finally, he burned his way through four ropes. Still naked, he hurried to the window, thinking it might be locked. It wasn't, but he now realised he was looking down from the second floor. Beneath him was a concrete path. He climbed onto the window-ledge, figuring he'd jump over the path and onto the grass opposite, but the sill collapsed and he fell straight down, fracturing bones in his feet. Adrenaline barely dulled the pain as he got up and raced forwards, out onto the street. He saw a utilities worker. "Hey, man," he yelled, "call the police for me. That son of a bitch is crazy. He's trying to kill me."

Together, they made for a house across the road and knocked on the door. The owner was shocked to open his door to a limping, scratched, naked man with a dog collar around his neck, swollen red eyes and a scratchy voice. He closed the door and called 911. By the time Bob returned home, police were waiting for him.

A search of the property, which was cluttered and scattered with dog faeces, revealed incriminating evidence: 334 Polaroid snapshots of naked men, both alive and dead, the instruments of torture in situ, a collection of starkly brutal images perpetuated by a sadist of extreme taste, inflicting humiliation upon pain. The fact was undeniable: he had used the camera as an additional weapon. The detailed torture logs confirmed the visual evidence. Elsewhere in the house were found the instruments of torture, pornographic material, a book on narcotics, property belonging to and identifying young men, newspaper clippings concerning missing Jerry Howell and a human skull in a second-storey closet. Further searches uncovered the tools Berdella had used to dismember human bodies and various body parts buried in the garden. Bob's Bazaar Boutique was revealed to contain

307

two skulls which appeared to be made of plastic but which were, in fact, deskinned, bleached human skulls. Robert Berdella seemed like a man with secrets to tell.

He did tell them. With the evidence stacking up nicely, and having been formally arraigned for the murder of Larry Pearson, Berdella pleaded guilty of first-degree murder of Robert Sheldon before Judge Alvin C. Randall. A month later, he agreed to a plea bargain to avoid the death penalty and confessed to the second-degree murder of four additional male victims. He made a full, detailed, vivid (and frankly shocking) confession under oath. When asked if his acts had been deliberate and with malice aforethought, the habitually rambling, bombastic braggart of a man simply replied, "Yes." He was sentenced to life imprisonment without the possibility of parole and sent to the state penitentiary in Jefferson City, Missouri.

Berdella's vast collection of antiquities and artefacts were seized and sold at auction, the proceeds going to pay legal costs. No. 4315 Charlotte Street was purchased by a local businessman and razed to the ground. The land was sold to local residents. It remains a vacant plot.

Within four years – and after making complaints to prison authorities that he hadn't received his prescribed medication for high blood pressure – Robert Berdella was dead at the age of 43, succumbing to a heart attack on 8 October 1992. He is buried in Oakwood Cemetery, Cuyahoga Falls. Prior to his death, he never expressed any remorse for his actions, instead, in an interview, referring to his victims as his "play toys". Judge Randall, upon hearing the news of Berdella's death, stately wryly, "It couldn't have happened to a nicer guy." Few mourned his passing.

# Luis Alfredo Garavito Cubillos

(active 1992-1999)

IT'S A HARD THING to say that one series of murders is worse than any other. The killings themselves may be differentiated by the *intensity* of their depravity. Edward D. Cowart, presiding judge at Ted Bundy's trial, described his acts as "atrocious and cruel, in that they were extremely wicked, shockingly evil, vile, and with utter indifference to human life". For the victims, the cost is still the same, for they are dead, having paid with their lives. However, when they are exposed, some series of murders stand out in terms of the sheer *quantity* of victims. And the numbers can be preposterous – bafflingly so.

Hamilton Howard "Albert" Fish (the "Gray Man") confessed to raping, killing and eating three children in the US in 1920s-30s. He once boasted that he'd "had a child in every state", and it's believed that he might've claimed over 100 victims.

Although Richard Kuklinski (the "Iceman") was convicted of three murders, it's believed that the true number is between 100 and 250. A hired killer, Kublinski not only performed assassinations under contract but for his own pleasure, often gruesomely. These included immolation, feeding live people to rats and beating to death with bare fists ("just for the exercise").

Donald Henry "Pee Wee" Gaskins Jr., the "Meanest Man in America", was convicted of nine murders, but the number could run into the 80s. A repeated rapist, killer and cannibal throughout the mid 20th-century, Gaskins claimed to have been a victim of his own short stature. He found that killing proved to himself, at least, that he could be his own master. He commented, "I have walked the same path as God. By taking lives and making others afraid I became God's equal."

Pedro Rodrigues Filho, a Brazilian, first started killing at the age of 14. In a career spanning four decades, he claimed to have killed more than 100 times, 47 whilst in prison. Known as "The Pedrinho Matador", Filho is also thought to be the world's most prolific killer *of serial killers themselves*. He was released from prison in 2018 under laws that limit jail terms to 30 years.

For over 30 years, Pedro Alonso López ("The Monster of the Andes"), targeted prepubescent girls across Colombia, Peru and Ecuador before being captured by indigenous tribespeople. He was given over to the police who promptly released him, allowing him to continue his spree, raping and strangling around three girls per week. Investigators only started to believe his confessions when a flash flood uncovered a mass grave containing many of his victims. Declared sane and released from psychiatric hospital in 1998, his whereabouts are currently unknown. He was convicted of 110 murders although he confessed to over 350.

Samuel Little ("The Choke and Stroke Killer") is now thought to be America's most prolific serial killer after making a credible confession to having taken 93 victims, often marginalised, vulnerable female sex workers or drug addicts whom he mostly killed by strangulation. Many of the bodies have never been found. So detailed was Little's memory that he was able to draw startling accurate portraits of several of his victims.

During his killing years, Rodney James Alcala appeared on the TV show *The Dating Game*, later earning himself the sobriquet "The Dating Game Killer". It's estimated that he killed at least 130 women and teenage girls, taking explicit photographs of many of them over his murderous career in the late '60s and '70s.

Dubbed "The Sunday Morning Slasher", mildly retarded Carl Eugene Watts, is estimated to have tortured and killed over 80 women between 1974 and 1982, kidnapping them from their homes and dispatching them in numerous ways, including strangling, stabbing, bludgeoning and drowning, across many US jurisdictions. Watts was caught after one victim feigned unconsciousness, only to escape whilst he was otherwise preoccupied with a second victim.

Daniel Camargo Barbosa is estimated to have raped, murdered and dismembered 180 young girls in Colombia and

Ecuador, targeting those whom he believed to be virgins. He earned the moniker "The Sadist of El Charquito" due to his habit of hacking his victims to pieces with a machete. He managed to escape jail once, swimming through shark-infested waters from his island prison, only to recommence his killing spree. He didn't escape a second time; a fellow prison killed him in 1994.

Theodore Robert "Ted" Bundy, a killer so notorious he doesn't have a nickname, was convicted of the kidnap, rape and murder of 30 women but it's thought that his victims number over 100. Bundy travelled widely across America in his search for prey, and in doing so strayed onto the patches of other killers, muddying the task for investigators of identifying ownership of the crimes. Charming and good-looking, Bundy was also a sadosexual predator who eventually blamed pornography for heightening his predilections for lust-killing.

Richard Cottingham tortured and killed women in New Jersey in the 1980s. He earned the nickname "The Torso Killer" for his habit of dismembering his victims, usually leaving only the torso behind. Although convicted of killing five women, he claims to have killed between 85 and 100 murders.

"The Red Ripper", Soviet serial killer Andrei Romanovich Chikatilo killed at least 52 women over a 12-year span from 1978. Travelling widely as a duty of his employment afforded him the opportunity to kill without detection. Also going in his favour was his indiscriminate victim profile type; he killed children, male and female, as well as women, thereby preventing investigators from initially linking the crimes. Mild-mannered and pleasant, he often had little difficulty in luring his victims towards isolated areas, where he'd suddenly pounce, brandishing razor-sharp knives for slicing at them.

Operating around the same time, also in Soviet Russia, was Nikolai Espolovih Dzhumagaliev, a schizophrenic maniac also known as "Kolya the Maneater". It's thought that he killed between 50 and 100 women, luring them to a park at night, hacking them to death with an axe in a bid to rid the world of prostitutes. He cannibalised some of his victims and also served up the flesh to unsuspecting others, disguising it as ethnic dishes.

Gary Leon Ridgway's victims were mostly prostitutes and underage runaways whom he strangled and dumped in water, earning himself the name "The Green River Killer". He would often return to the bodies to have sex with them. Convicted of 49 murders, he confessed to 71, although it is thought that the true number is actually over 90.

Robert William "Willy" Pickton was a Canadian serial killer who operated in the '80s and '90s, picking up women – many of them prostitutes – and murdering 49 of them on his remote pig farm. Investigators, realising that women were going missing, eventually searched Pickton's premises and found numerous body parts in freezers as well as human teeth strewn about the junk-littered farm. It's believed that Pickton's pigs ate many of the victims, earning him the epithet "The Pig Farmer Killer". It's also believed that he ground up and sold human flesh – even selling some to the police who eventually captured this most unsavoury of butchers.

The "Happy Face Killer" was so-called because of the smiles he drew on many of the missives he sent to the media. Keith Hunter Jesperson, a Canadian-American, claims to have strangled over 180 women during the first half of the 1990s, picking up hitchhikers, transients and sex workers in his truck. His preferred method of dispatch was strangulation, often bringing his victims close to death, reviving them only to repeat the torture.

Alexander Yuryevich Pichushkin, known as "The Chessboard Killer", is believed to have killed between 48 and 60 people in Moscow between 1992 and 2004. A chess-lover, his aim was to kill 64 people, the number of squares on a chessboard. Preying on the homeless, he would hit them on the head with a hammer and ram a broken vodka bottle into the wounds in their skulls.

Mikhail Viktorovich Popkov preyed upon women whom he considered immoral – prostitutes or the inebriated – in the years spanning the millennium. Dressed in his uniform, the Russian police officer would lure women with the promise of a free ride before raping and murdering them with a collection of tools that included knives, axes, screwdriver and baseball bats. It's estimated that "The Werewolf" killed some 80-plus women.

Moses Sithole is confirmed to have killed 38 black woman in the mid-1990s, and possibly as many as 76. Under the guise of being a charity worker, Sihole, a black South African, lured women to isolated fields where he would assault, rape and strangle them to death with their own underwear. His attacks occurred first in Atteridgeville, continued in Boksburg and concluded in Cleveland and so he became known as "The ABC Killer".

China's "Monster Killer", Yang Xinhai, killed 67 victims – mainly farmers and their entire families – by entering their homes at night and attacking them with axes, hammers and shovels. His motive, it is said, was revenge against society as a result of a break up from a girlfriend. "I have no desire to be part of society," he commented. "Society is not my concern."

Perhaps because they have close access to the unwell, medics and nurses feature highly in the rollcall of prolific serial killers. Harold Frederick Shipman was a much-loved English family doctor who, throughout his medical career, murdered patients with a swift injection of diamorphine. The crimes of "Dr Death" came to light after he forged the will of a patient he'd killed in 1998. Although found guilty of 15 murders, it's estimated that he killed over 215, mostly elderly women in good health.

Niels Högel, a German nurse and serial killer, admitted to dozens of killings, but the true number may well exceed 300. Tampering with intravenous medications, Högel's motivation, or so he claimed, was to see if he could revive them. The defence of Munchausen syndrome by proxy was scarcely exculpatory as he never seemed to succeed in his stated aim.

Similarly, Charles Edmund Cullen, a New Jersey nurse, spared many cardiac patients from going into arrest by administering them with fatal overdoses, simply because he didn't like to witness attempts to save their lives. Some authorities believe that the number of victims could be as much as 400.

But topping the list is Luis Garavito, a Colombian rapist and

serial killer. Known as *"La Bestia"* ("The Beast") or "The Monster of Génova", Garavito raped, tortured and killed boys between the ages of six and 16 over a period of seven years in the
1990s. His epithets were well earned; his deeds *were* truly monstrous. Although his compatriot, Pedro Alonso López, is thought
to have been the most prolific modern-day serial killer, Garavito
holds the dubious honour of having the largest number of
*confirmed* victims – 138 in total.

Luis Alfredo Garavito Cubillos was born on 25 January 1957
in Génova in Colombia's western coffee-growing region, to a
mother who, it's believed, was a hardened drug-addled prostitute. He lived in a toxic and abusive household. His mother suffered regular, severe beatings from his heavily alcoholic father,
Manuel, who, just for the fun of it, would also lay into Luis and
his six younger siblings. Indeed, Luis was so afraid of his father
that he used to hide in fear when he came home from work.

There was little respite at school. Luis, unpopular from the
onset due to his timid nature and the fact that he wore glasses,
soon became the frequent target of bullies. Occasionally, the
tension building within him would erupt and he'd lash out with
a violent temper. At the age of 11, Luis' father forced him to
drop out of school and get a job. Accordingly, Luis sold sundry
items on the streets in order to help support his family.

Luis' father would force young Luis to watch his mother engage in sexual activity with her clients. As Luis and his siblings
grew older, their father would allow these clients to sexually
abuse them also. Between the ages of 12 and 15, he was raped
and tortured by numerous of his father's friends. He kept the
details of the attacks to himself, however, fearful that he'd not
be believed if he came forward. During this time, Luis began to
sexually interfere with his own siblings. He also began to torture, kill and mutilate small animals.

Powerless to resist the abuse at home, and unprotected by his
drugged-out mother, at the age of 16 Luis ran away from home
to take his chances on the streets of Bogotá, Columbia's capital
city, some 150 miles away. There, he was arrested whilst trying

to molest a boy at a train station. After his release, he returned to the family home, only to realise that he was no longer welcome there. At this point, he became one of the countless itinerant youths who aimlessly wandered Colombia, drinking his way from one place to the next. A variety of jobs kept him afloat – a shop clerk, street vendor of prayer cards and trinkets, working in a bakery.

The drinking increased, and by the 1980s Garavito was deep in the throes of alcoholism. He continued to wander, but with the drink in him the aggression came out and wherever he went he soon outstayed his welcome and was encouraged to leave town – sooner rather than later. He drifted endlessly onwards. He lost a job in a bakery due to chronic alcoholism and now his problems only got worse. Complaining of voices in his head, Garavito sought help and remained under psychiatric care for five years. During this time, he spent 30 days in hospital due to malignant auditory hallucinations, but during this time he never once mentioned his proclivity for sadism or adolescent boys.

After discharge from hospital, Garavito found employment in a supermarket and began a relationship with an older woman called Claudia. It was at this point in his life, in 1992, that Garavito began killing young boys, crimes he committed when under the influence of alcohol and having been taken over by what he termed "a superior being".

Most of the victims were street children – boys from poor families, separated from their loved ones or displaced due to the political violence and upheavals then ravaging Columbia caused by its decades-long civil war. These were boys, in fact, who'd been just like himself. They were a familiar sight on the streets of Bogotá at the time – dirty, hungry, poorly-dressed and sad-looking. They begged, shone shoes and sold cheap, sundry items on street corners – scratching a living, in other words – and they were *everywhere*, yet they were at the fringes of society. During his two-hour lunchbreaks, Garavito would entice boys such as these to remote areas with sweets or money for doing odd jobs where he would rape and torture them. Aged between six and

13 (with the exception of one 16-year-old youth), all of the victims fell into the same victim type – homeless, peasants or orphaned boys. Often, Garavito would disguise himself in different garb in order to make himself look anonymous. Alternatively, he'd dress as if he worked as businessman who'd be legitimately seeking to offer work to boys, such as a farmer, a street vendor, a priest or a drug dealer. His capacity to change façade was remarkable, and draws comparison with another serial killer whose ability to change appearance seemed chameleon-like – Ted Bundy.

The first victim is thought to have been a teenager called Juan Carlos, who was unfortunate to have been spotted by Garavito on 2 October 1992, walking past a bar that the would-be killer happened to be drinking in that night. Garavito would later claim that the sight of the moonlight glinting off the boy had awoken something murderous in him, compelling him to kill. Three days after the sighting, Juan's remains were found with visible evidence of torture, including missing teeth and testicles. In less than a week, a second boy would be dealt the same treatment.

Garavito's *M.O.* was effective. Once gaining the trust of an impoverished boy, he'd take him on a long walk away from the crowded city streets until he was exhausted, stopping at a hidden area that was overgrown with plant foliage. There, the boy would be powerless to resist. First, Garavito would bind his hands. Then he would remove the boy's clothes. Next, he would torture them. The tortures were prolonged and painful, often involving biting the flesh, removing the teeth, impaling the buttocks or inserting sharpened items into the anus or hands. Sometimes he would emasculate the boy, stuffing his genitals into his mouth. He would anally rape him. One of his slow torture techniques was to bind the boy so that he could stumble off some distance, but not escape. There is not one known case of any child having escaped Garavito's clutches. They were all killed, probably by slitting their throats. And with each passing attack the violence would escalate. As he departed the scenes of the crime, Garavito would leave bottles of sexual lubricant lying discarded next to his victim's body, along with the empty bottles of the cheap schnapps of which he seemed to be so fond.

The bodies began to pile up, but connecting them to a single assassin didn't happen. People thought that the mutilated bodies had been caused by Satanic cults or human traffickers. Even the endemic political violence was blamed. Yet Garavito was killing regularly. Within a year, his hands accounted for 10 murders.

During this time, Garavito was living in Pereira and had begun dating a woman named Teresa. Teresa had a teenage son, but remarkably Garavito harmed neither him nor his mother. However, the relationship wasn't close, and Garavito would continue to travel Colombia's roads frequently and widely. Ostensibly this was in the search for work. In reality, it was to look for boys to kill.

Interestingly, Garavito managed to settle down somewhat during this period. He was regarded by locals as a friendly man who loved children, and they even gave him an affectionate nickname – "Tribilín", the Spanish name for Disney's cartoon character Goofy. Little did the townspeople imagine the monstrous epithets that were to come. What's curious, in retrospect, is that no one was suspicious of the odd man's activities with boys, even though much of the time he appeared to be heavily intoxicated.

Garavito began by collecting trophies from his victims. But by 1994, such was the rate of kills that he was unable to carry them with him anymore and so he left them in a bag at his sister Ester's house. He continued to travel, but somewhere along the line he injured his leg, which failed to heal properly. As a result, he now walked with a pronounced limp. But walk he continued to do …

He also continued to kill. With alacrity. He had progressed to disembowelment and decapitation. Sometimes he didn't bother to hide the bodies, merely leaving them exposed for others to find. He almost came close to being caught in 1996 after locals told police that they'd seen one of the their own, 12-year-old Ronald Delgado Quintero, in the company of Luis Garavito. Questioned by the police, however, Garavito was able to convince them of his innocence.

It seemed he couldn't stop himself – even in chancy situations. On 8 June 1996, in the town of Boyacá, Colombia, Garavito persuaded a boy to follow him on his (the boy's) own bicycle. The boy's mother instigated a search when he failed to come home. A group of local boys identified Garavito as the man whom the boy had followed. The mother informed the police, who in turn questioned Garavito. He told them that after buying the child some sweets he'd departed on his own. The boy's naked, emasculated body was found five days later, his penis shoved into this mouth. By this time, Garavito had left town, only to kill a 13-year-old boy in the nearby town of Pereira four days later.

The murders went undetected for many years due, in part, to the fact that the victims hadn't been reported missing. Although clusters of bodies began to turn up, the authorities didn't take much notice. Then, in 1997, came a shocking discovery. A group of children found a mass grave containing the bodies of over 30 young boys, just outside the city of Pereira. Although all of the remains had been bound with the same nylon rope and all had suffered the same types of torture, they were all in different stages of decomposition. The news hit the headlines and soon people wondered if the murders of a large number of boys, scattered throughout the country, could be the work of a single individual. Certainly, the similar *M.O.* seemed to point to a serial murderer. However, matters were complicated by the fact that many of the boys couldn't be identified. Severe purification, coupled with the tragic fact that many of the boys hadn't even been reported missing, hampered investigators' attempts to identify them, making tracing their families all but impossible.

Then, a few months later in 1998, the naked remains of two boys were discovered next to each other outside Génova. The next day, another set of remains were found only metres away.

All three children showed signs of having been tortured and sexually violated. Nearby were the signs of a recent fire: the murderer had clearly attempted to conceal evidence by burning it. Within the ashes, investigators found the murder weapon (a screwdriver), an empty bottle of cheap schnapps, a pair of men's shoes and a pair of red-framed spectacles. An examination of the spectacles revealed that they probably belonged to someone aged around 40-45 years. The shoes were heavily worn, moreso on one side, indicating that the wearer had probably walked with a limp.[1] But crucially, also found was a note with an address written on it. The discovery led investigators directly to Garavito's sister. It was a breakthrough. Ester informed police that she'd not seen Garavito in several months, but she did give them the bag that he'd left in her possession. In the bag were miscellaneous items including cut-out passport photos of young boys (the only trophies he collected), cryptic notes detailing Garavito's travels and murders, and an ominous "tally" of kills which looked to be shockingly numerous. A bill amongst Garavito's belongings led police to his address but when they arrived there he wasn't at home.

Meanwhile, in a park in Villavicencio, a city in central Colombia, a strange man had lured away 12-year-old John Ivan Sabogal, tied him up and was attempting to rape him. Fortunately for the boy, a homeless teenager passed by, saw what was happening and came to the boy's aid by throwing stones at his attacker. As a result of this incident, Garavito was arrested on 22 April 1999 on charges of attempted rape. However, police believed that if the teenager hadn't intervened at that point then Garavito would've killed the boy. Following a brief

---

[1] Another man was briefly arrested. A sex offender with a limp, he fit the bill, and police thought that they'd got their man. He was only cleared, however, after further bodies turned up during his incarceration, exonerating him.

interrogation, they confronted their prisoner with their suspicions that he was *La Bestia*. He denied it.

A confession wouldn't be enough anyway. Police covertly obtained DNA evidence from Garavito's cell. It matched DNA taken from the murder scenes. In addition, they tested the eyesight of all detainees in the jail, doing so in a way that their suspect's suspicions wouldn't be aroused. Garavito's optical examination matched the spectacles found at one of the recent murder scenes. Now, faced with the evidence against him, Garavito at last broke down and owned up to his crimes. One of the world's most wanted men had been caught. He confessed freely. He was able to recall all the details of his crimes, including dates; it was not understood why he needed to record the incriminating details in cryptic notes.

He never did appear in court. His confession, coupled with incontrovertible evidence against him, negated the requirement for a formal trial. Eventually, he was found guilty on 138 counts of rape, torture and murder. Some, however, have estimated the *actual* number of killings could exceed 400. Garavito was sentenced to 1,853 years and nine days in prison. He is currently in a maximum-security prison in Valledupar, held separately from other prisons due to fears that otherwise he'd be killed immediately. Due to Colombian law, however, Garavito could be freed after serving 40 years. The most prolific serial killer of all time is said to be a model prison. Reportedly, this sexually sadistic psychopathic paedophile can come across as friendly and sincere; his jailors like him. With good behaviour, and in consideration of cooperation and mitigation, he can apply to be released early – and there's a possibility he might even succeed. Once freed, he plans to start a political career and become an advocate for children's welfare. He says that he now has everything sorted out in his mind and he's no longer a danger. In reality, however, it is unlikely that Colombia's *La Bestia* will ever be allowed to roam its roads again.

# Colin Ireland
(active 1993)

IN EARLY 1993, a daydreaming loner made a fateful New Year's Day resolution: he decided to become a serial killer. At the time, Colin Ireland was living in an English seaside town with no job and few prospects. Life seemed to be passing him by and offering him little opportunity and no recognition. Well, now was the time to do something about *that*, and within months his reputation would be widely known. Colin Ireland was soon to become widely known as "The Gay Slayer".

He was born on 16 March 1954 to Pat, an unmarried 17-year-old, in West Hill Hospital in Dartford, Kent. The pregnancy was unplanned, and clearly unwelcomed by the teenage father, who left the scene shortly after the arrival of the new-born babe. His name was not documented on the birth certificate and young Colin was never to have any knowledge of his father.

Pat attempted to scratch an independent living working in a newsagents, but she was unable to make ends meet and, struggling emotionally as well as financially, she shortly returned to live with her parents and brother in Myrtle Road in Dartmouth.

After five years, in 1959, Pat, now in her early 20s, left home a second time. Trying to make it on her own again, she moved with Colin to a flat just 10 miles away in Burch Road, Gravesend. Desperate to provide a stable home for the pair of them, she found employment in a variety of positions. However, unskilled and unable to commit to a full-time job, she could only manage a meagre living. It wasn't enough. She soon returned to her parents' house. With Colin in tow, this was the start of six years of upheaval: Pat and her son moved house several more times during this period. In 1960, they moved to Sidcup, Kent. Within the year, they'd moved to Westmalling, a collective of timber huts for homeless women and children in Maidstone. More akin to a prisoner-of-war camp, as soon as Pat arrived there she burst into tears. She endured no more than three months in this grim, jail-like accommodation (which Ireland would later describe as "degradation personified") before heading back to her parents.

During this time, Pat had various partners coming and going in her life – and in and out of Colin's. By 1961, she'd met a new partner and the three of them moved into a house on Farnol Road, Dartford. The couple married and Colin's surname was changed from Ireland to that of his stepfather, Saker. Saker evidently treated Colin well and had a good sense of humour. He was an electrician by trade but work was sporadic and the family remained financially unstable. When Pat became pregnant, Colin, now aged 10, became an expense she could ill-afford and so he was placed into a foster placement in Wainscott, Kent. It was an unremarkable experience. After she and her husband found a new home Colin was invited back. Soon after this, however, the young couple fell into rent arrears and were evicted from their home. Pat returned to Wellmalling. Saker, unable to move into the accommodation (men were barred), went to live with his own parents. A half-brother was born and Pat, Saker and Colin moved into *yet another* house in West Kingsdown, Kent. Not long after this, however, Saker walked out on the family. Pat again became alone and broke.

She remarried a second time in 1966, to a man called Williams, when Colin was 12. The three found a home in Clyde Street in Sheerness, Kent and Colin's second stepfather proved to be a more stabilising influence. Nonetheless, this time Colin refused to take on a new surname, reverting to his mother's maiden name, Ireland. The marriage would turn out to be loving and enduring and Colin and Pat were both treated well and provided for over the coming years. Throughout all the upheavals, Colin's relationship with his mother for the most part remained strong. He would later remember Pat as being loving and affectionate, and he was able to recall the personal sacrifices she'd made in order to keep the family together and to provide for her children.

There'd been many school changes in Colin's short life. Having moved to different parts of Kent six times so far, he always seemed to be the "new boy". His thin, lanky frame, the bow-legged stance and, frankly, unappealing countenance made him an easy target for bullies. He always seemed to be on the periphery – a sad, lonely, withdrawn boy. What few friends he had were cast in a similar vein – unchallenging outsiders who wouldn't give him any trouble. He tried to avoid school. When forced, he would often turn up late. For this he was repeatedly punished with a severe caning. He'd later comment that it was a wonder he turned out to be a sadist rather than a masochist. Unathletic and morose, it was perhaps no surprise that he was never chosen to join team sports at school. He did, however, spend a two-and-a-half period in the Sea Cadets, which proved to be one of the few worthwhile experiences of his childhood.

As Colin approached adolescence, he began to receive the unwanted and unwarranted attention of others, all occurring in Sheerness. On the first occasion, the 12-year-old boy was working at a fairground during the summer. He'd spotted a necklace and locket that he wished to buy as a present for his mother. He asked the price of the stall-holder but it proved too high. The man suggested that Colin visit him in his caravan. When Colin did so, the trader offered to give him the necklace in exchange for a sexual act. Colin declined and left. In the second incident, not long after, Colin was using a public toilet. A young man peered over the cubicle wall and peered down at Colin. He offered Colin a few pence without specifying what he wanted in return. Colin was disturbed but did not respond. On a third occasion, Colin was at a local cinema when a local businessman approached, offering him drinks and ice cream in exchange for sexual services. The fourth instance occurred after a dealer in a bric-à-brac shop befriended Colin, only later to make repeated sexual advances in exchange for money. Although no sexual contact ever took place, the experiences left Colin upset, angry and feeling violated.

At the age of 16, Colin decided to run away to London. To do this he needed money, and so he stole £4. He got caught. He was served with a "fit person order" and sent to Finchton Manor

School in Kent, a fee-paying "free expression" establishment which only accepted boys exhibiting intelligence and emotional issues. Again, he was teased and bullied. In retaliation, he set fire to the belongings of one of his tormentors. Colin would later admit to a lifelong fascination with flames, stating that he also had nightmares about fire. The conflagration was quickly put out by a teacher, but Colin was expelled from Finchton Manor into the care of a social worker. He evaded the systems set up to look after him and immediately reactivated his primary plan, running away to London. He was now 17.

In London, he began hanging around Playland, an amusement arcade where he witnessed young runaways being picked up by paedophiles, selling their bodies for a place to sleep. Colin himself, however, was never abused. Homeless and penniless, he resorted again to robbery. It seems that Colin was a careless thief; he was soon caught again. Now he was sent to HM Prison Hollesley Bay – a borstal located a few miles east of Ipswich, Kent, known locally as "The Colony". Borstals were British reform institutions, which offered vocational training and therapy. Nonetheless, they were notorious for their brutal and austere regimes. Colin hated it. One summer's morning, he decided he'd had enough and ran away. He was caught by the police. He was sent to serve the remainder of his sentence at the much stricter borstals of Rochester and Grendon. When he turned 18 he was freed.

Colin Ireland now entered what he called his "lost period". To make ends meet he took a series of menial jobs. In December 1975, he earned further criminal convictions for car theft, burglary and criminal damage. For this he was sentenced to 18 months in prison. Less than a year later he was released. He moved to Swindon, Wiltshire. He met his first girlfriend – a black West Indian woman five years older than himself – and lived with her and her four children for a few months. It was with this lady that Ireland finally lost his virginity at the age of 22. Although the two planned to get married, for Ireland it wasn't a happy time. "In between custodial periods a lot of the

'70s were a blur," he said. "I spent my time detached and wondering." He was convicted of extortion in 1977 and sentenced to 18 months' imprisonment. In 1980, he was sentenced to two years for robbery. An attempted deception earned him another conviction in 1981.

Ireland met Virginia at a lecture on survivalism. She was nine years his senior and confined to a wheelchair after a road traffic accident – and Ireland adored her. They married in 1982 and settled down in the Holloway area of London. There, he worked in whatever unskilled, temporary jobs he could find, including restaurant work, a volunteer fireman, a stint as a bouncer ... even working the door at a gay club.

Virginia gave birth to their daughter but this didn't encourage him to mend his ways; he soon had another spell in prison for fraud. After his release, he had an adulterous affair which his wife found out about. She divorced him.

The following year, 1989, he met a pub landlady called Janet in Buckfast, Devon. She had two children aged 11 and 13, and Ireland moved in within a week. Within three months they were married. It didn't bode well. By now Ireland had grown tall and was a hulking man, more than capable of looking after himself ... or sorting out his wife. He turned his fists towards her, beating her harshly. He stole from her. One night he threw Janet out of the bedroom. She took refuge in another. Ireland entered, broke the lightbulb and plunged the room into darkness. Then he circled the room, taunting her, saying, "I'm over here, I'm over here." It was an exercise in control and the fear of violence.

During his time in Devonshire, Ireland, still fancying himself as a survivalist, would take himself off to Dartmoor wearing his camouflage gear. His plans to live off the land came to little; he always came home for his tea.

In April 1990, Ireland drove Janet and the children to his mother's house in Margate. Amidst the visit, he left Janet and the children there, stole her car and, knowing the PIN of her bank card, emptied her account, leaving her penniless. She hadn't even enough money to get home. At that point, only a few months into their marriage, Ireland disappeared from his wife's life. She and the children were forced to live in a homeless shelter. She wasn't to hear from him again.

With two failed marriages behind him, the next place Ireland popped up was Southend-on-Sea, a down-on-its-luck tourist resort on the coast of Essex. He was soon volunteering at a homeless centre, despite being homeless himself. He enjoyed his time there, feeling an empathy for the homeless people he worked with. Colleagues remembered him being homophobic, but otherwise he seems to have been well-enough liked by both staff and clients of the centre. Nevertheless, in December 1992, he was let go after female colleagues complained about being inappropriately touched by him. According to Ireland, the allegations were unfounded. By now, he was living alone in a dingy flat in Southend, unemployed and feeling frustrated and directionless. He simply didn't know what to do with his life. As the end of the year approached, Colin Ireland found himself stewing in resentment over his self-made troubles. He felt like a nobody. He didn't want to be a nobody; he wanted to be remembered. Two days into 1993, Colin Ireland travelled to London – his primary objective, to make a name for himself.

The Coleherne Arms public house began life in 1866 as a Victorian working men's pub. Due to its location on Old Brompton Road in London's fashionably bohemian Earls Court area it attracted an unconventional clientele from the onset. By the 1930s, it had become a firm favourite of the theatrical types piling in from local playhouses. Before long, the Coleherne had gained itself a reputation; this was somewhere where the homosexual population could find a welcome. In the early 20th-century, drag entertainers gave afternoon performances. By the mid-fifties, even though homosexual practice was still illegal in England it had become known as a gay bar. Over the next two decades it morphed into a leather bar, gaining such a wide reputation in the 1960s that tourists as well as locals came to its doors. The Coleherne's loyal patrons continued to flock to it after the decriminalisation of homosexuality in 1967,[1] and they remained loyal to the dark, subterranean, smoke-filled dive bar well into the early 1990s.

Its reputation was well-earned. The Coleherne had developed an air of seediness that could seem, quite frankly, menacing. There was always a hint of danger in the air. The windows were blacked out and the music was loud. In the underground cavern of the lower floor's murky depths the ceiling was low. It seemed oppressive ... and yet defiant. For here was a place where openly gay men and couples could come and be themselves. Through the '80s and into the '90s, celebrities, many of them still in the closet, felt free to come to the Coleherne, for this was a place where even the tabloid press didn't venture. Freddie Mercury, the front man of perhaps the world's biggest band, Queen, went there regularly. The celebrated TV and DJ star Kenny Everett and famous ballet dancer Rudolf Nureyev were well-known visitors. It even attracted the actor Anthony Perkins, the eponymous lead of Alfred Hitchcock's _Psycho_. Colin Ireland would fit right in.

From an early age, Ireland had been fascinated by true crime and serial killers in particular. He admired Peter Sutcliffe, "The Yorkshire Ripper". He avidly read non-fiction books about crime, so much that he became aware of geographic profiling, the process by which investigators determine the probable area of an offender's address by analysing locations of a connected series of crimes. Using the information he'd gleaned from reading an FBI manual, he strategically planned to mislead the police away from Southend-on-Sea, to make them direct their attention at densely populated Central London, consciously and conspicuously operating within a seven-mile radius. Furthermore, he calculatedly chose a certain pub as his hunting ground.

---

[1] The Sexual Offences Act 1967 made legal sexual acts between two (but no more) consenting males over the age of 21 in England and Wales, in private.

He knew of the appeal of the Coleherne to a certain subgenre of the gay population.

At the Coleherne (and other bars which catered to similar clientele), punters adhered to a code which let others know their sexual partialities. It was a recognisable rainbow of colours. Using a number of colour-coded handkerchiefs and bandanas, punters could advertise their interests, making trawling for partners easier, helping to avoid misunderstandings. A yellow hankie indicated a predilection for water sports (urine); light blue meant oral sex, dark blue indicated anal sex.

Three months after making his New Year's Day resolution, on 8 March 1993, Ireland was at the Coleherne. He knew the front door was covered by CCTV; he entered via a side-entrance. Hanging from a back pocket of his trousers was a hankie; it was likely to have been coloured black: this indicated S&M. It was also likely to have been worn in the right pocket, meaning that he was a "top", or the more dominant partner. Ireland was looking for a partner with a black hankie hanging from the left partner, a "bottom". That Monday evening, he found a "bottom": 45-year-old Peter Walker, a renowned choreographer and assistant theatre director from Liverpool who'd recently been hired to work on the West End musical *City of Angels*. Walker was a lonely man whose only real companions were his two dogs, Sammy, a white German Shepherd and Bessie, a black Labrador. Friends would later comment that Walker didn't like to go home to an empty flat. That evening, Walker approached a hulking stranger in the Coleherne, accidentally spilling his drink on him. Walker told the large man that he needed to be punished.

The two men, their respective hankies attracting each other as effectively as opposite poles on a magnet, soon got talking. Encouraged by what he believed were their compatible interests, Walker agreed to leave with his latest pick-up, exiting the Coleherne by the side door. They caught a cab to Walker's Battersea apartment.

They arrived in the early hours of the morning. Ireland was carrying his rucksack and in it was the "murder kit" he'd need

for his carefully prepared mission – gloves, cord, handcuffs …
and a complete change of clothing. On the way, he'd pulled on
the gloves. He was tense and nervous, mindful of what was
about to happen. Walker, though, was clearly unaware of the
thoughts running haywire through his bull-necked beau's mind.

In the apartment, Walker put Sammy and Bessie into another
room and closed the door. Then he willingly but unwittingly allowed Ireland to gag him with knotted condoms and restrain him
on the four-poster bed with cord. Now he was helpless. He
wasn't worried; this was all part of the S&M game he'd been
expecting. The foreplay was soon over. Ireland quickly unleashed extreme violence, whipping his helpless victim with a
dog lead and a belt and pummelling him with fists in a sustained
and brutal attack. At the height of his rage, he went into the
kitchen and returned with a plastic shopping bag. He pulled the
bag over Walker's head, suffocating him to the brink of death.
Then he removed the bag and allowed the man to revive, taunting him by saying how easy it would be to end his life. At some
stage during his torment Walker asked Ireland, "Am I going to
die?" "Yes," Ireland replied shortly. Walker simply gave up and
resigned himself to his fate. Ireland, soon tiring of his game,
pulled the bag over Walker's head a final time and made good
on his promise.

When it was over, Ireland burned off his victim's pubic hair,
purely because he wanted to know what it smelt like. He spent
a considerable amount of time meticulously cleaning the apartment, wiping down surfaces to rid them of fingerprints and
clearing away any items which may have connected him to the
scene of the crime. He'd read the FBI manuals; he knew how to
clean a scene. Whilst going through Walker's personal effects,
he was incensed to discover that the man had been HIV positive.
Enraged that he'd not been informed of this, he pushed condoms
into the man's mouth and nostril, and in a moment of grim
whimsy placed two teddy bears next to his first victim's body,
arranging them in the "69" position. It was an expression of disgust at the victim, his HIV status and the fact that he'd been

perfectly willing to engage in sex.

Then Ireland lingered a while in the apartment. Walker's two dogs, locked away in one of the rooms before the murder, gave him no trouble. He settled down to watch TV. In the morning, he prepared himself. Before leaving, he swapped his clothes with the new set he'd brought in his rucksack. These were both calculated acts. He felt that leaving the apartment in the middle of the night might arouse the suspicions of neighbours. Instead, he left the next morning, making his journey home amidst the hustle and bustle of the rush-hour commuters, hence making his movements less conspicuous. And the change of clothes, he calculated, would also help to stop the police picking up his scent. He dropped the keys to the flat into the Thames from Battersea Bridge as he made his way into Chelsea. The "murder kit" he tossed into a canal, unseen from the window of the moving train.[2]

The day after the murder, impatient that his crime hadn't been reported, Ireland phoned the Samaritans[3] and informed them of his worries for the dogs locked in the apartment. He wasn't concerned for the plight of the dogs; he wanted *his* murder to be discovered. To make sure, he also called a journalist from the tabloid newspaper *The Sun* to boast that he'd committed a murder. He told the journalist that the dead man had been into kinky sex. "You like that stuff, don't you?" he asked the journalist. For good measure he mentioned his plan to become famous for being a serial killer. "It was my New Year's resolution to murder a human being," he coldly admitted.

What Ireland didn't know was that the body had already been found by the building caretaker. Police were soon on the scene, but they struck a problem: there was little evidence that a crime had actually taken place. The rope-marks around Walker's

---

[2] He would always dispose of evidence within the same seven-mile radius.

[3] A suicide-prevention telephone hotline.

wrists pointed to a possible S&M accident. It seemed that Walker had a fondness for the practice, but by unfortunate coincidence, the day after his body was discovered the Law Lords ruled that S&M practices, even between consenting adults, were illegal. By cooperating with the police investigation, gay men indulging in such practices put themselves at risk of prosecution (as they might reasonably have presumed). The autopsy couldn't conclude whether the death was accidental or deliberate. Detective Inspector Martin Finnegan appeared on television to appeal for Walker's sexual partner to come forward. Ireland, not unexpectedly, made no approach. Nor did he make any further phone calls. Clues were non-existent. Detectives were stymied. With no leads to go on, the case quickly stalled.

Ireland lay low. The police investigation had quietened and the fears within the gay community would likely to have lessened. Ireland's murderous rage had increased, however. On 28 May, he travelled back to the Coleherne. His hunting technique remained the same. Soon he was chatting to a 37-year-old librarian named Christopher Dunn, a Coleherne regular and an S&M "bottom", just the victim type that Ireland sought. As before, the two left via the side door and went to Dunn's apartment in a Victorian cottage in Wealdstone in North London.

At Dunn's home, the two men had something to eat whilst getting in the mood by watching one of Dunn's S&M videos. When it was over, Ireland told Dunn to get prepared. Dunn went into the bedroom to do just that.

When Ireland entered the bedroom a short while later, Dunn was wearing only a studded belt and black leather body harness. Ireland ordered him to lie face-down on the bed. Dunn did so. Ireland then proceeded to tie his feet together. When Ireland asked how he felt, Dunn replied that he was scared but excited.

Then the play began with some whipping, and now Dunn's excitement was quickly replaced with a good reason to be scared as Ireland laid into him with a brutal beating with his fists. Then, perversely expecting to be reimbursed for the money he'd spent on this quest, Ireland now got Dunn's bank card and demanded to know the PIN. Dunn told him, but Ireland didn't believe him as three consecutive numbers were the same. To ensure that the information was correct, Ireland brought his lighter to Dunn's testicles and held the flame to them. After further beating, Ireland was satisfied that he had the correct PIN. He finished his victim off by ramming pieces of cloth into his mouth.

As before, the two-time murderer cleaned the scene thoroughly, wiping down anything he might've touched and bagging the plate and cutlery he'd used earlier. He changed his clothes and bagged them too. He remained in the apartment until the morning. After leaving, he used Dunn's bank card to withdraw £200. On the way home, he disposed of the "murder kit" by throwing it from the train window.

This time Ireland didn't contact anyone to report the crime. Dunn's body was discovered by a friend two days later. Police were later told that the dead man had been a homosexual who'd frequented gay bars. They initially believed that the death had been a sex-game gone wrong, but later, after realising that money had gone missing from his account, they concluded that it had been a robbery and murder. However, as the killing occurred in a different area from the murder of Walker, the two killings weren't linked. A lack of witnesses and forensic evidence hindered the investigation and it, like the previous murder, stalled. Ireland's desire for notoriety was likewise failing. A couple of days after the murder an anonymous caller phoned the police to taunt them for failing to link the two crimes. It could only have been Colin Ireland, the would-be serial killer.

Frustrated that the second crime hadn't been acknowledged either, he was back at the Coleherne one week later. Perry Bradley III was a handsome 35-year-old American from Sulphur Springs, Texas. A successful, wealthy businessman, he was also a closeted homosexual. After meeting Ireland in the underground bar, the two men left and made their way to Bradley's upmarket Kensington apartment. There, they had some food and wine whilst Ireland convinced his new friend that without the S&M element to their liaison he wouldn't be able to become aroused. And so Bradley removed his clothes and allowed himself to be cuffed and bound by the feet whilst he lay face-down on the bed.

At this point, it seems that Ireland wanted to get the business of reimbursement out of the way. He placed a noose around Bradley's neck and then demanded his bank card and PIN, casually mentioning that he would be quite willing to kill if it came to it. Bradley, realising the predicament he was in, immediately gave the hulking man the details he required. He even offered to go with the man to the bank to withdraw the cash. Ireland declined that offer, instead telling his captive that it was going to be a long night and proposed he get some sleep. As amazing as it sounds, Bradley did in fact drift off to sleep. Ireland hung around for a while debating with himself whether to allow Bradley to live or die. Realising that he could be identified, Ireland decided it would be just as easy to kill Bradley. "There was no way I could allow that man to wake up," he confessed to police. "That wasn't part of my plan anyway. My plan was to kill." While Bradley was asleep, Ireland went around to his side of the bed and then tightened the noose, strangling his host to death. He told police that Bradley hadn't put up much of a struggle.

After searching the apartment, Ireland found and stole £100. He listened to the radio as he wiped down the surfaces and then lingered until the morning. Before leaving, he placed a doll upon Bradley's body. Then, as he had done previously, he left during the rush hour, stopping at a bank to withdraw £200 from his victim's account. Again, he tossed the evidence bag from the moving train window.

Ireland's third killing was not linked to the others. Once again, it had occurred within another police area and so the serial element to the crime went unnoticed. Moreover, as far as anyone who knew Perry Bradley III was concerned, he wasn't gay. Links to S&M or the Coleherne bar were therefore missed. Ireland, by now irritated at the lack of recognition, went on to kill again … within a mere three days.

Victim no. 4 was 33-year-old Andrew Collier, a good-looking

man who sported a handlebar moustache. He worked as a warden for a sheltered housing complex and lived in Dalston, North East London with his pet cat, Millie. The pair courted each other in Ireland's familiar haunt, the Coleherne, and later went back to Collier's apartment. Just after they arrived, they heard a disturbance outside. Both men went to the window to look out. Whenever it died down, the two men got down to business. Collier allowed his new friend to handcuff him and bind him to the bed. Then Ireland placed a noose around the other man's neck.

His expenses were on his mind. Ireland demanded Collier's bank card and PIN. This time, however, the captive man refused to give them. As Ireland set about torturing his victim, Collier, with horror, realised that this was no S&M domination game. Ireland, however, needed that PIN and so he began a search through the apartment. During his rifling he came across documents that informed him that Collier was HIV positive. This incensed him. Collier hadn't told him of his status and yet he'd been willing to engage in sex. Ireland used his lighter as a torture instrument, burning Collier on several parts of the body.

The death of victim no. 1, Peter Walker, had made it to the papers. Due to the fact that the killer had phoned to report that Walker's two dogs were locked in the apartment, the article had described him as an animal lover. Now Ireland sought to dispel that misassumption. To Collier's horror, he caught Millie the cat and, before his captive's eyes, hanged her by the neck from the doorway. Collier must've known that he'd be next. He was right. Ireland pulled the noose tight around Collier's neck and strangled the life out of him. Then, to add insult to injury, he stuffed condoms into Collier's mouth and placed a condom on the dead man's penis, positioning the dead cat's mouth around his penis and her tail in his mouth.

As he had done before, Ireland wiped down the flat, tidied up and left as the rush-hour crowd thronged the streets. With him he took £70 of Collier's money for expenses along with a mug that he'd used.

*Yet another* investigating team took on the case and, as before, the killings were *still* not linked. Victim no. 3, Perry Bradley, hadn't been gay (so they believed) and so was no connection was made to *that* murder. However, as the team began to look into *other* recent deaths a familiar *M.O.* began to emerge. The teddy bears arranged in the "69" position was similar to how the dead cat had been left. Now the different teams began to talk to each other. At last, two of the deaths were linked. For Ireland, however, the police weren't moving fast enough and five days after his latest murder he called Kensington police to claim ownership of all four killings. He also called the Battersea station to ask if they were still investigating Walker's death. He told them that they weren't interested in the deaths of homosexuals and that he'd always dreamed of committing the perfect murder. *He'd kill again*, he told them ominously.

And he did. For the final time he went back to the Coleherne. There, he set his eyes upon 41-year-old Emanuel Spiteri, a Maltese national now living and working in London as a chef. Spiteri was a diminutive man whose pleasure it was to dress in leather pants and motorcycle boots. He gave all the appearance of outlandish bravado but Coleherne staff later reported that he was actually shy and reserved. Nevertheless, a hulking man had caught his attention and so they struck up a rapport. They returned by train to Spiteri's flat in South East London where Ireland was able to persuade his latest beau to be cuffed and tied to the bed. After this, Ireland placed a noose around Spiteri's neck and began to demand his bank card's PIN. Spiteri refused to give it and Ireland garrotted him to death.

After his usual tidy-up, Ireland watched TV as he waited until the morning. Before he left, however, he scattered some paper on the bedroom floor and set light to it with the idea that the entire apartment block would go up in smoke, obliterating any evidence. He briefly considered turning the gas on but decided not to.

The next day, he phoned the police and told them they'd find victim no. 5 in the burnt-out apartment in South East London. Now that he'd become a serial killer, Ireland decided that his spree would literally go out in flames. He told the police that this had been his last victim; he'd not kill again. Little did he know, though, was that his fire had gone out, leaving little damage. Spiteri's landlady discovered his body two days later, along with evidence of attempted arson, and reported her findings.

Now it was clear that there was a serial killer on the loose. Victims nos. 1-5 were officially linked.

And Colin Ireland now had the publicity he'd craved. The police called a midnight press conference, declared that the five London murders were linked and appealed to the gay community for information, also recommending that if they were meeting someone for a casual acquaintance they should let a friend know exactly where they were going. Two days later, they made an appeal directly to the killer to contact them. The newspapers, practically salivating over the torrid story, gave the killer a nickname he must surely have revelled in: "The Gay Slayer".

Ireland had made two errors that led ultimately to his downfall. One, his image was captured on CCTV in the company of Spiteri as the two made their way from Charing Cross to Hither Green. A man who'd been on the same train came forward and gave a description of the man who'd been with Spiteri. A photo composite was made up and a description of a man was widely publicised: "WHITE, 30-40 YEARS, HEAVY BUILD, 6FT PLUS, WITH FULL/FATTISH FACE, SHORT DARK HAIR, DIRTY/DISCOLOURED TEETH". The sketch was an accurate depiction. The day after its release, several men called in to the police claiming that they'd seen this man in the Coleherne.

Ireland's second error was more serious. During his time at Andrew Collier's flat, he'd gone to the window to look out at a disturbance. Whilst doing so he touched a bar. During his customary clean-up process he'd forgot to wipe the bar. Police subsequently found that single fingerprint.

Realising that his image had been caught on camera, on 19 July 1993 Ireland went to his solicitor, admitted that it was he who'd been caught on tape and said that he'd recognised the image of Spiteri. Ireland said that he and Spiteri had gone home (to Spiteri's) together, but there had been another man there and so Ireland had left. Meanwhile, police had already correctly identified Ireland and were on their way to Southend-on-Sea to speak to their one and only suspect. Whilst this was happening, Ireland's solicitor duly contacted them. They diverted to the solicitor's office, there to await the arrival of Ireland. When he showed up, he was immediately arrested and brought to Islington Police Station. He was fingerprinted. One of his prints matched the solo print found in Collier's flat. Confronted with this evidence, Ireland was shocked, but he said nothing. Until four weeks later …

On 19 August, he suddenly decided to come clean. He was the killer of five gay men. He was not gay himself and had no particular gripe against gay men. He'd picked them for convenience, because they were easy targets. It could just as easily have been women, he said. Robbery hadn't been the motive, he claimed; he'd stolen purely because he'd been unemployed and needed the cash to fund his hunt for victims. He'd not been under the influence of alcohol or drugs during the murders; he'd gained no sexual thrill from them and no sexual contact had taken place between him and his victims. Extreme male deviance had triggered his murderous rage, he claimed, as well as the fact that he'd had brushes with paedophiles in his youth. His mission, he claimed, had been to rid the world of vermin. His confession was detailed and frank.

At the Old Bailey on 20 December 1993, Colin Ireland put in a guilty plea, admitting responsibility without mitigation. He was given five life sentences for each murder. The presiding judge, Mr Justice Sachs, said:

> *"By any standards you are an exceptionally frightening and dangerous man. In cold blood and with great deliberation you have killed five of your fellow human beings. You killed them in grotesque and cruel fashion. The fear, brutality and indignity to which you subjected your victims are almost unspeakable. To take one human life is an outrage,*

*to take five is carnage. You expressed the desire to be re-garded as a serial killer. That must be matched by your de-tention for life."*

In February 2012, whilst walking in the yard at HM Prison Wakefield, Colin Ireland slipped and fractured his hip. Ten days later, he died of pulmonary fibrosis, a complication resulting from the fall. He'd been 57 years of age.

Ireland always claimed to be neither gay nor bisexual. Some doubt this. For a time, he'd worked as a bouncer at a Soho gay bar, and it's also thought that he'd frequented the Coleherne bar *prior* to the commencement of his murder spree. Others con-sider the strategic placing of childhood items – the doll, the teddy bears and the cat – as symbolic manifestations of his loss of childhood innocence. Rumours abounded that during his in-carceration he killed again, strangling a child killer in his cell. If true, this is possibly indicative of Ireland's pent-up rage against paedophiles. He took these secrets to the grave. What *is* certain, however, is that Ireland wanted notoriety. In allowing his mor-bid daydreams become a lethal "career choice", he managed to achieve this aim. He killed for no other reason than to make a name for himself.

# Daniel Owen Conahan Jr.

(active 1994-1996)

IN 1994, PORT CHARLOTTE, FLORIDA was a vast expanse of wilderness approximately 100 miles south of Tampa on the US Gulf Coast. Punta Gorda (meaning "fat point" in Spanish) is a popular place to live, and many are attracted to the low crime rates of the small historic town. Housing developers seeking to capitalise on this popularity had had plans to build across a huge swath of the land. Unfortunately, things somehow went awry and they'd gone bankrupt whilst in the midst of making subdivisions across the landscape, and so the area was left crisscrossed by numerous roads that provided easy access to hundreds of acres of unspoiled forests and swamps, but not much else. Dense vegetation wasn't far from the roadways, which seemed to be arterial routes going nowhere. Consequently, few people had any reason to come to this forsaken region of desolate Floridan wilderness.

With hardly any of the planned housing built, the surrounding woodland remained undeveloped, abandoned to the flora and fauna that had for millennia already been at home in this most richly mosaic of habitats. Amongst the woodland creatures that roamed beneath the canopy were clusters of hog, wandering their own crisscrossing networks of trails. Locally, the secluded wooded area was known as a good place to hunt; it was a particular magnet for hog hunters. For one man, however, it was also the perfect place to hunt humans – that is, until one of his victims turned up dead.

On 1 February 1994, a cool morning, two local hunters were making their way along the rural trails of Punta Gorda on a hog hunting expedition. Spotting buzzards circling above, they pulled over their car and walked into the wooded area hoping to find a dead hog. Instead they came across the corpse of a man. The body was unclothed and had few teeth. The genitals had been removed and rope marks were visible around the neck and wrist regions. There was nothing to identify the man. The two men immediately called their find in to the Charlotte County Sheriff's Office. Investigators scoured the scene and found further indications of a crime – rope marks around a nearby tree – but nothing else of evidentiary value.

The man had an estimated age of between 25 and 35 years old. He was white or Hispanic. His height was between 5'4" and 5'9"; his hair was brown. The eye colour couldn't be ascertained. Due to the state of decomposition, he'd probably lain dead for more than a month before being discovered. There were no distinguishing characteristics to help identify the decedent. The description didn't match anyone locally and so investigators surmised that the man may have come from a different state.

John Doe no. 1 was sent to the medical examiner in the hope of making an identification. Cause of death couldn't be determined; however, it was found that the victim had had a stainless-steel surgical rod inserted into his left ankle. He'd apparently had an injury, probably around four years prior to his death, and an operation had been performed to repair the damage. Investigators tracked down the manufacturers of the surgical rod via its serial number, but unfortunately this only returned a link to certain hospitals who used a number of the rods with the same batch number. Detectives issued subpoenas for patients who matched the physical description and general surgery description of John Doe no. 1. They managed to trace every patient who matched the descriptions; all were alive, well and accounted for. Their body was not one of them. The best viable lead turned cold.

As the months passed, no new leads appeared; no witnesses came forward. The media published pictures of a facial reconstruction in the hope that someone would recognise a long-lost friend or relative and provide a welcome break. None did. A screening of the dental charts and fingerprints of missing men yielded nothing. John Doe no. 1 currently remains unidentified.

So far, all that could be said about the case was that the unexplained death was a homicide – a single homicide. That changed on the first day of 1996 when a dog named Hollywood in the nearby city of North Port brought home to his owner, Wayne Brown, the gift of a human skull. The Browns' two dogs, Hollywood and her mother, Speedbump, had been bringing home pieces of bone for months and their owners had assumed that the bits were pieces of dead animals. This skull was clearly human. Mr Brown immediately ran to get his wife, Susie, and they quickly contacted local police.

A few further bones from the body found by the Browns' dog were discovered not half-a-mile away. He'd been a white male, 25-35 years of age, approximately 5'9" height, approximately 150-160lbs weight. The ravages of time, the Floridan weather and animal interference had caused the victim's head to disarticulate from the body. Cause of death could not be determined, but increased decomposition in the head, neck and low pelvis suggested that the victim had suffered severe injuries to those areas. He could not be identified.

Two months later, on 7 March 1996, a man driving along Route 75 in North Port stopped his vehicle on Laramie Circle in order to answer a call of nature. As he walked into the woods to relieve himself he was shocked to notice the corpse of a naked male on the ground. The man contacted local police.

A close search of the area uncovered tell-tale rope marks around a nearby tree. The man's clothes couldn't be found. The body itself provided its own evidence: scrapes and tears on the body and feet indicated that the victim had attempted to flee from his killer prior to his death, running through dense foliage, badly lacerating the skin. The wrists bore evidence of having been tied with rope. The body had four stab marks. It'd been posed face-up, in the shape of a cross. The genitals had been severed off and were never recovered.

The medical examiner determined that death had occurred around 10 days before being found. He'd been a white male with auburn hair, between 35 and 45 years of age, approximately 5'6" height with a muscular build. He had notably bad teeth. Despite efforts to identify the man, investigators had no success. He was labelled John Doe no. 3.

Two storm utility engineers were about their business on Highway 41 on 17 April 1996 when they made a startling discovery. Deciding to take a break from the searing sun, they'd entered the woods and wandered along the trail to check some hog traps they'd laid earlier. They climbed atop an embankment and looked about. Peering down, they noticed a suspicious object in the gulch. It was difficult to make out in the dim light. The two would-be hunters went down the embankment to inspect the object. Alarmed, they quickly realised it was a human skull.

The men made their way back to their vehicle and drove to the nearest gas station. There, they found a couple of police officers taking a break. The men told the officers of their find and the officers accompanied them back to the gulch. A closer inspection confirmed suspicions; this was a human skull.

Soon the area was swarming with police officers. They scanned the surrounding area and made *yet another* discovery: beneath old carpet padding was a young white male – dead. This one's remains were in similar condition to those of the previous find – unclothed, lying on his back, with genital mutilations and evidence of rope burns around his neck. Also near the victim was a human torso which clearly didn't belong to the victim.

Now investigators had three crime scenes and five bodies. The obvious explanation was that a serial killer had been using the wooded expanses of Port Charlotte as a killing and dumping ground.

The last corpse, having been made only the day before discovery, was in better condition and therefore able to give up its secrets. The pathologist was able to determine that the murdered man had been raped and strangled with a thin rope, possibly a clothesline. Like the other victims, this body's genitals had also been removed – with surgeon-like precision. And like the other victims, this man had also been a young, lean, fair-haired, white male. The killer's preferred victim-type had become clear. With fingerprints and dental records to work on, detectives were able to make their first identification: the fifth body belonged to 21-

year-old Richard Montgomery.

Richard Allen Montgomery had lived with his sister and mother at Palms & Pines Mobile Home Park in Punta Gorda. According to friends and relatives – and backed-up by a lengthy police charge sheet – Montgomery had been a problem child who'd grown up into a jobless, delinquent adult. In his short life, he'd been arrested countless times, and charges ranged from assault, burglary, disorderly intoxication and probation violation. Resident neighbours of the mobile home park were afraid of him, they reported. He was reportedly abusive towards his mother and had never had a job, preferring to lay low during the day and party at night. Others reported that he'd been a little slow but otherwise a nice guy, although one with a drink problem. He never kept a steady job and consequently never had any money. The word around town was that Montgomery had been doing drugs. Perhaps it was a craving for money for drugs that drew him to making money through a sordid photography session. On 16 April 1996, Montgomery had told a few of his friends that day that he was going out to make a few hundred dollars. He'd said he'd be back shortly. The friends asked him if it was legal. Montgomery smiled but said no more. Earlier, he'd mentioned to his mother that someone had offered to pay him $200 to pose for some nude photos. He didn't tell her who'd made the offer. However, in the same breath he mentioned that he'd made a new friend. The friend's name? Dan Conahan.

An autopsy conducted upon Montgomery's body revealed that he'd died of strangulation. There were two ligature marks at the fore of his neck, two horizontal marks on the chest and abraded groove marks around the wrists. All the marks were consistent with someone who'd been closely bound. The wounds appeared to have been caused by someone struggling for his life. There were also some crisscrossed abrasions which appeared to have occurred at the time of death or _post mortem_. Police who'd arrived at the scene came with search dogs, which had shown particular interest in a sabal palm tree which was somewhat flattened. It was an easy conclusion to draw:

Montgomery had been tied to the tree.

The next day, the Charlotte County Sheriff's Office compared notes on the unsolved homicides with the North Port Police. A task force was set up which began to meet daily. They didn't initially attribute the murders to a serial killer but it didn't take them long to consider the possibility. Inevitably, the press were ahead of them; they were already announcing that a homosexual or bisexual serial killer, most likely a schizophrenic sociopath, was roaming the area. They labelled the spate of murders "The Hog Trail Killings".

The second body found alongside Richard Montgomery turned out to be Kenneth Smith, whose sister came forward in response to the publication of a barely visible tattoo discovered on the body. Teresa Smith reported that she'd not seen her troubled brother in some while. Dental records confirmed the identification. Young, slim, good-looking and male – Smith fit the emerging victim-type specifications.

Investigators reflecting upon the assault of Richard Montgomery considered another assault which had been reported nearly two years earlier to Fort Myers Police. The victim, Stanley Burden, like Montgomery, was a high school drop-out who'd found it difficult to hold down a steady job. Burden had similar physical characteristics to Montgomery. Burden had complained to the police about a man who'd picked him up as he thumbed for a lift at the side of the road, then offered to pay him $100-150 in return for posing for nude photos. In that scenario, Burden had agreed, and the man had driven him along a rocky dirt road to an out-of-the-way area of the woods. There, the man had requested Burden remove his shirt so that the erotic photoshoot could commence with the showing of a little hip. The photographer's name? Daniel Conahan.

Allegedly, Conahan had taken numerous photos using his Polaroid camera. After a while, he'd taken a brand-new clothesline from his duffle-bag. Now he wanted to take some bondage shots, he'd said. He got his model to step close to a melaleuca tree and draped the clothesline over Burden to make it look like he was tied. At some point, Conahan moved behind Burden and pulled the rope tight, wrapping it twice around Burden's neck, around his chest also, and pulling his arms behind the tree. Then Conahan attempted to fellate and sodomise Burden. Burden resisted by keeping the tree directly behind him. After unsuccessfully attempting to rape his captive, Conahan drew the line tight and, bracing himself against the tree with his leg, pulled forcefully in an attempt to garrotte Burden. Burden manoeuvred himself back and forth in order to keep his windpipe open, a desperate struggle that lasted for some 30 minutes which Burden miraculously survived. Then Conahan hit Burden over the head and demanded to know him why he didn't die. Finally, giving up, he'd packed up his belongings and left. Burden freed himself from his binds and made his way to a local hospital where his injuries were treated. Police eventually located the scene of the attempted murder and found the melaleuca tree, which showed signs of the scuffle which had taken place around its trunk.

Based upon this information, police took an interest in this man. Born on 11 May 1954, Daniel Owen Conahan Jr. was now approaching his 42nd year. He'd come into the world in Charlotte, North Carolina, but the family had moved to Punta Gorda shortly after his birth. His early childhood was mired by drugs and alcohol use. Friends described him as a loner. His homosexual tendencies emerged early and his parents, disgusted by them, sent him to be cured by various psychiatrists. This failed. He was soon spending time around a local gay bar before being allowed to enter legally.

Conahan was a lacklustre student, only participating in school activities half-heartedly. He graduated high school in 1973, joined the US Navy in 1977, and was stationed at Naval Station Great Lakes in Illinois. The following year, he was nearly court-martialled for homosexual behaviour. The behaviour didn't stop. A few months later, further homosexual behaviour including several counts of sodomy, physical assault and attempts to lure men beyond the limits of the training centre and into motels for sex. This eventually led to a huge brawl within the ranks. He was finally discharged but remained in the Chicago area, spending much of his free time in gay bars. After 13 years, he moved back to Punta Gorda to live with his elderly parents in their condo, a couple of miles from Highway 41. He didn't have a job but he cooked and cleaned for them in lieu of rent. In 1993, after a three-month course, he graduated at the top of his class and became a licensed practical nurse and was duly employed by Charlotte Region Medical Center in Punta Gorda, becoming an assistant to a quadriplegic client. Meanwhile, he spent time propositioning men, occasionally taking pictures of them.

The police continued their investigation of this person of interest. On 23 May 1996, at 15:30, an undercover police officer, wearing shorts, boots, a tank top and an undercover transmitter, casually approached Conahan in a park and struck up a conversation with him. Shortly after this, the undercover officer went to the public bathroom. As he left the bathroom, he was approached by Conahan who again struck up conversation, offering the officer $7 if he would show him his penis. He then offered $20 if the officer would allow him to suck his penis. The officer acted reluctant and asked for the money upfront. Conahan then gave the undercover officer his telephone number and asked him to call.

The next day, the undercover officer returned to the park. He witnessed a white male leaving a trail, followed by Conahan. The unidentified man stormed into the bathroom, shouted a swear word and then left. The officer was then approached Conahan, who sat down beside him. Conahan asked the officer to pose for some nude photos to be taken using his Polaroid camera, saying this would take place at a beach or in a hotel room. He offered $150 for the job. Furthermore, he also offered $5 if the officer would there and then show him his penis. The officer declined the offer, which Conahan then repeated, and which the officer declined a second time.

Other witnesses came forward. One, 34-year-old David Allen Payton, informed law enforcement officers that he knew the identity of the man slaughtering men in Charlotte County. He described how he'd been returning home from a bar on Highway 41 one blisteringly hot summer day whilst under the influence of alcohol. He sat down in the shade to sober up, only to be approached shortly afterwards by a man pulling up in a blue Mercury Capri. The driver asked Payton if he'd like to drink some beer and smoke some pot. Payton took the man up on the kind offer and got into his car. There, the man gave him a beer and a Valium. As they travelled along the road, the man – who introduced himself as Dan – asked his new friend if he'd like to pose nude for photographs in exchange for $100. Payton declined to participate.

He then became anxious as the driver veered his car off the main highway and down an isolated dirt track. Some distance down the track, the car slid off the road and became stuck in a mud hole. Payton, wanting to get out of the car, said he'd get out and push, but Dan told him to stay in the car and steer whilst he got out to push. Fortunately, however, a four-wheel-drive vehicle came along and helped Dan free his car from the mud hole. Then, as Dan traded conversation with the driver of the four-wheel-drive, Payton suddenly decided to race off in the car, leaving Dan far behind.

The alcohol and Valium made Payton drowsy and when he later stopped the car in Fort Myers he fell asleep. The next thing he knew he was being rudely awoken and promptly arrested for auto theft. He was sent to prison for the theft of the car, and it was from prison that he spoke to law enforcement officers of the unusual encounter with the man named Dan. He was able to produce a description of his would-be abductor, and the resulting police sketch looked uncannily similar to the police's no. 1 suspect, Daniel Conahan.

Shortly after this, two further witnesses came forward. Charles Bateman and Robert Beckwith were acquaintances of Robert Montgomery. They reported Daniel Conahan as being the man who'd propositioned them. Whilst they couldn't positively identify him from a photo, they were able to identify the blue Mercury Capri belonging to his elderly father.

By the end of May 1996, Conahan was still living with his parents in their condo. His credit cards were subpoenaed and, pursuant to a warrant, police searched the condo and obtained paint samples from Conahan Sr.'s car, a blue Mercury Capri, which Conahan Jr. often drove. The police compared these samples with paint chips taken from the body of Robert Montgomery. The samples were indistinguishable.

The weight of circumstantial and witness evidence had become substantial. Hospital records strengthened Burden's story of attempted strangulation. Credit card receipts showed that Conahan had bought knives, ropes, leather gloves, plastic sheeting and dozens of Polaroid films. On 3 July 1996, Conahan was arrested for the first-degree murder of Robert Montgomery and the attempted murder of Charles Burden.[1]

Conahan was brought before the Lee County Courthouse on 2 August 1996 on charges of attempted first-degree murder, two counts of sexual battery and one count of kidnapping. He pleaded not guilty. A week later, he waived his right to a jury trial, citing that extensive media coverage and being tried by a conservative jury in the homophobic Deep South would prejudice the case against him. Whilst he awaited trail, on 22 May 1997, a further skeleton turned up under a pepper tree near Quesada Avenue. This turned out to be the remains of 24-year-old William "Billy" Charles Patten, who'd disappeared in 1993, who was identified by comparing skeletal DNA with that his parents' genes. He'd been a landscaper, last seen in 1993 carrying a cooler of beer towards a bridge connecting Punta Gorda and Port Charlotte. John Doe no. 3 would later be identified in June 1999 as 36-year-old John William Melaragno, a native of Cleveland, Ohio, who'd moved to North Port in November 1995 only to vanish the following year.

---

[1] In February 1997, after Conahan was indicted in the Montgomery case, the state dropped the charge of the attempted murder of Stanley Burden.

On 10 August 1999, the trial eventually began with opening arguments in front of Judge William Blackwell. The State Prosecutor, Robert Lee, presented Conahan as an evil, lethal phantom stalking the streets, soliciting transients to pose nude and bound for the satisfaction of his deviant fantasies. He presented Robert Montgomery as an easy victim, vulnerable in his need for money to fund his alcohol and drug use. He described the "near medical perfection" with which Conahan had severed Montgomery's genitals. He argued that the defendant had done this not only in order to remove saliva samples which could link him to the murder but to obtain a dreadful souvenir of the crime. He stated that he'd be seeking the death penalty.

Mark Ahlbrand for the defence claimed that his client's bad back made him incapable of committing the crimes, and that although he had an interest in sex with men there was no evidence that he'd ever been violent towards them.

The star witness was Stanley Burden. He recounted how, being flat broke, he'd agreed to pose for nude photos before Conahan's camera lens. His testimony was chilling. He told how Conahan had slung the rope around his neck, pulling it tightly with such deliberation that he'd become sweaty and breathless, doing everything in his power to kill, even putting his foot against the back of the tree in order to gain a better stranglehold. He remembered Conahan's terrible admonishment: "Why won't you die, you son-of-a-bitch!"

In the end, Burden's evidence, alongside microfibre evidence, proved conclusive. Conahan was found guilty on 17 August of first-degree murder and kidnapping. Now the guilty man chose to have the penalty phase of the trial heard before a jury. The ploy did not pay off. After the jury saw photos of the injuries on Richard Montgomery's corpse – the tight indentions caused by binding with rope; the cross-cross abrasions, presumably caused by attempts to escape from being tied to a tree; the gash site of the missing genitalia – they considered the arguments for just 22 minutes before giving a recommendation to enact the death penalty. Conahan was taken away to the Union Correctional

Institution in Raiford, Florida, there to await his execution.

All of the victims in the Hog Trail Killings were found within a 10-mile radius of Conahan's home. All were young, white, good-looking men. All were killed whilst naked. Four were posed on their backs *post mortem*. Three had had their genitals removed. Further skeletal remains were found within the murder zone after Conahan's conviction. Five of the sets of remains have yet to be identified.

Conahan has attempted to overturn the first-degree charge by arguing that the state did not conclusively prove premeditation. So far he has failed. He repeatedly insists upon his innocence.

# Andrew Phillip Cunanan
[active 1997]

FAME IS ONE THING; notoriety is another. It must seem that during the past few decades the difference between the two collapsed alarmingly. Individuals now obtain fame not through acknowledgement of their accomplishments, but by *being known*. The value of merit-based fame has become somewhat demerited, for want of a better word. The distinction between good and bad forms of fame has become rather obsolete. The trend continues. Wannabees seeking fame and fortune willingly set themselves up as the pantomime villains of so-called "reality-based" TV programmes such as *Big Brother*, *The Apprentice* and *The Real Housewives* series. The villains of such shows often draw the attention of the tabloid press more than the more newsworthy stories of the day. Social media is driven by their escapades. Being morally corrupt or spiritually bankrupt can therefore be an efficient shortcut to infamy. And these days, in the grinding machinery of publicity and promotion, infamy equals fame. And fame, as we all know, brings with it fortune.

For some, however, the achievement of notoriety is its own reward. Dennis Rader, the self-styled "BTK" of Wichita, Kansas, used to bind, torture and then kill his victims. Indulging in this cold campaign, he became so addicted to his own notoriety that it led to his undoing after he sent taunting documents to the police on a floppy disc. Likewise, "Zodiac" gave himself a self-appointed pseudonym in order to further his ill-repute. He is known to have killed five times, although the number is likely to be much higher. Like BTK, Zodiac sent taunting letters and cards to those who sought to capture him. Unlike BTK, Zodiac's true identity is unknown, but his notoriety is wide-reaching.

The victims of these two individuals were ordinary, everyday people, and if it were not for their killer's concerted efforts to publicise themselves the serial murder sprees would likely have faded into relative obscurity over time. One man, however, achieved worldwide fame on 8 December 1980 after he gunned down John Lennon, formerly of the pop band the Beatles and then still a major recording artist in his own right. Mark David Chapman has accounted for his motive in committing the murder. He stated that after a religious conversion he felt rage against Lennon's apparent blasphemy and hypocrisy.[1] However, he has also stated that he had an alternative list of potential victims, amongst them the talk show host Johnny Carson, the actor George C. Scott, the former first lady Jackie Kennedy, the singer David Bowie and, indeed, Lennon's former Beatles bandmate Paul McCartney. Chapman's only criterion was that they were all famous people and he chose Lennon out of convenience. He shot Lennon to death with five shots as the singer and his wife, Yoko Ono, left their Manhattan apartment. Then he remained there, reading the novel *The Catcher in the Rye* whilst awaiting to be arrested by police. He will forever he remembered for the crime due purely to the superstar status of the victim. Another killer, Andrew Cunanan, has gained everlasting fame due also, it must be said, to the celebrity of his last victim.

Andrew Philip Cunanan was born on 31 August 1969 in National City, California, the youngest of four children to Modesto "Pete" Cunanan, a Filipino who served as a hospital corpsman in the United States Navy, and MaryAnn, a former telephone operator of Sicilian Italian heritage. Andrew's siblings were Elena, Christopher and Regina.

Pete and MaryAnn's marriage, it's fair to say, was awash with acrimony from the start. Pete was convinced that MaryAnn had been unfaithful to him and adopted an attitude of total disgust towards her. A short but powerfully built man, Pete cast a commanding presence. His anger, fuelled by a belief in his wife's

---

[1] Lennon made a highly publicised comment in 1966 that the Beatles were "more popular than Jesus". His arguably most famous song, *Imagine*, contains the lyrics "Imagine no possessions". Chapman resented Lennon's attitude, which he felt was preachy and incompatible with Lennon's wealth.

infidelity, convinced him to consider that he could act however he pleased towards her. MaryAnn, on the other hand, eventually became fragile and needy – yet was not above using her womanly wiles to get what she needed, even withholding sex to get something from her husband. She was free and easy with money, spending it blithely, and Pete had to juggle three different bank accounts to hide his money from her. Pete was a go-getter with big dreams, but in the meantime the growing family were living in a small rundown home in National City, a humdrum part of San Diego, and Pete had to take a second job as a lab assistant to make ends meet. It wasn't until their youngest son Andrew turned four that the family were able to start a new life a few miles east in middle-class Bonita, buoyed by a recent inheritance from MaryAnn's father. It was a big step up.

Nevertheless, it still wasn't the sort of background that young Andrew wanted to present to the world. An inveterate liar, even from a young age, he was prone to telling tall tales. He was a good-looking boy, with thick eyebrows and large hazel eyes. His skin had the appearance of being permanently tanned. This came from his Filipino roots, but Andrew never mentioned this part of his heritage in school and he never befriended any of the other Filipino pupils.

He was an intelligent boy in class. It's said that he could memorise long passages from encyclopaedias and the Bible and recite them verbatim long afterwards. Reading became a retreat. If there were any upsets at home, he'd lie on his bed with his encyclopaedia and lose himself in its pages. In fact, this was what he enjoyed doing anyway. Whilst most boys his age were playing outdoors in the hot Californian sunshine, Andrew tended to stay inside with his mother, watching TV, reading his encyclopaedia and dreaming. He would cling to his mother's apron strings and allow himself to be smothered by her. With no male friends his own age, he was every inch the mother's boy. His father also lavished attention on Andrew, spoiling him with gifts from an early age, teaching him early on that he was better than others. It wasn't long before Andrew was inclined to accept his superiority as a given fact. When he scored 147 in an IQ test, allowing him to qualify for the mentally gifted programme, in the minds of both him and his parents the fact that Andrew was special had been indisputably confirmed.

If not a particularly popular pupil amongst his male peers, many of Andrew's female peers enjoyed his company immensely, who got a kick out of his colourful, over-embellished tales. He told them he'd spent the summer in Europe. He hadn't. He told stories about having stocks in various companies. It wasn't true. Everyone knew he was a pathological liar, but it mattered little as they didn't take him seriously, and it all added to the fun. Dressing in preppy-style, he strove for grandiosity, wanting to be part of that crowd. An avid fan of style magazines such as *GQ*, *Vogue* and *Vanity Fair* (his favourite), his interests were in celebrity and fashion; these were subjects (amongst others) in which he could easily converse – flamboyantly and at length. His precocious snobbery extended to food also. An early connoisseur of restaurants and gourmet cooking, he would spend all his money on lunch at Neiman Marcus. Spurning school cafeteria fare, he formed the Gentleman's Club and brought in fancy breads and cheese from a local French bakery. Once, when asked about food for an eighth-grade friend's birthday party, Andrew suggested serving cracked crab. He wasn't averse to having an elaborate lobster lunch delivered to him at school by his mother. Nevertheless, despite his pretensions and affectedness, he was generally liked by both teachers and pupils.

From an early age, Andrew knew he was different from other boys. He liked boys – in a sexual way. There was no internal struggle, but it did conflict with the religious teachings of the Catholic Church. Something had to give. It would be religion. In the end he rejected his Catholicism, later telling people that he was Jewish. It was all part of the act. In time, he embraced his sexuality fully.

In 1981, Andrew was accepted to attend the highly-regarded private Bishop's School in the affluence San Diego suburb of La Jolla, a 45-minute commute from Bonita. Upon matriculation at the exclusive school, he immediately made his presence known. He was always at the centre of the limelight, regaling the girls with his stories and entertaining conversation. The flamboyance continued, as well as the arch mannerisms and cultivated, charming pretentions. But it wasn't the girls' attentions he craved; his remarks on the "cute butts" of the boys around school indicted where his longings lay. He came out to his best friends and eventually to the rest of the school. His behaviours became more and more outrageous as he flirted with the stereotype of the mincing queen. He was flamboyant, entertaining, fun to be around. His sexuality proved to be another rich vein providing the attention he craved. In his last years at Bishop's, he began to hang out with the drug-taking set, taking ecstasy and cocaine and cruising Balboa Park, a recognised gay haunt. Soon he was boasting of having a sugar daddy who gave him expensive gifts and took care of him. It was a toe dipped into a life of prostitution. At school and beyond, his gay lifestyle were well known, but his family knew nothing of it. Andrew's ability to fabricate lies allowed him to compartmentalise his life so well that no single person saw the whole of it.

Meanwhile, Pete had taken night-classes in financial management, eventually earning two master's degrees. He would go on to complete a training programme with Merrill Lynch and find employment as a stockbroker at various companies, never staying more than a couple of years at any job, sometimes leaving on his own accord, more than once being let go. The family fortunes improved whilst the parents' marriage floundered. Pete bought an expensive Rancho Bernardo townhouse with ostentatious white carpeting throughout. MaryAnn slept in the maid's room, Pete on the couch. Andrew, obviously, got the master bedroom.

As senior year ended, Andrew became vague about what his future plans were. Academically, he hadn't scored well enough to win a scholarship to college and Pete had so overextended himself that there was little money to pay for it. Andrew, though, had no intention of getting his head down. He wanted to experience the lifestyles of the rich and famous without having to work for it. He chose not to submit any personal words to go beside his picture in the Bishop's yearbook. Instead, he submitted a pretentious phrase: *Après moi, le déluge.*[2] Nevertheless, he was voted "most likely to be remembered" by his 1987 classmates. He followed his sister and enrolled at the University of California at San Diego, majoring in history.

In July 1988, Pete disappeared amid suspicions about the legality of some of his financial dealings. He'd suddenly fled to his native Philippines to avoid embezzlement charges. The family home was sold, leaving MaryAnn with a mere $700. Her downward spiral brought her to seek psychiatric help. Andrew and Gina dropped out of college a year later. For Andrew, the shame was mortifying. He followed his father to the Philippines but survived only a few days of the sweltering heat. He was back within the week with wholly invented stories about the family sugar plantations back home, and his father, a Knight of Columbus. He was driven mad by the shameful secrets and self-pity. It was the beginning of his descent into instability and madness.

He accepted an invitation proffered by his lifelong best friend, Elizabeth Coté, a rich socialite whom he'd met through a friend-of-a-friend whilst at Bishop's. Lizzie rode horses and drove a BMW; she wore Chanel. She threw big parties at her upmarket place in Berkeley, a stone's throw across the bay from the Castro District of San Francisco, the centre of the city's gay culture. Cunanan had soon moved in and was making *himself* the centre of the Castro District, inveigling himself into the gay nightlife, befriending older men and living off their largesse. He also reportedly started dealing drugs (cocaine, opioids and marijuana), and taking an interest in creating violent pornography. And to

---

[2] Quote of Louis XV's favourite mistress, the extravagant Madame de Pompadour, translated as "After me, the flood", often thought of as a nihilistic expression of indifference to the aftermath of one's own ruination.

complement his perfectly compartmentalised lives he adopted several aliases, adopting the surnames of rich associates as his own in order to better himself by association: Andrew DeSilva, Drew Cunningham, Curt Matthew Demaris, Count Ashkenazy and, unfathomably, Lieutenant Commander Andy Cummings. He was also, by now, moonlighting as a gay prostitute to finance his elite lifestyle. Living rent-free in trendy Berkeley with the drug abuse, sexual license and self-destruction, it must've seemed as if his life were a fabulous movie, and that Andrew Cunanan were the top billing.

One of Cunanan's favourite haunts was the Midnight Sun. There, he'd hang out with a friend, Eli Gould, a young attorney whom Cunanan admired enough that he began to adopt his friend's identity somewhat as his own, claiming to be a New York Jew whose parents lived on Fifth Avenue.

Gould was friends with a choreographer of the San Francisco Ballet. The choreographer gave Gould VIP passes to a disco night at the popular gay club, Colossus, for 21 October 1990. Coincidentally, that night was also the première of the San Francisco Opera production of Richard Strauss' *Capriccio*. The costumes for the production had been designed by the celebrity designer Gianni Versace, a handsome, 43-year-old Italian designer and founder of the house of Versace, producer of fashion, fashion accessories, make-up, fragrances and home furnishings. He was also one of the world's most high profile openly gay men.

After the opera, the designer happened to go to the Colossus. There, waiting in the VIP lounge, was Eli Gould ... along with his friend, Andrew Cunanan. Cunanan had been to Italy several times, he told Gould, he knew the country well, he'd already met Versace, the two knew each other. All lies. Cunanan had never set foot on Italian soil.

Fifteen minutes after arriving at the Colossus VIP area, surrounded by his entourage, Versace's eyes surveyed the room. Noticing Cunanan, he cocked his head and approached. "I know you,' he said. *"Lago di Como, no?"* It was one of Versace's standard chat-up lines; it referred to his Lake Como house.

357

"Thank you for remembering, Signor Versace," replied Cunanan, to Gould's amazement. Cunanan introduced his friend Eli Gould. They made idle chit-chat about the opera (which Cunanan and Gould hadn't seen) and then the two friends drifted away towards the dancefloor. Retelling the story of their meeting to others, Cunanan couldn't resist an embellishment. According to Cunanan, when the famous fashion designed introduced himself, Cunanan had replied, "If you're Gianni Versace then I'm Coco Chanel!"

Versace was to attend the Colossus a total of three times during that visit to San Francisco. Whether Cunanan managed to wheedle his way back into Versace's presence there or at some other place is not known. What *isn't* known either is whether Cunanan had been engaged in any sex-for-hire business at the time. What *is* known, however, is that at a later date during Versace's stay Cunanan was seen showing off in big white chauffeured car alongside Versace, his boyfriend Antionio D'Amico and their friend Harry deWildt, before going partying together.[3]

Cunanan's party lifestyle abrupted ended when Lizzy and her husband moved to Sacramento. The Californian capital had none of the allure of San Francisco and so Cunanan moved to his mother's two-bedroom apartment in Rancho Bernardo, which had little allure either. He returned to the university, re-enrolling in an art history course, although not doing much actual studying. By day, he worked as a clerk at a local thrift store. MaryAnn was banned from entering Thrifty Drug, and he'd become angry if she tried. In fact, he would often lose his temper with his neurotic, chain-smoking mother, one time slamming her so hard against the wall she dislocated and fractured a shoulder. He warned her never to tell anyone about the incident otherwise he'd kill her. Despite the violence, she was very attached

---

[3] This is disputed by Harry de Wildt. The Versace family also deny that Versace and Cunanan ever met.

to him and would give him whatever he wanted, even if she couldn't afford it, whilst Andrew told her she was smothering him.

By night, however, Cunanan[4] was partying, often for days on end, presenting himself as a Yale graduate heir to various fortunes, coming home only to crash and recuperate from a hangover. He was mixing with a new crowd on the gay party-circuit. These tended to be quieter affairs – cocktails followed by a discreet dinner out, or civilised upper-class soirées. Cunanan hung around with the older, wealthier men, for that was where he felt he belonged. He could hold his own in their conversation, but always the lies and embellishments accompanied his stories. He had boyfriends – a surfer, a military man, a porn actor. A porn actor recruited him as a jet-setting escort. He was taking drugs (crystal meth), becoming involved in gay pornography trade as a producer and user. Then he began a career as a professional "kept boy". One of these rich lovers, Lincoln Aston,[5] who came from Texas oil money, eventually became sick of Cunanan's clutches and paid him a lot of money to go away. He did go, but not far. He could always be found amongst the older, richer gay men who liked to hang out with young, good-looking guys. One of these older men was Norman Blachford, a retired multimillionaire[6] in his late-50s who lived in Phoenix, Arizona but also spent time in a lavish seaside condo[7] in La Jolla, north of San Diego. Soon Cunanan had inveigled his way into Blachford's life and the sugar daddy had given him a sports car, was flying him to New York and Paris and was bankrolling him to the tune of $2,000 a month. They were eating at the fanciest restaurants,

---

[4] Now calling himself Andrew DeSilva.

[5] Aston was bludgeoned to death on 19 May 1995 by a stone obelisk from his art collection. Some thought that Cunanan had done the deed but a drifter pleaded guilty and was jailed for the crime.

[6] Cunanan had done in-depth research into the fact.

[7] The home had formerly been owned by Lincoln Aston.

where Cunanan would tip exceptionally generously – when everyone could see it. At Cunanan's insistence, Blachford sold his Arizona home and moved west. Not long afterward, Cunanan told Blachford he wanted to live up on Mount Soledad, the highest hill overlooking La Jolla. Blachford bought them a house there, keeping the condo for guests. Friends talked about the relationship, that Andrew had got himself a sugar daddy, but the relationship *did* remain platonic.

Soon the rot set in. Blachford became bothered that Cunanan showed no interest in continuing his education or getting a job. Cunanan complained that Blachford was cheap, all the while spending his benefactor's money on maxed-out credit cards. The relationship wouldn't last. By September 1996, they'd split.

By now, Cunanan had started to shoot crystal meth and was "drinking like there was no tomorrow", as one friend put it. After a month, he felt a need to move on, throwing a farewell dinner at an upmarket restaurant. The meal felt like a wake. He gave expensive designer clothes to friends and the next day left San Francisco for good with a one-way ticket to Minneapolis. This was the hometown of one of his friends, Jeffrey "Jeff" Trail, a handsome 28-year-old former naval officer, now working for a propane delivery company. Cunanan rang in advance of his coming, saying he'd be staying for a couple of weeks.

The news filled Trail with dread. He didn't want Cunanan to come. Trail had a new boyfriend, Jon, and he had an uneasy feeling that Cunanan wanted more than just a platonic relationship. Furthermore, Trail owed Cunanan money and Trail, an extravagant over-spender, didn't have it to return. Perhaps Cunanan had ideas about collecting a debt. Nevertheless, when Cunanan turned up on his doorstep on 27 April 1997, Trail let him in. They talked. Whether about love or money, the talk turned into an argument. Not long after, Trail phoned a friend and said that he and Andrew had "had a huge falling out", that he never intended to speak to him again. Cunanan had other ideas. He phoned Trail and left a message: "I'd like to see you." Trail returned the call. Cunanan told him that after their last meeting he'd taken a gun from the apartment; now he wanted to give it back. Trail agreed to meet Cunanan in a coffee shop sometime around 21:00, after which it is likely the pair made their way to a mutual friend's apartment.

The mutual friend was David Madson, a 33-year-old preppy-looking, blond, blue-eyed architect. He'd been the love of Cunanan's life but he'd ended the relationship after coming to think there was something "shady" about Andrew. Madson had had unpleasant experiences with an ex-boyfriend who'd stalked him, making his life a misery. Like Trail, he too was worried the same could happen with Cunanan.

Cunanan let Trail into Madson's loft apartment and it's possible that Madson wasn't in the apartment at the time. It was his habit to take his dog for a walk before the 10 o'clock news programme. Trail was killed at around 21:55. We know this because his watch stopped at that time, probably as a result of the 27 furious blows that Cunanan unleashed upon his former lover's face, head and body, using both the head and the claw ends of a hammer. The attack occurred near the doorway. Cunanan's hammer missed on one occasion, hitting the wall and leaving a large indent. Blood spatters were sent through the open door across the hallway, and pieces of brain became lodged in the doorjamb. Neighbours later reported hearing shouting ("Get the fuck away from me!"), the sounds of a door slamming and thumping noises that went on for around 30-40 seconds.

Whether Madson had been present to witness the murder or returned after it'd already happened is not known. However, it's likely that Cunanan later dominated him with threats – either by threatening to implicate him in the violence (the attack had taken place in Madson's apartment) or intimidating him into cooperating with the clean-up of the aftermath. Madson *did* help; there were two sets of bloody hand- and footprints left on the floor, and there had been *a lot* of blood to clear up. Then, he and Cunanan remained at the apartment for two day as Trail's body lay wrapped in an oriental carpet next to the sofa.

When the usually reliable Madson didn't turn up for work the next day, a Monday, his colleagues became concerned. One of them arrived at his apartment with police the following day and knocked the door. They thought they heard whispering and the sound of Madson's Dalmatian pup, Prints, scratching at the door. The police had no probable cause to enter the property and left. Then neighbours witnessed Cunanan and Madson leaving, leaving Prints alive and well in the apartment with the already bloating body. It would be found later that Tuesday, two full days after the murder. Police initially believed that the body was that of Madson. When they realised it wasn't him, and that Madson was missing, they then assumed that *he* was the murderer.

Cunanan was more than likely holding Madson hostage with a gun. They drove around, ate lunch together at a bar. On Saturday morning, 3 May, a male body was found of the shore of Rush Lake near Rush City, Minnesota. He'd been shot three times – in the eye, the cheek and the chest – with a gun belonging to Trail. The body would later be identified as David Madson. For a week, law enforcement had been searching for this man as their main suspect; now he'd turned up as a victim. Both of the men, who'd had the audacity to dump Andrew Cunanan, now lay dead. Meanwhile, one of Trail's friends fingered Cunanan as the man who'd come to Minneapolis only last weekend. Now the focus of attention turned to this other man who'd mysteriously gone missing.

Two days later, he was in Chicago. On the same day he arrived, Marilyn Miglin was leaving. Fifty-nine-year-old Marilyn, a prominent entrepreneur, known as the Queen of the Makeovers for her appearances on the Home Shopping Network, left for Canada to promote her wares and wouldn't be back until late the next day. She left behind her 72-year-old husband Lee, a wealthy, successful real estate developer. Lee was fastidious and reliable. When he didn't pick Marilyn up from the airport the next day she knew something was wrong. She called a cab, but when she got home she noticed things were amiss: a sliced ham and a tub of ice cream had been left out on the kitchen counter, something her meticulous husband would never have done. She crossed the road to her neighbours, the Byers, and together they returned to the Miglin home.

Stephen Byers wandered around the inside of the large house whilst the two women waited outside. There was further evidence that the elderly man hadn't been alone that weekend: clothes were strewn around the bedroom, as if picked up and hastily discarded; black shavings from a few days' beard growth were in the hand basin and scum covered the bathtub; towels were scattered around the bathroom floor; and on the bathroom counter, a gun that looked all too real. Still, the house was in deathly silence.

Byers continued his exploration, half expecting to find a sleeping drug addict. Finding nothing upstairs, he went down into the basement, there to be confronted by the bizarre sight of the Miglins' underground chapel. But still, no sign of Lee.

A check of the garage revealed that Lee's Lexus was missing. Then four police officers arrived. They made a perfunctory search of the garage and found nothing. But Barbara Byer hesitated and took a closer look. She was disconcerted to notice some brown wrapping paper on the floor near the Jeep. Lee Miglin would *never* have left that there, she thought. She took a closer look, then let out a piercing scream.

Although the crime scene itself had been left pristine, the murder had been hideously vicious. Lee Miglin was found lying supine, fully clothed but for one shoe, the zipper of his jeans open. His ankles were bound tightly with cable and he'd been gagged with a garden glove and his head wrapped several times around with masking tape that left just a gap at the nostrils for breathing. Gay pornography magazines were set down near the body.

Prior to his death, Miglin had been tortured with a screwdriver and gardener's bow saw. He'd been slashed numerous times in the neck and the head had been almost completely severed using the saw. Every single rib was fractured, caused by having two bags of cement thrown onto the chest. There were over two dozen bruises. Bruises do not form after death; Miglin had been beaten whilst still alive. There were no defence wounds; the elderly man hadn't put up any fight. Despite the severe wounds, the white shirt was unstained with blood. Miglin had either been attacked without a shirt on or dressed afterwards.

There was no evidence that the killer had been in a hurry. It's possible that Cunanan had been invited into the house by Lee on the understanding that, as his wife had gone to Canada, he'd have the place to himself for the night. This is speculation. Certainly, there were hints given to the press that "the killer had made himself comfortable in the home" and "there is an indication the person or persons occupied and used the victim's apartment", which could easily be interpreted as a belief that the victim had known the assailant. And just like David Madson's puppy, the Miglins' golden retriever, Honey, had been left unharmed. This also suggested that there'd been no forced entry.

The question of motive persisted. It was not a Mafia hit; the fact that the killer had hung around suggested otherwise. Sexual gratification and the extortion of money were considered possibilities. That the killer had wreaked brutal revenge on the victim's face indicted a "very personal" impetus, an FBI consultant suggested. Then a check was made on a nearby red Jeep which had collected three parking tickets. The vehicle belonged to David Madson, the victim of suspect Andrew Phillip Cunanan. Now the media leapt on the story, hypothesising a "homosexual love triangle"; a revenge attack by a HIV-positive killer; or even an S&M bondage session, played out between an openly gay male prostitute and a millionaire businessman, gone wrong. The press tried their best to dig up the dirt on Lee Miglin; they only found unprintable hearsay. And the only one who seemed able to shed any light on the case was a fugitive. Cunanan now became the subject of a major manhunt.

Once again, Cunanan had a considerable headstart. However, he knew he was been tracked via the Lexus electronics and a witness had already seen him rip the antenna from the car. He cut the in-car phone wire but because he couldn't find the power box in the trunk the phone was still activated whenever the ignition was turned on.

Heading east, by 9 May 1997, he'd passed through historic Wilmington, crossed the Delaware Memorial Bridge and was in Finn's Point National Cemetery at Pennsville Township, New Jersey. Bill Reese, aged 45, was the cemetery's caretaker. He was a devout Christian who loved the outdoors and animals and was interested in history. The job was a vocation to him. That Friday afternoon, he had the misfortune to be observed alone by his office in an isolated part of the cemetery by a man obsessed by an undeactivatable car phone.

When Bill's wife, Rebecca, arrived home she became concerned at her husband's non-appearance. She drove to the cemetery and found the caretaker's office door open, the radio playing and a Lexus parked outside, but no sign of Bill. She called the police. When they arrived they went through the house, finding the basement locked, bizarrely, from both in the inside and outside. They broke in and found Bill, slumped at the base of the stairs, shot dead. Since there was no murder weapon they quickly concluded it'd been a cold-blooded execution-style murder. Cunanan had wanted Reese's truck ... and he'd killed for it. He'd left bloodstained evidence in the Lexus tying him to the murder of Miglin including the shoe taken from his foot. The only reason police could think of? He was leaving breadcrumbs: Cunanan wanted credit for his crimes. Even now he still craved the limelight.

Now travelling down the I-95 in a stolen red Chevrolet pickup truck (stopping mid-way to steal a licence plate), Cunanan made his way to Miami Beach, Florida, arriving on 11 May. He took a room in the Normandy Plaza Hotel, a rundown establishment near the gay nude beach. He signed himself in as Curt Demaris; he paid his bills in cash. There, he "hid in plain sight" for two months. Just over five miles away in upmarket South Beach was Gianni Versace's plush home at 1116 Ocean Dive, smack in the middle of gay capital of the world.

Cunanan stayed indoors during the day. He emerged from his seedy room only at night, wearing baseball cap and sunglasses, to eat takeaways, wander the streets and buy crack or vodka.

Occasionally he pimped himself out with older rich men, hustling on the beach. He took to burglary, stealing jewellery, and credit card theft, using what cash he obtained to buy more drugs or books and magazines. His appetite for reading hadn't left and he immersed himself in history, art and fashion, his favourite subjects. For two months straight he wore the same clothes. He was no longer shaving regularly. His skin paled; he put on weight. He tried to find work as a nude model for a gay magazine publisher and at a health club. He was rejected by both. In the meantime, he'd made it to the FBI's Ten Most Wanted list, but no one in Miami Beach suspected that a spree killer was living in their midst.

In mid-July, Cunanan informed the hotel receptionist that he'd be gone within the week. On Friday, 18 July, he left the hotel, dressed preppily. A member of the public recognised him from *America's Most Wanted* and reported the sighting to the police but, not being able to remember any more, the tip-off led nowhere. Cunanan went to Twist bar and hustled. One of the regular punters, a news-junkie, got bad vibes about him and even went to check the wanted posters. There was none of Andrew Cunanan.

Cunanan went to Twist the next night, only staying a short while. As he left, he was recognised by the same news-junkie patron who commented, "That's probably the serial killer." As Cunanan left, the customer said to some friends, "There goes the serial killer." Another chance to apprehend Cunanan somehow slipped by.

The next morning, Saturday, Cunanan skipped out the back gate of the Normandy Plaza without paying. In his room he'd left hair clippers and the box for a lady's girdle.

The following week, on Tuesday, 16 July 1997 at around half-past-nine in the morning, Gianni Versace visited a local café where he picked up a coffee and some fashion magazines. Upon his return home, Cunanan was standing waiting. Versace, now 50 years of age, bent over to unlock the wrought-iron gate to his opulent seafront mansion. He looked over his shoulder, glancing and smiling at a local woman who happened to be passing. Cunanan stepped forward and aimed Jeff Trail's .40-calibre semi-automatic pistol at Versace's neck and pulled the trigger. The first bullet destroyed the lower part of his brain.[8] Cunanan let loose a second bullet into Versace's face, next to the nose. Versace slumped on the steps, a bloom of blood forming beneath him. Cunanan, utterly calm, walked coolly away down Ocean Drive. Police showed up within two minutes. The scene seemed so staged they thought it was part of a movie setup. Paramedics were quick to arrive and the victim was rushed to hospital. There, Versace's heart fluttered briefly, but within minutes he was dead.

Inevitably, the press went wild. The assassination received an enormous amount of coverage and Cunanan's face was plastered all over the front pages. Bill Reese's stolen pickup truck was discovered at a local garage. It contained Cunanan's clothes and clippings of newspaper reports about his murders. The driver of the truck, however, was nowhere to be found.

The end came eight days later on Wednesday, 23 July at around 15:45 in Indian Creek, around four miles from Versace's home. A caretaker, whose job it was to look after berthed boats, noticed that one of them had been broken into. He and his wife entered the houseboat and saw evidence that someone had been sleeping there. Something told him that the person was on the boat – right at that very moment.

Then he heard a gunshot. He and his wife ran to shore and hid in some nearby bushes The caretaker called his son, who called 911. Police were on the scene within four minutes. Chaos quickly descended. The news media flocked to the scene en masse. Circling helicopters broadcast the events as they unfolded. Reporters began to suspect that the shot was linked to

---

[8] As the bullet left Versace's body it also struck and instantly killed a resting mourning dove.

Cunanan case. At around 20:30, the police found a body – killed by a gunshot wound – in the houseboat's upstairs bedroom. By around 05:10 the next day, it was all over. The victim was confirmed as Andrew Cunanan by fingerprint comparison. The press went wild; for days the story flooded the news cycle. It was the number one story in the country, if not the world. Now everyone knew the name of Andrew Cunanan. Finally, the strutting peacock with delusions of grandeur had achieved the attention he'd craved all his life.

The gunshot wound had been self-inflicted; gunpowder burns between Cunanan's fingers confirmed it. Nevertheless, the conspiracy theorists began to mutter. Cunanan had been set up to kill Versace by the Mafia, they proposed. He'd been tricked into dealing drugs for a high-powered syndicate and had stumbled into something so big he couldn't be allowed to live. He'd gone to the houseboat expecting to be rewarded, only to serve as the fall guy. He'd learned he was HIV-positive[9] and had tasked himself of killing past paramours out of vengeance.

So why did Cunanan kill Versace? It's known that he came to hate the fashion mogul in the period after their first meeting; he'd often spoken of him in extremely disparaging terms. The HIV conspiracy theory does not ring true. Whilst Versace's HIV-status became a much-publicised topic *after* his death, it had not been common knowledge *before* his death. It could be that Cunanan chose to kill Versace simply because of his fame. Murdering the world's most renowned fashionista would make the killer famous. The answer is unknown and unknowable.

Whatever the truth of the matter, Cunanan's 1987 classmates' predications had come true: the pretentious high-flier who never actually made it to the top where he felt he belonged *did* become the one "most likely to be remembered".

---

[9] Cunanan had not been HIV-positive.

# Ronald Joseph Dominique
(active 1997-2006)

WHEN ANDREW CUNANAN gunned down the famous Italian fashion designer, Gianni Versace, he achieved his dream: he became famous. Killed by his own hand, however, he never got to live that dream. Other serial killers do come out from the shadows, whether by their own cognisance or due to having been caught, and embrace their "celebrity" with alacrity.

In 1977, American David Berkowitz introduced his own "brand name", the legendary moniker "Son of Sam",[1] which became perhaps the most famous serial killer identifier in the world. In a badly spelt missive, Berkowitz used a few alternative names for himself, including "Mr Monster", "Beelzebub" and "Chubby Behemouth" [*sic*]; but the Son of Sam moniker stuck and the killer adopted it and came to savour it.[2] He was delighted to see his letters printed in the papers and has subsequently relished his evil celebrity status, his criminal infamy boosting an otherwise unstable, disturbed ego, giving him a perverse sense of self and purpose.

Richard Ramirez, the "Night Stalker", was keenly aware of the public's fascination with him. An avowed Satanist, after his capture he never expressed any remorse for the brutal slayings of his 14 known victims in the mid-1980s. Instead, the American killer rejoiced in his notoriety, mugging for the cameras and even wearing large sunglasses at his trial, as if he were an eminent Hollywood superstar.

Englishwoman Joanna Dennehy was in the business of killing for kicks. In 2013, she stabbed to death three randomly-chosen

---

[1] "Sam", Berkowitz claimed was a demon, manifested in the shape of a neighbour's dog.

[2] When apprehended on 10 August 1977, Berkowitz referred to himself as "Sam", rather than "Son of Sam".

men and attempted to kill another two. Although she has consistently refused to shed any light on her motive, it's known that she actively courted notoriety as a serial killer, even dancing a jig as she saw a television news report of her misdeeds. She wanted to become a "celebrity monster" and enjoyed, for a while at least, being Britain's most wanted person.

When we think of serial killers, the name of Ronald Joseph Dominique doesn't necessarily spring to mind. Even to devotees of the true-life crime, Dominique's small face in its large head mightn't be immediately recognisable. Twenty-three men died at his hands in a decade, and that body count makes him one of American history's most prolific killers. But his name hasn't entered the annals of serial killer fame in quite the same way that Gacy's, Bundy's or Dahmer's have. Yet his offences were no less monstrous. Lamentably, why this has happened isn't difficult to ascertain: Dominique was homosexual, and when he was detained he confessed freely to his misdemeanours. But perhaps the most shameful reason is this: some of Dominique's victims were gay African-American men – often homeless sex workers or drug users living on the fringe of society – yet others were from hard-working families, and others were high school students. It could almost seem, however, that the world just didn't care enough about them to remember.

The landscape of Louisiana is wide-open spaces, dominated by waterways and lush, verdant vegetation. Its climate is characterised by subtropical humidity, with long hot summers and short mild winters. There is ample precipitation, and the area is subject to tropical storms which, for a while at least, clear the air. But it is the humidity, rather than the heat, that dominates: clammy days lead to muggy nights. It's difficult to escape the uncomfortable weather.

Thibodaux, the parish seat of Lafourche, is halfway between New Orleans and Baton Rouge, along the banks of the Bayou Lafourche. It's a small city of around 15,000 where everyone knows everyone else's business, but little is remembered of a couple called Eldred and Josie Dominique or their large brood of seven children. One of them was Ronald Joseph Dominique, who was born on 9 January 1964 into a life of poverty and disruption. An unappealing child, Ronald was short and squat, with deep-set green eyes that gave him the look of one perpetually dejected. His family history reads like a Dickensian novel, with tales of neglect and abuse. Neighbours recall that whilst the parents ate well ("steak for supper"), the children had to make do with a hotdog weenie between them. They'd get so hungry they often scrounged food from the same neighbours. There were also rumours that the mother used to meet her brother in a remote camper in the middle of the woods for whatever pleasures a man and a woman might get up to when alone together. The father, hearing about this, marched the children through the woods in order to catch their mother in the act. When he did an almighty ruckus erupted. The children saw it all.

From a young age Ronald was a loner. He didn't make many friends in elementary school. He had difficulty maintaining friendships. Classmates remember little about him. Once, he claimed that a priest had molested him but he wasn't believed by his parents and the accusation did little to endear him to them.

In Thibodaux High School he joined the glee club, singing in the chorus. He was ridiculed for his camp mannerisms and peers teased him for being gay although he never admitted to being so at school. Here too he struggled to make friends, and he certainly didn't leave school having managed to make any lasting friendships.

Dominique's first run-in with the law was in June 1985 when he got caught harassing local residents by making obscene phone calls. He was arrested and charged, but he pleaded guilty and paid the $75 fine in order to avoid jailtime. He managed to stay out of trouble until May 1994, when he was arrested for driving under the influence of alcohol. Again, he paid the fine and fell off the law enforcement's radar. When he next came to their attention, two years later, it was for a more serious transgression. After he'd tied up a man and tried to rape him, the scantily-clad victim made a frantic escape through Dominique's bedroom window. This time Dominique was booked and spent three months in custody. He would later claim that whilst inside he was himself raped, so violently that his anus split. The experience made him determined never to return to jail. However, after the complainant could not be found a legal loophole meant that Dominique had be freed. He'd escaped justice. As he left the prison gates he made himself a vow: he'd do whatever it took never to return. Whatever it took …

By 1997, Dominique was a regular on the New Orleans gay scene, in the neighbourhood known as "the French Quarter". Now aged 33, he hadn't aged well. He was a short and stocky, unattractive man with a fat face and those emotionless deep-set eyes which still gave off a permanent air of disappointment. He knew he'd never find a date with his looks alone. Nor with his charm, for he had none. Any sex coming Dominique's way would be the result of a business transaction.

On 13 July 1997, David Lavon Mitchell Jr., a 19-year-old black man, was last seen in St Charles Parish, Louisiana, not far from where Dominique was now living in Boutte. He'd been attending a birthday party with his mother, after which his mother dropped him off at his grandmother's house in Killona. He'd arranged to wait here to be picked up by his uncle. For whatever reason, the uncle didn't show up and it's believed that Mitchell then tried to hitch a lift back home to nearby Luling. His body showed up in an open patch of industrial land off Highway 18. He'd been sodomised and drowned. Police were able to gather no DNA evidence, suggesting that the killer had used a condom.

Five months later, Gary Pierre, a 20-year-old black man, was found dead in St Charles Parish. Like David Mitchell, he'd been raped and asphyxiated. Like Mitchell, Pierre's body had also been dumped in plain sight. Then, seven months later, the body of 38-year-old Larry Ranson turned up. Again, the brutal circumstances of the murder were similar. Three months later, the body 27-year-old Oliver LeBanks, a gay prostitute, was discovered. He too had been choked to death and dumped out in the open, pushed over the edge of a freeway overpass. His body was found on 31 July 1998. So far all the victims had been black. A killer's _M.O._ was emerging.

With this latest victim, the pathologist was able to glean evidence from hair cast at the scene that the killer had been Caucasian. He recorded that LeBanks had been bludgeoned on the cranium and bound by the wrists, raped and manually strangled to the point of death.

Investigating detective, Lieutenant Dennis Thornton, conjectured: so far, four bodies had been found – four black men. They'd been left in accessible places. It seemed that the killer had _wanted_ the bodies to be found. What's more, the rate at which the bodies were turned up was increasing. The killer's cool-off period was becoming shorter. It was likely that he would kill again, and kill again soon. Lamentably, Thornton was to be proved correct.

Fourteen days after the discovery of Oliver LeBanks' body, another body turned up dead. Joseph Brown, at the age of 16, would prove to be the youngest of the killer's victims. There was no alteration to the now-familiar _M.O._; Brown had been raped and strangled and dumped in a public area. A month later came a similar murder, that of Bruce Williams, aged 18. Lt. Thornton found that, like LeBanks, Williams had been a hustler who'd simply vanished without reason that last Friday night of November 1998.

The predator took a six-month break before striking again, killing three men in four months: Manuel Reed, aged 21, Angel Mejia, aged 34, and Mitchell Johnson, also aged 34. There was no variation to the _M.O._ Each man had been black, tied up, raped, strangled and dumped in public.

With the discovery of the last victim, Johnson, the police caught a break. Witnesses provided a description of a white male in his 30s with a receding hairline and fat cheeks. Though they didn't yet know it, the police sketch drew a good comparison to Ronald Dominique. It's likely that Dominique had seen himself in that sketch. After it was publicised on local television and print media the killings stopped (at least for a while).

In November, Dominique quietly quit his maintenance job, left Boutte and towed his trailer along the I-90, some 60 miles southeast of New Orleans. He headed back home and parked his trailer on his sister Lainie's property at 2215 Bayou Blue Road in Houma, Terrebonne Parish. This area is what people think of as *classic Louisiana*, with its bayous – long, narrow, slow-moving rivers which leak into the Gulf of Mexico. The surrounding land is marshy – often called wetland, for the distinction between shore and water is ill-defined and can change with the tides. In the sleepy South, it's not uncommon for rural residents to live in shacks in relative isolation. Indeed, the region as a whole is quite distinct from the rest of the mainland, and locals have resisted the encroaching "Americanisation" upon their unique Cajun culture. Many locals make their living from the gulf by shrimping and trapping oysters. In Houma, illiteracy is higher than the national average. Here, Dominique connected his trailer to the electricity and water supplies and settled down, keeping his head low, drawing as little attention to himself as possible. He found work as a labourer and caused no problems. People who met him found him pleasant and polite.

It wasn't to last …

Michael Rydell Vincent was a small-time, small-town criminal of small stature. A 23-year-old black man sporting a thin moustache and goatee, his charge sheet showed that he'd made a career of hustling men for sex. This career came to an abrupt end on Millennium Eve when his slim, 5'7" body was thrown onto a barbed-wire fence just off the side of the road, where it hung for any passer-by to discover.

Vincent had been strangled to death. Burst blood vessels in the eyes and marks around the neck confirmed the fact. Abrasions around the wrists indicated that he'd been restrained prior to the killing. In the pocket of his jeans, Vincent had carried four pieces of crack cocaine, which suggested a motive for his decision to engage in sex work. If the body had been discovered 50 miles north or northeast, police might've linked it to the recent killing spree which had taken place in the surrounds of New Orleans – but it hadn't been. No connection was made. The killer had left no forensic traces; no one came forward to report having seen Vincent in the company of any individual that New Year's Eve; no one witnessed the body being dumped. And to complicate matters, now the killer decided to lay low – for over two whole years. Local police were stymied, whilst back in New Orleans Lt. Thornton was left scratching his head. The reason for the hiatus may have been practical: in May 2000, after arguing with someone public so loudly that the police had been called, Ronald Dominique was summonsed to appear in court on charges of disturbing the peace. The brush with the law may have quenched his appetite for murder; after all, he'd come to Houma in order to *avoid* the law, to lay low. He simply couldn't afford to draw any attention to himself by getting into trouble.

It wasn't to last ...

On 10 February 2002, Dominique slapped a woman during an altercation at a Mardi Gras parade. He'd accused her of bumping her car into a baby stroller at a parking lot and, although the lady apologised, he continued his verbal onslaught. The fury, simmering just beneath the surface, had now broken free and could barely be contained. He made a deal with the police, entering an offenders' programme that kept him out of jail. He kept his nose clean and met all conditions of the programme. In October that year, he was discharged and entered society with a clean slate, getting a second job as a pizza delivery man at Domino's. Seemingly, he was a good employee and a model citizen. He enjoyed helping people and volunteered calling out bingo numbers at the Lions Club.

It wasn't to last ...

Before long, Dominique was to kill again. His victims were the same – young black men on the fringes of society. The wide, open cane fields were his ally – desolate, remote spaces miles from anywhere. He targeted his victims in the gay bars he frequented, luring them to these isolated rural areas by offering them money for sex. If the men were straight he would conjure up fake drug deals, or tell them that his wife was willing to pay to have sex with a black man, even carrying around a photo of a woman in order to add authenticity to the story. He must've cut a persuasive figure, for not once did he have to use force, instead using verbal inducements and money so that the men would allow themselves to be restrained with a rope or a belt. Between October 2002 and October 2006, Dominique killed a further 13 times, varying the gaps between attacks, sometimes killing two victims in the same month. The victim-profile remained much the same – young, black men[3] – all of them raped and strangled. Most were disposed of in an open place, although some were left in a closed off spaces, for example, dumped in a storage-rental facility. In each case, however, Dominique killed in order to keep a promise he'd made to himself some years before – that he'd never go to prison again.

By 2004, he was reading meters. This worked to his advantage: in his travels around Houma he became familiar with the old dirt roads that led to farms, utility areas, bayous. He knew the best places to dump bodies, places where he'd be less likely to be stopped by a passer-by, or to get stuck in his car, or otherwise draw the unwelcome attention of inquisitive gazes.

Meanwhile, Lt. Thornton had assembled a taskforce and was continuing to investigate every lead. He noticed a common thread: some of the victims had been picked up near the Sugar Bowl Motel. Another area of interest was around the Lake Houmas Inn, where sex workers and drug dealers congregated. It made sense to consider these as part of the killer's trawling grounds. An FBI profiler suggested that the killer lived near the airport. Everyone wondered, however, how the killer had managed to tie up and immobilise several young, virile men with toned bodies. Maybe there were two or more killers, working together … The answers, however, wouldn't come.

---

[3] Their ages ranged 17-46. Some of Dominique's later victims were white.

A clue came in 2005. John Banning, a young African-American man, was walking along the highway one day, minding his own business. A black Sonoma pickup truck pulled up alongside him. The driver, a fat white man with a pudgy face and sad-looking eyes, leaned out and asked him if he wanted a beer. Then he quickly produced a photo of an attractive woman. "How'd you like to fuck this attractive white girl?" he asked. "She'd like to make it with a guy like you."

Having just come out of prison on parole, Banning's loins were already atwitch. This driver didn't look dangerous, he thought. He got into the vehicle and allowed the strange man to drive him through town and onto the Bayou Blue Road.

Stopping at a trailer, the pair got out of the vehicle and entered the trailer. Once they were inside the man began his ploy.

"I'll tie you up," he said. "Take off your clothes."

Banning wondered what was going on. Something seemed amiss. The trailer was a mess, littered with clothes and what looked like jars of urine. It was festooned with Christmas decorations even thought it was nowhere near Christmas. And on the floor were stack upon stack of gay pornographic magazines.

At this point, Banning made a wise decision. He turned and left. The strange man made no attempt to stop him. The move probably saved his life.

Lt. Thornton and his team, meanwhile, were discussing possible leads. They'd been going through the archives of sex offenders but found nothing connective. By felicitous coincidence they decided to approach a local parole officer. The officer agreed to ask his parolees if they'd lately encountered anything sexually bizarre – for example, anyone who had requested they engage in bondage as part of the sex act. The parole officer did just that. Going through his list of parolees he eventually came to John Banning. Banning had a story to tell. He was able to bring the detectives along to Bayou Blue Road and point out the trailer at no. 2215. Detective Dawn Bergeron opened the mailbox and pulled out an envelope. The addressee: Ronald J. Dominique. It was their first real lead.

They invited Dominique down to the police station for an interview. He came willingly – cool, calm and collected. He declined legal representation.

The detectives began with the complaint from John Banning.

Dominique admitted to tying him up as part of a sex game. He admitted to being gay. He consented to giving DNA samples. He'd be willing to undertake a polygraph. "I don't have anything hide," he said. He looked very much like a man willing to help the police with their enquiries.

The detectives obtained the DNA samples, gave their suspect a lift back to the trailer and returned to the office. Then they decided to take another look at the database of sex offenders.

Dominique's charge sheet was suspicious, to say the least. Three allegations of rape, false imprisonment, assault, disturbance of the peace, making obscene phone calls. Then Bergeron and Thornton drove an hour north to consult with their counterparts in Terrebonne. They discovered charges that'd been dropped for the lack of corroborating evidence, which was hardly a declaration of innocence. Nevertheless, with little evidence by which to go on, the detectives were forced to proceed slowly.

They decided to put up a roadblock around the Sugar Bowl Motel, where at least three of the victims had done business. They'd meant to cut off the killer's trawling ground. Instead, the killer simply shifted location.

Nicholas "T-Nick" Pellegrin was a 21-year-old white hustler in need of money. On 5 November 2005, Ronald Dominique turned up at Pellegrin's house to read the meter. Dominique propositioned him, suggesting they have some fun together. Pellegrin was busy, but he agreed that this short, fat man could come back later.

Dominique did just that. He arrived at dusk to collect Pellegrin and drive him back to the trailer on his sister's property. They entered the second trailer nearby. Now, however, Dominique was on dangerous ground. With his sister living nearby and a church just across Bayou Blue Road he couldn't afford to let his victim make any noise. The manner of the killing was similar to the previous ones – a strike on the head, presumably to knock the victim out, so that he could be gagged, tied up and strangled. The serial killer didn't waste any time afterwards. Using his knowledge of the backroads of Houma, Dominique avoided the roadblocks and drove the body to a wooded area in Lafourche Parish.

Understandably, when the detectives found the body they were enraged and outraged. How had this homicidal maniac managed to evade capture yet again? Nevertheless, they had some good news – of sorts: the DNA analysis of semen taken from the rectum of Angel Mejia had just been returned. Dominique's DNA was a mitochondrial match to the DNA found on the victims. This proved a familial match, but it wasn't the conclusive nuclear match that would've confirmed beyond doubt that Dominique was the killer. They needed more evidence. Now they threw more resources at the case, tightening the net by setting up reconnaissance, eavesdropping and deploying a night scope from the grounds of the church across the road. Yet, despite the increased surveillance, Dominique still managed to shake the tail, leaving him free to kill – one last time.

On 14 October 2006, he picked up a 27-year-old white hustler, Christopher Sutterfield, from the Hebert Motel, where he'd been visiting friends, and drove him to a storage facility. His dead body was dumped near a little-used boat launch at White Castle, next to the Mississippi River. It was found the following day. This time Dominique had travelled much further afield to find a dump site. The manner of death followed the now-familiar *M.O.* The detectives were certain this was yet another in the serial murderer's canon of victims.

Meanwhile, Dominique's sister had become irritated by the intrusive police presence. She put pressure on her brother to leave. He went to a cheap dosshouse and settled in. With pressure from their superiors and press editorials mounting, the detectives decided to throw the dice and make an arrest – *without* the airtight evidence needed for a sure-fire conviction. On 2

December, they drove to the dosshouse and found their suspect lying on his bed. Showing the warrants, they arrested Ronald J. Dominique on two charges of first-degree murder of Oliver LeBanks and Manuel Reed.

He confessed quickly. It was almost as if he were bragging about his exploits. Manual Reed had been a 21-year-old African American with a slim, muscular build whose body had been found discarded next to a dumpster under an overpass in Kenner, Louisiana on 30 May 1999. Dominique calmly explained in detail how he had been approached by Reed in the New Orleans French Quarter, how he'd been offered sex, how the two had gone to his vehicle. How they driven off and parked up somewhere. How they'd undressed, and then fellated each other. Now Dominique introduced a new element: he said that Reed had forced him onto this stomach and then produced a knife, telling him he was going to sodomise Dominique and that he wanted his money. It sounded as if the suspect were attempting to raise the spectre of self-defence.

Then Dominique stated that he'd had anal intercourse with Reed – at knifepoint. It didn't make sense. Perhaps Dominique suspected that DNA profiling would be able to be used to prove that he'd sodomised Reed.

Then, in another bizarre twist, Dominique told the detectives that Reed had flipped him over and was about to rape *him* – at knifepoint. He explained that some years in the past he'd got a tear in his rectum, caused by ingesting too much black pepper, and that this build-up of pepper caused his rectum to rip, meaning that now he couldn't have anal intercourse. The way he told it, it was almost as if Dominique had been the victim of Reed. It was an unbelievable story – and an unbelievable self-defence scenario.

Giving precise details that could only have been known to someone who'd been there, Dominique went on to describe immobilising Reed by bludgeoning him with a tyre iron, tying him up with a clothesline, kneeling on top of him with his full weight, and then choking him with the seat belt. He recounted pulling it so tight that Reed couldn't get his fingers in to relieve the pressure. He remembered witnessing Reed grappling against his restraints as he fought for his life, and how the life had eventually ebbed away from him.

What Dominique claimed then was *even more* incredible. He recalled that after discarding Reed's body by the dumpster he'd panicked ... panicked because he hadn't wanted to go back to jail. His justification for killing Reed was self-protection. He'd used the tyre iron merely to incapacitate Reed, only to find himself having to kill him ... in self-defence. The story stank. But by now the detectives had enough to pin the killing firmly on Dominique. He was no longer their suspect; he was the perpetrator. He'd be going nowhere.

Dominique continued to spill. He gave details, so many details, but always there was that defensive whine and the suggestion that he'd only done what he'd done out of panic or fear of being raped. It was pure bunkum, and the cops weren't buying any of it. "All these guys want is money," was a constant theme. When the guys threatened to go to the cops, "I was scared they [the cops] wouldn't believe my story and they'd bring me to jail." More phoney justification ... but at least he was still talking.

The next morning, Dominique led the investigators on a morbid tour of the bayous. A caravan of police cars wound its way along the old rural roads of Southern Louisiana as their navigator pointed out site after site of dump spots. At times he would get out of the car and indicate a particular place of interest. Never once did he show any remorse. For the detectives, it was about bringing closure to 23 families; the weight of it was a heavy pressure on their shoulders.

*So why had Dominique been so cooperative?* The answer was simple: self-preservation – he wanted to avoid the electric chair. But the detectives wondered about his motivation for killing. His response: because his family had made fun of him when he was young, calling him "queer" and "fag". *How had he managed to pick up straight men?* By showing them a picture of an attractive woman and asking if they wanted to fool around with her. Only after they were tied up did he reveal that it was *he* the men would be having sex with – whether they wanted to or not. In other words, rape. *How did he keep them quiet?* He shoved a towel in their mouths. *What about the men who didn't allow themselves to be tied up?* They were allowed to go.

It was a full confession, but could Dominique's version of events ever be trusted? Only the confessor knew the full truth. But he'd admitted to killing for nigh on a decade, taking 23 victims to the grave, giving enough detail to prove beyond doubt he'd killed as many men as he'd claimed to have done. He'd been the archetypal serial killer, disguising his deceptions behind a mask of normalcy, hiding in plain sight, a man without distinction, who'd lived without distinguishing himself. That's how he'd managed to be so effective. But now he'd given his statement, although whether the motive had been power, revenge or fear of being sent to jail will probably never be known for definite. Thornton and Bergeron were satisfied though. Now they had their man.

On 23 September 2008, Dominique pleaded guilty to eight counts of first-degree murder. Any more charges than that and the case risked being tied up in appeals for the next decade or more. Besides, the remaining ones had no inculpatory forensic evidence and so were unlikely to lead to convictions. Prosecutors felt that pursuing additional charges would be a waste of public money.

The defendant cut a pathetic figure in court, shuffling into the dock supported by a walking stick. Nevertheless, this was the man who'd admitted to brutally cutting short the lives of 23 men after raping them. He was given eight life sentences, to be served consecutively. Ronald J. Dominique wouldn't be roaming the streets of Houma any time soon. He remains at this time incarcerated at the State Penitentiary in Angola, Louisiana.

Incredibly, the case received little press at the time, barely rating a headline on the national stage. Nowadays, few people have heard the name of one of America's most prolific serial killers and he hasn't even had the dubious honour of being dubbed with a serial killer moniker. Languishing in jail, Ronald J. Dominique remains Mr Nobody.

# Bruce McArthur

[active 2008-2017]

A COMPARISON BETWEEN THE US and its neighbourly state, Canada, could not yield greater dissimilarity in at least one respect: its rate of murder. The statistics speak for themselves; homicide in Canada is rare and multiple killers are almost unheard of. In 2019, there were 658 homicides in the whole of Canada. There were slightly more homicides, 669, in the US state of Pennsylvania over the same period. However, at around 12.8 million, the population of Pennsylvania is less than a third of that of Canada, which stands at 37.5 million. The comparison couldn't be greater: Canada is not a country used to homicide. In fact, so rare is murder in Canada that in 2019 there existed just a single full-time forensic anthropologist working in the country.

Dr Kathy Gruspier's expertise was called upon one cold January day in 2018 when she was asked to investigate a number of planters. Twelve of these large fibreglass tubs had been used to display plants and trees outside a property in Leaside, a district northeast of downtown Toronto. They were taken from the chill Ontario air and removed to Dr Gruspier's office, where they were allowed to defrost over several days.

After a week thawing, however, the fetid stench emanating from the planters alerted the anthropologist that something was amiss. She x-rayed one of the planters and saw that it contained a foreign object. Then, watched by a cohort of police, Dr Gruspier peeled away the sides of the planter. She soon made a grisly discovery. Buried within the large vessel were dismembered human remains – heads, limbs and torsos. As the investigators uncovered more from the gruesome harvest, the tally from the planters yielded a total of eight victims. Most of them turned out to be of Middle Eastern or South Asian descent, and most of them had disappeared from the vicinity of Toronto's gay village. And several of the victims' families had had no idea that their loved ones had been leading double lives in the Village.

It turned out that the owner of the Leaside property (from where the planters had been removed) had had an arrangement with a local landscape gardener. The Leaside property owner allowed the gardener to store landscaping equipment in her garage in exchange for gardening work. After police had found a suspect for the unexplained disappearances of gay men from the Village, they'd made a search of several properties associated with the suspect. At one of the properties, cadaver dogs took an interest in several planters on the site. The planters happened to belong to a local landscape gardener, and that gardener's name was Bruce McArthur.

Born Thomas Donald Bruce McArthur on 8 October 1951 in Lindsay, Ontario, Bruce and his sister were raised on a rural farm on Palestine Road just outside the village of Argyle, near Woodville in the Kawartha Lakes region. The McArthur parents were of good stock. Their roots in the area went back generations. In addition to the McArthur clan, the sturdy bungalow was also often home to several troubled children from Toronto, whose parents sent their children to live with the family for respite from the troubles of city life, hoping to straighten them out away from the concrete jungle. At times, there could be eight or 10 children living in the house. There were always kids coming and going, and none of them ever complained about being sent to live in such an idyllic, outdoorsy environment.

Malcolm "Mac" McArthur was a good but strict father. He and his wife were quiet, well-respected people. There was said to be "tension" within the home due to the parents practising different religions. Having two parents, equally devout in their respective faiths, young Bruce would often side with Islay, his Irish Catholic mother, instead of his Scottish Presbyterian father. This would earn Bruce some derision from his father, who may already have sensed his son's homosexual leaning. In rural Ontario in the 1950s and '60s, homosexuality would not have been seen as normal and it would be well into his adulthood before Bruce began to accept this part of himself.

The "prissiness" of Bruce McArthur was remembered by his

classmates. In the one-room primary school, whilst his peers were capable of messing about, Bruce would suck up to the teacher, even rushing inside to snitch on the others if they were to get into mischief. He'd never get into trouble himself; he was a stick-in-the-mud. Perhaps this was his method of achieving the validation he didn't receive at home. "He wasn't like the rest of the boys," one classmate recalled. Another recollected him as being "prim and proper" but all the same "a nice kid". Other than having a pleasant singing voice, Bruce's spell at the school was quite unremarkable.

By the time he transitioned to high school, Bruce was a handsome young man. His tenure at Fenelon Falls Secondary, in the four-year arts and technical stream, also proved to be unremarkable, other than by the fact that it was here that he met and began dating Janice Campbell, a slight, light-haired girl whose ambition was to be a nurse. In the Fenelon Falls yearbook of '69-'70, McArthur's picture shows a neat-looking, dark-haired and strikingly good-looking young man. His nickname was "Snoopy"; his probable future read: "Your guess is as good as mine." Meanwhile, Janice's pet peeve (with unwitting irony) was: "Someone who can't decide what they want."

At that time, in that place, Bruce would've felt an enormous pressure to conform. He would've been waging an internal battle against his natural inclinations. There weren't many options left for a closeted young man – often it was either a sham marriage or a calling to the priesthood. McArthur would turn out to be Janice's pet peeve: someone who couldn't decide what he wanted. They married in 1974 at the age of 23. McArthur began work as a buyer's assistant for Eaton's department stores.

By the time they were in their mid-30s, the McArthur family had expanded by two children, Todd and Michelle;[1] and Bruce

---

[1] The family contracted again with the death of McArthur's mother in 1978, of cancer, and his father in 1981, from a brain tumour.

was working as a travelling salesman, soliciting department stores to sell his company's wares – socks and long johns. He was regularly on the road, criss-crossing the country for most of his working day. It's not known if McArthur was now killing, but he wouldn't be the first killer to have taken advantage of a roaming lifestyle to disguise his crimes. Certainly, though, to his friends, family and colleagues, the good-looking salesman with the smooth patter was a pleasant and amenable individual who never seemed to cause anyone any trouble.

By 1986, the McArthurs had moved to a red-bricked home on Cartref Avenue in suburban Oshawa. Neighbours remember that it was Janice who tended to the garden, not Bruce, and that they both attended church regularly, keeping himself active in ecumenical business. He was friendly with his neighbours and no one had a bad word to say against him. Bruce McArthur was viewed as a friendly guy – a regular guy – always having a smile on his ruddy face, never betraying any hint of anger or moodiness. There was no hint at all that anything was amiss. Life seemed good.

Then it all began to unravel …

In the 1990s, Bruce left his job and his career as a salesman came to an end. In his early '40s, he began to hang around Ontario's gay village and cheat on his wife with men. A year-and-a-half later, he came out to his wife, confessing to her that he was gay. By now the pair were experiencing financial hardships, and perhaps because of these Janice and Bruce continued to live together. However, in the late 1990s, after 25 years of marriage, the two eventually separated. The family home had already been mortgaged in an attempt to consolidate their joint debts. Following their separation, Janice remained in the home whilst Bruce moved to Toronto. After a lifetime of suppressing his true self, he'd decided to further explore his sexuality.

The divorce was finalised in 1999. Declaring liabilities that outweighed the assets by around $90,000, now McArthur had no choice but to file for bankruptcy to pay off debts. In 2000, the Oshawa property was sold.[2]

McArthur's new Toronto home was a three-bedroom condo on Don Mills Road, which he shared with a roommate, a dark-skinned immigrant who'd not yet come out to his family – just the type of man Bruce liked. Here, he decorated the wall of his en suite bathroom with photos of naked men with erections. Most of the men appeared to be of East Indian heritage. The photos weren't exactly hidden from sight. Todd, McArthur's son, who was now living with him, believed that the photos were of men his father knew. It seems that by now McArthur was openly gay and didn't care who knew it.

He was now regularly frequenting the watering holes of the Church-Wellesley district, almost becoming part of the fixtures and fittings. He was seen as a jolly-looking man, agreeable and polite, but still as straight-laced as he'd been as child. The looks were deceptive. In 2001, McArthur met up with a male sex worker he'd been talking to on a chat line. The two were soon having sex. On 31 October 2002, the man invited McArthur to his apartment to view his Halloween costume. There, McArthur assaulted the sex worker with a metal pipe, striking him on the back of the head and beating him several times and causing bodily harm. The victim was knocked out. When he regained consciousness he dialled 911 and was taken to hospital where he was treated for serious injuries.

For some reason, McArthur reported himself to the police, confessing that he may have hurt someone. It may have been a ruse to obtain leniency for a crime which he knew would come

---

[2] It was around this time that Todd, the McArthurs' son, began to get into trouble for making obsessive obscene phone calls to random women. The couple's financial difficulties stemmed in part due to ensuing legal issues. By 2014, Todd had amassed more than two dozen convictions for similar offences, and would spend 14 months in jail for these crimes. There, he would be diagnosed with "telephone scatalogia", an obsessive need to make obscene phone calls.

out anyway. Regardless, in April 2003, he was before the court for the first time, arriving with no criminal record. He entered a guilty plea. He said that he didn't remember the incident or why he'd done it. His defence argued that the unexplained behaviour may have been due to taking anti-seizure medication along with amyl nitrate, a muscle relaxant popular with gay men that's often taken before sex. It was a weak argument. The victim himself failed to provide a statement. A psychological assessment submitted during sentencing indicated that McArthur was a "low risk" of reoffending, and that he presented "absolutely no signs of psychopathy". He was handed a conditional sentence of a day shy of two years followed by three years' probation.

Avoiding prison, McArthur was under house arrest for the first year of his sentence, followed by a six-month curfew. He was banned from entering the Church-Wellesley district and could not use the services of male sex workers. He was not to consume drugs without a medical prescription and specifically barred from using amyl nitrate. In addition, he was compelled to give a sample of DNA to be added to the national database and had to take an anger management course.[3]

Things changed in 2003 when his four-year relationship with his male lover ended, around the same time that his divorce was finalised. He saw a psychiatrist and was prescribed an antidepressant. Around this time, he sought work as a landscape gardener. In his private life, he was enjoying the benefits of gay fetish dating sites for men in to BDSM. He was active on many websites, the names of which betray his proclivities: Bear411, BearForest, DaddyHunt, Grindr, Growlr, Manjam, Scruff, Silverdaddies and Squirt. His profiles advertised his interest in "submissive men of all ages", often under a variation on the username "silverfox". "I am a bit shy until i [*sic*] get to know

---

[3] In 2014, McArthur's sentence was expunged from his criminal record, and wouldn't have appeared in any subsequent criminal background checks.

you, but am a romantic at heart," his profile noted. However, his reputation for rough sex was already going before him. On one occasion in 2003 (during the period when he'd been banned from the Church-Wellesley gay village), he was rebuffed in a coffeehouse. His volcanic temper exploded and he swept all the glasses from the counter, screaming, "I'm tired of these fuckin' faggots, telling stories about me! You're just like the rest of them – you think I'm crazy." He wasn't exactly providing evidence to the contrary. Friends warned each other off the now-rotund bear, telling each other to be careful. He liked to play the master role, they told each other, and he had a terrible temper. Everything he was into was freaky, they said, and none of his sexual encounters ever ended well. Bruce McArthur was a man to stay away from.

Perhaps the signs of McArthur's nefarious doings were already there, waiting to be discovered. Then it happened – at the end of 2013, when he was in a South Asian-influenced bistro in the heart of Toronto's gay district. As a regular at this particular establishment, he would come in and order the "Big Bear" breakfast, or an extra spicy chicken tandoori omelette. He would often arrive with his usual companion, but on this day he came in by himself and sat down at a corner table. The proprietor asked him what was going on, to which McArthur replied that his boyfriend was on vacation. "But I saw him only yesterday," the proprietor replied. At this, McArthur became "very angry" and got up and left, never to return again.

If he had not already done so before, certainly, by this stage McArthur had already killed. He was living in a 19th-floor apartment at Leaside Towers, an area populated mainly by immigrants. He had a Facebook profile and, in addition to the usual photos of cats and vacations, he was uploading pictures of himself with younger men of Middle Eastern or South Asian heritage. He was a part of the gay community and a regular fixture at its downtown bars. Working alongside his son, he was now working as a self-employed landscaper, operating his small-time business under the name Artistic Designs. Also working at his side were an older man, with whom it is thought he was in a romantic liaison, and a South East Asia or Middle Eastern day labourer.

To all intents and purposes, Bruce McArthur was hiding in plain sight. He had a large social circle, but to those closest to him there were no tell-tale signs of the smouldering malevolence inside. McArthur looked and acted like a roly-poly benign uncle – not unlike the Santa he portrayed at Christmas as he dressed up for the local mall. He even earned the nickname "Santa" at a couple of the bars he frequented, such as Woody's and Zipperz. He presented such an affable, agreeable face to the world that no one suspected a thing. It seems that he cultivated this revamped image in his sex life too. A few of his ex-partners described their trysts as little more than vanilla – basically, conventional, uncomplicated sex with very little expectations upon either partner. He'd come a long way since being barred from the district in 2003.

But the kinky side was still there – online. In his dating sites, his profiles alluded to his more controlling side. On the dating app Scruff his profile said he was looking for "men that have a kinky side", that his aim was "finding a guys [*sic*] buttons and then pushing to them to your limits". But he also sought to sweeten the image he presented. On at least two websites, he described himself as "romantic at heart but don't let that put you off".

During sex, the benevolent image could evaporate quickly, as some later testified. One man agreed to meet up with McArthur after connecting on a dating app. As McArthur's partner was out, the pair went back to his apartment. There, they engaged in consensual BDSM roleplay games which suddenly turned sour. The man stated that McArthur didn't respect his limits, ignored his safe words and took it to the extreme of completely cutting off his airway (with his hands, his penis, and by sitting on the man's chest with his not inconsiderable weight) so that the man couldn't breathe. He fell unconscious, only to be revived, he believed, by the early return of McArthur's roommate who'd unwittingly interrupted the ritual McArthur had intended to play out with him.

Essentially, serial killing is about the need to control. Sex play involving bondage is also about control. Mixing in the circles McArthur did allowed him to find and lure partners who are willing to play BDSM games, and once they were bound he had them exactly how he needed them – fully under his control. McArthur had become adroit at concealing his malevolent intent by hiding in plain sight – beguiling and deceiving his friends right at the centre of the gay community.

In his native Sri Lanka, Skandaraj Navaratnam had been forced to hide his sexuality. Known as "Skanda" to his friends, the 40-year-old refugee had come to Canada in order to be himself and give his family back home a better life. Those who knew him remember him as a kind and charming man with a "jovial character" who loved to laugh. He took care of his appearance, liking others to see him in a positive light. An educated man with a strong interest in global affairs, he loved animals and was a keen environmentalist who sought to protect the forests of Sri Lanka. He worked as a home nurse.

At some point in 1999, Navaratnam met McArthur, and by the early 2000s they were in a romantic relationship, and, according to reports, they were Facebook friends. They split due to McArthur's refusal to stop flirting with other men and his controlling behaviours.

Over the Labour Day weekend of 2010, Navaratnam went missing after having last been seen at the 1980s retro night in Zipperz in Ontario's gay village. It was around two o'clock in the morning and he was with two unidentified men. When he failed to reply to a friend's texts after several days he was reported missing. His former lover, McArthur, continued to frequent Zipperz, often expressing concern to others about the disappearance of his friend.

Abdulbasir "Basir" Faizi, a 42-year-old immigrant from Afghanistan, was last seen on 28 December 2010, He was a married father of two daughters who lived a double life as a gay man. According to friends, he was funny, clever and adored his children. Family and friends had no idea that Faizi was frequenting the gay village.

Faizi worked at a printing facility. On 29 December 2010, he phoned his wife to tell her he'd be working late with colleagues and would come home later that night. It wasn't true. In fact, he'd visited a Church Street sauna and the notorious Black Eagle leather bar. That would turn out to be the last time anyone other than his killer is known to have seen him alive. The next day he was reported missing. A week later, his abandoned car was found a short distance from Mallory Crescent. That weekend, the couple who owned the property where McArthur stored his planters were away. Around a kilometre away, McArthur had been housesitting for another couple. Upon their return, the owners noticed a dark stain on the carpet of one of their bedrooms. McArthur explained that he'd spilt Coca Cola which he'd tried to clean up.

Faizi's wife claimed that the police had told her that he'd abandoned her. She didn't believe it. Because no one knew at the time of Faizi's links with the gay village his disappearance initially wasn't recognised by Toronto's gay community.

Majeed Kayhan, aged 58, kept an apartment on Church Street and could often be found in the gay bars of the district. Like the two previous men to disappear, Kayhan led two separate lives. An Afghan immigrant and the son of a Muslim cleric, Kayhan had a wife and children, but he'd also been in a brief relationship with McArthur. In 2002, the Kayhans separated. Now able to embrace his sexuality more, Majeed would often be seen at Toronto Pride sporting traditional Afghan dress. However, life was still not easy. Kayhan was crippled by loneliness and turned to alcohol. One of his favourite drinking haunts was a bar called Woody's, where it was known he was attracted to older, white-haired men – men just like Bruce McArthur. Indeed, the owner of the Mallory Crescent property where McArthur stored his planters later stated that he'd brought Kayhan to her house. But on 18 October 2012, Majeed Kayhan suddenly vanished without explanation. He was reported missing two weeks later by his concerned son.

In November 2012, the Toronto Police Service launched a taskforce to probe the disappearance of Navaratnam, dubbing it "Project Houston". Utilising demographic and geographic profiling, the project soon identified the disappearances of Faizi and Kayhan as remarkable. An anonymous tip fingered McArthur as a person of interest and he was interviewed. He admitted being in a romantic relationship with Navaratnam and to having known Kayhan but it wasn't enough to connect him to the disappearances. At the same time, the police also tracked another man, who seemed a more likely suspect in the Navaratnam disappearance. Eventually, however, this line of enquiry fizzled out.

At the age of around 30, Soroush Mahmudi came to Canada as a refugee from Iran. He had no family in Canada until meeting his future wife in the country, moving to Toronto to be closer to her family. There, he found work in a manufacturing plant. Described by friends as likeable and easy-going, Mahmudi enjoyed soccer, playing pool and camping. On 14 August 2015, he disappeared, shortly to be reported missing by his wife.

Prior to this, however, not long after arriving in Canada, Mahmudi had met and had a a four-year relationship with a transgender woman. They eventually moved in together. Following an argument, Mahmudi came home to tell his lover he was leaving. She told him to go. She turned, and he hit her over the head with a blender and dragged her around by the hair. Other than this episode, Mahmudi is not known to have had any connections to Toronto's gay scene. And if his remains hadn't been discovered buried within a planter in 2018, any connection to Bruce McArthur would've remained unknown also.

In the hope of a "bright future", Kirushna Kumar Kanagaratnam, aged 37, came to Canada in 2010 aboard a ship carrying 492 Sri Lankan refugees fleeing from the country's civil war. However, his claim for asylum was denied and he was ordered to be deported. He ended up in Toronto, doing odd-jobs such as moving furniture, sending what money he could home to his family, who described him as "the responsible one".

At the time of his disappearance, sometime in August 2015, it was presumed that Kanagaratnam had gone into hiding, and so he wasn't reported missing by his family at the time. Eventually, his sister posted a notice on Facebook requesting anyone who knew of her brother's whereabouts to get in touch. No one did.

By the time he was killed, 47-year-old Dean Lisowick had fallen under the radar. Known as "Laser" to his many friends, Lisowick was a polite, gentle, artistic young man. As a child, he'd been removed from his single father's care and placed in a foster home in Udora, Ontario. He became a surrogate older brother to one of the other foster children, and together they would explore the creeks of the surrounding countryside. It was a brief, idyllic interlude in a troubled life.

Estranged from his family, he developed mental health problems and drug addiction (crack cocaine), eventually becoming homeless and living on the streets around Toronto's gay village. At other times, he would sofa-surf, sleeping in spare space in friends' houses – but always paying his rent on time. He'd take lowly work such as cleaning and stocking shelves to earn money, but when it came to it he'd also resort to making money as a sex worker. Those who knew him remembered him as a "sweet guy", but "street savvy", not someone likely to end up a victim. He'd unhesitatingly come to the aid of others in need, often volunteering to help out the community with odd jobs.

Lisowick was last seen at a homeless shelter sometime in April 2016. A cousin reported that when she'd last seen him he was making plans to change his life, setting goals, working out how to accomplish them. Friends assumed that he'd decided to do just that – to change his life and move on, like many in the sex business are wont to do. He was never reported missing. Having slipped *under* the radar, now he slipped *off* the radar. Lisowick had been exceptionally handsome in his youth. Now, the ravages of drugs and a hard life had taken their toll. Looking rough and unkempt, he wouldn't seem to have been McArthur's preferred victim-type. Nevertheless, their paths must surely have crossed, for two years later, in 2018, body parts found stashed within the planters found at the Mallory Crescent property were identified as belonging to Lisowick.

By the end of 2016, Project Houston's efforts to find out what had happened to the missing men had stalled. There was no evidence to link the disappearances, and nothing to indicate that any crimes had been committed. It's easy to blame the police for the lack of progress, to accuse them incompetence or lacking commitment, but this would not be accurate. The truth of the matter is that such little progress was made due to the fact that McArthur covered his tracks, and he covered them well. He left no trails of his interactions with the men he murdered, abstaining from using his real name, avoiding using mobile phones (probably using public payphones instead) and, if his victims had a mobile phone, he turned that off too. Additionally, he purposefully never met any of them in areas monitored by CCTV. Furthermore, he targeted men who were low-profile, who were still in the closet, who were drug users or who had no fixed address. That changed with the disappearances of his final victims.

Selim Esen, aged 44, had grown up unhappy being a gay man living in Turkey. He emigrated first to Australia and then to Canada in 2013 to marry his boyfriend. Although the relationship didn't last, Esen remained in Toronto where he managed a café. Friends described him as "full of compassion, wisdom and a desire to help others". He was also said to be independent-minded, deeply curious and philosophical, as well as a romantic who believed in the power of love. With past issues of drug use, Esen had now turned his life around and was hoping to offer support to other recovering addicts. A good friend to many, when Esen uncharacteristically didn't respond to a text during Easter weekend in 2017 he was reported missing. It was said after his vanishing that Esen "was convinced something bad was about to happen".

Andrew Kinsman was an openly gay man who had deep connections within Toronto's busy gay community, working as an activist. Unlike the seven previous known victims, Kinsman was Caucasian. Erudite and intelligent, 49-year-old Kinsman had had more than a passing interest in serial killers (before becoming a victim of one himself). When police later searched his apartment they found on his computer literature and films about infamous serial killers who'd targeted gay men. With profound irony, he was known to have discoursed on the mind-set of serial killers with a friend, and had admitted as much to a colleague (without, unfortunately, mentioning that friend's name).

Kinsman was a champion of social justice. He enjoyed helping others and baking, often combining these two pleasures by baking cakes for others and volunteering at the food bank. He and his best friend would often make weekend road trips and go camping, where they could indulge their love of the outdoors and hiking.

One day after Pride Toronto, 26 June 1997, Kinsman disappeared from Cabbagetown, the central Toronto district where he lived. Two days later, friends gained access to his apartment and discovered no signs of disturbance, although unusually his elderly cat had been left without food and water and Kinsman's medications were still there. Unable to believe that their stable and responsible friend would suddenly leave, they reported him missing.

A new task force – Project Prism – was set up to investigate the disappearances of Esen and Kinsman, and to search for any linkages between these and the missing men of Project Houston. Within 72 hours of Kinsman's vanishing the detectives had some viable leads. In a diary amongst Kinsman's possession the word "Bruce" was written against the date 26 June, the last day Kinsman had been seen. CCTV images of that day showed a person matching Kinsman's description approaching a red 2004 Dodge Caravan. Only five of the 6,000 registered in Toronto belonged to someone called Bruce. On his computer, police found photos of Kinman engaging in home-made porn, and some images labelled "Bruce" which were portraits of a burly white middle-aged male. By early October 1997, the search for the red vehicle and its unidentified owner, "Bruce", had yielded results, which were narrowed down to reveal the name of Bruce McArthur. His now-sold Dodge Caravan was traced to an auto parts business some 40 miles from Toronto. Traces of blood identified as belonging to Kinsman and Esen were found in the vehicle.

Events moved quickly now. Cadaver dogs found nothing at the Mallory Crescent residence where McArthur stored his planters, but a camera was covertly installed to monitor any comings and goings. Police investigators also covertly entered McArthur's apartment and cloned the hard drive of his computer. Forensic analysis of the digital information revealed deleted files and hundreds of graphic photographs of the victims after they'd been killed. Many of the photos had been posed, some of which had the victims naked or wearing fur coats, whilst others had them with cigars placed in their mouths. Most of the victims had been shorn of their hair. Some of the photos clearly showed Kinsman, with a rope connected to a metal bar around his neck, as well as ligature marks around his neck and wrists. Missing posters of three of the victims were also recovered from the deleted files.

In addition to the digital evidence, the detectives retrieved DNA samples from McArthur's pillow and a metal bar found in his property. Trophies from the victims were also found – including jewellery and a notebook.

Armed with this information and a mine of circumstantial evidence, the police began round-the-clock surveillance. They watched as McArthur enjoyed a meal at a café. After he left, they swept in quickly, gaining a sample of his DNA from the plate he'd been using.

On 18 January 2018, they saw a young man enter McArthur's apartment and, believing the young man's life to be at risk, decided they had to intervene. When they entered the apartment they found the man bound to the four-poster bed with tape on his mouth and a black bag over his head. At that point they arrested McArthur.

Police executed search warrants on 18 January and a thorough search of the planters at the Mallory Crescent property later revealed their macabre contents. Ziploc bags full of hair were found in a shed at Mount Pleasant Cemetery, although it's not known if any of it belonged to the victims.

By 16 April 2018, after identifications of all the victims had been made, Bruce McArthur was charged with his eighth count of first-degree murder. Serial killers do not normally commence their disturbing careers late in life, and so it's likely that there are further victims, yet to be uncovered. The investigators were well aware of this, and so the scope of their investigation widened. All of the properties that McArthur had either lived in or worked at – more than 100 in total – were considered potential crime scenes. They currently remain suspicions about the disappearances of other men who fit McArthur's victim-type profile, but so far no discoveries have been made.

On 29 January 2019, in a packed courtroom, McArthur pleaded guilty to each of the eight charges levelled against him, thereby ending the spectre of any trial. He was sentenced to life imprisonment with no possibility of parole for 25 years. Given that the convict is overweight, has type-2 diabetes and would be aged 91 by then, it's unlikely that he will ever be freed. He serves his sentence at Millhaven Institute, a maximum-security facility located in Bath, Ontario, where he is on 24-hour suicide watch. He has shown no remorse for his crimes.

# Stephen Port
(active 2014-2015)

WHEN GRINDR LAUNCHED in 2009, it was one of the first-ever developed geosocial online dating apps for gay men. It has since extended its remit to include lesbian, bisexual, transgender and other service users under an expanded umbrella service to become the most used and most popular gay mobile app in the world. Downloadable for Android and iOS devices, the app is available in both free and premium versions, accounting for its widespread use and appeal. Grindr is not the only dating app available that targets gay men, but with over 3 million active daily users it is definitely the most well-known and most used.

Much of the appeal of Grindr comes from its geolocation function. Members who have signed up to Grindr create a personal profile. Using members' GPS positionings, the user is presented with a list of other members, whose profiles are sorted by proximity to the user. In other words, one Grindr user can check out which other Grindr users may be nearby. Clicking on a profile photo will bring up that member's details, other photos, and the option to send instant messages. Additionally, users may share their precise locations with likeminded users, and if they so wish, decided to meet up in person. Using Grindr, sex is accessible – right at the user's very fingertips – and getting it is quick and easy to arrange.

It is a relatively new phenomenon, but since its inception the practice of arranging to meet strangers, after exchanging only a few words or pictures online, has become normalised. Not only has it become *normal* to talk to strangers, people are now meeting up with them in their own homes. It can be a daunting experience, yet for many who are prepared to do it, the elements of curiosity and trepidation are arousing. Millions use the app every day, and the majority of interactions go without incident – but as the conviction of Stephen Port shows, the so-called "Grindr Killer", the need to be cautious is real.

Little is known of Stephen Port's early years. He was born on 22 February 1975 in Southend-on-Sea, a large coastal town about 40 miles east of central London. His father, Albert, worked as a cleaner for the local council whilst his mother, Joan, was a supermarket cashier. Stephen has a sister, Sharon, three years his elder. When he was one year old, the family moved to a small, semi-detached house in Dagenham in East London, and it was here that he grew up and where his parents continue to live. It is a "rough 'n' ready", tough working-class region dominated by Ford Motor Company's major automotive factory.

As a child, he was said to have been shy and quiet – so much so, in fact, that his school at one stage even thought he might be deaf because he wouldn't speak up in class. He was often bullied at school, and this may have been in part due to the fact that he had an obvious squint to his right eye and wore large, unfashionable spectacles. As a result, he became a friendless loner who retreated into childlike mannerisms and playing with toys, behaviours he continued to do well into adolescence and early adulthood. Certainly, he was withdrawn and found it difficult to engage socially with his peers. If he was diagnosed with autism it is not publicly known, and yet the evidence would suggest that such a diagnosis may be reasonable. The difficulties with social understanding, delayed emotional growth, incapacity to empathise, struggles with connecting to one's peers – they are all indicators of autism, but they do not explain Port's later offences. And there is nothing in his childhood to illuminate the path he took towards his adult self. Other than this, there is little to remark upon Stephen's upbringing. His parents were hardworking and considerate and it seems they treated him and his sister well.

Stephen left school aged 16 with three GCSEs to his name – mathematics, English and art. He enrolled in art college, but was obliged to leave the course as his traditional working-class father couldn't afford the fees. Determined to succeed, however, he plunged into training to become a chef, and at the age of 18 he got his first job.

As a qualified chef, Port now obtained kitchen work at local business events, including weddings, before finding more permanent work with Stagecoach, at its West Ham bus depot, where he cooked for staff. He continued living at the family home with his parents (and would remain there until his 30s), but his coming out as homosexual in his mid-20s caused some friction within the Port household. Neither of his parents was particularly happy with Stephen's declaration about his sexual orientation. His mother, who wanted grandchildren, had a problem with it, but to his sister Sharon it was a non-issue as she "always kind of knew". Whilst his working life as a cook remained unchanged, his private life stayed just that – private. Little is known of his movements and doings in the community during this period of his life as he kept his private life well away from the domain of work. However, friends and neighbours were certainly aware of his sexual inclinations and that he was an active pursuer of men, and thereafter his *specific* sexual preferences became clear: Stephen Port liked young, attractive, boyish-looking men, commonly known in gay circles as "twinks". With some skill, he was able to compartmentalise his quotidian existence, putting on a front to his work colleagues and, to some extent, to his family, whilst maintaining his *other* life outside the confines of the home domicile – that of a sexual predator of young men.

Port had grown into a tall adult of 6'3". He worked out and had a trim, muscular body that many men would be proud of, but he didn't seem comfortable in his own skin. He still found it difficult to make eye contact, and his stride was awkward, almost lumbering. As his thin hair was now balding, he took to wearing a toupée, bought from a specialist hairdresser's in Woolwich, reapplying eyelash glue every six months or so. Unfortunately, as his real hair changed shade, that of the toupée remained the same, and the fact was clearly obvious to anyone who cared to notice it – Port was sporting a wig. Nevertheless, the cosmetic enhancement seemed to give him a jolt of the confidence he was severely lacking.

In 2006, he moved out of the family home to a small flat at

no. 62 Cooke Street, Barking, not far from where he'd grown up. This was the beginning of his spiral downwards into depravity. He became acquainted with a neighbour, Ryan, who'd also just moved into the area, and the two became friends, going out to gay venues together. Port's new-found freedom brought parties and, now that his sexual partners were now able to stay the night, promiscuity. He had an insatiable appetite for young men. He invited Ryan to these parties, often leaving his beaux with him whilst he went out. They would rarely have a good word to say about the older man, describing him as argumentative and difficult, always wanting to be in control.

Port had still retained that eccentric childlike characteristic, often spending time watching cartoons and even going alone to Toys R Us to buy himself items to play with. He took an interest in Transformer figures and lined them up on a shelf above his bed. But he was becoming increasingly promiscuous. He had partners, but he also cheated on those partners, and was also exploitative of them. Still, he struggled at making real, meaningful relationships. He coped better on social media, where he could hide behind the impersonal communication of the keyboard. In 2007, at the age of 32, he met and started a relationship with a 16-year-old youth whom he'd met online. Port made a sex video featuring the teenaged boy and showed it to third parties. The teenager was told about this by another. The relationship dissolved after the teenager discovered Port was being unfaithful.

Port had also started working as a male escort, commanding £165 for a session, But with his looks (and his hair) receding upon his approach to middle age, he began to act as a go-between for sexual liaisons – in other words, he was a pimp. With his next partner, Port would bring his escort clients back to his flat. There, he would expect his partner to join in with group sex activities, and the partner, in order to placate Port, would do so. Later partners, often vulnerable young men, also found themselves in this position – impromptu prostitutes in Port's seedy business. He even began to advertise their wares, including on his escort profiles naked photographs of these unknowing young men as they slept on a bed.

And he began to take drugs. He enjoyed cocaine, but his preference was GHB, a drug which can induce feelings of euphoria.[1] Port began to obsessively search the Internet for information on these drugs. He scoured sites for drug-rape pornography. When police later investigated his browsing habits they were shocked by the depravity they witnessed. Many of these videos involved depictions of men slipping drugs into an unwitting partner's drink. Port re-enacted the stories in real life in his own sinister porn scenarios. His fully-evolved interest now lay in having sex with unconscious young men. In one of his online conversations, he crowed with delight recounting an encounter with a boy which was "like having sex with a rag doll he was so out of it". This shows the dichotomy of Port's existence – a grownup child who liked to play with toy cars, but also an adult addicted to deviant sexual lusts.

By 2012, Port was using the gay dating app Grindr and had started to retreat deeper into the online world. The medium suited him. He was able to exploit the open-ended format of various social media applications to select his victims in privacy. To this end, he uploaded different profiles to a range of social networks, often using made-up names in the construction of entirely fabricated identities and biographies. In one, he claimed to be an Oxford graduate; in another, he stated he'd served in the Royal Navy. He even professed to be a special needs teacher. He routinely took decades off his age and used out-of-date photographs in an attempt to appear younger. A teenage student he encountered later remembered a romantic date gone wrong. He

---

[1] GHB or gamma hydroxybutyrate ($C_4H_8O_3$) is a central nervous system depressant that can, in small doses, lead to feelings of euphoria. In larger amounts it can lead to unconsciousness which, if too much is taken, can result in respiratory failure and death. GHB usually comes in the form of a powder which is dissolved in water prior to administration. It is commonly referred to as a "club drug" or "date rape" drug.

reported being collected by Port at Barking station and that his prospective paramour had been "quite polite, friendly, nothing that would ring any alarm bells". They went back to Port's flat where the host supplied cheap red wine that "tasted bitter". After draining the wine, the student noticed a "sludge in the bottom of the glass". The pair watched an animated film, during which the guest began to feel woozy. Port suggested the student retire to the bedroom, which he did. Immediately the younger man lay on the bed, he passed out.

He came to to the horror of Port raping him. Hardly aware of what was going on, he lapsed again into unconsciousness. In the morning, he awoke feeling disoriented. Too scared to say anything about the previous night's activities, the student let Port drive him to the station, during which he talked "as if nothing had happened".

In 2014, Port met another partner, a Muslim man in his early 20s, on the Fitlads website. As a Muslim, the man was unaccustomed to taking drugs or alcohol. Their first meetings were unremarkable, but on the fifth Port gave him a phial of amyl nitrate to sniff. After doing so, the man fell asleep. When he awoke, Port was standing over him holding a glass of water. Shortly after drinking the liquid the man fell into unconsciousness. He later awoke to find his underwear had been removed.

The man began to scream as panic set in. He told Port he needed to get home. Port brought him to Barking station, helping the almost insensible man who could only walk with an unsteady, wobbly gait. Passers-by thought the man was either drunk or mad. British Transport Police soon attended and someone called for an ambulance. Port, they noted, was "worried and jittery". He told them the young man had arrived at his flat in that state and that he'd been trying to get the man home safely.

The man declined any further police involvement. His strict Muslim family were not aware of his sexuality and he didn't want them discovering it. He didn't make any allegations and so the pair were allowed to leave the scene.

Later that evening, the man phoned Port, wanting answers.

But the more he asked the more Port clammed up. It was almost as if this had been an everyday occurrence for him. When the man found out about subsequent events, he realised he'd been lucky to have escaped with his life, because, two weeks later, Port met another man whose outcome *wasn't* to be as fortunate.

A second-year fashion student at Middlesex University, 23-year-old Anthony Walgate had hopes to become a fashion designer. Anthony was originally from Hull, north England, but came to London to study, renting a room in Golders Green. He occasionally supported himself by working as a male escort, advertising himself on the Sleepyboys website. The aspiring designer was a talented student who was known to be popular amongst his peers. He was blond and slim and he was Stephen Port's type. Friends who knew how Anthony made extra cash said he was "choosy" about which jobs he would commit to, and would turn down clients he felt were risky.

Port met Anthony through the Sleepyboys website and offered him £800 for an "overnight".[2] They agreed to meet at 22:00 on 17 June 2014 and Port picked up Anthony (using the name Jo Dean) at Barking station. Prior to their meeting, Anthony texted a friend with the details of his assignment, ending with a joke: "In case I get killed." As an extra precaution, he said, he was taking with him a pair of scissors.

One can only imagine what went on in Port's flat from that point, but it's likely that Anthony Walgate was raped whilst unconscious or dead. Certainly, he was dead by the time his body was removed from the premises. On 19 June, two days after meeting Port, his body was set on the ground outside the Cooke Street apartment complex, propped up against the wall, with his top pulled up to reveal the midriff. Port himself called the emergency services early that morning, anonymously reporting that

---

[2] Since Port had little savings and no access to £800 in cash, it's possible that he'd already made the decision to murder Walgate.

a young man had "collapsed or had had a seizure or was drunk". Police and an ambulance attended the scene and a doctor pronounced the victim dead shortly before eight o'clock. It was evident that he had died for some hours before. Next to the body was a holdall containing a phial of GHB. Blood work indicated GHB in Walgate's system, at a high enough level to cause intoxication and death.

Police traced Port via the telephone call, entered no. 62 Cooke Street and found him asleep in his bed. He told them that he'd found the body lying unconscious and, thinking the young man had had a seizure, propped him up against the wall. Then he'd returned to his flat where he'd fallen asleep. In his witness statement, he told police that he'd returned home from a nightshift to find a man lying in the doorway, "gurgling". According to his statement, Port "tried to rouse him by slapping his face", and then propped him up before going inside and into bed. All lies!

The incident seemed similar to the previous event which had occurred three weeks ago in the same area involving the same man, Stephen Port. In that case, a Muslim man had also been drugged. The comparisons were somewhat suspicious ...

A week later, Port was arrested after police discovered that he'd hired Anthony as a male escort. His account of the discovery of the body was not believed and two days later he changed his story, saying, "Can I just say for the scenario, if it was an accident, and if he did have a fit in my place, is that still my fault?" Confronted with the evidence against him, Port admitted that he'd met Walgate via an escort site, that they'd taken drugs and that they'd had sex. He stated that after Walgate had put on his clothes to leave he'd suddenly become tired and got into bed fully dressed. According to Port, he'd gone to work, leaving the escort sleeping in the flat, and that when he returned he got into bed beside him. Upon wakening, he found the body cold and stiff and panicked that it would be thought that he'd murdered him. He denied knowing that had happened to Walgate's mobile phone.

Port was charged with perverting the course of justice. His

laptop was seized and his DNA collected. However, evidence connecting him directly to the death was missed by those investigating the incident and so Port, not accused of involvement in the death, was instead released on bail. Had the police examined Port's computer they would've been alarmed by his Internet browsing history on the same day he'd accessed Anthony Walgate's escort profile: "sleeping boy", "unconscious boys", "taking date rape drug", "drugged and raped", "gay teen knocked out raped" and "guy raped and tortured young nude boy".

Gabriel Kovari, a 22 immigrant from Slovakia, was well-educated and spoke good English. He'd left his native home because he felt the people were "conservative and intolerant", finding work in a Slovakian shop in London amid his tour around Europe. He was creative and had ambitions to become a great artist. Tall, young, slender and good-looking, Gabriel was Port's type, and he had the misfortune to catch the older man's eye. Port made his move and soon the two were in a sort-of relationship.

Gabriel had been staying in the spare room of a friend's flat in south London. After several weeks there, he suddenly announced that he'd found another room to rent in Barking and on 23 August he moved out. Three days later, the friend texted Gabriel to ask how things were going in Barking. He never got a response.

Port was in the mood for showing off to Ryan, his neighbour across the road. He texted, inviting Ryan to meet his "new Slovakian twink flatmate". Port proudly showed off Gabriel to Ryan when they met briefly that same night.

Port's feelings of joy were not reciprocated by Gabriel. The next day, Gabriel messaged Ryan: "I'm not happy at Stephen's. Stephan is not a good man." He didn't elaborate further, but something had made him unhappy in his new home. He was sleeping on the sofa and no longer wanted to sleep in the same bed as Port. Ryan allowed Gabriel to stay at his place for a while whilst he sought alternative accommodation.

The following day, Port received a message from Ryan

asking, "How is Gabriel?" Port sent a reply: "He's gone to stay with another local guy ... some soldier guy he had been chatting to online". In all likelihood Gabriel was by now already dead.

On 28 August 2014, a woman walking her dog in the grounds of St Margaret's Church on Broadway, Barking found a body, about two hundred yards from Stephen Port's apartment complex. The young male had been propped in an upright position in the southwest corner of the churchyard wall. He was wearing his sunglasses and two bags beside him contained his few possessions. Like Anthony Walgate, the young man's top was pulled up to reveal the midriff. He was soon to be identified as Gabriel Kovari. As he was found to have traces of GHB in his system, police deemed his death to be non-suspicious.

By dreadful coincidence, less than a month later, the same woman walking her dog found another body in the same churchyard. Like Gabriel Kovaria, this body belonged to a good-looking young white male of slim build, and when discovered he too was in propped-up position.

Daniel Whitworth was a 21-year-old from Graveshead, Kent who was passionate about cooking and enjoyed working as a chef in the London business centre of Canary Wharf. He loved life, the outdoors and exploring the countryside on his bicycle. Furthermore, Daniel was an openly gay man who'd lived with his long-term boyfriend in Kent for the past three years. When Daniel failed to return, his partner raised the alarm.

Daniel was last seen leaving Canary Wharf on 18 September 2014 after having mentioned to a work colleague that he was going to meet up with a friend in Barking. What happened after he arrived only Stephen Port knows. What *is* known is that by the next morning Daniel's Fitboys account had been deleted.

When found, Daniel's body was leaning against the graveyard wall atop a blue bedspread, and his top was raised, exposing the midriff. It seemed that Daniel's body had been dragged into position. The top he wore was later identified as having belonged to Gabriel Kovari. Daniel's mobile phone was missing, but found along with his body were found a phial of GHB and a handwritten note.

> *I am sorry to everyone, mainly my family but I can't go on anymore, I took the life of my friend Gabriel Kline, we was just having some fun at a mates [sic] place and I got carried away and gave him another shot of G I didn't notice while we was having sex that he had stopped breathing. I tried everything to get him to breath [sic] again but it was too late, it was an accident but I blame myself for what happened and I didn't tell my family I went out. I know I would go to prison if I go to police and I can't do that to my family and at least this way I can at least be with Gabriel again, I hope he will forgive me.*
>
> *BTW. Please do not blame the guy I was with last night, we only had sex then I left, he knows nothing of what I have done. I have taken what g I have left with sleeping pills so if it does kill me it's what I deserve. Feeling dizey [sic] now as took 10 min ago so hoping you understand my writing.*
>
> *I dropped my phone on way here so it should be in the grass somewhere. Sorry to everyone.*
>
> *Love always*
> *Daniel P W.*

Those who knew Daniel were appalled – both at the suggestion that he'd killed someone, and that he'd ended his own life. The note suggested that he'd been responsible for the death of "Gabriel" whilst also attempting to rule out the possibility of any other individual being responsible (*"Do not blame the guy I was with last night ... he knows nothing of what I have done"*). The police failed to fully check the handwriting on the note purportedly written by Daniel; they didn't investigate his movements in the hours preceding his death; nor did they attempt to trace the "guy I was with last night", referred to in the note. Had they done so, the trail would've led them straight to Stephen Port's door, and DNA on the blue bedspread, which was already on the police database, would've directly implicated him in a crime.

It later transpired that Daniel had connected with Port on the Fitlads website in the month before he died. He was Port's type. Port had asked him to go for a drink before dinner at his Barking flat, adding, "Just so you can get to know me a bit so you know I'm not some psycho."

The autopsy recorded evidence of bruising around Daniel's armpits, consistent with having been manually handled, possibly _post mortem_. Nevertheless, detectives deemed the death "unusual and slightly confusing", but not, evidently, suspicious. Confirmation that he'd ingested GHB – as well as sleeping tablets – validated their belief that the death had been the tragic suicide of a guilt-ridden man. Stephen Port seemed to have got away with it again.

His murder spree was interrupted by jailtime. On 23 March 2015, Port was convicted and sentenced to eight months in prison for perverting the course of justice (due to his varying accounts concerning the death of Anthony Walgate). He served half the sentence and was released on licence in June, having been electronically tagged.

Jack Taylor was a 25-year-old man from Dagenham, east London who lived with his parents and worked as a forklift truck operator. A young man who wanted to make a difference, Jack volunteered alongside St John's Ambulance, raised money for charities and donated blood. He was said to have loved life and was always laughing. Although he'd had girlfriends, Daniel, was actually gay and in the closet. He was youthful-looking. He was Stephen Port's type.

In the early hours of 13 September 2015, Jack left the local social club where he'd been drinking and went home. There, he logged into Grindr and in due course was contacted by Port. They agreed to get together and Jack left his house, meeting his new friend at 03:00 at Barking station.

The circumstances surrounding the finding of his body were uncannily similar to two previously discovered bodies just a year ago. Jack had been propped up against the wall in St

Margaret's Church graveyard and his shirt was pulled up. He had no mobile phone, but there was a syringe in one pocket and a phial of liquid in the other. The death was treated by police as an accidental overdose. Jack's family didn't buy that conclusion. They initiated their own research and uncovered a shocking catalogue of police failings that included ineptitude, flagrantly disinterested attitudes and botched investigative procedures.

Little did Jack Taylor's family know that Gabriel Kovari's unhappy flatmate had already begun his own investigation. It wasn't long before he noticed the pattern of deaths near and around St Margaret's Church in Barking. Alarm bells were ringing. Further research brought up the name "Jon Luck", who admitted to having spent the night with Kovari, expressed surprise at hearing that he'd died, and gave the information that Gabriel had been collected by an older Irish man called Tony driving a green Toyota. "Will the police want to speak to me as my DNA would be on him [Kovari]?" Jon Luck asked.

The man called Jon Luck then contacted the Internet sleuths with a message:

> *I text him and asked what happene [sic] to Gab and he said h [sic] left with a young guy about his age named Dan and they was heading to a party/orgy in Barking ... Dan is tall, light brown hair he said, loks [sic] similar to Gab just a bit taller, very slim, when I told him Gab is dead, he said he don't want anything to do with it, leave him alone.*

"Jon Luck" was actually Stephen Port, and it looked as if he'd been trying to pin the blame for Kovari's murder on Daniel Whitmore a second time. Desperate to cover up his tracks, Port continued spinning more and more lies, creating a tangled web of deceit he was finding it difficult to maintain.

Collective pressure from various interested parties was put on the police – and the coroner – to take the matter more seriously. Inevitably, when the police decided to trace the messages they came back to Port and truth started to emerge at last. Once the police had accepted that they had a series of homicides and a viable suspect they began dig deeper. On 13 October 2105, they issued a CCTV screenshot of Jack Taylor near Barking station with a lanky man with blond hair. It was Stephen Port. Two days later he was arrested for causing death by administering poison. He was interviewed over the next four days, during which he continued to lie, denying knowledge of the deaths. Daniel Whitworth's handwriting was eventually analysed and it bore no resemblance to the "suicide note". Its author was Port, and the paper upon which it was written was traced to Port's flat. DNA belonging to the dead men was found at Port's flat. A mobile phone owned by Port was found to contain over 80 homemade porn videos, including videos of himself sodomising unconscious men.

In court, Port no longer looked anything like his online profile photographs. Gone was the too-blond toupée, and the shuffling, mumbling defendant – pale and prematurely balding, with pockmarked skin and a thin, ill-kempt moustache – looked a decade older than his 41 years.

He gave an admission, of sorts: "The truth sounded like a lie, so I lied to make it sound like the truth." But it was an implausible truth, jumbled up with utter fabrication. He admitted to writing Kovari's "suicide note", alleging that it had been dictated by Whitmore. He stated that Taylor, known to be a modest non-drug user, had indulged in a marathon drug-fuel sex session. Again, more lies!

On 23 November 2016, Port was convicted of four counts of rape and murder, as well as other rapes and sexual assaults. The crimes were devious and planned. They were committed purely in order to satisfy Port's unquenchable lust for anally penetrating unconscious men. And he didn't have to travel far to find his victims; he simply turned on his phone and logged into a dating app. There was little to be offered by way of mitigation. Port was sentenced to imprisonment with a whole-life order, a rare tariff shared by the likes of Ian Brady and Myra Hindley, Ian

Huntley, Dennis Nilsen, Colin Ireland, Rosemary West and Harold Shipman. He was taken away to HMP Belmarsh, Britain's high security unit near Woolwich. Stephen Port, who came to be known as "The Grindr Killer", will die in prison.

Following the conviction, the police issued a short statement describing the convicted man. Said Detective Chief Inspector Tim Duffield of Port:

*"He's a voracious sexual predator who appears to have been fixated, nay obsessed, with surreptitiously drugging young, often vulnerable men for the exclusive purpose of rape. This is a highly devious, manipulative and self-obsessed individual."*

Port might not necessarily agree; he has yet to show any remorse for his crimes.

# Dishonourable Mentions

# Michele del Marco Lupo
(active 1986)

THE WORLD WAS HIS OYSTER. He had a thriving business and a wealthy clientele list; he was fit, young, handsome; and his sex-life was one that many gay men would admire and envy. But when his life began to unravel it did so abruptly, rapidly and savagely – and there was simply no going back.

Michele del Marco Lupo came into the world on 19 January 1953 in Genzano di Lucania, northern Italy. As a child he was known to be creative and especially talented at art. From a winsome youngster who sang in the church choir, he grew up to be an admirable man with fine facial features and a lean, fit body. After leaving school, he took a correspondence course in languages before being drafted into the army to complete his two years' obligatory national service, ending up in an elite commando unit. There, amongst other skills, he learned to kill with his bare hands. During this time, he discovered his preference for sex with men, indulging his enormous appetite for sex wherever he went. With his handsome looks he had no difficulty seducing many of the gay men who crossed his path. On his travels, he discovered a partiality for sadomasochism, and in his sex games he developed a fondness for playing the dominant role. With no shortage of sexual partners, he was able to boast that over the years he'd bedded more than 4,000 men, the details of which he recorded in his numerous journals.

Leaving the Italian military unit, Lupo made his way to London, England in 1975. Now aged 21, he soon found work as a hairdresser. When he was able to do so he opened up his own salon, a boutique that catered for well-to-do society gentlemen who were keen to conceal their sexuality. The establishment did well, attracting many men who were rich, vain … and available. Lupo was soon attending to many of their sexual needs as well as their styling requirements. With his good looks and body, he realised he could use these to his economic advantage and advertised himself as a sadomasochist who'd service gay men. For three years, he flogged and smacked and applied nipple clamps. Business was brisk and before long he was able to buy himself an expensive home in Roland Gardens in upmarket South Kensington.

Here, he built an underground torture chamber, complete with black-pointed walls, where he was able execute his deviant sadomasochistic business and desires in privacy and comfort. Trawling London's bars, looking for a pretty face, he would bring them back home to his underground chamber. He would rarely spend the night alone, bedding men insatiably. Often his "dates" left the next morning with incision marks, bruises, bloody noses and the marks of strangulation around their necks. How consensual these men were to this treatment is not known; less so is how much they enjoyed the suffering at the hands of the handsome Italian stud. Aside from being fined £40 after being caught sodomising a man in a public toilet in 1977, life for Lupo was good.

Then, in the 1980s, the spectre of AIDS reared its head. Gay men became more aware of the dangers of promiscuous sex. Word was also getting out that Lupo was too sadistic even for willing BSM clients. Hence the custom for Lupo's sex trade dried up. He was obliged to find work as a sales assistant at the Yves Saint Laurent boutique on Brompton Road. His fortunes revived and he eventually became the store's manager, a post which brought him in touch with wealthy admirers. Once again, Lupo was sleeping around with abandon. Life was looking good again, until something unknown happened which caused Lupo to depart his store manager's post and take a lowly-paid store assistant job. Life went downhill fast.

In early March 1986, at the age of 34, Lupo received earth-shattering news: he was diagnosed as HIV-positive. For many, this would have ended (or at least curtailed) their sexual careers. Not Lupo. The news enraged him. The inner monster emerged and the men he encountered were now at *even greater* peril as he began to fantasise about torturing and killing his sex partners.

Lupo met 31-year-old Kevin MacDonagh at the Coleherne pub in Earl's Court on 10 March 1986. Utilising the colour-coded accessory system (of handkerchiefs and gloves) known to the patrons of that bar, the two picked up each other's signals and were attracted to each other. They left together for their agreed liaison, going to the basement of a nearby derelict building. Immediately they got there, Lupo wound a scarf around MacDonagh's neck and strangled him until it appeared he was lifeless before stealthily slipping away. After an hour, Mac-Donagh revived and stumbled home. He never reported the incident to the police.

Five nights later, on 15 March 1986, Lupo returned to the Coleherne. Here, he openly masturbated in the toilets before engaging in conversation with a lonely 37-year-old man, James Burns, who'd been diagnosed as HIV-positive only two weeks before. They agreed to repair to a derelict flat in Kensington.

There, Burns was bitten, beaten about the head and slashed with a razor. Lupo also attempted to gouge Burns' eyes out before strangling him with a scarf or a sock. As he died, Burns lost control of his bowels, and Lupo smeared the man's own excrement over his corpse. In a final act of defilement, he also bit off the man's tongue and threw it across the room.

The body was found the next day by vagrants. As no connection could be found between Burns and any potential suspect the police investigation stalled.

On 4 April 1986, Lupo arrived at the Prince of Wales pub in Brixton where he met 26-year-old Anthony Connolly, who was wearing ripped jeans that exposed the pink tights he had on beneath. At around 01:00, the two men left and made their way to a nearby railway line. There, Connolly dropped his trousers in the hope of a romantic encounter. Lupo had other ideas: he punched Connolly, bit his chest, chewed his penis and finally strangled him to death with the same sock or scarf he'd used on MacDonagh. After the killing, he went socialising at a nightclub.

Connolly's body, smeared with excrement, was found by local

children the next day. It was a carbon-copy homicide of the murder of MacDonagh. When the coroner discovered that Connolly had lived with a man who was infected with HIV they delayed the autopsy. Understandably, this created tensions between police and the gay community, who accused the police of not taking their safety seriously enough.

After leaving a gay bar on 18 April, Lupo impulsively slaughtered an elderly tramp on Hungerford Bridge, kicking him in the groin and strangling him to death before tossing the body over the railings and into the waters of the Thames.

The next day, Lupo approached 22-year-old Mark Leyland at Charing Cross station.[1] The two agreed to go to a derelict outbuilding to have a sexual liaison. Whilst Leyland was fellating Lupo, he had an instinct that he was in danger. He was right. As the younger man disengaged his mouth, Lupo suddenly punched him about the head. Lupo then left the building, grabbed a plank of wood and began beating Leyland with it through the open window. When Leyland fell to the ground unconscious, his attacker left.

Leyland later revived and reported the incident to the police, omitting the sexual nature of the encounter. Somewhat understandably, the police treated it as a mugging, but with little information to go on the investigation drew a blank.

Lupo went out to kill again on 25 April, and this time he succeeded. He met 24-year-old Damien McCluskey at the Copacabana club on Earl's Court Road and struck up a conversation. The pair left, and Lupo directed him towards a derelict building. There, McCluskey fellated Lupo who reciprocated by slashing the man with a razor, raping him and strangling him to death with a ligature. The disintegrating remains were found in the

---

[1] Hungerford Bridge spans the Thames between the Charing Cross and Waterloo railway stations. It's possible that Lupo was in the area to check on the status of the murder he'd committed the night before.

building three weeks later.

Less than two weeks later, the urge to kill grew again. A second time Lupo botched the attempt. His victim escaped. He gave a good account of the handsome man who'd tried to strangle him with a pair of black tights, and he and a police escort toured the gay bars in order to identify the culprit. The victim spotted his would-be murderer on 15 May and Michele Lupo was arrested at last.

He confessed, sparing the need for a lengthy trial. He gave himself a nickname – "The Wolf Man" (*lupo* is the Italian word for wolf). The Press anglicised his name to Michael. At the Old Bailey, in July 1987, he pleaded guilty and was sentenced to four life sentences for murder, plus 14 years for the two attempted murders. The adjourning judge recommended that "life means life". It did. On 12 February 1995, at the age of 42, Michele del Marco Lupo died in the hospital of HMP Frankland Prison, Durham of AIDS-related complications. He had shown no remorse for his crimes.[2]

---

[2] Whilst living the high life, Lupo had visited various cities, including Los Angeles, New York, Hamburg and Berlin. These were all places in which young gay men had been found dead, their bodies mutilated and putrefying. Although their deaths have not been conclusively linked to Lupo, he remains a suspect. Interpol continues to investigate similar killings around the world.

# Steven John Grieveson
(active 1990-1994)

THE METAPHOR "coming out of the closet" might be viewed as an evolution of the "skeleton in the closet" metaphor. Non-heterosexual individuals often feel confused and experience turmoil as they begin to come to terms with their sexuality; they can believe that those in society view their homosexuality as something shameful to be hidden away (the *skeleton*), and that revealing their secret (*coming out*) can only result in a backlash of rejection and discrimination. They believe that it can only lead to a life of misery, shame and loneliness. As a consequence, some gay individuals can be very reluctant to disclose their sexual orientation; their closet door must stay closed … at any cost.

Steven John Grieveson was born on 14 December in Sunderland, North East England, one of seven siblings. He was a quiet and self-conscious child but also a naturally gifted footballer. Neighbours knew the household as "troublesome". Certainly, it was a violent household, his mother Cathy reported, and accordingly the relationship with Steven's father didn't last. Cathy would later state that Steven had been a "mammy's boy" and "a good little boy" up until the age of 11; that was when he first started to get into trouble.

By this time, it is believed, Cathy was a single parent. She found it difficult to be available to care for the children, preferring to go to bingo instead. Because of this (and also due to the fact that Steven had got into trouble before and had been cautioned by the police), when he was found to have stolen (the item in question was a single nail) he was removed from the family under a Care Order and sent to a children's home in Carlisle, there to remain until he was aged 18.

Contemporary reports described him as having "no insight into his behaviour", casting him as an "emotionless boy who appears to have a couldn't care less attitude … a nervous, insecure boy who has little stability from his background or from within himself", adding that "he has a very low opinion of himself".

Soon he was sniffing glue on a daily basis. He found himself getting into exploitative situations in which he would masturbate older men for money, whilst also having feelings of wanting to be the *exploiter* of these men by taking their money. During later psychological counselling, Grieveson would allege that as a child he'd been sexually abused by an older male, as well as being gang-raped. The Carlisle children's home subsequently closed down following allegations that physical and sexual abuse had taken place there. Later psychiatric evaluation would identify Steven as having a personality of psychopathic traits marked by emotionlessness, callousness and remorselessness. It's difficult to ascertain to what extent the regime there had on its residents but it's unlikely to have been entirely constructive.

When Grieveson turned 18 and returned home from Carlisle he was still able to get himself into trouble. He was smoking cannabis and sniffing glue, and soon the police were making regular trips to the Grievesons' front door with enquiries about burglaries and stolen cars. It wasn't long before he got his first spell in prison, and then another, and then another … Life on the straight and narrow was not for Steven Grieveson.

With his regular features and strawberry-blond hair he could easily have been described as a good-looking young man. He had relationships with girls but they didn't make him happy and they never lasted long. It was all an act. Sunderland's working-class Roker area, in Grieveson's mind anyway, was not a place to come out as gay. In May 1990, after playing football, he met Simon Martin, a 14-year-old boy. Simon had left his home to go play with friends a few hours earlier. Grieveson lured Simon to a derelict building. There, Grieveson (now a 19-year-old man) and Simon performed a sex act. Afterwards, Grieveson got scared and pleaded with Simon not to tell anyone about it. Simon said he wouldn't tell, but for some reason Grieveson didn't believe him. He started to shout at the boy and then, whether it was rage or a blind panic that drove him, he battered the boy to death, smashing his skull in with a large piece of rubble. Another boy was charged with the murder, but the case against the innocent individual was later dropped. Nevertheless, at the time, Grieveson said nothing. He only admitted to the crime in February 2013, denying murder and claiming diminished responsibility for his actions.

On 26 November 1993, Thomas Kelly, aged 18, was strangled with a scarf and his body set alight in an allotment shed near to his home. When found, it was still burning and a can of lighter fuel and glue was beside it. On 4 February 1994, the charred remains of David Hanson, aged 15, were found in similar circumstances in a derelict house in Roker Terrace. Three weeks later, the remains of David Grieff, aged 15, were found on an allotment, just 50 yards from where Thomas Kelly's body had been found.

All three boys had been pupils of Monkwearmouth Academy, and naturally suspicion grew that the perpetrator had also gone to that school and had known the victims. It was a faulty line of enquiry. Before going into care, Grieveson had gone to Hylton Red House School in Sunderland.

Grieveson was eventually arrested on 11 March 1994 after making a schoolboy error: he returned to the scene of the crime and attempted to break into the derelict house on Roker Terrace where David Hanson's charred remains had been found. A DNA profile of semen found in Hanson's mouth and stomach matched Grieveson's. By November of following year, he was charged with the three latter murders and in January 1996 he stood trial. By now the Press had dubbed him "The Sunderland Strangler" and the sexuality he'd sought to hide was the subject of television news headlines and splashed across all the front pages.

The prosecution argued that Grieveson was a homosexual either "unable or unwilling to accept his sexuality". They reasoned that he'd killed the three youths for either of two reasons: "to prevent them from revealing that he had demonstrated his sexual preference to them" or that he was "simply because he enjoyed killing them and firing their bodies".

Grieveson didn't give evidence in his own defence, but the court heard that he claimed the murders had been accidental and that he'd killed them unintentionally whilst threatening the victims not to report that he was bisexual. The jury weren't fooled. He was found guilty of the three counts of murder and given three life sentences The presiding judge ordered that the "plain evil" killer serve at least 35 years. He is currently incarcerated at HMP Full Sutton in the East Riding of Yorkshire, England. He'd gone to extraordinary and terrible lengths in an attempt to keep his homosexuality a secret. He failed.

# Gary Ray Bowles
(active 1994)

SOME SERIAL KILLERS, knowing that the bodies will soon be found, "sign" their works with macabre identifiers. They might position the corpse for degrading exposure, tie ligatures with a curious knot, lacerate or stab the body in a particularly individual or rit- ualistic manner. Albert DeSalvo left his victims exposed – sometimes spread-eagled; other times kneeling over, their bare buttocks elevated. Randy Kraft staged his victims with a tree branch forcibly thrust into the rectum. Charles Albright de- tached the eyes of three prostitutes with such surgical precision that it soon became clear the killings were linked. These "signa- tures" are designed to further punish and desecrate the victims, and to establish *even more control* over them *post mortem*. But the killer is thinking ahead; he also wants induce shock and re- vulsion in those who find the body. Bowles, a one-time prosti- tute turned brutaliser, was one such serial killer.

Born on 25 January 1962 in Clifton Forge, Virginia, Gary Ray Bowles would be raised in Rupert, West Virginia. He was the second of two sons to Frank and Frances Bowles. Frank, a coal miner, had died six months prior to Gary's birth and his mother later remarried. Gary's early childhood was relatively unevent- ful – up until the point his mother remarried. When Gary was around the age of seven his first stepfather began to abuse him. His mother married a second time. Her next spouse turned out to be an even more abusive man, who was violent to both of his stepsons, flying into alcohol-induced rages and beating them with his fists or a belt. When their mother tried in intervene, she too suffered attacks that resulted in hospitalisation on more than one occasion. Meanwhile, Gary began to sniff glue and experi- ment with drugs. At the age of 12, he dropped out of school. The abuse continued unabated until finally, at the age of 13, Gary and his brother fought back, seriously injuring their stepfather by smashing a rock onto his head, nearly killing him.

Gary's mother decided to remain with her second husband. That's when her younger son decided to leave home.

As a good-looking teenage boy and then young adult living on the streets, Gary was able to provide for himself by hustling, engaging in homosexual activity with older men, earning just enough to get by. He would always deny that he was homosexual and that he'd engaged in same-sex activities strictly for pay. He always prohibited actual intercourse and, according to his own admission, only ever received oral sex from the men he encountered. His true interest lay in women. He had girlfriends and lived with some of them for a time. These were mostly unsuccessful relationships, marred by brutality. One of Bowles' girlfriends was subjected to bites, battery and choking as well as receiving internal damage to her vagina and rectum. The woman's bedroom, a crime scene, exhibited blood spattering on the ceiling above her bed. It was evidence enough of Bowles' violent nature. For these attacks, he was sentenced to eight years imprisonment in 1982.

He was released in 1990, manifestly unrehabilitated. Shortly afterwards, the unconcerned recidivist was stealing cars. He also attacked an elderly woman, pushing her over violently whilst stealing her handbag. Sentenced to four years' incarceration, he was released after two.

Bowles' killing career started in Daytona Beach, Florida on 15 March 1994. Fifty-nine-year-old John Hardy Roberts was an insurance salesman who'd met Bowles at a popular gay bar. He offered Bowles a temporary place to stay at his beachfront home. It's believed that Bowles provided sexual services as part of the arrangement. According to Bowles' own account, however, after staying there for two weeks the two fell into a dispute over a woman. "Make up your mind. It's me or her," was Roberts' ultimatum. Bowles, flying into a sudden rage, grabbed a glass lamp and battered Roberts about the head. Roberts, falling over a coffee table in an attempt to escape, was overpowered by his assailant, who strangled him to death on the spot. Such was the level of violence that one of Roberts' fingers was almost

427

severed.

Before leaving the scene, Bowles stuffed a rag down Roberts' throat. He escaping in his victim's car, having also stolen his wallet and credit cards.

Roberts' putrefying remains were found a month later, on 14 April, by a friend who'd been unable to contact him. He called the police. It was quickly clear from the disarray of the room, as well as the widespread blood spattering, that a violent struggle had taken place. The rag stuffed into Roberts' mouth provided further proof of his killer's rage. The potential suspect had left evidence in the aftermath which pointed in his direction: fingerprints in blood and probation papers, as well as records of phone calls made to Bowles' family from the victim's home. The escape car was eventually found in Georgia but there was no sign of Bowles. Unbeknownst to them, he'd already made his way northwards.

On the same day that police discovered the body of John Roberts, a maintenance man in Silver Spring, Maryland found the decomposing remains of David Jarman, a 39-year-old loan officer. He'd last been seen leaving a local gay bar with a man resembling Bowles. When found, he was lying dead in a pool of his own blood. A sex toy had been forcibly shoved into his throat cavity.

On 5 May, the decaying remains of 72-year-old Milton Bradley, were found behind a shed at a golf club. Bradley was a World War II veteran who'd suffered a shrapnel injury and later underwent a lobotomy which changed his personality and made him vulnerable. He was known to his neighbours in Savannah, Georgia as a "kind, gentle old man" who enjoyed feeding pigeons in the park. He'd met Bowles at a gay bar where they spent the night shooting pool.

Bowles offered to drive Bradley home. Instead, he took a detour. At the golf course, he went into a blitz, beating the elderly man to death with a discarded toilet and shoving leaves down his throat. Police described the action as an "overkill".

The next kill took place eight days later, over 250 miles away in Atlanta, Georgia. Alverson Carter Jr., a 47-year-old gay man, was found fatally stabbed on 13 May, several days after the murder. The murder scene resembled those of the other murders and bore the signs of the now familiar *M.O.* The FBI believed the crime was linked to the others in the spree. Forensic evidence later confirmed it.

Moving onwards to Florida, there Bowles killed a 37-year-old convenience store owner, Albert Morris, savagely beating him with a marble dish and shooting him in the chest. He "signed" the gruesome death by stuffing a towel into Morris' mouth. After this, Bowles assumed another identity, Timothy Whitfield, whilst he went on the run for four months, even serving time in jail for a minor transgression which Whitfield had committed.

By November 1994, he was on the FBI's 10 most wanted list of fugitives. Walter Jamelle "Jay" Hinton, a 42-year-old florist, would become the final victim of Bowles's spree. Hinton offered "Whitfield" a place to stay in his mobile home. On 16 November, he and Hinton had been drinking and smoking marijuana. Hinton retired to bed whilst Bowles stayed up drinking. At some point, something in Bowles just "snapped". He went outside and got an 18kg concrete block. Moments later, he dropped it onto Hinton's head as he lay sleeping, fracturing the jaw. Hinton awoke, stunned, and tried to get off the bed, but Bowles strangled him before stuffing toilet paper and a rag down the dead man's throat. He remained in the home for two days with the body (even at one stage bringing back a homeless woman, who remained unaware of the body inside) before stealing Hinton's car and disappearing to a Jacksonville Beach motel.

Hinton's body was found in the mobile home by day labourers, strangled and stabbed. They knew that "Whitfield" had been living with Hinton and they informed the police. When he was picked up by the police, Bowles told then, "Look, I'm tired of this. Do you want to know who I really am?" He quickly confessed, giving the reason for the final killing as "it was time to move on". He also stated that a girlfriend had terminated her pregnancy after learning that he was a sex worker, and as a consequence he blamed homosexuals for the abortion.

As Bowles had made a full confession, court proceedings now moved apace. The state prosecutor argued that the crimes had been committed for financial gain, the targets being gay men, for whom Bowles allegedly held a great hatred. Defence arguments that Bowles' actions were the result of ingestion of alcohol and marijuana secondary to being abused as a child counted for little. He was sentenced to death for three counts of murder.

After decades of legal wrangling, on 22 August 2019, Gary Ray Bowles, who is sometimes referred to as "The I-95 Killer" due to the fact that most of his victims lived close to that highway, enjoyed a calorific last meal of three cheeseburgers, French fries and bacon before his execution by lethal injection at the age of 57. His last words were a written statement, released from beyond the grave: "You don't wake up one day and decide to become a serial killer."

# Peter Howard Moore

(active 1995)

SERIAL MURDERERS DON'T NORMALLY wake up one morning with a new-found urge to torture and kill. The compulsion within them has usually been nurtured over many, many years, stemming from incidents or situations that occurred much earlier in their past. In the case of Peter Moore, that impulse probably was stimulated by the fractured relationship he had with his disapproving, alcoholic, homophobic father.

Peter Howard Moore was born on 19 September 1946 in St Helens, a large town in Merseyside, England. The small family of parents Ernie and Edith and their only child Peter moved to the small coastal village of Kinmel Bay in Cowny, North Wales when Peter was still a young child. It was a pleasant rural area, buoyed by tourism in the summer but becoming much quieter once the season had passed. The town itself didn't amount to much; other than some run-of-the-mill houses, there was little more than a chip shop, a post office and a newsagents, all surrounded by fields. The Moore family, however, moved into a grand, custom-built building on St Asaph Avenue called Darlington House, which made an imposing presence in the town. Beneath the house, on the street-front, was the shop, a hardware store that was run by Ernie. It provided good business and what would've been viewed by others as a privileged life for the Moores.

Edith doted on young Peter, whom she called her "miracle son" based upon the fact that he'd arrived when she was in her 40s when she thought she wouldn't be able to have children. She loved him unconditionally, often sticking up for him against her husband. Edith didn't have much affection for Ernie, however. Neither did there appear to be much love lost between Ernie and his wife or, for that matter, between father and son. Ernie dedicated himself to the successful business. Previously a military man, he liked to run things in a certain way. He also liked to drink, and could often be seen swallowing the odd snifter of whiskey during his day's work in the shop. Sometimes the odd snifter would turn into a sizeable amount, and it wasn't unknown for Ernie to be quite drunk on duty.

Living in one of the area's most prestigious homes, Peter possibly began to develop feelings that he was better than the other boys of the town, who lived in smaller houses. He may even have developed a delusion of grandeur. He certainly found it difficult to relate to his peers, and he struggled to make friends. On the other hand, it was obvious to others from an early age that Peter was odd and effeminate. He was not at all like the other boys in the village. The difference was clear to them and consequently they treated him differently. What's more, Peter's father could see his son's camp mannerisms. He grew suspicious that Peter was gay and he couldn't tolerate this. He made it clear that he would've preferred a manlier son. He'd often reprimand Peter harshly, and in the outside community rumours began to fly that there was violence within the Moore household. Whether these rumours were true or not, Peter began to resent his father, the hard-drinking, domineering bully who'd eventually become the source, and the symbol, of his anger.

As he grew older, Peter developed an interest in filmmaking. He owned a Super 8 camera, in those days an expensive home-movie camera, undoubtedly one of the few in the area. With his camera he would immerse himself in making films, and inevitably the star of the show was his mother. He'd produce films of himself declaring undying love to her, bounding towards her with bouquets of flowers and a huge smile on his face.

He still couldn't tell her about his sexuality: this was the 1960s, a time when homosexuality in the UK was illegal and any sexual activity between men had to be done in secret. It's not known if Moore indulged in sexual activity at this period. However, his passion for cinema continued to grow, and by now he'd joined a group of film buffs to watch "B" movies. His entrepreneurial side emerged, and he took over and began to manage small, local cinemas, renovating them but still maintaining the "old-style" feel. By now, he was dressing entirely in black. He would tell people that this was the traditional mode of dress of the theatre worker, but the truth of it was that he wore such garb outside the auditorium also. The softly spoke giant (his stature was now well in excess of six feet) projected a positive image of himself in the local community, and he was looked upon as some sort of saviour of the cinema industry. He set up a Saturday cinema club for youngsters that proved very popular and he expanded his business to include a chain of four cinemas in North Wales. He appeared on television to promote his love of cinema. His neighbours thought of him as conventional, easy-going and courteous. They were mistaken.

It was around this time that he began to scour the area far and wide, searching for men to attack and rape. He did so with impunity. Wearing all black, Moore would carry a knife or truncheon and target men, going to specific areas where he knew homosexual men congregated. He did this for over a decade, going to gay meeting places wearing his Nazi-style cap, coat and leather boots, searching for men to dominate and take them – willingly or otherwise – as his lover. With his height, black costume and disagreeable face he cut an imposing presence.

Ernie died sometime in the late 1980s and Moore now became an openly gay man, visiting gay nightspots whilst living in Darlington House with his elderly mother. Then, in 1993, tragedy struck: his beloved mother passed away. When his two dogs, his cat and some koi fish also died, he began to feel an unusual sense of peace. He would later comment: "Death seemed to be literally following me," He became fixated, in 1995, with the film _Friday the 13th_ and its fictional antihero, Jason Voorhees. Moore was approaching his 50th year. As a birthday treat, he bought himself a gift – a combat knife. It wasn't long before the killing spree started – once a month over a period of four months.

Henry Roberts was a retired railway working living in semi-squalor on an isolated farmhouse. The harmless 56-year-old man wasn't found immediately. In September 1995, his body was discovered dumped in the farmyard. His pet Labrador was found safe but trapped inside the house. Roberts had been subjected to 27 stab wounds in a violent, frenzied attack, many of them in the groin and buttocks.[1] Police could find no motive for the attack.

Edward Carthy was last seen in a Liverpool gay bar in October that year. The 28-year-old man who had problems with addiction met his assailant there and the pair drove to a dense forest near Ruthin, North Wales, where Carthy was horribly mutilated in the groin area and killed.

A month later in November, Keith Randles, a 49-year-old traffic manager, went missing after going to buy fish and chips. His body was found the next morning outside the caravan on the construction site where he'd been working. He'd been stabbed to death, many of the wounds in the groin.

Anthony "Tony" Davies was a 40-year-old married man and father-of-two who'd gone to Pensarn Beach in Abergele, known as a cruising spot for gay men. Peter Moore happened to be in the vicinity at the time. Moore later alleged that when they met Davies had his trousers around his ankles, exposing himself. Moore stabbed his victim to the point of death six times and left the body on the beach.

The police opened a confidential hot-line for information. One name kept coming up as a suspect: Peter Moore. One man even talked of being tortured by Moore at his house, but he'd not reported the incident due to the shame. DNA profiling of blood on the beach matched that of Peter Moore and he was arrested. When police searched his house they discovered his collection of Nazi memorabilia displayed amongst cuddly toys, handcuffs and rubber gags, a lethal-looking knife stained with the blood of a number of men and a collection of trophy items belonging to

---

[1] Piquerism (from the French, *piquer*, "to prick") is a sadistic form of paraphilia involving the penetration of another person's skin with sharp objects. Moore, it seems, took this interest to an extreme.

the victims. Hanging in his wardrobe was a police sergeant's uniform.

Moore was unrepentant and happily admitted his crimes to an investigating officer, stating that he'd killed "just for fun", that he took a "certain excitement" from it. "But it certainly wasn't a sexual excitement. Like everything, it was a job well done." He sniggered as he drew a map of the burial spot of Edward Carthy's body, saying, "I think he got a bit frightened actually." And John Roberts, he said, had just been "unlucky" to have been on Moore's route home. "When driving around, I would sometimes notice someone walking along the road late at night and I would stop and attack them."

Nevertheless, at Moore's trial he pleaded not guilty and blamed his crimes on a fantasy gay lover named Jason, inspired by the killer of the _Friday the 13th_ films. The prosecution argued that Moore's psychopathic frenzies were fuelled by rage against his own sexuality, and that he was a "dominant homosexual", a "violent and predatory sadist" whose lust was stimulated by causing pain and suffering. He was reprimanded by the judge several times for "insolence", and he would even wave to the news cameras as he was led into the court building, almost as if he were the star of his own movie.

The jury found him guilty of four counts of murder. At sentencing, Mr Justice Maurice Kay remarked that Moore, "The Man in Black", was "as dangerous a man as it is possible to find" and recommended that he never be released from prison. Despite numerous appeals that the whole-life term is against his human rights, Peter Moore remains inside, a guest of Her Majesty at Wakefield Prison in West Yorkshire.

# Javed Iqbal Umayr
(active 1998-1999)


THE CONCEPT OF RETRIBUTIVE JUSTICE goes back to the dawn of civilisation. An eye for an eye. Measure for measure. Let the punishment fit the crime.

> *Judicial punishment can never be used merely as a means to promote some other good for the criminal himself or for civil society, but instead it must in all cases be imposed on him only on the ground that he has committed a crime.*[1]

According to these words of the 18th-century philosopher Immanuel Kant, retribution is the only legitimate form of punishment prescriptible by the court. It must be carried out *by* the state and *on behalf of* the state, not on behalf of the victim. Hence, in criminal proceedings, the state – the living embodiment of the people – is the prosecuting party. Cases are brought in the name of state justice – for example, *Regina v. Burrell (appellant)* or *The People of the State of California v. Orenthal James Simpson*. They are *not* brought on behalf of the victim. There are many reasons for this, but perhaps the most significant one is that the victim could be seen as too close to the crime and therefore *must* be removed from the process of administration of justice. It makes common sense in that justice must not only be *done*, but must be *seen* to be done.

On 16 March 2000, a court in Pakistan dealt an unusual punishment. The defendant was ordered to be strangled to death, chopped into 100 pieces which were to be dissolved in a vat of acid. It was a replication of the fate to which a murderer had

---

[1] Immanuel Kant, *Die Metaphysik der Sitten (The Metaphysics of Morals)*, 1797

subjected his 100 victims. It was literally a case of "an eye for an eye". But the sentence never got to be carried out, and in his own twisted way the convicted man managed to escape retribution.

Javed Iqbal Umayr was born in Lahore, Punjab, Pakistan on an unknown date (but probably in 1956), the sixth of eight children (and one of four boys) of Mohammad Ali Mughal, a well-to-do businessman. As a teenager, Javed owned a 200CC motorcycle and he would use it lure young boys to him. He would also make pen-pals of boys whose names he got from magazines, maintaining friendships only with the ones he found attractive, spending thousands of rupees on sending them gifts such as coins, tickets and fragrances. Javed himself was a pampered child who indulged his interest in young boys from an early age. Apart from this, little else is known about his childhood.

He matriculated at the Government Islamia College as an intermediate student and started up his own commercial enterprise, a steel recasting business, whilst still in college. His father bought two villas in Shad Bagh, Lahore, giving one of them to Iqbal. From here he operated his various businesses, living surrounded by young boys.

Surprising everyone, Iqbal married in 1983 after declaring that he'd found himself a bride. It was the sister of one of his group of boys, and he'd chosen her in order to keep the boy by his side. He also arranged for the sister of one of his boys to marry one of his sisters. Again, it was a ploy to keep the boy nearby.

In 1993, his father died and Iqbal inherited enough money to make him a wealthy man. He built a large villa in Rana Town, Shahdara Bagh, a pleasant, historic upmarket area of Lahore. There, he enjoyed that trappings of his wealth, driving around town in any one of this four expensive cars, often with several boys joining him for the ride.

Some of Iqbal's family members became concerned about his interest in the company of youths and came to Shad Bagh to confront him, but Iqbal rejected their interference and refused to speak about it. Family members of the boys themselves made allegations but these were summarily dismissed. On some date in 1990 (when Iqbal may have been in his mid-40s), a complaint was made against Iqbal: a father accused him of sodomising his son. Iqbal refused to surrender himself for over a week. It was only when the police arrested one of the boys at his house that Iqbal gave himself up in order to secure the boy's release.

One charge, however, did stick, and Iqbal was sent to jail for rape, although he vehemently professed his innocence. Upon his release from prison, Iqbal was shocked to find that his assets had been sold. During his incarceration, his mother died and it was this that sent him into a descending spiral of rage and revenge. At that point, he made a pledge to himself: he would kill 100 boys in order to vent his infuriation at the perceived injustice he'd experienced at the hands of the Lahore police for the rape of a runaway boy in the early 1990s. His anger, he would later state in a detailed letter, had been on behalf of his mother, who'd "been forced to watch [his] decline" before succumbing to a fatal heart attack. Iqbal intended 100 mothers to cry for their sons, just as his own mother had cried for him before her death.

Iqbal's *M.O.* was cunning, specific and ruthless. He opened a video arcade business in the Shad Bagh, the first of its kind in the area. To boys he felt an attraction towards he would give reduced-rate tokens ... or sometimes free tokens. He was also in the habit of "accidentally" dropping a note of cash on the floor and watch to see which boy would pick it up. Then he'd announce the theft and the boy would be taken to an adjacent room where he'd be intimately searched. Inevitably, the search ended with the boy being raped. Sometimes, as a gesture of goodwill, Iqbal would let the boy keep the cash.

Sometimes, however, he'd also take one of the boys back home to his villa where he'd strangle them to death. He trawled the streets of Lahore, targeting runaway boys or orphans who wouldn't immediately be missed. Incredibly, many of them weren't. Iqbal managed to kill exactly 100 boys and youths, aged between 6 and 16, throttling them with a bicycle chain and dismembering the bodies. He disposed of the remains by dissolving them in vats of hydrochloric acid and then dumping the solution into a local river. When locals stopped allowing their sons to visit Iqbal's arcade he invested in a gym and an aquarium to lure them in. He also set his hand to other enterprises – a discount shop and an air-conditioned school. Both of these failed after a few weeks, boycotted by the locals.

With astounding callousness, when Iqbal reached his target of 100 murders he simply stopped. He wrote a letter confessing to the crimes and stated his intention to drown himself in the Ravi River. The letter told of his crimes in detail, and he sent it to both the police and a local newspaper.[2] Now that he'd reached his promised target, Iqbal coldly stated, there was no need to continue. He made no attempt to hide his identity. This was a public confession.

The police searched Iqbal's villa and found evidence of his deeds. The walls and ceilings were spattered with blood and, most damning of all, two vats of acid containing partially dissolved human remains had been left there deliberately so that the authorities could validate his story.

They dredged the Ravi for a month but found nothing of Iqbal's body. A manhunt ensured. When he was ready, on 30 December 1999, Iqbal presented himself to the offices of the *Daily Jang* newspaper and awaited the police to come and get him.

Despite his letter, when it came to trial Iqbal recanted his confession, alleging that he'd only been making a political statement about runaways and missing children. He claimed that the entire affair had been an elaborate pantomime, staged to draw attention to the plight of Lahore's street children. He insisted

---

[2] The police officer who received the letter allegedly tossed it into the bin, thinking it was a spoof, and so news reporters arrived at the crime scene before the police did.

that all the boys mentioned in his detailed journals were still alive and well, and were "living with different people and were surely compulsive homosexuals". It did him little good. Photographic evidence, his own journals and forensic evidence from his villa (including the two vats of dissolving human remains) were presented before the court. The overwhelming tide of evidence could only eat away at Iqbal's rather weak defence.[3]

Javed Iqbal was found guilty and sentenced to death in accordance with sharia law. In this case, it was deemed that he should be killed in the same way that he'd killed his victims and in a manner which he very much deserved – strangled, cut into 100 pieces (each piece representing a single boy) and placed in a vat of acid, all before the eyes of the parents of the decedents.

They were to be denied retributive justice – not because the state intervened, but because Iqbal himself took matters into his own hands. On 8 October 2001, authorities at the Kot Lakhpat Jail announced that he and his main accomplice, 20-year-old Sajid Ahmed, ended their own lives by hanging themselves with bedsheets in their prison cell. Others weren't so sure. Some investigators insisted that the evidence didn't support the theory of suicide, believing that vengeful employees of the prison had helped the two men on their way. At the time of his death, Javed Iqbal, also known as "*Kukri*" (Nepali, "The Knife"), had probably in his mid-40s.

The fact remains that Iqbal's killing spree only came to an end after he'd reached a target that he'd set himself. Had he not given himself up, he might've been able to double that number … or more. That fact alone is a savage indictment of society itself.

---

[3] Iqbal didn't act alone. He'd recruited four teenage boys – boys just like the murdered victims – in his campaign of revenge. One of these boys died in police custody by throwing himself out of a second-storey window whilst being interrogated by police. Two of the remaining three, were sentenced to 182 years in prison whilst a third received 63 for their parts in the deeds.

# Mohammed Bijeh
(active 2004)

THE CRIMES OF MOHAMMED BIJEH have not been widely publicised outside his native country, Iran. Yet the punishment he would receive was photographed, videoed and circulated widely, and anyone who has access to the Internet can search for and view the execution in full. It was a barbarous end to a barbaric life, and yet the customs of the country in which Bijeh committed his crimes demanded it. Few can say that he didn't deserve to be punished severely for this actions, for they were premeditated and wicked beyond belief. But the man was a victim himself, and in the end he became a victim of his own making.

Mohammed Bijeh (*né* Basjee) was born on 7 February 1982 in Quchan, Iran, one of six brothers born to an unnamed father and unnamed mother. His father was a merchant who was allegedly abusive toward his wife. Mohammed's mother died of cancer when he was aged four, after which his father immediately married another woman, with whom he had six more sons, half-brothers to Mohammed.

The father was also allegedly brutal towards his son Mohammed. He would chain his legs, beat him with a cane and even, on one occasion, attempt to kill him with a stick. Mohammed enjoyed going to school, but at the age of 11 the family relocated to Khutanabad, Iran, where, at his father's insistence, he had to give up his education and begin work at a furnace. Here, he was sexually abused and raped multiple times. The incident affected him profoundly and left him driven by on overwhelming compulsion to seek revenge.

Bijeh began his revenge in 2004, at the age of 22, but the targets of his lust for blood wasn't his attacker (or attackers); he directed it towards at least 17 young boys and adolescents, and three adults, all chosen randomly from the slums of Pakdasht, near Tehran. He stated that he'd wanted to take revenge on his community, citing his mother's death and the lack of affection he'd received as a child as the motives for the murders: "I suffered cruelly from childhood," he said, "and when I compared my life with others', I had to commit such acts."

Bijeh used a small brick bird coop by which to lure small children, telling them fabricated stories of performing doves to gain their interest. He also enticed them into the desert with promises of digging foxes and rabbits from their burrows.

He didn't work alone; he had an accomplice, Ali Baghi, a 24-year-old heroin addict, who also claimed to have been abused by men as a young child. After they had their victims alone in the desert, they either bludgeoned them to death or poisoned them. Together they waged a campaign of cruelty which included vampirism, necrophilia, rape and murder. To disguise the shallow graves in which they buried their victims the two slaughtered animals, leaving the carcasses nearby so that the stench of rotting flesh would mask the smell of their victims' decomposition.

Bijeh's crime spree lasted a year, after which he was caught. At the moment of his capture he'd been reportedly watching young boys swimming in a canal.

Bijeh admitted his crimes, confessing to killing 16 boys between March and September 2004. Locals believe the amount to be much higher. His sentence was 100 lashes followed by execution by hanging. Some called for him to be burned alive in the furnace kilns where he'd worked but this request was ignored. Baghi the accomplice was given a 15-year term in prison for his part in the crimes.

"The Vampire of the Tehran Desert", as Bijeh came to be known, was flogged 100 times in front of a crowd of over 5,000, some of whom cried out for the officials to strike him harder. He fell to the ground more than once during this part of the punishment but he didn't cry out. As Bijeh walked towards his final execution site, a brother of one of the murdered boys rushed forward and stabbed him in the back, only to be grabbed and held back by soldiers. Then, whilst mullahs read a prayer into the loudspeakers, a mother of one the victims placed a blue nylon rope around Bijeh's neck. Finally, he was hoisted high into the air above the dusty square as the crowd cheered and applauded. There was no sudden breakage of the neck, as is the case in conventional hanging executions. It wasn't a swift death. Bijeh's execution would've been prolonged and painful. There were many children amongst the crowd, also cheering and applauding. After a while, the victim-turned-abuser was dead, and within moments, the entire episode was uploaded to social media sites and shared around the world. In the eyes of many, justice had not only done ... but had been seen to have been done.

# Afterword

THERE ARE CERTAIN SITUATIONS that most of us cannot imagine because we haven't experienced them, and that is something to be thankful for. How many of us can *truly* imagine what it is to be in the object of a serial killer's rage, under his murderous psychopathic control? It doesn't even bear thinking about, but the truth of the matter is we are unlikely to find out.

Nevertheless, such killers *have* existed and *do* exist, and the statistics suggest that the prevalence of the homosexual serial murder is certainly significant. The data are not irrefutable, but they do suggest that the proportion of gay killers roughly correlate to the proportion of homosexuals in society, at least when it comes to the male demographic – that is, around 5-10%. (There is a scarcity of reliable statistics for the lesbian population.)

Like their heterosexual counterparts, the homosexual serial killer's motives are myriad, and they often overlap. Dean Corll, Randy Kraft, Robert Berdella and William Bonin killed for hedonistic reasons, pursuing their lustful agenda. Brutally killing the men they were attracted to aroused powerfully lustful feelings within them that were intensely stimulating and addictive. Yet their motives often strayed into the dominions of the torture killers such as Patrick Kearney, John Wayne Gacy and Daniel Conahan. There is little comfort to be had here, however: it seems that gay serial killers are capable of inflicting just as much pain and torment as their heterosexual equivalents. In fact, for whatever reason there might be, it appears that they are capable of subjecting the objects of their rage to the most heinous brutality possible – all in the name of lust.

Jeffrey Dahmer and Dennis Nilsen were also hedonistic killers, although they sought comfort and, in a dreadfully irrational way of thinking, company. Gain was the motive; they sought and achieved company – a playmate who could not answer back, who could not leave them. Only when these playmates' bodies became too putrefied to retain did these serial killers let them go.

The motive of Colin Ireland might be thought of as the pursuit of fame – or notoriety. Certainly, he claimed this himself. But his motive may also have been mission-oriented. It's known that he was sexually assaulted as a youth. Despite rationalising that he chose to kill gay men because they were easier targets, revenge may also have some part in his victim choice. Andrew Cunanan likewise – whilst he slaughtered men whom he believed to have slighted him in some way, he also chose to kill a fashion designer with one of the most recognisable names in the world. Both murderers would no doubt have decried allegations that they killed out of *lust*.

Ronald Dominique, Luis Garavito and Larry Eyler were also mission-oriented killers, venting their rage upon victims like themselves. And like *all* serial murders – crossing every demographic classifications and boundaries – power and control figured largely in their motives. Above all, they wanted *power and control* over their victims, as if dominating them totally and absolutely during the murder process inferred in them the self-validation they otherwise lacked. Carl Panzram seems to have been in a class of his own in this respect – in his own words, at least. He just wanted to kill. And Henry Lee Lucas and Ottis Toole – according to their dubious confessions, they killed to pass the time.

Let us not worry overmuch, however. Serial killers are literally a dying breed. Modern technology and improvements in forensics mean that sociopathic monsters are either caught before they can do too much damage, or they decide that it is easier to curtail their appetite for torturing and killing than to risk capture and detainment.

But let us also be heedful. For inside a psychopathic serial killer lies a fantasy abandoned by reason, and one does not wish to become the object of this impossible monster's twisted desires. The gay serial killer is *more than capable* of executing the ruthless overkill. And as we have seen, when that happens the outcome (for one party at least) is rarely good.

Printed in Great Britain
by Amazon